THE CAMBRIDGE
COMPANION TO
# MEDIEVAL FRENCH
# LITERATURE

EDITED BY
## SIMON GAUNT
AND
## SARAH KAY

CAMBRIDGE
UNIVERSITY PRESS

CAMBRIDGE UNIVERSITY PRESS
Cambridge, New York, Melbourne, Madrid, Cape Town, Singapore, São Paulo

Cambridge University Press
The Edinburgh Building, Cambridge CB2 8RU, UK

Published in the United States of America by Cambridge University Press, New York

www.cambridge.org
Information on this title: www.cambridge.org/9780521679756

First published 2008

Printed in the United Kingdom at the University Press, Cambridge

*A catalogue record for this publication is available from the British Library*

ISBN 978-0-521-86175-5 hardback
ISBN 978-0-521-67975-6 paperback

# CONTENTS

ILLUSTRATIONS

# NOTES ON CONTRIBUTORS

ADRIAN ARMSTRONG is Professor of Early French Culture at the University of Manchester. He is the author of *Technique and Technology: Script, Print, and Poetics in France 1470–1550* (2000), and is currently co-directing a research project on poetic knowledge in late medieval France.

MATILDA TOMARYN BRUCKNER is a Professor of French at Boston College. Together with Laurie Shepard and Sarah White she edited and translated *Songs of the Women Troubadours* (1995; rev. paperback 2000). She is currently finishing a book on Chrétien de Troyes's *Conte du graal* and its dialogue with the four verse continuations.

WILLIAM BURGWINKLE is Reader in Medieval French and Occitan at the University of Cambridge and a Fellow of King's College, Cambridge. He published *Sodomy, Masculinity, and Law in Medieval Literature* with Cambridge University Press in 2004 and is currently finishing a co-authored book (with Cary Howie) on hagiography and pornography.

KEITH BUSBY is Douglas Kelly Professor of French at the University of Wisconsin, Maddison. An expert on manuscript studies, his major recent work is the two-volume *Codex and Context: Reading Old French Verse Narrative in Manuscripts* (2002); he is now working on the text–image relationship in English, Italian and Burgundian manuscripts of French secular narrative.

EMMA CAMPBELL is Assistant Professor and RCUK Academic Fellow in Medieval French Studies at the University of Warwick. She is the co-editor with Robert Mills of *Troubled Vision: Gender, Sexuality and Sight in Medieval Text and Image* (2004) and is currently finishing a monograph provisionally entitled *Unholy Relations: Reading Social and Sexual Connections in Medieval Saints' Lives*.

MARILYNN DESMOND is Professor of English and Comparative Literature at Binghamton University. Her books include, most recently, *Ovid's Art and the Wife of Bath: the Ethics of Erotic Violence* (2006) and (co-authored with Pamela

Sheingorn) *Myth, Montage and Visuality in Late Medieval Manuscript Culture: Christine de Pizan's* Othea (2003).

SIMON GAUNT is Professor of French Language and Literature at King's College London. His most recent book is *Martyrs to Love: Love and Death in Medieval French and Occitan Courtly Literature* (2006). He is currently working on a book on the use of French in Italy with particular reference to Marco Polo.

JANE GILBERT is a lecturer in French at University College London, and a comparatist working in English, French and modern theory. She is currently completing a monograph on the interface between life and death in medieval French and English literature.

NOAH D. GUYNN is Associate Professor of French at the University of California, Davis. He is the author of *Allegory and Sexual Ethics in the High Middle Ages* (2007) and is currently working on a book on ethics and parody in late medieval and early modern French farce.

SYLVIA HUOT is Reader in Medieval French Literature and a Fellow of Pembroke College at the University of Cambridge. Her most recent book is *Postcolonial Fictions in the 'Roman de Perceforest': Cultural Identities and Hybridities* (2007). She is co-director with Adrian Armstrong of a project on poetry and knowledge in late medieval France.

SARAH KAY is Professor of French at Princeton University. She recently completed *The Place of Thought: the Complexity of One in Late Medieval French Didactic Poetry* (2007) and is now researching the use made of quotations from the troubadours in Occitan literature.

PEGGY MCCRACKEN is Professor of French and Women's Studies at the University of Michigan, Ann Arbor. Her most recent book is *The Curse of Eve, the Wound of the Hero: Blood, Gender, and Medieval Literature* (2003). Her current research focuses on literary representations and reactions to crusade and crusade rhetoric.

DEBORAH MCGRADY is Associate Professor of French at the University of Virginia. She is the author of *Controlling Readers: Guillaume de Machaut and His Late Medieval Audience* (2006). She is currently writing a study entitled *The Gift of Literature: Reinventing Patronage during the Hundred Years War*.

JAMES R. SIMPSON is Senior Lecturer in French at the University of Glasgow. His monograph *Fantasy, Identity and Misrecognition in Medieval French Narrative* appeared in 2000 and he has just completed a book on Chrétien's *Erec et Enide*.

HELEN SOLTERER is Associate Professor of French at Duke University. She is the author of *The Master and Minerva: Disputing Women in French Medieval Culture* (1995). Her latest work, *Medieval Roles for Modern Times*, is forthcoming. It focuses on the function of pre-modern culture in twentieth-century France.

JANE TAYLOR is Professor of French at Durham University. She specializes in the literature of late medieval France: François Villon, the late medieval Arthurian romances, late medieval courtly lyric. She is past President of the International Arthurian Society, and co-editor of *Medium Aevum*. Her *The Making of Poetry: Poetic Anthologies in Late-Medieval France* appeared in 2007.

# CHRONOLOGY

| | Historical events | Medieval French and Anglo-Norman authors and texts | Other cultural events in France and its neighbours |
|---|---|---|---|
| 1050 | | *Vie de Saint Alexis* (c.1050, or later?) | |
| 1060 | Philippe I, king of France (1060)<br>Battle of Hastings (1066) | | |
| 1090 | First Crusade (1095–9)<br>Foundation of Cistercian order (1098) | *Chanson d'Antioche* (1098) | |
| 1100 | Henry I, king of England (1100)<br>Louis VI, king of France (1108) | Oxford *Roland* (c.1100, or earlier?)<br>*Chanson de Guillaume* (c.1100, or later?) | Death of Anselm (1109) |
| 1110 | Foundation of Bologna University (1113) | | |
| 1120 | St Bernard founds Clairvaux (1115)<br>First Lateran Council (1123)<br>Foundation of Templars (1128) | | *Sponsus* (macaronic theatrical piece) (c.1120)<br>Abelard's *Sic et non* (1121)<br>First known troubadour Guillaume de Poitiers dies (1127)<br>Earliest version of the Alexander romance in Franco-Provençal (first third twelfth cent.) |
| 1130 | Louis VII, king of France (1137)<br>Construction of abbey at St-Denis begun (1137) | *Couronnement de Louis* (?)<br>Wace, *Vie de sainte Marguerite* (before 1155) | Geoffrey of Monmouth, *Historia* (c.1135–8)<br>Marcabru's poetic activity begins |
| 1140 | Second Crusade (1147–50) | *Jeu d'Adam* (between 1146 and 1174) | *Poema de mío Cid* (1140, or possibly early thirteenth cent.)<br>Abelard dies (c.1142–4)<br>Jaufre Rudel probably dies *outremer* (1148) |

| Historical events | Medieval French and Anglo-Norman authors and texts | Other cultural events in France and its neighbours |
|---|---|---|
| **1150** Foundation of Paris University (1150) Louis VII divorces Eleanor of Aquitaine, who marries Henry of Anjou (1152) Henry II, king of England (1154) | *Charroi de Nîmes* (?) *Floire et Blancheflor* (after 1150) Wace, *Roman de Brut* (c.1155) *Roman de Thèbes* (c.1155) *Roman d'Apollonius de Tyr* (c.1150–60) | *Sententiae* of Peter Lombard Troubadours Bernart de Ventadorn and Raimbaut d'Aurenga active *Girart de Roussillon* (c.1150) |
| **1160** Work begins on Notre Dame de Paris (1163) Foundation of Oxford University (1167) | *Sept sages de Rome* (c.1160) *Roman d'Eneas* (1160?) Benoît de Sainte-Maure, *Roman de Troie* (c.1160) Wace, *Roman de Rou* (begun c.1160) *Pyramus et Thisbe* and other Ovidian *contes* Béroul, *Tristan* (? could be earlier or later) Earliest French and Anglo-Norman versions of the *Roman d'Alexandre* | Alan of Lille, *De planctu naturae* (c.1160–5?) |
| **1170** Thomas Beckett murdered | Thomas, *Tristan* (c.1170) Chrétien de Troyes, *Erec et Enide* (late 1160s or 1170), *Cligès* (c.1176), *Yvain / Le Chevalier au lion* (c.1177–81), *Lancelot Le Chevalier de la charrette* (c.1177–81) Clemence of Barking, *Vie de Sainte Catherine* (c.1175–c.1200) Blondel de Nesle (c.1175–1200s) Marie de France, *Lais* (before 1178 and maybe as early as 1160) | |

| | | | |
|---|---|---|---|
| 1180 | Philippe Auguste, king of France (1180)<br>Philippe Auguste begins to confirm municipal communes (1182)<br>Saladin retakes Jerusalem (1187)<br>Richard I, king of England (1189)<br>Third Crusade (1189–92) | Gautier d'Arras, *Ille et Galeron*, *Eracle* (between 1176 and 1184)<br>Gace Brulé (between 1179 and 1212)<br>*Roman de Renart* begins<br>*Roman d'Alexandre* continues<br>Bertran de Bar-sur-Aube, *Girart de Vienne* (c.1180)<br>*Prise d'Orange* (c.1180)<br>Rhymed *remaniement* of the *Chanson de Roland* (c.1180)<br>Chrétien, *Perceval / Le Conte du graal* (c.1180–92)<br>Hue de Rotelande, *Ipomedon* (c.1180–5)<br>*Partonopeu de Blois* (c.1182–5, but could be earlier)<br>Châtelain de Couci first known of in 1186<br>*Roman de Renart* continues | Andreas Capellanus, *De amore* (c.1183–6)<br>Hartmann von Aue, *Erec* |
| 1190 | John Lackland, king of England (1199) | First Continuation of the *Conte du graal*; also Second Continuation (by Denain)<br>First surviving *fabliaux* (or earlier?)<br>Renaut de Beaujeu, *Le Bel Inconnu*<br>*Raoul de Cambrai* (or early thirteenth cent.?)<br>*Renaut de Montauban* (existed in some form before the end of the twelfth cent.)<br>*Cycle des Lorrains* begins with *Garin le Loheren* and *Gerbert de Metz* in the late twelfth cent.<br>Jean Bodel, *Les Saisnes* | Old English Katherine Group (c.1190–1225)<br>Averroës dies (1198) |

| | Historical events | Medieval French and Anglo-Norman authors and texts | Other cultural events in France and its neighbours |
| --- | --- | --- | --- |
| 1200 | Capetians begin to impose royal currency (c.1200)<br>Charter of University of Paris (1200)<br>Fourth Crusade (1202–4); crusaders capture Constantinople (1204)<br>Albigensian Crusade begins (1209)<br>Foundation of Franciscan order (1209) | Jean Bodel, *Jeu de Saint Nicolas* (1199–1201)<br>*Ami et Amile* (c.1200)<br>Thibaut de Champagne born 1201<br>*Jourdain de Blaye* (early thirteenth cent.)<br>French translations of the *Pseudo-Turpin* (c.1202)<br>Châtelain de Couci dies outremer (1203)<br>Villehardouin, *Conquête de Constantinople* (after 1207)<br>*Chansons de geste* about Guillaume d'Orange recast into cyclical form<br>*Huon de Bordeaux* (?)<br>Raoul de Houdenc, *Meraugis de Portlesguez* (between 1200 and 1220) | Alan of Lille dies (1203)<br>Layamon, *Brut* (1205?)<br>Walter Map dies (c.1209)<br>Wolfram von Eschenbach, *Parzival* (c.1205–12) |
| 1210 | Battles of Bouvines (1214)<br>*Magna carta* (1215)<br>Third Lateran Council (1215)<br>Dominican order founded (1216)<br>Fifth Crusade (1217–21)<br>End of Albigensian Crusade (1219) | Conon de Béthune dies (c.1219)<br>Jean Bodel dies (1210)<br>Jean Renart, *Roman de la rose* (1210s–20s?)<br>Non-cyclic *Prose Lancelot* (c.1215–20?)<br>Third Continuation of the *Conte du graal*, by Manessier (1214–27)<br>Raoul de Houdenc, *Roman des eles* (First third of thirteenth cent.)<br>*Athis et Prophilias* (between 1210 and 1225) | *Chanson de la Croisade Albigeoise* (1212–19)<br>Gottfried von Strassburg's *Tristan* interrupted by his death (1216?) |

| | | | |
|---|---|---|---|
| 1220 | Louis VIII, king of France (1223)<br>Louis IX, king of France (1226)<br>University of Salamanca founded (1227)<br>Sixth Crusade (1228)<br>University of Toulouse founded (1229) | Fourth Continuation of the *Conte du graal*, by Gerbert (1220s)<br>Cyclic *Prose Lancelot: Lancelot Proper*, followed by the *Queste* and *Mort* (c.1220–35?)<br>*Gaydon* (between 1225 and 1234) | Death of Wolfram von Eschenbach (c.1220; born c.1170)<br>After 1220, death of Hartmann von Aue (born c.1160–70)<br>Francis of Assisi dies (1226)<br>*King Horn* (1225?)<br>German prose *Lanzelet* (1225? Or late thirteenth cent.)<br>Occitan romance of *Jaufre* (c.1225–8)<br>Sicilian School (c.1220–67) |
| 1230 | Inquisition established in Languedoc (1233)<br>Cordoba falls to Christians (1236) | Guillaume de Lorris, *Roman de la rose* (c.1225–45)<br>Expansions of the cyclic *Prose Lancelot*, *Estoire del saint graal* and *Estoire de Merlin* (c.1230–40?)<br>*Tristan en prose* (c.1230–5)<br>*Aucassin et Nicolette* (or earlier?) | Death of Walther von der Vogelweide (c.1230, born. c.1170)<br>*Ancrene Wisse* (c.1230)<br>Translation into Castilian of the *Prose Lancelot* (1230–40) |
| 1240 | Seventh Crusade; Saint Louis captured (1248)<br>University College, Oxford, founded (1249) | Gerbert de Montreuil, *Roman de la violette* (before 1250)<br>Rutebeuf, *Dit des cordeliers* (1249) | Peter of Spain, writings on logic (first half thirteenth cent.) |
| 1250 | Treaty of Paris between France and England (1259) | Thibaut de Champagne dies (1253)<br>Rutebeuf, *Dit de Guillaume de Saint-Amour* (1258) | Aquinas lectures in theology at Paris (1256–9); composition of the *Summa theologiae* begins (1259) |
| 1260 | | Brunetto Latini, *Li livres dou trésor* (c.1260–6, or later?)<br>Rutebeuf, so-called *poésies personnelles* (1260–2), *Frère Denise* (1262), *Marie l'Egyptienne* (1263), *Miracle de Théophile* (1264) | Thomas Aquinas resumes teaching in Paris (1269–72), completes the *Summa*, dies 1273 |

| | Historical events | Medieval French and Anglo-Norman authors and texts | Other cultural events in France and its neighbours |
|---|---|---|---|
| 1270 | Philippe III, king of France (1270)<br>Marco Polo leaves Venice (1271)<br>Condemnations at Paris University by Bishop Tempier (1276–7) | *Châtelaine de Vergy* (c.1270?)<br>Adam de la Halle, *Jeu de la feuillée* (c.1276)<br>Jean de Meun, *Roman de la rose* (between 1268 and 1285) | *Flamenca* (c.1270 or earlier)<br>Bonaventure dies (1274; born c.1221)<br>Thomas Aquinas dies (1274) |
| 1280 | Foundation of Peterhouse, Cambridge (1284)<br>Philippe IV (the Fair), king of France (1285) | Jakemes, *Castelain de Couci* (c.1280?)<br>Adam de la Halle, *Jeu de Robin et Marion* (c.1283)<br>Heldris de Cornuailles, *Roman de Silence* (late thirteenth cent.) | Albertus Magnus dies (1280; born c.1220)<br>Cavalcanti and *dolce stil novo* (c.1280–c.1300)<br>Alfonso the Wise dies (1284; born 1221) |
| 1290 | War between France and England (1294)<br>Marco Polo returns to Venice (1295) | Jean de Meun, *Testament* (before 1305)<br>Marco Polo, *Le Devisement du monde* (1298) | Dante, *Vita Nuova* (1293–4) |
| 1300 | Avignon papacy begins (1309) | Joinville, *Saint Looys* (c.1305–6) | Dante, *De Vulgari eloquentia* and *Convivio* (1304–7)<br>Duns Scotus dies (1308; born c.1266) |
| 1310 | Louis X, king of France (1314)<br>Philippe V, king of France (1316) | *Roman de Perceforest* (c.1314–c.1340) | Dante completes *Inferno* (1314)<br>Raimon Llull dies (1316? born 1235?) |
| 1320 | Charles IV, king of France (1322)<br>Philippe VI, king of France (1328) | | Dante dies (1321)<br>Meister Eckhart dies (1327; born c.1260) |
| 1330 | Beginning of 100 Years' War (1337) | Machaut, *Jugement du roi de Behaigne* (1330)<br>Machaut, *Dit dou vergier* (1330s)<br>*Miracles de Nostre Dame par personnages* (c.1339–82) | First version of Juan Ruiz, *Libro de buen amor* (1330)<br>*La tavola ritonda* (c.1330) |

| | Historical events | French literature | Other literature |
|---|---|---|---|
| 1340 | Battle of Crécy (1346)<br>English capture Calais (1347)<br>Black Death (1347–50)<br>Dauphiné ceded to France (1349)<br>Foundation of the University of Florence (1349) | | Harley Lyrics (c.1340)<br>Second version of Juan Ruiz *Libro de buen amor* (1343)<br>William of Ockham dies (1347; born c.1285)<br>Boccaccio, *Decameron* (1349–52)<br>Petrarch, *Trionfi* begun (finished 1374) |
| 1350 | Jean II, king of France (1350)<br>Battle of Poitiers (1356) | Machaut, *Jugement dou roy de Navarre* (1350s)<br>Machaut, *Remede de Fortune* (1350s)<br>Jean de Mandeville, *Voyages* (1356)<br>Machaut, *Confort d'amy* (1356–7) | |
| 1360 | Second wave of plague (1361)<br>Charles V, king of France (1364) | *Ysaïe le triste* (c.1360)<br>Froissart begins his *Chroniques* (c.1360)<br>Machaut, *Fonteinne amoureuse* (c.1361)<br>Machaut, *Voir dit* (1363–5)<br>Christine de Pizan born (c.1364)<br>Froissart, *Espinette amoureuse* (c.1369) | Chaucer, *Book of the Duchess* (c.1369–70)<br>Langland, *Piers Plowman* A-Text (1367–70) |
| 1370 | End of Avignon papacy (1377) | Froissart, *Prison amoureuse* (1372–3) and *Joli Buisson de Jonece* (1373)<br>Machaut dies (1377) | Nicole Oresme translates Aristotle's *Ethics, Politics, Economics,* and *Meterologia* into French (1370–7)<br>Petrarch dies (1374)<br>Boccaccio dies (1375) |
| 1380 | Charles VI, king of France (1380) | | Wyclif and others translate the Bible into English<br>Chaucer, *Troilus* (c.1382–6)<br>Chaucer begins *Canterbury Tales* (c.1387) |

| Historical events | Medieval French and Anglo-Norman authors and texts | Other cultural events in France and its neighbours |
| --- | --- | --- |
| 1390 | Deschamps, *Art de dictier* (1392)<br>Jean d'Arras, *Mélusine* (1392–3)<br>Christine de Pizan, *Cent ballades* (??), *Epistre au dieu d'amours* (1399) | Gower, *Confessio amantis* (c.1390) |
| 1400 Assassination of Louis d'Orléans (1407) | Froissart finishes *Chroniques* (1400 probably) and dies (after 1404)<br>Christine de Pizan, *Epistre Othea* (1400), *Querelle du Roman de la rose* (1399–1402), *Livre du chemin de long estude*, and *Livre de la mutacion de Fortune* (1403)<br>Coudrette, *Mélusine* (c.1402)<br>Eustache Deschamps dies (1404)<br>Christine de Pizan, *Livre de la cité des dames* (1405), *Livre des trois vertus* (1405), *Livre de l'advision Cristine* (1405), *Livre du corps de policie* (1407) | Chaucer dies (1400)<br>*Sir Gawain and the Green Knight* and related texts (MS dates from c.1400) |
| 1410 Battle of Agincourt (1415)<br>Assassination of Jean sans Peur (1419) | Christine de Pizan, *Livre des fais d'armes et de chevalerie* (1410), *Lamentacion sur les maux de la guerre civile* (1410), *Livre de la paix* (1413), *Epistre de la prison de vie humaine* (1418)<br>Alain Chartier, *Le Livre des quatre dames* (c.1416) | Hoccleve, *Regiment of Princes* (1411)<br>Lydgate, *Troy book* (1412–20) |

| | | | |
|---|---|---|---|
| 1420 | Charles VII, king of France (1422)<br>Jeanne d'Arc's victories (1428–9) | Alain Chartier, *La Belle Dame sans mercy* (1424)<br>Christine de Pizan, *Ditié de Jehanne d'Arc* (1429) | Circulation of earliest Spanish *Romanceros* (1421) |
| 1430 | Jeanne d'Arc burned at Rouen (1431)<br>Treaty of Arras between France and Burgundy (1435) | Jean Gerson dies (1429)<br>Alain Chartier dies (1430)<br>*Mystère du siège d'Orléans* (c.1430–40)<br>Christine de Pizan dies (c.1431)<br>Martin Le Franc, *Champion des dames* (1441–2) | |
| 1440 | | | |
| 1450 | France retakes Normandy and Gascony (1450–3) | Arnoul Gréban, *Mystère de la passion* (c.1450)<br>Antoine de la Sale, *Jehan de Saintré* (1456)<br>*Cent Nouvelles nouvelles* (1456–61)<br>François Villon, *Lais* (1456) | Malory, *Morte D'Arthur* (after 1450)<br>Ausias March dies (1459; born c.1397) |
| 1460 | Louis XI, king of France (1461)<br>Philip the Good, duke of Burgundy, dies (1467) | Charles d'Orléans dies (1465)<br>*Farce de Maître Pierre Pathelin* (1460)<br>François Villon, *Testament* (1461–2)<br>Jean Meschinot, *Lunettes des princes* (1461–5)<br>François Villon dies (after 1463)<br>Jean Molinet, *Complainte de Grece* (1464)<br>*Mystère des Actes des Apôtres* (c.1470) | |
| 1470 | First printing press in Paris (1470)<br>First printing press in Lyon (1473)<br>Charles the Bold, last duke of Burgundy, dies (1477) | | Career of Caxton (from 1473) |
| 1480 | Division of Burgundian lands between France and empire (1482)<br>Charles VIII, king of France (1483) | Jean Michel, *Mystère de la passion* (c.1480)<br>Jean Molinet, *Ressource du petit peuple* (1481)<br>Philippe de Commynes, *Mémoires* (1489–98) | Birth of Martin Luther (1483) |

| Historical events | Medieval French and Anglo-Norman authors and texts | Other cultural events in France and its neighbours |
|---|---|---|
| 1490 French annexation of Brittany (1491)<br>Columbus lands in West Indies (1492)<br>Fall of Grenada (1492)<br>French invasion of Italy (1494)<br>Louis XII, king of France (1498–1515) | | Skelton, *The Bowge of Courte* (1498)<br>Earliest edition of *La Celestina* (1499)<br>Marsilio Ficino dies (1499; born 1433) |
| 1500 | Jean Marot, *Voyage de Gênes* (1507) and *Voyage de Venise* (1509)<br>Lemaire de Belges, *Temple d'honneur et de vertu* (1504) and *Epitres de l'amant vert* (1505)<br>Jean Molinet dies (1507)<br>Lemaire de Belges, *Illustrations de Gaule et singularités de Troie* (1511–13) | Wynkin de Worde's new press established (1500) |

SIMON GAUNT AND SARAH KAY

# Introduction

French was the most influential vernacular literature of the European Middle Ages. Early texts such as the *Chanson de Roland*, the Old French *Tristan* romances, the prose *Lancelot*, and the *Roman de la rose* were widely translated into other European languages and had an enormous impact on other vernacular traditions; later writers such as Guillaume de Machaut, Christine de Pizan, or Charles d'Orléans, had an international readership and saw themselves as working in an international context. The prestige and dissemination of French were such that writers whose mother tongue was not French wrote major texts in French (in Italy Brunetto Latini and Marco Polo, in England John Gower); even in instances where robust national traditions emerged in the wake of major authors such as Dante and Petrarch in Italy, or Chaucer in England, they did so in part at least by emulating French models.

The literary production to which this *Companion* is devoted dates *c.* 1100–1500, but there is evidence the tradition began earlier. The earliest surviving written French is found in the *Serments de Strasbourg* (842), a record of oaths supposedly taken by two of Charlemagne's grandsons one of whom swears in French, the other in German. The equally brief *Séquence de Sainte Eulalie* (*c.*878), the fragmentary *chanson de geste Gormont et Isembart* and the *Vie de St Léger* (both eleventh century), suggest French was already being used sporadically for written texts before 1100, and that the *Serments de Strasbourg* were not therefore a flash-in-the-pan. The general lack of surviving evidence and the undoubted loss of many texts, especially from the early Middle Ages, mean that it is not always possible to delineate this production precisely. What we know is that, after uncertain beginnings before 1100, there is more sustained literary activity in French in the first half of the twelfth century, that this increases markedly after *c.*1150, and that texts in French (and books containing them) start to be produced in far greater numbers from the early thirteenth century onwards. We have indicated the probable dates of all the texts that are the subject of substantive discussion in this volume in the

Chronology, but before 1200 especially these reflect informed guesswork rather than secure knowledge.

The language in which this literature was composed comprises various forms of medieval French. Like all romance languages, French emerged from the linguistic and cultural melting-pot that followed the disintegration of the Roman empire, initially from contact between Latin and the languages of the inhabitants of the territories that had been occupied, then from contact with invaders from the north and east in the fifth and sixth centuries.[1] In the northern part of the Roman province of Gaul Latin underwent the influence of a Celtic 'substrate' (largely lexical), then a Germanic 'superstrate' brought by invading tribes, notably the Franks, who had a major impact on pronunciation, vocabulary and syntax, and who gave France its name ('Frankia'). In Brittany the Celtic substrate survived more or less intact, while south of the Loire, where Latin was more entrenched and the Germanic invasions less aggressive, there developed instead a distinct group of dialects nowadays classed as 'Occitan'. Medieval and modern linguists alike use the terms *langue d'oïl* and *langue d'oc* to refer to French and Occitan, *oïl* being the medieval Northern French word for 'yes' and *oc* its Occitan counterpart. It is hard to tell at what point exactly the Latin spoken in Northern France became the *langue d'oïl*, but in 813 the Council of Tours decreed sermons should be preached in the vernacular rather than Latin, suggesting a retrospective recognition that the language of the people was so distant from Latin as to be a separate language.

Histories of the French language usually divide medieval French into three periods: early Old French (before 1100), Old French (c.1100–c.1300), and Middle French (c.1300–c.1500 and beyond). Initially, French was less a language than a collection of dialects. They relied heavily on what linguists call 'inflections': tense and person endings for verbs, and case endings for nouns and adjectives which distinguished the subject forms of most masculine nouns and adjectives (and a few feminine ones too) from forms other than the subject. As a result of these two features, early Old French used fewer grammatical markers (such as subject pronouns with verbs and articles with nouns) than more recent forms of French, and its syntax was more flexible than the now standard subject-verb-object word order. Early Old French also had a wide range of consonants and vowel combinations (called 'diphthongs' or 'triphthongs', depending on how many vowels are combined), but these began to reduce in the Old French period. By the twelfth century a number of mutually comprehensible dialects had gained prominence, notably *picard*, *champenois*, Norman, Anglo-Norman (the French spoken by much of the ruling classes in England after the Norman conquest in 1066), and *francien* (a term used to designate both the dialect spoken in the region around Paris and then the written *koinè* based upon it that was promoted for use in certain types of official document); *francien* progressively became the norm from about 1300. Old French continued to use case endings with nouns and adjectives, albeit not consistently, together with the complex verb endings of the earlier period. Its literary style was characterized by a greater use of tense switching than is the norm in modern written French,[2] and by the accumulation of discrete clauses without any markers of grammatical connection (a style known as 'parataxis', in contrast to the marking of grammatical relations in 'hypotaxis'). The case system gradually fell into disuse in the Old French period, and its loss inaugurates the language known as Middle French. Middle French also saw a major overhaul of verbal morphology, as a result of which the language starts to look more like Modern French. Syntax became more fixed and 'determiners' such as subject pronouns started to be used more frequently. Major changes in pronunciation also took place in the fourteenth and fifteenth centuries; whereas Old French spelling coincided to a large extent with pronunciation, the Middle French period witnessed the divergence between the two that still characterizes Modern French. Some Middle French texts are, in addition, marked by Latinisms, as humanist writers consciously imitated classical models. A guide to reference works on various aspects of medieval French language is included as an Appendix.

As mention of the Norman conquest indicates, the geographical range of medieval French literature was not coterminous with present-day France. Not only was a significant part of what we now call France not French-speaking in the Middle Ages, but a large number of texts in French were composed outside the territories directly controlled by the French king: in England, for instance, in the often extensive continental domains of the English crown, or in the various border regions which moved in and out of the French or English spheres of power throughout the Middle Ages (for example, Flanders, Burgundy, Lorraine).[3] As a result of French or English military or dynastic interests, French was also spoken in the Near East (Jerusalem, Syria), in Sicily, and parts of central Europe (Bohemia). The major historical figures and events that mark the period are set out in the Chronology above.

Medieval French literature first attracted interest in the late eighteenth and early nineteenth centuries (under the influence of the Romantic movement then prevalent in Europe) and became an object of intensive study in the last third of the nineteenth century. Initially enormous effort was needed to identify, catalogue, and edit texts. Critical evaluations, at first overshadowed by methods prevailing in the study of classical literature were, in the twentieth century, increasingly influenced by the development of critical study of modern European literatures. Different national cultures have evolved distinctive approaches. In the French-speaking world, where medieval French texts are the earliest form of the national literature of most scholars concerned, the approach has been largely literary-historical; British attention has been predominantly devoted to the extensive Anglo-Norman tradition; the strong philological and historical tradition in Germany is now, sadly, continued by only a handful of scholars; Italian scholarship continues to be focused on philology and textual transmission. In North America a wide range of philological and critical methods have been pioneered, and it is from here that the most adventurous works of synthesis have come.

To some extent the canon of medieval French works studied in university curricula has been fluid, depending on the historical moment and the national tradition, but the canonical status of some texts is constant: the *Chanson de Roland*, for example, because of its monumental importance to the conception of French literature *as French*; Chrétien de Troyes's five Arthurian romances because of their seminal contribution to courtly romance and thereby to the prehistory of the novel; the *Roman de la rose* because of its extensive pan-European dissemination; François Villon's *Testament* because of its play with poetic voice, often vaunted for its modernity, but in fact characteristically medieval. We have endeavoured, in this *Companion*, to strike a balance between works of undoubted canonical status, texts that are now widely taught (for example Marie de France's *Lais* and *Aucassin et Nicolette*), and texts or figures to which recent innovatory research has been devoted (for instance, Christine de Pizan, the *Perceforest*, hagiography). We could not include everything, and to our regret there is no discussion of medieval historiography, and much less than we would have liked of some other major works like the *Roman de Renart*. In order to structure and guide the reader towards future as much as existing work in medieval French studies, we have divided the volume into four sections that address the following four questions: what is a medieval French text? What do we mean when we talk about an author in the medieval French literary tradition? How useful is it to think in terms of literary genres when reading medieval French literature? And how can we read medieval French texts historically? The next four sections of this Introduction outline the problematic encapsulated by each of these questions, and indicate how it is developed in the chapters that follow.

### What is a medieval French text?

Modern conceptions of a text are conditioned by a culture in which authors are directly answerable for what they write, in which printing fixes the wording and presentation of texts, in which copyright and censorship laws regulate who has the right to reproduce and read them, and in which high levels of literacy encourage a strong disassociation of the written from the spoken word. Our emerging digital culture marks a revolution in practices of textual production, transmission, and reception that may well prove as far-reaching as the invention of printing, and this will perhaps help us in some ways to understand better a world in which texts were manipulated and changed by those who transmitted and read them. In other crucial respects, however, digital culture distances us yet further from a world in which texts had to be copied laboriously by hand, using quill pens on parchment that was harder to work with and far more expensive than modern paper. These differences separating medieval from modern forms of text are not simply a matter of external material conditions: they profoundly influence the character of medieval French literature.

In the Middle Ages the recording of any French text in writing meant aligning it, to some degree, with Latin culture since literacy was almost always taught through the medium of Latin, more was written in Latin than the vernacular, and the main business of *scriptoria* (workshops of scribes devoted to producing manuscripts), at least before the fourteenth century, was to copy Latin texts.[4] It is not uncommon for early French and Latin texts to be found together in manuscripts and, in the Old French period particularly, French works often claim to be translations or adaptations of Latin models.

The profession of copyist tended to be regarded as menial and technical, and far more people knew how to read than write. Consequently, most Old and Middle French texts were composed to be recited to an audience (for a variety of reasons the norm – even in Latin – was to read aloud) or indeed to be sung, possibly with accompanying instruments (*trouvère* lyrics, the *chansons de geste*), or to be performed or mimed by a group (like drama). 'Reading' medieval literature was thus a social, public activity, sometimes committed to professional performers, either travelling troupes of *jongleurs* or else minstrels attached to a particular court. In the case of narratives recited from a book, the figure of the narrator would have been physically embodied by the reader, and thereby distinguished from the author, who tends to be referred to in the third person as the absent authority behind the text. But early French literature was composed exclusively in verse, which continued to be widely used even after the emergence of prose in the very late twelfth century,[5] and some of these verse texts (such as *chansons de geste*, *lais*, and lyrics) may have been performed without the presence of any written text.

There has been much debate – some acrimonious – among medievalists about the origins of early verse genres in oral culture, but by definition the texts that have survived were written down, and were consequently, at this stage at least, part of a written tradition.[6] Rather than opposing writing and orality in this period, we should seek to understand how the rhythms and practices of the spoken language inflected the written word. Most Old and Middle French works, for example, are scripted for oral delivery, featuring a first-person voice who addresses an audience of listeners in the second person, and uses spatial and temporal deictic markers to locate delivery 'here' (ci, as in 'at this place in the book') or 'now' (or, as in 'at this stage in my narration').[7]

Only in the late Middle Ages, and then only rarely, do we have copies of texts that were made by their authors, or overseen by them. The poet Charles d'Orléans has left us an autograph copy of his poems (see Chapter 10); the efforts made by Machaut and Christine de Pizan to control the circulation of their works are described in Chapters 7 and 8. But the temporal gap between the composition of most medieval works and the written sources by which we know them exposes texts to the vagaries of transmission: for example, almost our entire canon of twelfth-century French literature is known only from manuscripts produced in the thirteenth century or later. Variations from one copy of a text to another – sometimes termed *mouvance* – pose problems for editors and by the beginning of the twentieth century two distinct editorial methodologies had emerged.[8] The method named as Lachmannian after Karl Lachmann (1793–1851) seeks to reconstruct what an author originally wrote; the so-called Bédieriste or 'best manuscript' method, named after its formidable proponent Joseph Bédier (1864–1938), opts instead to edit a single manuscript on the grounds that the resulting text will be more authentically medieval. But whichever method is followed, modern critical editions of medieval texts necessarily occlude the mobility to which they were subject in transmission.[9] For throughout the Middle Ages texts were frequently adapted in far-reaching ways (rewritten, abridged, expanded) to suit the tastes of a new group or generation of readers, and/or to foreground certain interpretations according to the tastes of a scribe, audience, or patron. This process (known as *remaniement*, 'rehandling') can lead to the circulation of a number of versions that are so divergent that they may in effect be viewed as constituting separate works, even where they clearly derive from a common source.

*Remaniement* is well illustrated by the *Chanson de Roland*, the subject of Chapter 1. The version with which most readers are familiar – the late eleventh- or early twelfth-century Oxford *Roland* – has iconic status in literary histories as the founding monument of French literature and as the archetypal *chanson de geste*, but it was not widely disseminated in the Middle Ages, and subsequent *remaniements* can be seen as quasi-independent poems that are more typical of the genre. And yet as these multiple versions of the

*Roland* suggest, *remaniements* move a textual tradition forward while remaining melancholically attached to the spectre of an earlier textual core. Chapters 2–4 go on to demonstrate, in different ways, that the aesthetics of writing in the Middle Ages entail some form of *re*writing. This phenomenon, a specifically medieval form of what modern critics call 'intertextuality',[10] is as much in evidence in Villon's *Testament* (*c.*1461–2), discussed in Chapter 4, as in the *Chanson de Roland*. Though not a close reworking of Villon's earlier *Lais*, the *Testament* explicitly supersedes it, while also containing a series of lyrics (some of which may have been initially composed independently) and frequent covert references to other texts. All these features unsettle the status of the text we are reading, the more so given the *Testament* explicitly acknowledges its own susceptibility to reworking at the hands of others, positioning itself thereby in a dynamic, constantly evolving process of textual transformation. Villon was acutely aware that texts could change over a period of time, either independently of their first author or in some cases as part of an author's own developing writing project, and Villon builds an awareness of this instability into the aesthetics of his *Testament*.

Another source of intertextuality that is specific to the Middle Ages arises as a result of another aspect of manuscript culture. Although there are some manuscripts that contain only one work, most are compilations. In the later Middle Ages the principle of compilation can be to assemble the works of a single author (see Chapters 4, 7, and 8), but in the earlier period a compilation is typically one of *texts* not authors. Sometimes these collections seem random, the result of idiosyncratic choices on the part of the scribe or the person commissioning the manuscript, but sometimes they have thematic, generic, or narrative unity:[11] consider the St Albans Psalter discussed in Chapter 14, the *trouvère chansonniers* discussed in Chapter 6, or the manuscripts of the early thirteenth-century Vulgate *Lancelot* cycle discussed in Chapter 2.

In this last instance, a story (inspired by earlier verse romances) provides the impetus for the composition of a series of related texts by different writers that then circulate as a cycle. The great cycles of medieval French literature – the Vulgate cycle, the *cycle de Guillaume d'Orange*, and the *Roman de Renart* – illustrate the extent to which some texts are subordinate to and generated by a story that exceeds the boundaries of just one text.[12] Whereas the prequels and sequels of the Vulgate cycle usually present themselves in manuscripts as separate entities within a *sequence* of texts, Jean de Meun's continuation of the *Roman de la rose* (see Chapter 3) is so skilfully grafted onto Guillaume de Lorris's apparently unfinished poem that the two are often presented as a single text. But whereas multiple authorship in the Vulgate *Lancelot* cycle produces a sequence whose various parts seem

by and large (albeit problematically) subordinate to a relatively unified ideological agenda, multiple authorship in the *Rose* produces a work which opens
up a space for dialectic, play, and uncertainty. The 'text' in both cases is
inherently multiple, incorporating – like Villon's *Testament* – the play of
material circumstances into its literary nature.

## What is a medieval French author?

The study of literature is often organized round the study of authors. But in
many instances the instability of medieval texts makes it impossible to
ascertain what an author wrote (all we can be sure of is what a text becomes
in transmission), while what it means to be an author is problematic when a
text results from the interventions of multiple authors (including anonymous
performers), or has undergone a series of *remaniements*. Furthermore,
authors have no proprietorial control over their texts, as Villon acknowledges in his *Testament*, and appropriately enough many texts, particularly
before 1300, are anonymous. When authors are named, they are generally
shadowy figures, known only by a name that does not allow us to identify the
writer (this is the case with Guillaume de Lorris, for example), sometimes by
a name that is not a real one but a *nom de plume* adopted by the writer
himself (Rutebeuf, perhaps also Chrétien de Troyes), or a name confected
by modern scholarship (Marie de France). An author's name – whether used
in a text or by a critic – often seems primarily to *authorize* a text, that is, to
explain its provenance and/or guarantee its authenticity. The example of
Chrétien de Troyes (see Chapter 5), the most influential figure in the emerging genre of courtly romance, illustrates that a writer can develop his own
authorial style, seek to delineate his corpus for his readership, and thereby
generate an awareness of his work as a distinct entity. But in the twelfth
century this is the exception rather than the rule and as the *Conte du graal*'s
continuations show, an author's work may elude his control and always
remains susceptible to appropriation and reorientation by others. Even in a
case such as Chrétien's, where author-centred criticism is practised by French
medievalists, the vagaries of manuscript transmission and uncertainties of
attribution mean that it is impossible to demarcate the corpus definitively, as
Chapter 5 also shows.

Another illustration of the uncertainties surrounding authorship is the
implausible (sometimes impossible) attribution of texts to a well-known
figure, usually a bid for the authority conferred by a well-known name.
A celebrated instance is the attribution of *La Mort le roi Artu*, the last segment
of the *Lancelot* cycle, to Walter Map, Henry II of England's secretary and
courtier (see Chapter 2), who died several decades before the *Mort* was

written. Chapter 6 examines the case of the Châtelain de Couci, one of the best-known lyric poets (*trouvères*) of the late twelfth century. His life and work seem to have captured the imagination of several generations of readers and writers in the thirteenth century, leading to the ascription to him of lyrics that were probably by other poets. That he also becomes the hero of a romance narrative loosely based on his life, but citing his lyrics, shows how the reception of lyrics is grounded in the perceived presence of an author-figure, but the move into fiction also suggests the extent to which the figure of the author is an effect as well as a cause of the text.

In the later Middle Ages, some authors emerge from the shadows and, while continuing the play with conventions and formal experimentation typical of the earlier period, they start consciously to inject autobiographical elements into their work, also seeking to take control of how it is transmitted. Thus Guillaume de Machaut (*c*.1300–77) – the subject of Chapter 7 – foregrounds the processes and circumstances of the writing of his texts, and towards the end of his career seems to have played a key role in the compilation and circulation of manuscripts of his complete works, some clearly for specific patrons. Although his influence on the transmission of his corpus fades after his death, he is, as Deborah McGrady felicitously puts it, both 'the last troubadour and a prototype for the modern author' (p. 121).

Authorial presence in a corpus goes a stage further in the work of Christine de Pizan – the subject of Chapter 8. As her writing evolves, she uses it increasingly to negotiate her position as an author in the public sphere, commenting on her own circumstances, on her development as a writer, and on events in the world around her. She also does so, of course, as a woman, and an awareness of gender is a constant in her life-long engagement with the question of authorship. Does one have to be a man in order to have the authority of an author? Clearly not, but the authority implicit in the very notion of authorship is nonetheless tacitly gendered masculine, so whereas a male writer may assume his right to it automatically by dint of his gender, a woman must constantly negotiate and renegotiate it.

Christine de Pizan's professionalism as a writer and publisher reminds us that, as in all periods, writing in the Middle Ages had an economic basis. Manuscript books were labour-intensive and costly to produce, requiring a team of skilled craftsman. Only in centres with a sufficiently large adminis-trative machinery to require the production of texts or with relatively high-level educational establishments – initially just secular courts and large religious foundations, but by the early thirteenth century also some towns – were the conditions right to sustain and create the demand for the composi-tion of long texts and book production. For this demand to be realized there also needed to be sufficient surplus wealth to pay for non-essential luxury cultural and recreational activities such as the production of texts. Some writers may have earned a living from performing their own works at fairs or in other popular gatherings. Others may have had sufficient wealth and leisure to write. But most relied on support to do so. In the Middle Ages, more often than not, this came in the form of a patron.

In the earlier Middle Ages, writers seem to have been integrated into their patron's household and rewarded with items (such as horses, furs, or goblets) that marked their inclusion in a courtly lifestyle. Such arrangements were not permanent, permitting authors to move from one court to another; but they seem to have been pretty exclusive while they lasted, and indeed 'professional' poets were probably often professional as a result of being employed in some capacity *other* than poet, such as clerk or chaplain. However, from at least the time of Machaut in the fourteenth century, patterns of patronage changed.[13] It became more common for authors to solicit the attentions of several patrons concurrently, and to be rewarded with an income or cash payments. Thus Machaut held office in the church (see Chapter 7), as did Froissart. The reason why Christine de Pizan felt her position to be especially precarious was because, as a woman, she was denied the possibility of holding a church benefice and relied on monetary payments. Such payments could be enjoyed by male authors in addition to their stipend. For instance, at the beginning of his *Joli Buisson de Jonece* Froissart runs through his account book, noting with satisfaction how much money he has received from his various protectors. Nonetheless, the impoverishment claimed by other writers (such as Villon, see Chapter 4, or Rutebeuf) suggests that not all writers were so fortunate: as today writing was not necessarily the best path to either fame or fortune.

## What is the value of genre for medieval French literature?

Unlike comparable literatures, French is not dominated by a small number of major authors (like Chaucer or Dante), nor by a fixed canon of texts, but by distinctive forms, each with their own lifespan. Many works are regularly studied *as* a group: for example, lyric poems, *fabliaux*, or farces. Even longer works like *chansons de geste* or mystery plays are often studied together with other texts of the same kind. The most obvious term for these forms or groups is 'genre'. If not as a concept, at least as a practice, genre has played an unusually large part in the study of medieval French literature. But there is by no means consensus as to its meaning.

To what extent was genre perceived to exist in the Middle Ages? Probably it was more palpable for some types of text than others. From early on a vocabulary existed to refer to different kinds of lyric; medieval terms like *grand chant courtois* (a formally elaborate love song), *aube* (dawn song), or *ballade* (a form marked by the repetition of a refrain) are still used by poets and critics today. Lyrics were usually transmitted in anthology collections (see Chapter 6), which reinforce the sense that they belong together, and within these collections a generic organization is not uncommon. The terminology of medieval drama evolved from the blanket term *jeu* ('play') used in the twelfth and thirteenth centuries, so as eventually to discriminate a wealth of different religious and secular dramatic categories (see Chapter 12). Medieval generic terms for narrative existed, but were more fluid (see Chapter 9). The word *chanson de geste* is used to refer to epic or heroic poems, but sometimes manuscript rubrics refer to them as *romans*, a term which can in fact designate almost any kind of vernacular narrative text, including chronicles, saints' lives and beast epic (*Le Roman de Renart*). Similarly some *fabliaux* are hard to distinguish from fables or short courtly narratives,[14] and the term *dit* can refer to texts of varying form on a wide range of topics, but most commonly a first-person reflection on personal, amorous, or political themes based on octo-syllabic rhyming couplets. Although there are manuscripts exclusively devoted to one genre, compilations of a variety of different sorts of texts are just as or more common, especially for the literature of the earlier period (Chapter 9).

Lacking unambiguous evidence from the Middle Ages, medievalists have long debated the meaning and value of the concept of genre. Given the broad spectrum of literature in verse, criteria based on verse form are widely used, and they can be useful to distinguish *chansons de geste* from lyrics or verse romance. But formal definitions work well for some genres, badly for others. If the *rondeau* is entirely defined by its form, saints' lives can be written in a wide range of verse forms, or in prose; they can even be turned into plays. Accordingly, different types of hagiographic text are usually categorized not by form but by content, according to whether they narrate the saint's whole life, martyrdom, or miracles.[15] Perhaps saints' lives, like medieval vernacular history-writing, should be defined by their formal variety; historiography, however, was formally innovative whereas saints' lives adopt forms pioneered by other narratives.

Invoking the model of linguistics, Fredric Jameson proposed that as well as assigning significance to form one could give a formal account of content. Using the example of medieval verse romance, he argues that form is ideologically overdetermined.[16] An influential essay by Hans Robert Jauss brilliantly sidesteps the 'form'/'content' dichotomy altogether to define genre as a 'horizon of expectation'.[17] Most literary production falls within the expected horizon; but the cultural horizon, like the terrestrial one, moves when we do and is therefore constantly challenged and displaced. Jauss's great strengths are his recognition of dynamism and change, and the value he accords to 'limit' texts that stretch existing paradigms. The most radical contribution to the debate over genre was made by Paul Zumthor, who dismissed the concept as unproductive for the French Middle Ages and instead substituted the term 'register'.[18] Register is a discourse that combines lexical and semantic features as much as purely formal ones (such as rhyme); different registers constitute different kinds of texts, much as classical and medieval rhetoricians distinguished between the high, middle, and low styles. Zumthor finds an ally in Mikhail Bakhtin, for whom what characterizes medieval literature is not the purity or fixity of forms, but their hybridity. For Bakhtin, medieval texts characteristically consist of fragments of competing discourses cited from earlier texts.[19] They are thus precursors of the novel as Bakhtin envisages it.

Each of the four chapters in this section of the *Companion* adopts a distinctive approach to genre. Chapter 9 confirms the fluidity of generic boundaries in the Old French period, pointing to the hybridity of texts such as *Ami et Amile* and *Huon de Bordeaux*, and suggesting how readers' perceptions of genre could have been shaped by the organization and selection of individual manuscript compilations. Later medieval self-consciousness about lyric is examined in Chapter 10, which shows how fixed-form lyrics such as the *ballade* and *rondeau* developed from the thirteenth century onwards, involving adherence to predetermined patterns of repetition that are discussed in quasi-scientific terms. Chapters 11 and 12 experiment with ways of conceiving genre that do not involve form or language, Chapter 11 by taking theatricality as a model for considering the role of spectatorship in various short comic tales together with the texts' own potential as spectacle, Chapter 12 by focusing on the social and political interaction implicit in medieval theatre.

What is certain is that any account of genre in medieval French literature needs to be able to explain not just the persistence of recognizable codes or forms, but also the constant emergence of the new. Innovation, whether it took the form of shifting the horizon (in Jauss's terms), or contriving some new hybrid (Bakhtin), was the key to success with patrons and audiences (see Chapter 9). Medieval French writers were constantly inventing new literary forms: from verse romance to prose romance, from the *dit* to the *dit amoureux*, from the *grand chant courtois* to the *formes fixes*, whether we call them 'genres' or not. What was the relation between such changes and historical conditions? Interdependence between literary and social activity forms the main thrust of the study of theatre in Chapter 12, paving the way for the next section.

## How can we read medieval French literature historically?

The success of French literary culture over such a long period owes much to the historical context in which it was produced, and which inevitably inflected its course. The increase in textual production in French from *c.*1150 was undoubtedly linked to a marked increase in literacy. The initial impetus for this was pragmatic: as the English monarchy (initially under Henry II), then the French (under Philippe Auguste) sought to centralize power, writing was increasingly used to keep accounts and records.[20] Other determining factors include the prosperity of regional courts; the concomitant growth of courtly and chivalric culture; the monarchy's rivalry with regional magnates as it progressively asserted its control; a high level of intellectual activity, initially in church schools and later in universities, particularly Paris which was a European beacon from the thirteenth century onwards; the rapid growth of urban communities avid both for entertainment of their own and for a share in the glamorous culture of the courts; travel, including crusade and pilgrimage, both of which led as much to cultural exchanges as religious development, often enriching their participants materially as much as spiritually. Such factors not only fostered the production of literary texts but also made up much of their content.

To what extent, then, do texts reflect historical circumstance? The chapters in this section of the *Companion* directly address four crucial fields in which this question is posed: the domains of government (Chapter 13), religion and the church (Chapter 14), sex and marriage (Chapter 15), and relations with other cultures (Chapter 16). But the traces of historical issues are legible in other chapters: Holy War and relations with Islam in the *Chanson de Roland* (Chapter 1); love and chivalry in different ways in the Vulgate cycle (Chapter 2) and the romances of Chrétien (Chapter 5); pilgrimage and crusade in the texts associated with the Châtelain de Couci (Chapter 6); sexual and class difference in short comic tales (Chapter 11); clerical and lay experience in the *Roman de la rose* (Chapter 3); and, as already noted, in medieval theatre (Chapter 12).

Although occasionally practical matters can be documented in literature (such as knighting ceremonial or methods of combat), overwhelmingly literary texts reflect not so much material events as people's ideas, desires, or anxieties; as a result they influence their historical environment as much as they mirror it. This is especially true of the mutual interference between courtly milieus and the ideology of courtly literature. The emergence of a refined literary model of love (*fine amour*, from the Occitan *fin'amor*, often termed 'courtly love') first in the courts of Occitania and later in France, where it fused with ideas of chivalry, is widely regarded as one of the great paradigm shifts in western European sensibility. Treated with a bizarre combination of fervour and irony by medieval writers, the themes of love and chivalry have excited controversy over the extent to which they are literary fictions or social practices, debates that have often been paralyzed by naive assumptions about literature merely reflecting a 'reality' which in fact it helps to shape, and of which it is therefore part. Chapter 15 indicates a way of avoiding these pitfalls by looking for evidence of fissures between marriage as represented in medieval texts, the desires it appears to serve, and the desires that may find expression outside the institution of wedlock.

Among medieval historians, those of the French Annales school have been the most successful at exploiting literary texts as sources, thanks to their recourse to the concept of the 'imaginary': the recognition that literary texts map a world of mental images (and not directly a set of material conditions) subscribed to by their authors and audiences.[21] The most important of these medievalists, Jacques Le Goff and Georges Duby, have fruitfully explored the domains of feudalism, knighthood, love and marriage, religious belief, and many other topics, using literary texts in ways that are often of immediate value to literary scholars.[22]

Another successful, though contrasting, approach is the Marxist methodology developed by the German scholar Erich Köhler. Köhler used contradictions in medieval texts as a means of progressing beyond their depiction of conscious ('imaginary' or 'ideological') thoughts to the political and economic conflicts that they masked, most notably in his book on Chrétien de Troyes.[23] If Marxist-inspired criticism has most commonly been addressed to romance, Peter Haidu's iconoclastic study of the *Chanson de Roland* is an important exception,[24] while reading medieval French texts as 'political fictions' is an approach that has been fruitfully applied more broadly.[25] Chapter 13 draws on this tradition to show how economic realities are partially concealed, partially revealed in literary representations of government. This chapter also demonstrates how, in addition, individuals' desires are often in contradiction with the institutions within which they ostensibly operate. A similar conclusion is reached in Chapter 15 which, like Chapter 11, shows the continuing influence of the feminist criticism that flowered in the 1980s and 1990s in the English-speaking world. Like the Marxist-oriented criticism on which they drew, feminist readings influentially revised the received, male-dominated, perception of most medieval texts, using literary analysis as a means of 'demystifying' representations, though in this instance so as to discern the power relations of sex and gender that underlie them.[26] As a result of the rearticulation of Lacanian theory by Slavoj Žižek, a Marxist slant also informs much recent psychoanalytic criticism, thereby making it far more historically engaged than previous writings by the likes of Jean-Charles Huchet and Charles Méla.[27]

The rise in the anglophone world in the 1970s of New Historicism was responsible for theorizing the relation between history and literature in a new way. R. Howard Bloch produced a series of ground-breaking studies all premised on the illuminating potential of homology (the analogy between structures), an intellectual strategy repudiated by traditional Marxists.[28] In his first book, medieval literature and law are shown to be reciprocally related, forensic procedures (for example) favouring deposition over combat just as narrative became more circumstantial and less focused on action.[29] This strategy of seeking out a dialogue between social or political discourses and literary ones has been pursued by Bloch himself and also, with *éclat*, by other North American scholars.[30]

Currently, perhaps, some of the most forward-looking work relating French medieval literature to the social and political circumstances of its production has been done under the aegis of post-colonial or queer theory.[31] Although there are many kinds of theoretical assumption at work in these approaches, they are united by their interest in recuperating the marginal and the occluded from the hegemonic. Chapters 15 and 16 explore how medieval French literature represents (and thereby includes) desires and figures that the period's dominant cultural forces apparently seek to repress. As we see in Chapter 15, literary texts seem open to a range of sexual desires, identities, and practices that do not sit easily with the somewhat restricted and restrictive models of medieval sexuality and marriage propagated by the church; similarly, we learn in Chapter 16 that medieval French texts are often more open to otherness than they might at first seem, blurring the boundaries between 'us' and 'them' as characters cross over confusingly and freely between the supernatural and natural worlds (sometimes grounding the latter troublingly in the former), or between the Christian and Saracen faiths, thereby unsettling what is often taken to be one of the most rigid oppositions of medieval culture.

We should note one further way of seeing a connection between vernacular literary production and its historical context, namely through intellectual history. What is at stake here is not the relation between a literary representation and a political or social 'reality', but the continuity (or discontinuity) between literary discourse and other forms of thought, such as rhetoric, philosophy, or theology. A pioneering, if now discredited, version of this approach was the criticism of D. W. Robertson, a giant of English studies who also wrote extensively about French, and who maintained (for example) that the literature of courtly love was so incompatible with orthodox Christian belief that it could not be taken at face value.[32] But the study of medieval thinking remains an extremely fertile way of seeing how literary texts – which were after all often written by educated men, by clerks and sometimes even by priests – continue in an imaginative arena the intellectual problems and debates of their age. Thus the pervasiveness in the Middle Ages of philosophical traditions deriving from Plato, Aristotle, or the Stoics illumines many important studies of medieval French texts, though such studies often diverge in how receptive they are to modern theory as well as medieval thought.[33] By exploring the relationship between lay and clerical interests, Chapter 14 illumines the ideological intentions of medieval saints' lives and conjectures on their appeal especially to women readers, given women's exclusion from the clergy. That the life of one particular woman reader, Christina of Markyate, was so deeply influenced by the *Vie de Saint Alexis* graphically illustrates how medieval French literature has impacted on history, as well as the other way round.

These, then, are the problems and issues explored in this *Companion*. It is not a literary history, and although within individual sections most chapters are ordered chronologically there is no overall chronological trajectory. What we seek to offer, rather, is an agenda for students and teachers of medieval French literature, and hopefully too for further research. This agenda is not grounded in a single approach; indeed the approaches adopted in some chapters contrast noticeably to those adopted in others. We wish to foster, not finesse, such differences. We have also taken a conscious decision not to make extensive use of 'theory' in this volume, even though our own publications, and those of many of our contributors, are at the theoretical end of the spectrum of medieval French studies, and even though theoretical assumptions (for instance about intertextuality, authorship, gender, genre, class, race, and so on) are implicit in *all* the chapters. What we want to show, by foregrounding above all the rich and varied textual traditions in medieval French, is that they elicit and encourage a variety of approaches in and of themselves.

## Notes

1. See W. D. Elcock, *The Romance Languages*, 2nd edn (London, Faber, 1975).
2. See S. Fleischman, *Tense and Narrativity: From Medieval Performance to Modern Fiction* (London, Routledge, 1990).
3. For an account of the emergence of France and its fluid borders in the earlier period, see J. Dunbabin, *France in the Making 843–1180* (Oxford University Press, 1985).
4. On the relation between Latinate culture and medieval romance vernacular traditions, see E. R. Curtius, *European Literature and the Latin Middle Ages*, trans. W. R. Trask (London, Routledge and Kegan Paul, 1953).

5. On the emergence of prose in French, see particularly G. M. Spiegel, *Romancing the Past: the Rise of Prose Historiography in Thirteenth-Century France* (Berkeley and Oxford, California University Press, 1993).
6. For a summary, see S. Gaunt, *Retelling the Tale: an Introduction to Medieval French Literature* (London, Duckworth, 2001).
7. See S. Fleischman, 'Philology, Linguistics, and the Discourse of the Medieval Text', *Speculum*, 64 (1990), 19–37; S. Marnette, *Narrateur et points de vue dans la littérature française médiévale* (Bern, Peter Lang, 1998).
8. See A. Foulet and M. B. Speer, *On Editing Old French Texts* (Lawrence, KS, The Regents Press of Kansas, 1979), pp. 1–39.
9. B. Cerquiglini, *L'Eloge de la variante: histoire critique de la philologie* (Paris, Seuil, 1989).
10. See J. Still and M. Worton (eds.), *Intertextuality: Theories and Practice* (Manchester and New York, Manchester University Press, 1990).
11. On compilations, see in particular S. Huot, *From Song to Book: the Poetics of Writing in Old French Lyric and Lyrical Narrative Poetry* (Ithaca and London, Cornell University Press, 1987) and K. Busby, *Codex and Context: Reading Old French Verse Narrative in Manuscripts*, 2 vols. (Amsterdam, Rodopi, 2002).
12. On the general phenomenon of cyclicity, see S. Sturm-Maddox and D. Maddox (eds.), *Transtextualities: of Cycles and Cyclicity in Medieval French Literature* Medieval and Renaissance Texts and Studies (Binghamton, NY, Center for Medieval and Renaissance Studies, 1996).
13. See D. McGrady, 'What Is a Patron? Benefactors and Authorship in Harley 4431, Christine de Pizan's Collected Works', in M. Desmond (ed.), *Christine de Pizan and the Categories of Difference* (Minneapolis, Minnesota University Press, 1998), pp. 195–214.
14. See W. Spiewok, 'La division en genres à l'intérieur du récit bref. Pour une typologie du récit bref au Moyen âge', in *Le récit bref au Moyen âge. Actes du colloque des 8 et 9 mai 1988* (Amiens, Centre d'études médiévales, Université de Picardie, 1989), pp. 151–67.
15. Charles F. Altman, 'Two Types of Opposition and the Structure of Medieval Saints' Lives', *Medievalia et Humanistica*, n.s. 6 (1975), 1–11.
16. F. Jameson, *The Political Unconscious: Narrative as a Socially Symbolic Act* (London and New York, Methuen, 1981).
17. H. R. Jauss, *Toward an Aesthetic of Reception*, trans. Timothy Bahti (Minneapolis, Minnesota University Press, 1982).
18. P. Zumthor, *Essai de poétique médiévale* (Paris, Seuil, 1972), pp. 239–43.
19. M. Bakhtin, *The Dialogic Imagination: Four Essays*, trans. Caryl Emerson and Michael Holquist (Austen, University of Texas Press, 1981).
20. M. T. Clanchy, *From Memory to Written Record: England 1066–1307*, 2nd edition (Oxford, Blackwell, 1993); see also H. J. Chaytor, *From Script to Print: an Introduction to Medieval Vernacular Literature* (Cambridge, W. H. Heffer, 1945).
21. As enshrined in Georges Duby's title, *Les Trois Ordres ou l'imaginaire du féodalisme* (Paris, Gallimard, 1978).
22. For example, J. Le Goff, *Les Intellectuels au moyen âge* (Paris, Seuil, 1976); G. Duby, *Le Chevalier, la femme et le prêtre* (Paris, Hachette, 1981).
23. E. Köhler, *L'Aventure chevaleresque: Idéal et réalité dans le roman courtois*, trans. Eliane Kaufholz (Paris, Gallimard, 1974).

24. P. Haidu, *The Subject of Violence: the Song of Roland and the Birth of the State* (Bloomington and Indianapolis, Indiana University Press, 1993).

25. S. Kay, *The Chansons de geste in the Age of Romance: Political Fictions* (Oxford University Press, 1995).

26. E.g. E.J. Burns, *Bodytalk: When Women Speak in Old French Literature* (Philadelphia, University of Pennsylvania Press); S. Gaunt, *Gender and Genre in Medieval French Literature* (Cambridge University Press, 1995); R.L. Krueger, *Women Readers and the Ideology of Gender in Old French Verse Romance* (Cambridge University Press, 1993); H. Solterer, *The Master and Minerva: Disputing Women in Medieval French Culture* (Berkeley and London, University of California Press, 1995).

27. See, for example, J.-Ch. Huchet, *Le Roman médiéval* (Paris, PUF, 1984) and *Littérature médiévale et psychanalyse: pour une clinique littéraire* (Paris, PUF, 1990), and C. Méla, *La Reine et le graal: la conjointure dans les romans du Graal de Chrétien de Troyes au livre de Lancelot* (Paris, Seuil, 1984). Post-Žižekian psychoanalytic criticism includes S. Huot, *Madness in Medieval French Literature: Identities Found and Lost* (Oxford University Press, 2003); S. Gaunt, *Love and Death in Medieval French and Occitan Courtly Literature: Martyrs to Love* (Oxford University Press, 2006); S. Kay, *Courtly Contradictions: the Emergence of the Literary Object in the Twelfth Century* (Stanford University Press, 2001).

28. See the attack on analogy by Jameson, *Political Unconscious*, pp. 1–101.

29. R.H. Bloch, *Medieval French Literature and Law* (Berkeley, California University Press, 1977).

30. Especially R.H. Bloch, *Etymologies and Genealogies: a Literary Anthropology of the French Middle Ages* (Chicago and London, Chicago University Press, 1983); but also K. Gravdal, *Ravishing Maidens: Writing Rape in Medieval French Literature and Law* (Philadelphia, University of Pennsylvania Press, 1991), and P. McCracken, *The Romance of Adultery: Queenship and Sexual Transgression in Old French Literature* (Philadelphia, University of Pennsylvania Press, 1998).

31. See for example W. Burgwinkle, *Sodomy, Masculinity, and Law in Medieval Literature* (Cambridge University Press, 2004) and S. Kinoshita, *Medieval Boundaries: Rethinking Difference in Old French Literature* (Philadelphia, University of Pennsylvania Press, 2006).

32. D.W. Robertson, *Essays in Medieval Culture* (Princeton University Press, 1980).

33. See, for example, D. Heller-Roazen, *Fortune's Faces: the Romance of the Rose and the Poetics of Contingency* (Baltimore and London, Johns Hopkins University Press, 2003); T. Hunt, *Chrétien de Troyes: Yvain* (London, Grant and Cutler, 1986); Kay, *Courtly Contradictions*; S. Nichols, *Romanesque Signs: Early Medieval Narrative and Iconography* (New Haven and London, Yale University Press, 1983); E. Vance, *From Topic to Tale: Logic and Narrativity in the Middle Ages* (Minneapolis, Minnesota University Press, 1987).

PART I

# What is a medieval French text?

# I

JANE GILBERT

# The *Chanson de Roland*

The *Song of Roland* functions as what Pierre Nora terms a *lieu de mémoire*: 'any significant entity, whether material or non-material in nature, which by dint of human will or the work of time has become a symbolic element of the memorial heritage of any community (in this case, the French community)'.[1] Nineteenth-century antiquarians seeking a national epic which would be to France what the *Iliad* was to Greece – at once a glorious military legend, an exposition of core ethical values and a great literary production from its finest political and cultural moment – directed their energies to discovering a *Song of Roland*.[2] Since then the *Roland* has been invoked in wartime to symbolize and galvanize French resistance; during the siege of Paris in 1870 the great medievalist Gaston Paris lectured at the Collège de France on '*La Chanson de Roland* et la nationalité française', and Raoul Mortier published clandestinely all the extant French *Roland* versions under the Occupation in 1940–4.[3] Even to those who have not read it, the *Roland* epitomizes 'une certaine idée de la France', the evocative phrase with which de Gaulle characterized the roots of his political outlook and which has been borrowed ever since (not always without irony) to express patriotic attachment to a romantic conception of France. The poem's heroes – combative, passionate, pious, unwavering in their commitment to *France dulce, la bele* – personify virtues foundational to French collective identity. Histories of French literature devote substantial attention to the *Roland*, and studies of medieval French (including the present volume) give pride of place to what is generally considered the first masterpiece in the French tongue and foundation stone of the world's foremost tradition of *belles-lettres*.

The national memory invested in the *Song of Roland*, as in any *lieu de mémoire*, represents a retrospective fantasy serving a modern audience's sense of its own identity rather than an accurate reflection of the medieval past. We need to look beyond the myth to see the real complexity of the *Roland*'s history. In the first place, there is not one *Chanson de Roland* but many. Much the most famous is the Oxford *Roland*, the text preserved in the

Bodleian Library's manuscript Digby 23. It is, however, only one of seven versions, each of which is a distinct 'version' by virtue not only of its particular wording but also of the selection of other works with which it was copied or bound, its date, provenance, and dialect.[4] Duggan's edition localizes and dates the manuscripts containing these versions as follows:[5] Oxford (O) 1125–50, Anglo-Norman; Venice 4 (V4) early fourteenth century, Franco-Venetian, possibly copied at Treviso or Bologna; Venice 7 (V7) and Châteauroux (C), a pair of closely related manuscripts containing similar texts, end of the thirteenth century, Franco-Venetian; Paris (P), 1265–90, northern French (Picard or Ardennais), possibly from near Laon; the Cambridge manuscript (T) shows traces of an older text in a western French dialect, greatly modernized by the scribe who copied it not much after 1431; finally Lyon (L), late thirteenth or early fourteenth century, northern French (Burgundian), possibly from around Lyon itself.

Besides its written forms, surviving or lost, the *Chanson de Roland* circulated orally in versions of which we have little notion; our comprehension of the tradition can therefore only ever be partial. The surviving texts employ rhetorical devices commonly associated with orality, such as repetition, formulae, and parataxis. These features have led critics to debate whether the written texts were intended for use by *jongleurs* (minstrels) who would have intoned them in live performance, or whether they deploy literary strategies mimicking orality for stylistic purposes. Such questions are relevant to medieval textuality as a whole but particularly to *chansons de geste*. A long dispute over the Oxford *Roland* once opposed 'traditionalists' who viewed the surviving text as the accretion of generations of oral narratives stretching back to the battle of Roncevaux in 778 to 'individualists' who considered it the self-conscious creation of a single author. Present scholarship adopts an intermediate position, holding that oral and written, 'far from being simple alternatives, were in fact interactive and operated in tandem in a complex symbiotic relationship' in the production and transmission of medieval literary works.[6]

In this chapter orality is considered mainly in the thematic significance it acquires from Roland's repeatedly expressed concern over his *los* (public esteem, glory, reputation) and over the song which, he is certain, people will sing about his deeds. The protagonist's anxiety to avoid a *male chançun* (O, 1466: 'bad song') plays a determining role in his strategic decisions and thence in the direction of the battle of Roncevaux. I shall comment upon individual *Roland* texts in the accidental or intentional forms in which they have survived. I shall also draw upon the conventional division of *Roland* narratives into two redactions, referred to by formal criteria: in one (represented by O and V4) the *laisses* are unified by assonance, in the other (represented by all the other manuscripts) by rhyme. (A *laisse* is the *chanson de geste* equivalent of a stanza. By 'rhyme' is meant that at the end of each line in a *laisse*, 'the last stressed vowel and any sounds following it are the same' (*OED*); by 'assonance', that the last stressed vowel and any vowel sounds following it are the same but any following consonants may be different.) While the Oxford *Roland* is generally dated to shortly after 1098, the rhymed *Roland* is dated after 1180. It is thought to represent a *remaniement* or reworking in which the earlier, assonanced tradition was adapted to tastes, interests, and political imperatives of the late twelfth century. Such modification is typical of medieval literature, and it was until recently equally typical of medievalist scholarship that many later revisions, including the rhymed *Rolands*, remained neglected. More recent studies, recognizing the diverse and changing cultures of the Middle Ages, have turned again to less celebrated works including *remaniements*.

The core narrative of the *Chanson de Roland* tradition goes as follows:

> In Charlemagne's long war against the Saracens of Spain, King Marsile of Saragossa, the last unconquered Muslim city, offers to capitulate, secretly intending to renege once the invaders have returned home. The Frankish barons wonder whom to send on the risky mission to negotiate. Roland, Charlemagne's heroic nephew, nominates his stepfather, Ganelon, who promptly swears vengeance on his stepson. Ganelon plots with the Saracens to ensure that when the Franks withdraw Roland, his friend Oliver, and the twelve peers (Charlemagne's major barons) will lead the rearguard, which the Saracens will then ambush at Roncevaux. During the first assault, Oliver asks Roland to blow his horn, the oliphant, to recall the emperor and the main body; Roland refuses. The Franks repel the first Saracen wave but gradually succumb before the second. Oliver now rejects Roland's proposal that the oliphant be sounded, but Archbishop Turpin (one of the twelve peers) insists and Charlemagne returns. The Saracens are in flight but all the Franks are dead, including Roland and Oliver. Charlemagne mourns and takes revenge on the fleeing and on the African emir Baligant, Marsile's overlord, who arrives with a large army. On his return to Aix-la-Chapelle Charlemagne informs Aude, Roland's betrothed and Oliver's sister, of Roland's death; she laments and dies. At trial, Ganelon's plea that he is innocent of treachery is accepted by Charlemagne's council. He is nevertheless convicted and sentenced to death after a judicial combat between his kinsman Pinabel and Charlemagne's champion Thierry d'Anjou, who wins with divine assistance.

Naturally the various manuscripts show idiosyncratic differences in their presentations of this story, but between the assonanced and rhymed traditions there are substantial narrative differences, in particular in the aftermath of Roland's death, where the rhymed tradition greatly expands the treatment of both Aude and Ganelon. Aude's protracted anxiety and anticipatory mourning enhance Roland's status, while Ganelon's escape and the comic and cruel pursuit which follows emphasize his wickedness and whet the audience's appetite for his brutal punishment. Thematic differences are also evident. The heroes of the assonanced tradition are much more divided, quarrelsome, and destructive, their treatment by the texts much less straight-forwardly laudatory. Their actions are set within an assortment of sometimes overlapping, sometimes contradictory ethical and strategic frameworks. At various times they dedicate their service to country, king, kin, peer group, friend, god, co-religionists, or simply self; moreover they do not always agree on the best way to serve any one of these. All the main characters including Ganelon and the Saracens are treated as worthy barons, while no individual is wholly righteous. Up until Roland's death, the assonanced *Rolands* ambiguously encourage discord as well as unity within the noble Christian community and maintain an uneasy tension between those forces. In cons-picuous contrast, the rhymed tradition harmonizes the conflicting values of the assonanced tradition into a comprehensive ideology in which the Christian God, Carolingian emperor, and French king, country, family, and military unit form a single allegiance. All its characters are carefully placed on one ethical scale stretching from an idealized Roland to Ganelon, a pantomime villain. The Saracens are uncomplicatedly demonized, with little evidence of the problematic similarities which in the assonanced tradition cut across distinctions between faithful and infidel.[7] Ironically, given its relative neglect, the rhymed tradition tallies much more closely with the *Song of Roland* of modern memory-myth than does the assonanced.

The idea of a *Song of Roland* was for medieval writers and audiences also a bearer of imaginary investments in community and struggle, different from but analogous to those it has borne in modern France. Reading medieval French writing, one is struck by how widely known and how influential was the story of Roncevaux. Other *chansons de geste* return tirelessly to the subject; Roland's death is the foundational event of the *cycle du roi*, the group of around twenty *chansons* centred on Charlemagne's foreign cam-paigns. The conventional dating of the Oxford text to the end of the eleventh century makes it one of the earliest surviving works of French literature, while the rhymed tradition was still being re-copied in the fifteenth century. Just as Gaston Paris and Raoul Mortier invoked the *Roland* to give courage in times of war, twelfth-century historians felt inspired to report (truthfully or not) that a *cantilena Rollandi* was sung to lead Duke William's troops into the battle of Hastings.[8] Norman conquests were thus ennobled by absorption into a communal heroic tradition. Rendered helpfully indeterminate by its territorial extent as well as by its temporal distance, 'Frankish' identity lent itself to multiple appropriations. The *Roland* circulated well beyond modern France; indeed the assonanced tradition survives substantially in only two manuscripts, neither of which can be considered unproblematically 'French'. O is written in Anglo-Norman, the dialect of post-conquest England, and V4 (which follows the assonanced tradition only until the end of the Baligant episode) in Franco-Venetian, a *koinè* devised for the diffusion of French works in northern Italy.[9] In fact a substantial number of the surviving *Roland* texts have either Anglo-Norman or Italian connections. Within what would become modern France, but outside the sphere of Old French, *Roland* is more frequently cited in the Occitan lyric tradition than are such major figures as Tristan, Alexander, Charlemagne, and Arthur. The *Song of Roland* was a *lieu de mémoire* significant to various medieval communities, not limited to those which we today would call French; it could permeate national boundaries as much as consecrate them.

This is not surprising given the protagonist's will to found a glorious memorial tradition in his name. But is the song that Roland intends should be sung about him the *Song of Roland*? In what relation does that song stand to the surviving *Chansons de Roland*? A brief exploration of the theory behind Pierre Nora's model of the *lieu de mémoire* will help us to approach these questions.

## Memory, history, and melancholia

Nora's definition of a *lieu de mémoire* rests on a fundamental contrast between 'history' and 'memory'. Whereas memory, 'unconscious of the distortions to which it is subject, vulnerable in various ways to appropriation and manipulation' (3), constantly reinterprets past events to fit present purposes, history engages in methodological reflection aiming at an impersonal rendering which respects the discrepancy between then and now. Memory is primary, spontaneous, and sacred, oral or silent (for its plenitude makes voice unnecessary), identified with a living present conceived as eternal, continuous with past and future: 'experience, still lived in the warmth of tradition, in the silence of custom, in the repetition of the ancestral' (1) (much the same has been said of the *chansons de geste* in general and of the Oxford *Roland* in particular).[10] History is secondary, artificial, and godless, a grammatology embedded in impermanence and in matter, melancholically contemplating a past perceived as dead and gone. Nora sees the modern condition dominated by the historical ('Our consciousness is shaped by a sense that everything is over and done with, that something long since begun is now complete' (1)), while memory is associated with 'primitive and archaic societies ... whose secret died with them' (2).

There may be something in this characterization of modernity, but the notion of a human society which experiences no loss and no mourning in relation to the past is untenable.[11] The nature of Nora's antinomy becomes clear when we compare it to Freud's distinction between normal and pathological mourning (melancholia); the latter relates less to physical loss of an object than to 'a loss of a more ideal kind' where the subject feels betrayed or abandoned, robbed of some abstract ideal such as love, courage, or generosity.[12] Similarly, Nora's past is valuable less for itself than as representing a capacity lost to modernity. 'Memory is constantly on our lips because it no longer exists' (1). 'Memory' itself is a *lieu de mémoire.*[13] Nora's constructs are therefore best taken as hypothetical poles facilitating analysis of representations of the past in complex societies. Such analysis will involve refining, even redefining its own conceptual tools. Of course different relationships to the past, to death, to loss, to memory and memorialization are always possible, and the *Rolands* may manifest a number of these in ways which do not necessarily fit the conceptual schemas that structure Nora's essay or even Freud's. But it can be particularly fruitful to examine texts such as the *Roland* as *lieux de mémoire* because, as Nora acknowledges, they are 'hybrid places, mutants in a sense, compounded of life and death, of the temporal and the eternal' (15). It is as such 'Möbius strips, endless rounds of the collective and the individual, the prosaic and the sacred, the immutable and the fleeting' (15) that I shall approach the various *Chansons de Roland*, focusing on Roland's death and on responses to it.

## The loss of Roland

A significant death behaves, in Freud's memorable description, 'like an open wound, drawing to itself ... energies ... from all directions' in an effort to heal the damage it threatens to cause.[14] Roland's death is a trauma generating the energy which powers the various *Chansons de Roland* and beyond them the *cycle du roi* and other *chansons de geste*. In the present section I shall elaborate on the different ways in which the assonanced and rhymed traditions handle the dynamics of Roland's loss; in the next I shall consider these approaches' capacities to generate memorial and textual traditions.

Charlemagne's nephew Roland is portrayed as his chief military support and instigator of the territorial expansion and unification the emperor has achieved. The death of this captain is already momentous enough. While battle rages at Roncevaux, France suffers the storms, earthquakes, and noontide darkness that signify loss on a cosmic scale. I quote here from the less familiar V4 as a means of challenging the dominance of O:

Hom nol vid che tut no s'espavant.
Dïent plusur: 'Quest el difenimant.'
Cil no savent mot, nel dïent veramant.
Deo li fist tot per la mort de Rollant.
(V4, 1343–6; equivalent to O, 1433–7)

(No one who saw it was not overcome with fear. Many said, 'It is the end [of the world].' They know nothing about it, they do not speak true. God did all this for the sake of Roland's death.)

Still more critical would be the loss of Roland as an ideal: his discrediting as a leader worthy of esteem and love. Yet precisely this is threatened when Oliver, Ganelon, and the Saracens question his status as military hero. The Saracens portray him as a hollow man, Ganelon as quarrelsome, rash, and irresponsible, Oliver as something perhaps worse. All thereby oppose themselves to the Song that Roland is bent on creating (although in another sense Ganelon and the Saracens assist in its creation). Many critics have attempted to determine which of the pair is tactically or morally correct. My interest here is in the different approaches adopted by the *Chansons de Roland*.

Simon Gaunt's analysis of the famous 'first horn scene' contrasts its handling in assonanced and rhymed versions.[15] The assonanced tradition keeps questions about Roland's value in suspension until after his death. In O, *laisses* 83, 84, and 85 (equivalent to V4, *laisses* 79, 80, and 81), Oliver appeals three times in similar terms to Roland to summon Charlemagne and Roland responds with dissimilar refusals. This is an example of the technique known as *laisses similaires*, in which successive *laisses* depict what appears to be a single event in qualitatively different ways.[16] The effect is one of narrative disturbance, since the audience is unsure how to make sense of what it has heard. *Laisses similaires* are associated in the assonanced tradition with moments in which Roland's loss is envisaged and its value discussed. Characters evaluate that loss differently, contributing to the debate which animates the text as a whole, and audience members are pressed to decide which version of events to credit. The scene culminates with the claim that 'Rollant est proç, Oliver est saçe' (V4, 1038: 'Roland is valiant, Oliver is wise'; equivalent to O, 1093). Often taken to imply the superior value of one of the heroes, this line is nevertheless followed immediately by one that rejects hierarchy: 'Ambes dos ent bon vassalaçe' (V4, 1039: 'Both have the qualities of a good vassal'; equivalent to O, 1094). The audience is faced with a double challenge: to assess the relative claims both of valour and prudence and of the two lines. Weighing these potentially but not necessarily competing alternatives requires us to reflect on the question of what will be (has been) lost in Roland, a problem which the assonanced texts do not allow us to answer with finality. By contrast, in the rhymed *remaniement* the equivalent couplet reads: 'Rollanz fu proz et Oliver fu ber; / per igal furent et compeignon et per' (CV7, 1887–8: 'Roland was valiant and Oliver valorous; they were absolutely equal and companions and peers'). The virtually synonymous adjectives *proz* and *ber* uniformly denote martial qualities, the second line unambiguously reinforces the first and the audience knows what to mourn. Thus there is no longer any difference of principle to ground the quarrel between Roland and Oliver and thence to unsettle the audience's attachment to its hero.

Significantly, the rhymed tradition emphasizes the fact that Oliver repeats his request to blow the horn: 'Sire compeing, car sonez la menee; / je le vos ai autre foie rovee' (CV7, 1839–40: 'Sir companion, sound the blast; I have already asked you to do so'). The provocative *laisses similaires* of the assonanced tradition are thus replaced with *laisses parallèles*, a technique in which numerically different events are described in qualitatively similar terms, buttressing a single interpretation. Roland is the greatest of heroes, a paragon among men and among leaders, whose tragic loss we can mourn wholeheartedly, following the examples of Aude and Charlemagne in adding lustre to his image. No ideal is lost in him; on the contrary, he incarnates the ideals of leadership and *vassalaçe* the more fully for being dead. Therefore he is presented as effectively a dead man from an early point in the narrative, as witness his response on first seeing the Saracen army: '"Deus," dist Rollant, "qui feïs mer salee, / men esïent, ma mort est hui juree"' (CV7, 1532–3: '"God," said Roland, "who made the salt sea, to my knowledge, my death is sworn today"'). Believing it too late to call for help, he reasons that his task is to ensure that his troops' final battle and the *chanson* that will be sung of it become inspirational *lieux de mémoire*. At once that of a sacrificial victim and a self-sacrifice, his death is eagerly embraced for the impetus it gives to future undertakings. Thus Charlemagne urges his men on:

> Ferez, baron! Ne vos atargez mie!
> Ge ai grant droit, tort a la paienie!
> Il m'ont tolu tant de ma compeignie
> dont dolce France est lasse et apovrie!
> Rollant m'ont mort, mon nevo, par envie,
> et Oliver a la chiere hardie.　　　　　　　(CV7, 5566–71)

(Strike, barons! Do not delay! I am completely in the right, the pagans in the wrong. They have deprived me of so many of my retinue, which is why sweet France is wretched and impoverished! They have killed my nephew Roland out of malice, and bold-faced Oliver.)

France may have lost its champions but their exalted memory will be translated into glorious actions encouraged by their example. Hence the rhymed texts repeatedly compare the surviving warriors to the lost hero: 'Dist l'uns a l'autre: "Cist fiert bien par vigor! / Unques Rollant ne dona cop meillor!"' (CV7, 5677–8: 'One says to another, "This man strikes with great force! Roland never delivered a better blow!"').[17] The rhymed tradition thus embodies that exploitation of the past in the service of present and prospective politics that Nora associates with 'memory'. Not Roland but his idealized image is to be kept alive, a socially useful resource. This one-dimensional endorsement of Roland's myth may truly be said to constitute a Song of Roland.

The rhymed tradition represents one possible response to the cultivated ambiguity of the assonanced tradition. We find a complementary response in such *chansons de geste* as *Girart de Vienne* (late twelfth century) and *Gui de Bourgogne* (early thirteenth century), both prequels to the *Roland*; the former relates the first encounters between Roland and Oliver in the war which opposes Oliver's uncle Girard to Charlemagne, the latter how the sons of Charlemagne's army, grown to adulthood during their fathers' long absence, come to Spain to help the militarily and spiritually bankrupt older generation. Both these texts expand on and polarize the *prouesse/sagesse* distinction, contrasting a pugnacious, arrogant Roland to an idealized counterfoil (Oliver and Gui, respectively). They emphasize that the hero's military usefulness is offset by the imprudence which leads him unnecessarily to risk his mens' lives and by his willingness to quarrel with fellow Christians and thus weaken the social order. This Roland's death, when it comes in the narrative future (but intertextual past) will inspire mainly relief at the passing of a source of too often inappropriate conflict. These texts conclusively bury Roland while resisting the loss of an ideal which threatens the assonanced tradition, for they provide alternative candidates for the role of model hero and leader – better men, they imply, than Roland ever was. Sacrificing the character and myth of Roland allows text and society to move on from an unsatisfactory past to a brighter future.

To summarize: the texts examined offer three distinct treatments of Roland's loss. The rhymed tradition makes of itself a memorial to Roland's enhanced and clarified reputation. Those *chansons de geste* which reject Roland and the Song that lionizes him firmly shut the door on a past to be remembered only as a warning. In its early stages the assonanced *Roland* tradition rejects either form of closure and keeps open the wound by emphasizing the uncertain value of what is lost in Roland. It is worth noting that several strategies used to this end are associated with orality; repetition, formulae, and parataxis are deployed to create a kind of perpetual present which prevents us from leaving the past and its dead hero behind, as Nora suggests in his discussion of memory. However, the effect in this case is not one of serene continuity; instead the past disrupts the present and forecloses the future, a condition which has much in common with Freudian melancholia. We cannot generalize about the effect of this oral rhetoric, though, for no less oral techniques work in the rhymed tradition and in other *chansons de geste* to establish a more settled relationship to the past.

## Memory and memorial

We might expect that the rhymed tradition's unequivocal elevation of Roland would constitute the more successful and politically effective memorial tradition. Certainly its survival in six manuscripts (if we include V4, the final part of which is rhymed) and three fragments suggests a respectable level of popularity. (The relative paucity of manuscript evidence for the assonanced tradition does not allow us to assume that it was unpopular. There is a huge rise in the number of manuscripts of all sorts surviving after the mid twelfth century, and the Oxford *Roland* is one of a tiny handful of *chansons de geste* surviving in earlier manuscripts, the majority of which come from what is now considered the precocious Anglo-Norman literary culture.) However, each of the extant rhymed texts departs in some way from the 'tradition' as it can be pieced together from other witnesses, and there is a striking tendency for such departures to disturb the smooth handling of Roland's death. Both C and V7, for example, include assonanced as well as rhymed material in the first horn scene, disorienting the audience with a narrative discord comparable to *laisses similaires* (but with the added jolt of the formal shift from rhyme to assonance). V7 includes only two extraneous *laisses* (printed in appendix as 92 A and 108 A by Duggan) but in C the effect is carried to a grand scale, the text containing first the assonanced account of the whole first horn episode (*laisses* 90–9) and then the rhymed (*laisses* 100–28). Both versions of the couplet comparing Roland and Oliver, discussed earlier as emblematizing the two traditions' different conceptions, are found in C (1465–6 and 1939–40).[18]

Such indifference to strict coherence is typical of medieval textuality. Although often edited out of modern published texts, textual inconsistencies of this kind repay close attention. They invite speculation on the conditions of textual production; where multiple versions of a story were circulating, individual redactors might be unable or unwilling to choose between alternatives. They also allow us to consider the effect on readers or audiences of the end product regardless of the intentions or accidents which brought it about. Thus, in manuscripts C and V7, the idealized Roland of rhyme is periodically and inconsistently cut through with the problematic figure of assonance as if the former, however rationally desirable, lacked some quality that only the more disturbing persona could bestow; yet the texts' primary allegiance to the rhymed tradition's approach is clear. The archaic material and form intrude on the 'official' text as indices of Roland's troubling past and of the past as troublesome: the return of a kind of textual unconscious.[19] Reintroducing in these slippages a confusion and ambiguity which the rhymed 'tradition' works to erase, C and V7 (though particularly C) reanimate the debate over Roland and thereby refuse his passing. This could be compared to manuscripts L and T, which open up the Roland question by omission: L commences its narrative in the middle of the first battle just after the horn scene; T, whether intentionally or accidentally (Duggan, 3, V, pp. 25–6), starts in the middle of Roland's nomination to the rearguard and thereafter loses much of the first horn scene to a lacuna between lines 411 and 412. P, which has lost a quire, now begins just before the first horn scene.

Roland's loss engenders various responses which all in their way aim to resolve that loss. Within the narrative there is the aftermath of Roncevaux: Charlemagne's immediate revenge and subsequent war with Baligant, the massacre of the Saracens and Bramimonde's conversion, Charlemagne's and Aude's mourning, Aude's death, Ganelon's trial and execution. All the surviving versions are also themselves part of the aftermath. Because none represents the original version of the story and each brings its own solution, they must be considered along with other *chansons de geste* among the reactions to Roland. The story of Roncevaux is reworked, with episodes added or omitted and with shifting emphases; it is furnished with sequels and prequels (like those discussed above) and it is inserted into manuscript compilations with other works whose selection invites us to read it in particular ways.[20] All these responses constitute so many explanations which attempt to render Roland's death acceptable according to some literary, historical, spiritual or moral logic and thereby to remove its outrageous, offensive, traumatic quality – to close up the wound. Their effect is not only palliative, however, for they also exploit the energies generated by Roland's loss. The greater the trauma, the more powerful are the energies attracted in the effort to heal it and the greater the opportunity for those energies to be mobilized politically to form new attachments, which in turn have their part to play in the healing process. This may explain why O's early encouragement of controversy over Roland's worth does not lead to a more discriminating or detached pose in the heavily ideological sections following his death, sections which many critics have considered to be later additions because they are so different from the earlier ones.[21] After Roncevaux the conflict centring on Roland, characterized by obscure particularities and internal inconsistencies, is translated to two theatres of political combat – the religious and the governmental – where the principles at stake are clearly articulated and resolution brought about by divine intervention (see Chapter 13). The ideological claims there formulated derive considerable force from the poem's aesthetic and psychic dynamics.

An important conclusion to be drawn from the above argument (though of course not the only one possible on the basis of the textual evidence considered) is that the intrusion of assonanced material and form into the rhymed *Rolands* reflects the possibility that seamless idealization in practice provides a weaker political impetus than do more problematic portrayals. O's traumatic presentation of Roland's loss attracts the energies which power the strenuous political investments of the second half of the poem. Moreover, it is crucial to the legend's literary life that Roland's loss should meet no final resolution, for only as a still open wound will it continue to attract further efforts at closure; hence the potential for future action stressed at the ending of all the extant texts. It seems that the vitality of the *Chanson de Roland* tradition – its ability to generate further textual responses – is not best served by the imposition onto it of Roland's meaning or by the success of his intention to make of it a *Song of Roland*, but depends on the opposition to that Song within the text. I shall leave the last word to Nora:

> For although it is true that the fundamental purpose of a *lieu de mémoire* is to stop time, to inhibit forgetting, to fix a state of things, to immortalize death, and to materialize the immaterial (just as gold, they say, is the memory of money) – all in order to capture the maximum possible meaning with the fewest possible signs – it is also clear that *lieux de mémoire* thrive only because of their capacity for change, their ability to resurrect old meanings and generate new ones along with new and unforeseeable connections (that is what makes them exciting). (15)

## Notes

1. P. Nora, in *Realms of Memory: the Construction of the French Past*, ed. P. Nora and L. D. Kritzman, trans. A. Goldhammer, 3 vols. (New York, Columbia University Press, 1996), 1, xvii. Subsequent references to this volume will be in parentheses in the text.
2. A. Taylor, *Textual Situations: Three Medieval Manuscripts and their Readers* (Philadelphia, University of Pennsylvania Press, 2002), chapter 2.
3. J. J. Duggan, 'Franco-German Conflict and the History of French Scholarship on the *Song of Roland*', in P. J. Gallacher and H. Damico (eds.), *Hermeneutics and Medieval Culture* (Albany, NY, State University of New York Press, 1989), pp. 97–106.
4. See Duggan's indispensable *La Chanson de Roland: the French Corpus*. References to this edition of different versions of the *Roland* will give Duggan volume number,

part, and page number. All versions are quoted from this edition except the Oxford text, where Ian Short's 1990 edition is used. A slightly amended form of Short's text, which is proudly interventionist, is printed in Duggan 1, I.

5. See the introductions to the different texts in Duggan's edition.

6. See Short in Duggan, I, I, p. 44. For recent views on the *Roland*'s orality, see Taylor, *Textual Situations*; Short, in Duggan I, I, pp. 39–62; S. Gaunt, *Re-Telling the Tale: an Introduction to Medieval French Literature* (London, Duckworth, 2001), pp. 25–37.

7. S. Kinoshita, *Medieval Boundaries: Rethinking Difference in Old French Literature* (Philadelphia, University of Pennsylvania Press, 2006), chapter 1. See also Chapter 16 in this volume.

8. William of Malmesbury, *Gesta regum Anglorum: the History of the English Kings*, ed. and trans. R. A. B. Mynors *et al.*, 2 vols. (Oxford, Clarendon Press, 1998), chapter 242. See D. C. Douglas, 'The *Song of Roland* and the Norman Conquest of England', *French Studies*, 14 (1960), 99–116.

9. This is typical of the diffusion of *chansons de geste* in northern Italy, on which see J. Vitullo, *The Chivalric Epic in Medieval Italy* (Gainesville, FL, University of Florida Press, 2000). On the precocious Anglo-Norman literary culture, see S. Crane, 'Anglo-Norman Cultures in England, 1066–1460', in D. Wallace (ed.), *The Cambridge History of Medieval English Literature* (Cambridge University Press, 1999), pp. 35–60.

10. S. Kay, 'Introduction', in *The Chansons de geste in the Age of Romance* (Oxford University Press, 1995).

11. On a similar sense of modernity in late medieval French literature, see J. Cerquiglini-Toulet, *The Color of Melancholy: the Uses of Books in the Fourteenth Century*, trans. L. G. Cochrane (Baltimore, Johns Hopkins University Press, 1997).

12. 'Mourning and Melancholia', in *The Standard Edition of the Complete Psychological Works of Sigmund Freud*, gen. ed. and trans. J. Strachey, 24 vols. (London, Hogarth, 1953–74), XIV (1957), 237–58 (245).

13. For an important critique of Nora's project, see F. Hartog, 'Temps et Histoire: "Comment écrire l'histoire de France?"', *Annales Histoire, Sciences Sociales*, 50 (1995), 1219–36.

14. 'Mourning and Melancholia', p. 253.

15. S. Gaunt, *Gender and Genre in Medieval French Literature* (Cambridge University Press, 1995), chapter 1; also *Re-Telling the Tale*, pp. 118–26. Gaunt discusses O and P.

16. J. Rychner, *La Chanson de geste: Essai sur l'art épique des jongleurs* (Geneva, Droz, 1955), pp. 74–93.

17. Compare O, *laisses* 242, 249.

18. C. Segre, 'La première "scène du cor" dans la *Chanson de Roland* et la méthode de travail des copistes', in *Mélanges offerts à Rita Lejeune*, 2 vols. (Gembloux, Duculot, 1969), II, 871–89.

19. Compare Kay's analysis of romance and *chanson de geste* as each other's political unconscious in *The Chansons de geste in the Age of Romance*. Manuscript L provides its *Roland* with a romance introduction.

20. Keith Busby in Chapter 9 discusses the cycle of *chansons de geste* into which the Paris manuscript inserts the *Chanson de Roland*; see also Taylor, *Textual*

*Situations*; Gaunt, *Gender and Genre*, and Reejhon in Duggan 3, IV, pp. 40–76. L is included with orthodox religious texts, thus emphasizing the *Roland*'s Christian dimension. T was copied with the letter from Prester John (a fictional Christian monarch of the Indies) to the Roman Emperor Frederick Barbarossa.

21. V4 is differently discontinuous, including an account of the taking of Narbonne (usually associated with the cycle of William of Orange) before concluding in the rhymed tradition.

# 2

## PEGGY McCRACKEN

# The Old French Vulgate cycle

The quest for the holy grail, the story of Merlin, the adventures of King Arthur and the knights of the Round Table, the love affair of Lancelot and Queen Guenevere – these are familiar stories that have their first sustained development in the early thirteenth-century Old French Vulgate cycle, also known as the Lancelot-Grail cycle or the Pseudo-Map cycle.[1] The Vulgate is a compilation of five prose romances composed between 1220 and 1240. Together the five texts recount a story that unfolds across generations, but the texts were not composed in chronological sequence.[2] The oldest part of the compilation and its central text is the *Lancelot en prose*, also known as the *Lancelot Proper*, which recounts the story of Lancelot's birth and education by the Lady of the Lake, his arrival at King Arthur's court, his early feats of chivalry, then his love affair with Guenevere, his many adventures and those of Arthur's other knights. The *Lancelot* comprises roughly half of the Vulgate and it is the centre around which the cycle grew. In the decade and a half following its composition, four other narratives were added to the *Lancelot*: *La Queste del saint graal* continues the story of Arthur's knights in the quest for the grail and *La Mort le roi Artu* recounts the destruction of Arthur's kingdom after the grail quest. Each romance refers back to events narrated in the *Lancelot*, but each is also a complete, independent romance.[3] Two romances were also added to the beginning of the *Lancelot* to recount the early history of the grail (*L'Estoire del saint graal*) and the early history of Arthur's kingdom (*L'Estoire de Merlin*); these two texts contain prophecies or references to events recounted in the stories that follow chronologically, but they too may stand alone as independent narratives.

The Vulgate is long and digressive. It has many protagonists, and the tone and style of the narrative change from text to text. The religious history of the grail story in the *Estoire del saint graal* yields to the story of feudal strife in the *Estoire de Merlin*; courtly and chivalric values dominate in the *Lancelot*, but in the *Queste del saint graal* worldly chivalry is subordinated to heavenly chivalry; impending and then unfolding tragedy is the story of *La Mort le roi*

*Artu*. Such changes are due in part to the changing authorship of the individual texts that make up the Vulgate, but they are also in part dictated by the stories told in the compilation – the history of the grail and the Christianization of Britain promote values different from those that structure the story of courtly adultery – but how do these stories fit together? How does the grail story, a story imbued with theology and religious values, relate to the story of Lancelot and Arthur's court, a place associated with love and chivalry but not explicitly with religion, and how does the combination of these stories generate a text, the Old French Vulgate cycle? How might the Vulgate, as a text, be seen to generate the stories that give it coherence? And finally, what narrative strategies provide coherence to this long text, where does coherence fail, and what might such failures tell us about the values that organize the story?

## Composition and compilation

The Vulgate develops stories found in a number of earlier texts. The history of King Arthur comes from Geoffrey of Monmouth's *Historia Regum Britanniae*, the story of Lancelot's love affair with Guenevere comes from Chrétien de Troyes's *Chevalier de la charrette*, the story of the grail and the association of Arthur's court with the grail quest come from Chrétien's *Conte du graal*, and the Christianization of the grail and the story of Merlin are recounted by Robert de Boron. The authors of the Vulgate texts elaborate the earlier material, expand it and shape it into a narrative that incorporates the history of the grail into the history of Britain.[4]

The Vulgate is written in prose, and it is a product of the growing interest in prose fiction and romance cycles in thirteenth-century France. Earlier vernacular romances, including the Old French romances that the Vulgate takes as sources, were written in verse; prose was reserved for chronicles, for history. The Vulgate's claim to transmit history is thus reflected in its form, and its persistent attention to historical development allows the Vulgate to be read as a single narrative, rather than a series of individual texts. The events, episodes, and characters borrowed from its sources are embedded in extended narratives that place them in a historical development. The early history of the grail recounted by Robert de Boron becomes a narrative about the conversion of Britain to Christianity, and the night that Guenevere and Lancelot spend together in Chrétien's *Chevalier de la charrette* is expanded into the story of Lancelot's life-long love for the queen. The religious history of the grail converges with the political history of Britain in the Vulgate, and historical explanation – the consequences of the past for the present and the future – is a fundamental organizing principle of the narration. It is articulated through the many examples of prophecies and prophetic dreams that announce future events, and it is articulated through genealogy and the importance of genealogical destiny.[5]

The lineage of the grail kings, guardians of the holy grail, is established in the *Estoire del saint graal*, where the birth of Galahad, the good knight who will bring the adventures of the grail to an end, is foretold. Galahad is descended from the grail kings through Lancelot, however his father Lancelot himself will never be worthy to approach the grail because of the sin of his adultery with Queen Guenevere, and because of his own father's adultery: King Ban slept with another woman after his marriage and engendered a son, Hector des Marches, who later, like his half-brother Lancelot, becomes a knight at Arthur's court (*Lancelot*, III, 293–4). Genealogy has consequences in the Vulgate, though not always in predictable ways – Lancelot is the sinful son of a sinful father, but he produces a son who is without sin: 'Des pechiez mortiex porte li peres son fes et li filz le suen; ne li filz ne partira ja as iniquitez au pere, ne li peres ne partira ja as iniquitez au filz; mes chascuns selonc ce qu'il avra deservi recevra loier' (*Queste*, 138; Lacy, IV, 45: 'The father carries his burden of mortal sin and the son carries his. The son will never share in his father's iniquities, nor will the father share in the son's faults. Each will be compensated in accordance with his own merits'). King Arthur's illegitimate son Loholt does not play a significant role in the Vulgate, but Arthur's lineage is important in the narrative. He is the son of a king, but does not know it until he claims his own kingdom. His nephew Gauvain is his greatest champion and a model of chivalric courtesy, but Gauvain's half-brother Mordred, who is Arthur's own son, betrays his father and brings about the destruction of his kingdom.

The multigenerational narrative has at its centre the great knight, Lancelot. Just as the *Lancelot* provides the core narrative that other romances expand, so the character himself is a unifying presence, even in the *Estoire del saint graal* and the *Merlin*, whose stories predate his birth. In other words, because of the way that the cycle develops around the *Lancelot*, the narrative is always already about Lancelot, and while the later additions that situate Lancelot's story in relation to the grail and the grail quest may condemn the queen's adulterous liaison with her knight, the central point of reference for the narrative is the story of Lancelot's love for Queen Guenevere.[6]

In its accretion of related stories around Lancelot, the Vulgate forms a cycle, a group of narratives united by a focus on a single character or group of characters in a chronological sequence; episodes within the cycle develop common themes, and the narrative has a defined point of origin and closure beyond which elaboration cannot logically extend the story.[7] The incremental narratives added to the *Lancelot* push the story toward origin and closure: the early history of Arthur's court in the *Merlin* is added to the story of Lancelot's birth and infancy in the *Lancelot*, and the *Mort* recounts the fall of Arthur's kingdom and Lancelot's death; the *Estoire del saint graal* offers an early history of the grail to balance the end of the grail quest recounted in the *Queste*.

The compilation of discrete narratives into a cycle organized around the peregrinations of the holy grail and the adventures of Arthur's knights would seem to imply that a single compiler organized the work. Critics have long debated the role of such an 'architect' and what hand he might have had in dictating the composition of the various parts of the story. It is hard to explain the extent to which the Vulgate is in fact a coherent composition without recourse to the idea of some kind of architect – although the individual romances that make up the Vulgate can stand alone (and indeed, they are commonly studied as individual texts), they also continue narrative threads that subtend the entire compilation, they refer back to events recounted in earlier texts, and they look forward to events to come. In fact, manuscript evidence suggests that the process through which the individual texts were linked as a whole continued through their transmission. Scribes often amended or changed passages to eliminate incoherence or contradictions in the development of the story.[8] They may also have contributed to marking the story's many examples of narrative interlace: the technique of weaving in and out multiple storylines that is typical of prose romance.

Interlace orients the reader by explicitly identifying shifts among different narrative developments. Since Arthur's knights typically separate from each other to pursue adventures alone or in pairs, interlace helps the audience to follow two or more storylines as they develop: 'Si se tait atant li contes de mon seignor Yvain et de Lancelot et retorne a parler avant del duc de Clarence' (*Lancelot*, I, 179; Lacy, II, 282: 'At this point the story stops speaking of Sir Yvain and Lancelot and goes on with the duke of Clarence'); 'Si se tait ci endroit li contes et de lui et de sa cosine et retorne a mon seignor Yvain la ou il se parti del duc et de Lancelot' (*Lancelot*, I, 186; Lacy, II, 283: 'At this point the story stops speaking of [the duke of Clarence] and his cousin, but turns back to Sir Yvain just as he took leave of the duke and Lancelot'). Interlace deliberately interrupts the linear development of the story, and in this it is the counterweight to cyclicity: it allows the narrator to follow simultaneous events sequentially in the narrative while maintaining the various narrative threads in a common chronological sequence.

## Chivalry and the value of violence

The Vulgate recounts stories whose trajectories are shaped through battles. Severe justice is imposed on the enemies of God in the *Estoire del saint graal*, and in the *Merlin* Arthur claims his kingdom through war. Whereas in the early story of the grail and of Arthur's kingdom, violence is the means to religious and political order, in the *Lancelot* chivalric violence structures the court: battles among knights establish hierarchies of worth, whether in war, in tournaments, or in battles outside the court. However the value of chivalric violence is also put into question in the *Lancelot* and particularly in the *Queste del saint graal* where 'li chevalier terrien' (worldly knights) fail in the grail quest, while 'li chevalier celestiel' (heavenly knights) succeed (*Queste*, 143). Moreover, the end of the grail quest seems to provoke a crisis in chivalric values. *La Mort le roi Artu* begins with the identification of how many of Arthur's knights have been killed – and which knights have killed fellow knights of the Round Table. In this concluding section of the Vulgate, tournaments and adventures give way to war among Arthur's knights and the destruction of his kingdom.

The meaning and value of violence are different in the texts that make up the Vulgate compilation: the violent conversion of pagans in the *Estoire del saint graal* is different from the adventures that structure battles in the *Queste del saint graal*. Violence is perhaps most clearly ritualized as a form of symbolic action in the *Lancelot*, where knights participate in tournaments to prove their prowess and gain reputation, they leave court to seek challenges which consistently involve battles, and the narrative itself is presented as a record of their adventures made by scribes at Arthur's court. King Arthur's knights fight battles to end enchantments or to fulfill one of the customs that organizes the world outside Arthur's court, they fight battles to save fellow knights from prison or from harm, and of course knights fight battles to rescue and defend women.

Battles participate in defining the gender system of the Arthurian world: knights fight, ladies are rescued. Chivalric heroism demands the public display of prowess, and ladies are often the pretext for that display. One of Hector's adventures in the *Lancelot* suggests the extent to which chivalric contest is grounded on women's bodies. Hector comes to a castle that a knight may enter only if he agrees to deliver it from the custom that dictates that every passing knight must do battle with Marigart le Ros, the lord of the castle. After he wins his battles, Marigart has his defeated opponents stripped naked and dragged through all the streets of the city. After Hector promises to fight Marigart, a porter describes the second custom of the castle:

> Mais encore en i a une plus vilaine, et si est a nostre oes; kar il n'est nus des
> mois de l'an qu'il ne preingne une de nos files, por qu'ele soit pucele, et gist a
> force a li et puis la livre as garçons a tenir en soignantage. Et ensi en a honies
> plus de .XL. dont nos tuit somes hontels et dolens si que nos voldrions miels

morir que vivre. Ce sont les malvaises costumes del chastel: si covient que vos
metois paine a oster les ou vos serrois parjures.                    (*Lancelot*, II, 392)

(But a yet more evil custom has been devised, one that involves us. For no
month goes by that he doesn't take one of our daughters, providing that she's
a virgin, and rape her and then release her to his serving boys to use as a
whore. He has disgraced more than forty maidens this way, and we're so
ashamed and upset about them that we'd rather be dead than alive. These are
the evil customs of the castle. You must try your hardest to banish them or
you will have perjured yourself.)                              (Lacy, III, 104)

The two customs of the castle dictate that if a knight can protect his own
honour, he will also save the virgins of the city from rape and shame, but a
knight's defeat will be re-enacted in the continuing abuse of the virgins'
bodies. The fate of the knight's body is tied to the fate of the women's bodies,
but only the knight can change that fate.

Violence ends violence. Hector's defeat of Marigart le Ros ensures justice
for the city and acclaim for Hector: 'Bien viegne la flors des chevaliers del
monde qui nos a delivrés del grant hontage ou nos estions!' (*Lancelot*, II, 397;
Lacy, III, 105: 'Welcome to the flower of all the knights in the world who has
delivered us from our state of shame!'). Interestingly enough, however,
although Hector's defeat of Marigart demonstrates his prowess, the episode
ends with praise of Lancelot. The lady of the castle, raped and imprisoned by
Marigart and rescued by Hector, learns that her champion is from Arthur's
court and immediately asks him for news of Lancelot. She loves Lancelot
more than any man in the world because of the stories she has heard of his
great prowess (*Lancelot*, II, 399–400).

This episode follows what appears to be a conventional logic: through
battle, a knight rescues women from violence and enhances his reputation.
Yet the text seems to undermine this structure in the lady's recognition not of
Hector, but of Lancelot. Rather than proclaiming her debt to the knight who
has saved her, she regrets Lancelot's absence, and Hector recognizes
Lancelot's superiority when he asks her to accept him as her knight for the
sake of her love of Lancelot. Lancelot is indeed the greatest knight of King
Arthur's court, his adventures prove this status over and over, and it is not
surprising that he is a standard of chivalric prowess. Nonetheless, in the initial
recognition of Hector's accomplishment (he is 'the flower of all the knights in
the world') and in the subsequent subordination of Hector to Lancelot, the
narrative seems to question the equation between battle and reputation. The
description of the excessive violence – both toward women and toward
defeated knights – of the castle's customs may also voice an implicit critique
of the chivalric violence that structures hierarchies among Arthur's knights.

A more explicit questioning of the value of violence is found in the episode that immediately follows Hector's defeat of Marigart le Ros in the *Lancelot*. The story turns from Hector to Yvain who meets a damsel whose sparrow-hawk has been taken from her by a knight. Yvain responds to this classic pretext for chivalric battle by claiming the bird, challenging the knight, and winning the sparrow-hawk in a battle, but only after killing the knight who took the hawk and being wounded himself. The damsel is unhappier having regained her bird than she was at losing it, 'ele voit .I. chevalier ocis et .I. autre navré, et por si petit d'acheison' (*Lancelot*, II, 407; Lacy, III, 107: 'she had seen one knight dead and another wounded for such a trifle'). Even before the battle she had explained to Yvain that 'je voldroie miels que vos le me poissiés rendre a pes que a guerre' (*Lancelot*, II, 405; Lacy, III, 107: 'I would rather you returned it to me peacefully than by fighting').

This damsel's voice does not carry far, it is not explicitly recalled in the *Lancelot*, though her critique can be seen to resonate in the excessive violence of the grail quest where Arthur's knights kill other knights and they kill each other. The end of the grail adventures seems to come in a moment of frustration that emphasizes the separation of the grail knights, Galahad, Perceval, and Bors, who are with the grail in Sarras, from Arthur's knights, who no longer find adventures in which to prove their worth. The narrative thus offers critiques of its values from within the story itself. This is not to say merely that the text deconstructs its own values, although this may be one of the things it does. More interesting is the way in which this composite text speaks across the individual narratives that compose it to debate values and to imagine alternative scenarios to what seem like inexorable developments.

## Love stories

Although the grail story frames the Vulgate, the story of the great love of Lancelot and Guenevere is its heart. Lancelot's love for the queen is the source of his great prowess, he claims in the *Lancelot* (V, 3), even if that same love is later identified as a sin that prevents him from attaining the grail. Lancelot's fidelity to Guenevere is unwavering, but he is twice tricked into making love to another woman, Amite, the daughter of the Fisher King, with whom he engenders Galahad. The first time Lancelot is drugged by Amite's nurse, but the second time he is simply led to her bed in darkness and he thinks he is making love to the queen. When Guenevere discovers his second infidelity she exiles him from court, and the queen's rejection drives Lancelot into a madness that is later cured by Amite, with whom he goes to live chastely at the Isle de Joie for seven years until summoned back to court by the queen (*Lancelot*, VI, 236). Lancelot's love for Guenevere is a basic premise of the text and it is never seriously questioned in the narrative – after all, her rejection causes him to go mad. However, the text does open a narrative space for imagining an alternative scenario to the enduring love of Lancelot and Guenevere in Lancelot's repeated sexual encounters with Amite and in his retreat with her to the Isle de Joie. The text insists that Lancelot lives chastely with Amite, and an audience is more likely to expect a reconciliation with the queen than to expect that Amite might replace the queen in Lancelot's affections, but this episode recounting Lancelot's encounters with Amite questions, even if only obliquely, Lancelot's exclusive devotion to the queen.

Lancelot, too, is subject to doubts about Guenevere's fidelity. Drugged by Morgan, he dreams that he discovers the queen in bed with another knight and he believes that the dream is real. Lancelot stays away from Guenevere and Arthur's court, again he suffers from madness until cured by the Lady of the Lake (*Lancelot*, II, I). Episodes like these recount obstacles to their love that test the queen and her knight, but they also suggest that the lovers are none too sure of each other's fidelity. They may also suggest alternative love stories that are not developed in the narrative, in part because the devotion of the two lovers to each other grounds the representation of adultery in the story, and in part, it seems, because the lovers cannot love without adversity.

Guenevere and Lancelot live together, although chastely, when Guenevere is exiled from court during the False Guenevere episode. The queen's half-sister (the False Guenevere) arrives at court and claims to be the king's rightful wife. She also claims that the woman the king has known as his wife is an imposter. The king is deceived, he believes the claim, and Guenevere leaves the court. Galehaut, a former enemy of Arthur who abandoned his war with the king because of his great love for Lancelot, offers Guenevere the Kingdom of Sorelois. The queen spends two years there with Lancelot and Galehaut before the False Guenevere's plot is uncovered and Guenevere again assumes her place as the king's wife (*Lancelot*, I, 153). Guenevere never accepts the exile as a place in which to live freely with Lancelot – the lovers remain chaste while in Sorelois and do not entertain the possibility of continuing to live together away from Arthur's court. It may be logical that Guenevere would not wish to give up the honour and status of queenship, even to live with her lover. And perhaps Lancelot, too, would be dishonoured by living openly with the queen, so that the possibility of the lovers leaving Arthur's court to live together is not one the narrative can seriously entertain. But it is a possibility imagined in the narrative. When Galehaut offers his lands to the exiled queen, he explicitly states the possibility that the queen will gain love and a kingdom, even as she loses Arthur's realm: 'si vos enmenrai en mon païs et donrai a vos et a mon conpaignon lo reiaume de Sorelois qui assez est riches et biaus, si sera rois et vos reine et manroiz boenne vie ansanble comme genz qui molt s'antr'aiment' (*Lancelot*, III, 42; my translation: 'I will take you to my country and will give you and my companion the rich kingdom of Sorelois, and he will be king and you will be queen, and you will live a good life together as lovers'). The Vulgate imagines a love story that depends on status, perhaps on secrecy, and without doubt on the context of Arthur's court. But it also continuously imagines alternative ways in which the story of Lancelot and Guenevere's love might unfold.

The narrative tests outcomes in ways that expose the values on which the development of the story depends. Although Lancelot and Guenevere ultimately remain faithful to each other, they never achieve a legitimate union, even after Arthur's death. The tension around the adulterous relationship reveals not just the tension at the heart of the Vulgate between the religious values associated with the grail and the courtly values associated with Arthur's kingdom, but also a key narrative strategy of this long and unwieldy compilation. Alongside the prophecies, dreams, and narrative forecasting that announce the future developments of the story, the Vulgate tests alternative scenarios, paths that the story does not take, but that it glimpses, and through which, perhaps, it debates the values that structure the narrative.

## Sex and secrets

If the love of Lancelot for Guenevere is the central story of the Vulgate, both because it is recounted in the central text of the compilation and because of the way it organizes much of the narrative, it is also a focus for the conflicting values of the two major narrative threads: the religious history of the grail and the secular history of Arthur's kingdom. Lancelot enters the grail quest, but he will not succeed because of his sin with the queen, a corruption that, as a hermit explains to him, coincides with his entry into chivalry:

> Lancelot, cest essample t'ai mostré por la vie que tu as si longuement menee puis que tu chaïs en pechié, ce est a dire puis que tu receus l'ordre de chevalerie. Car devant ce que tu fusses chevaliers avoies tu en toi herbergiees toutes les bones vertuz si naturelment que je ne sai juene home qui poïst estre tes pareuz. Car tout premierement avoies tu virginités herbergiee en toi si naturelment qu'onques ne l'avoies enfrainte ne en volenté ne en oevre ... Et lors affermoies tu qu'il n'ert nule si haute chevalerie come d'estre virges et d'eschiver luxure et garder son cors netement ... Lors entra en la reine Guenievre, qui ne s'ert pas bien fete confesse puis que ele entra primes en mariage, et l'esmut a ce qu'ele te resgarda volentiers tant come tu demoras en son ostel, le jor que tu fus chevaliers. Quant tu veis qu'ele te resgarda, si i pensas; et maintenant te feri li anemis d'un de ses darz a descovert, si durement qu'il te fist chanceler. (*Queste*, 123–5)

(Lancelot, I have told you this tale because you have led a life of sin for so long, ever since you received the order of chivalry. Before becoming a knight, you were endowed by nature with all virtues; I know of no young man who could have compared with you. First, you had a natural virginity, so pure that you never violated it in thought or in deed ... Then you would affirm that there could be no more chivalrous act than being a virgin, avoiding lust, and keeping one's body pure ... [The devil] entered into Guenevere, who had not made a good confession since her marriage, and encouraged her to glance longingly at you when you were in her household, the day you were dubbed a knight. When you noticed her looking at you, you began musing about her. Just then the devil shot you unawares with one of his arrows, striking so hard that it made you stumble and wander off the straight path.) (Lacy, IV, 40–1)

The association of chivalry and sexual sin is part of the *Queste*'s valorization of heavenly chivalry over worldly chivalry, and it is also part of this romance's representation of sin as sexual sin. The values associated with the grail are articulated through discourses about sexuality and, above all, through the valorization of virginity.

Joseph of Arimathea, the first guardian of the grail, remains chaste after he receives the grail. He has sex with his wife only at God's command, so that he engenders a son, Josephé, who will be the next guardian of the grail and who will remain a virgin (*Livre du graal*, I, 58). In the *Estoire del saint graal* even the conversion of pagans is represented as a conversion to legitimate sexuality – when Josephé converts King Mordrain, he commands him to renounce his carnal relationship with a wooden image of a woman that Mordrain dresses in rich clothes (*Livre du graal*, I, 164). In the *Estoire del saint graal* religious orthodoxy is described in terms of sexual purity, and that equivalence is echoed in the *Queste* where the grail knights are Bors, a chaste knight, and Galahad and Perceval, the only two knights in Arthur's court who have retained their virginity (*Queste*, 74, 80).

The emphatic endorsement of virginity in the *Queste* redefines chivalric worth as grounded in bodily purity rather than in the pleasures of the body – battles and love – associated with Arthur's court. When the narrative returns to Arthur's court in the *Mort le roi Artu*, the grail quest has changed the Arthurian world. Although Lancelot's great love for the queen, which inspired his prowess but made him unworthy to succeed in the grail quest, is no less in evidence (in fact, it is apparent to almost all), its role in the narrative has changed because of its earlier characterization as a sin and because the lovers no longer hide their liaison as carefully as they did before the quest. If the values that organized the court have changed, the secrets that depended on those values no longer hold.

Much of the Vulgate is structured around keeping and discovering secrets: secrets are announced and their revelation anticipated in the narrative; secrets are revealed, sometimes to great effect and sometimes to almost none; above all, secrets invite consequences and they invite narration. Secrets are prominent at the beginning of the Vulgate in the mysteries of the grail and in the disguise that allows Utherpendragon to take the place of Ygerne's husband without her knowledge and engender Arthur, and at the end of the cycle, the revelation of the queen's secret launches the destruction of Arthur's kingdom.

In the *Mort*, Arthur's nephew Agravain learns of Lancelot and Guenevere's love affair, but his brothers Gauvain and Gaherriet protest when he states his intention to tell the king – they do not dispute Agravain's discovery of the secret adultery, but they refuse to tell the king because to reveal the secret will lead to war between the king and Lancelot. The dispute between the brothers centres not on what betrayals the secret hides, but on the results of the telling of the secret, on the effects of the revelation.[9] The secret adultery is ultimately less important in the moral universe of the romance than the events it sets in motion – events that in this case seem like inexorable moves toward a tragic end.

Part of that inexorable motion is related to the revelation of Mordred's identity as Arthur's son. Earlier in the story, Lancelot learns from a hermit that Arthur engendered Mordred with his sister and that Mordred will kill his father, and he tells Guenevere of the hermit's prediction. Guenevere does not believe the prediction and she keeps it secret – a secret for which the narrator reproaches her: 'se ele eust dit au roi ce que Lanceloz li dist, il qui se sentoit soupeçonneus de ceste chose l'eust chacié fors de sa cort et ainsi remainsist la guerre et la bataille qui fu puis es plains de Salibieres, dont li rois et maint prodome morurent a grant pechié' (*Lancelot*, VI, 60–1; Lacy, III, 293: 'if she had told the king what Lancelot had told her, then the king, suspicious of this matter, would have chased Mordred from his court, and thus the war and the battle that later took place on Salisbury Plain would not have occurred'). The narrator suggests that Guenevere might have averted the final tragedy by warning Arthur.

These two examples of revealed secrets point to the functions of secrecy in the Vulgate. In the first example, the revelation of the queen's adultery, the discovery of a secret leads indirectly to disaster, it is a catalyst to a conflict that persists even after the crisis provoked by the secret is resolved and Guenevere and Arthur are reconciled. In the second example, the revelation of a secret could have prevented disaster – in fact, it could have prevented the very disaster launched by the revelation of the queen's secret. Or at least that is what is suggested by the narrator's commentary on Guenevere's failure to speak, although the signs that portend Arthur's death would seem to suggest that it cannot be averted.

This tension between what must be and what might have been is a persistent one in the Vulgate and it defines the very space of narration in the cycle. Early events, prophecies, and predictions forecast and explain later narrative developments, but at the same time the narrative also imagines alternative outcomes for the story and suggests that prophecies may not come true. It is in the narrative space between the inexorable development of the story and its possible diversions that the Vulgate develops as a narrative cycle and in which it questions the extent to which the present explains the past and the past determines the future, offering to its modern readers as, perhaps, to its medieval audiences, the pleasures of a story that both defends and debates the values that give it meaning.

## Notes

1. 'Vulgate' because it is the vulgar, vernacular source for Arthurian material, particularly the Lancelot story; 'Lancelot-Grail' after the two main narrative threads of the cycle; and 'Pseudo-Map' because the compilation was traditionally attributed to Walter Map, a scribe at the court of Henry II Plantagenet, but who died in 1210, well before the narrative cycle was completed. I am using lower case for 'grail' in order to emphasize the circulation of the grail as part of the larger Vulgate narrative, rather than the mystical quality of the object itself.

2. The texts are published as: D. Poirion with P. Walter *et al.* (eds.), *Le Livre du graal*, vol. 1 (for the *Estoire del saint graal* and *Merlin*); A. Micha (ed.), *Lancelot: roman en prose du XIIIe siècle*; A. Pauphilet (ed.), *La Queste del saint graal* and J. Frappier (ed.), *La Mort le roi Artu: roman du XIIIe*.

3. However, the individual romances that compose the Vulgate rarely appear alone in manuscripts. For an overview of the manuscript tradition, see E. J. Burns, 'Introduction', in N. Lacy (gen. ed.), *Lancelot-Grail: the Old French Arthurian Vulgate and Post-Vulgate in Translation*, 5 vols. (New York and London, Garland, 1995), I, xix–xx.

4. That the story might have developed differently is suggested by the existence of a non-cyclical *Lancelot* which does not include the grail story, and a post-Vulgate *Roman du graal* which eliminates much of the Lancelot material. See E. Kennedy, *Lancelot and the Grail* (Oxford University Press, 1986) and F. Bogdanow, *The Romance of the Grail* (Manchester University Press, 1966).

5. E. J. Burns, *Arthurian Fictions: Reading the Vulgate Cycle* (Columbus, Ohio State University Press, 1985); R. H. Bloch, *Etymologies and Genealogies: a Literary Anthropology of the French Middle Ages* (University of Chicago Press, 1983); E. Baumgartner, 'From Lancelot to Galahad: the Stakes of Filiation', in W. Kibler (ed.), *The Lancelot-Grail Cycle: Text and Transformations* (Austin, University of Texas Press, 1994), pp. 14–30.

6. D. Kelly, 'Interlace and the Cyclic Imagination', in C. Dover (ed.), *A Companion to the* Lancelot-Grail *Cycle* (Cambridge, D. S. Brewer, 2003), pp. 55–64; A. Leupin, *Le Graal et la littérature* (Geneva, L'Age d'Homme, 1982).

7. D. Staines, 'The Medieval Cycle: Mapping a Trope', in S. Sturm-Maddox and D. Maddox (eds.), *Transtextualities: of Cycles and Cyclicity in Medieval French*

*Literature*, Medieval and Renaissance Texts and Studies (Binghamton, NY, Center for Medieval and Renaissance Studies, 1996), pp. 15–37; J. H. M. Taylor, 'Arthurian Cyclicity: the Construction of History in the Late French Prose Romances', *Arthurian Yearbook*, 2 (1992), 209–223; Kennedy, *Lancelot and the Grail*.

8. E. Kennedy, 'The Scribe as Editor', in *Mélanges Jean Frappier*, 2 vols. (Geneva, Droz, 1970), pp. 523–31.

9. N. Lacy, 'The *Mort Artu* and Cyclic Closure', in Kibler (ed.), *The Lancelot Grail Cycle*, pp. 85–97.

# 3

NOAH D. GUYNN

# *Le Roman de la rose*

There can be no doubt that the composite *Roman de la rose*, an allegorical love poem begun between 1225 and 1245 by an otherwise unknown court poet, Guillaume de Lorris, and completed between 1268 and 1285 by the scholastic author Jean de Meun, was the most admired, influential, and controversial literary work of the French Middle Ages. With nearly 300 extant manuscripts (several times the number for Chaucer's *Canterbury Tales*), the *Rose* clearly enjoyed exceptional renown among medieval literate populations. The reason for this popularity may well be the poem's encyclopaedic range of themes and styles and its openness to diverse interpretive approaches. Not only does Guillaume's mannerly, euphemistic, and concise *Rose* stand in stark contrast to Jean's ironic, explicit, and sprawling continuation, but also each of the two authors complicates the production of meaning in his poem by eschewing thematic unity, singular perspectives, and structural stability. Some medieval readers sought to straighten out these problems, emphasizing the passages they considered edifying or amusing, and minimizing or expurgating the rest. Others were evidently fascinated by the hermeneutical challenges posed by a hybrid text and sought to exaggerate its contradictions.[1] Likewise, some modern scholars have claimed that the poem teaches Christian ethics by promoting sensuality ironically, others that it revels in moral indeterminacy and sexual liberation.[2] Regardless of critical bent, most readers would agree with the early humanist Jean Gerson that the *Rose* contains a remarkably wide range of themes and styles and could 'rightly [be] called a formless chaos, a Babylonian confusion, and a German broth, like Proteus changing into all his shapes'.[3] Indeed, even those scholars who insist on the poem's orthodoxy acknowledge that it teaches its lessons through the juxtaposition of contradictory viewpoints and ironic reversals of meaning.

In this chapter, I will argue that the *Rose* proliferates alternate meanings only after it has posited an essential core of truth immanent within the text. On one hand, the *Rose* announces that it contains an overarching design and didactic message that will subsequently be made evident to the reader; on the other, it fails to disclose these and thwarts attempts to impose them from the outside. If the *Rose* initially suggests that full consensus about textual meaning is not just possible but necessary, it eventually demonstrates that exegesis is itself a fictional construct subject to the vicissitudes of interpretation. Indeed, the authors themselves are described both as the originators of the poem and repositories of its message, and as fictional constructs created by the poem and indissociable from it. Finally, though the *Rose* is aware of the impact a poem may have in shaping its audience's views, it frustrates attempts to locate its ideological content. In short, the *Rose* both endorses and debunks claims to mastery, including the author's over his poem and the reader's over interpretation. The result is a work in which we may grasp the concomitant desire for and resistance to totalization in medieval texts. The *Rose* signifies by means of internal conflict, including, most crucially, between theories of discursive presence (in which essential truths are unveiled through exegesis) and discursive difference (in which language has no stable ground whatsoever).

In the ensuing pages, I will draw attention to some of the more spectacular forms of internal conflict in the *Rose*, including antithetical theories of rhetoric and hermeneutics, language and meaning, love and desire. Though my emphasis will be on the expressivity of the *Rose* independent of authorial intention and the poem's relation to tradition, I will nonetheless examine in turn the two authors and their distinctive uses of allegory: perspective and meaning are constantly fluctuating in the *Rose* even as the work announces its own rigorous consensus and coherence. I will conclude by sketching an ideological critique of the *Rose*, but one attentive to the fictional, fluctuating nature of ideology itself.

## Guillaume de Lorris

The relationship between fiction and truth is addressed almost immediately in Guillaume's poem. In the opening prologue, the narrator declares that his text should be called *The Romance of the Rose* and that the reader will find in it 'l'art d'Amors ... tote enclose' (38; 3: 'the whole art of love ... contained').[4] He proposes to reveal this art of love by recounting a dream he once had. Contrary to popular belief, dreams are not deceptions or illusions but 'senefiance' (signs) that show things 'covertement' (covertly) only to reveal them later 'apertement' (16, 19, 20: 'overtly'). The dream the narrator will recount in fact foreshadows real events: 'En ce songe onques riens n'ot / qui tretot avenu ne soit / si con li songes recensoit' (28–30; 3: 'There was nothing in the dream that has not come true, exactly as the dream told it'). The reader is alerted from the outset, then, that the dream-narrative contains an ulterior truth, one pertaining both to the essence of love and to a particular love the dreamer has experienced. If the reader's role is to seek out that truth, the text's is to conceal it, at least temporarily. The *Rose* thereby seduces the reader into a process of interpretation fuelled by promises of emotional and erotic fulfilment.

Having named his romance and described its signifying mode, the narrator offers his recollection of the events of the dream. The narrator's dream-double, who is nameless but is usually called Amant (the Lover) in manuscript rubrics, discovers the garden of Deduit (Pleasure) while on a springtime walk. Oiseuse (Idleness) admits Amant into the garden, where he witnesses the courtly virtues dancing a round with Amor (Love). Eventually, Amant wanders off to visit the garden; Amor pursues him stealthily, armed with bow and arrows. Amant arrives at the fountain where Narcissus fell in love with his own image and perished. Gazing into the fountain, he perceives the reflection of a rosebush and is seized by mad desire for a particular rosebud. Amor strikes Amant with his arrows and compels him to submit to his authority. Thus begins the love quest, which follows the traditional *gradus amoris* (stages of love): sight, converse, touch, kiss, and deed (that is, the plucking of the rose). Though Bel Acueil (Fair Welcome) initially encourages Amant's advances, Dangier (Rebuff), Male Bouche (Evil Tongue), Honte (Shame), and Poor (Fear) repel him. With Venus's help, Amant is allowed to kiss the rose, but Male Bouche informs Jalousie (Jealousy), who builds a fortress to protect Bel Acueil and the rose from further advances. Guillaume's work ends shortly thereafter, with Amant lamenting the loss of Bel Acueil. It is unclear whether Guillaume abandoned writing because he saw the love story as necessarily incomplete (the last *gradus* being suppressed for decorum's sake), or because (as Jean later surmises) death prevented him from completing it.

In keeping with traditional rhetorical theory, a literal reading of this allegorical narrative must be supplemented by figurative meanings. Ancient and medieval rhetors define allegory as 'speaking otherwise': a technique whereby one thing is said and another is meant. Obviously, the poem anticipates the imposition of 'other', extra-literal meanings on the story, and indeed the narrator promises he will eventually reveal such a meaning himself: the reader will know a great deal about Amor's games if he will simply wait to hear the narrator disclose 'dou songe la senefiance' (2070; 32: 'the significance of the dream'). If the truth is now 'coverte' (hidden), it will be 'toute overte / quant espondre m'oroiz le songe, / car il n'i a mot de mençonge' (2071–4; 32: 'completely plain when you have heard me explain the dream, for it contains no lies'). This explanation is missing from the poem, however, and the reader is left to wonder what hidden content might have been revealed if Guillaume had fulfilled his promise. Is the poem a fragment? Or did Guillaume withhold his gloss deliberately, in an attempt to frustrate his reader's expectations, elicit doubt about the text's veracity, or invite speculation about its meaning? Many critics agree with D. F. Hult that Guillaume's *Rose* is indeed a finished work, but one that reflects a 'prevailing penchant for indefinite, open-ended texts'.[5] Far from containing its truth, the *Rose* self-consciously refers to its absence; rather than foreclosing interpretation by imposing a *senefiance* on the dream, it opens itself to semantic play.

The open-endedness of Guillaume's text is perceptible not just at the macro-level of textual design but also at the micro-level of individual personifications. If the *Rose* initially appears to encode a literal story allegorically (a young man's awakening to love and his beloved's responses, both warm and cold), it quickly becomes apparent that literal and allegorical meanings are never fully transparent or distinct. Thus whereas Bel Acueil embodies willingness to please, he becomes timorous and reserved when Amant reveals his desire for the rose. Behaving like Honte, Bel Acueil is ashamed of having offered the warm reception for which he is named: 'Frere, vos beez / a ce qui ne puet avenir. / Coment! Me volez vos honir?' (2892–4; 45: 'Brother, you aspire to something that cannot happen. What then, do you want to shame me?'). Venus rushes to Amant's aid and accuses Bel Acueil of being 'dangereus' (3425: 'withholding') as well. Dangier, by contrast, is overly accommodating and is reproached by Honte for not living up to his name: 'Il n'afiert pas a vostre non / que vos faciez se anui non' (3677–78; 56: 'It does not befit someone with your name to cause anything but distress'). Punning on *non* ('name'/'not'), the text evinces the unreliability of allegorical signs, which may invert or negate the meaning they allegedly contain. Honte's admonition thus reveals two contradictory things: first, that the goal of allegory is to bind words securely to meanings; and second, that it not only fails to do so but also repeatedly draws attention to that failure.

These inconsistencies are far from incidental; indeed, all the figures in the *Rose* are unsettled by the production of allegorical meaning 'otherwise'. Amor, whose meaning is intrinsically paradoxical (love and war, affection and assault), describes his art as so elusive and unpredictable that it could never be contained in a book: 'Nes qu'em puet espuisier la mer, / ne poroit nus les maus d'amer / conter en romanz ne en livre' (2591–3; 40: 'The pains of love can no more be recounted in a book or a romance than the sea can be drained dry'). Punning on *la mer* (the sea) and *amer* (to love), Amor belies the stated goal of the very poem in which he appears: to enclose the art of love. The narrator later returns to this pun, comparing the fickleness of love to the windswept sea and concluding, 'Amors n'est gueres en un point' (3480: 'Love is never in a single place'). Far from being an embodiment of an unchanging truth, Amor is clearly subject to an inexorable ebb and flow.

The meaning of the beloved rose tends to eddy and drift as well. In the prologue, the narrator dedicates the poem to 'cele qui tant a de pris / et tant est digne d'estre amee / qu'el doit estre Rose clamee' (42–4; 3: 'she ... who is so precious and so worthy of being loved that she ought to be called Rose'), and therefore ostensibly links the rose to a female beloved. Yet, mysteriously, the identity of this dedicatee is never any more substantial than the absent antecedent of a demonstrative pronoun. The rose is, moreover, not actually a personification in that she/it lacks human traits and never speaks or acts. Oddly enough, the rose even lacks unambiguous gender markers. Though it is often taken as a genital symbol, critics are divided as to whether it is vaginal or phallic. The narrator describes the stem as 'droite con jons' (straight as a reed) and adds, 'Par desus siet li boutons / si qu'i ne cline ne ne pent' (1663–5; 26: 'The bud was set on top in such a way that it neither bent nor drooped'). Later, he perceives it as a bud tightly enveloped in leaves; though swelling as it matures, it has not yet unfolded to expose its seed (3339–52). Do these descriptions suggest an intact hymen, an erect penis, or both? Is the beloved male, female, or androgynous? Is Amant's desire heterosexual or homosexual, normative or transgressive? The association of the rose with Narcissus's fountain certainly contributes to the ambiguity. According to Ovid, Narcissus was pursued by boys and girls and eventually fell in love with himself – a man. Guillaume does little to disguise his source's homoeroticism but instead lovingly describes Narcissus's comely visage and the burning desire Narcissus feels for himself. If Amant discovers the rose by gazing into Narcissus's 'miroërs perilleus' (1569; 25: 'perilous mirror'), might the love quest not be inflected by similar semantic, sexual, and moral difficulties?

The relationship between Amant and Bel Acueil, which dominates the last third of Guillaume's poem, suggests as much. Bel Acueil (who, by dint of grammatical gender, is male) personifies a kind of sexual receptivity that courtly readers would have considered distinctly unmanly. When he is approached by Venus armed with 'un brandon flanbant ... dont la flame / a eschaufee mainte dame' (3406–8; 52: 'a burning torch whose flame has warmed many a lady'), he promptly yields, granting 'un bessier en dons' (3457; 53: 'the gift of a kiss'). It soon becomes clear that Amant kisses the rose and not Bel Acueil. Yet the temporary ambiguity subsequently takes on broader meaning since Bel Acueil largely replaces the rose as the object of Amant's desire. In the closing pages of Guillaume's *Rose*, Amant uses lyrical language (including repeated use of *joie*, a ubiquitous term in love lyric) to refer to the bliss he would experience if Bel Acueil were restored to him. The rose is now little more than an afterthought, and courtly love metamorphoses into its apparent contradiction, an amorous bond between men:

> Je n'oi bien ne joie onques puis
> que Bel Acueil fu em prison,
> que ma joie et ma guerison
> est toute en li et en la rose
> qui est entre les murs enclose;
> et de la covendra qu'il isse,
> s'Amors veut ja que j'en garisse,
> que ja d'aillors ne quier que j'oie
> honor ne bien, santé ne joie.
> Hai! Bel Acueil, biau douz amis,
> se vos estes em prison mis,
> gardez moi seviaus vostre cuer.          (3966–77)

(I have had no blessings or joys since Fair Welcome was put in prison, for all my joy and my salvation is in him and in the rose that is confined within the walls. He will have to come out from there if Love wants me to be cured, for I seek neither honour nor good, neither health nor joy from any other source. Ah, Fair Welcome, fair sweet friend, if you are imprisoned, at least keep your heart for me.)          (61)

Guillaume's *Rose* concludes soon afterward, leaving the narrator's promises of a truthful revelation unfulfilled. In the absence of this gloss, the poem yields an array of incompatible meanings – literal and allegorical, proper and improper. Simon Gaunt has shown that this semantic openness and sexual indeterminacy have a long afterlife in *Rose* manuscripts. Some illuminations depict Bel Acueil in female dress in an attempt to 'normalize' Amant's erotic drives. Yet this does little to resolve the problem, since the image yields 'either the troublesome spectacle of the textual and visual contradicting each other, or alternatively ... the even more troublesome spectacle of a cross-dressed Bel Acueil'.[6] The ubiquitous reading of the *Rose* as an allegory of heterosexual seduction and of the rose as the beloved lady flies in the face of manuscript evidence, which highlights contradiction and deviation in the text. More to the point, this reading is belied by the text's own fascination with semantic and sexual uncertainty. For as Hult argues, Guillaume's signal achievement is to have attached 'the problem of incompletion ... to a larger question of the poetic expression of human desire'.[7] Just as the love quest remains in suspense, so, too, the allegory of love remains equivocal and incomplete, even to the point of compromising the moral value of the lessons it purports to teach.

## Jean de Meun

As Daniel Poirion remarks, '[Medieval] literature, like [medieval] architecture, is a work in progress, pursued as need be from one generation to the next.'[8] It is not unusual to encounter texts in which major narrative elements remain unresolved, and it is precisely these enigmatic, open-ended texts that yielded continuations (for example Chrétien de Troyes's *Conte du graal*, see Chapter 5). Typically, the continuation exaggerates the ambiguities of the original work through structural, thematic, or stylistic changes. Indeed, Poirion remarks, 'One must not evaluate this kind of undertaking on the basis of fidelity to the model', for continuators typically reinterpret the original text according to the cultural and ideological expectations of a new audience.[9]

This is certainly the case with Jean's 18,000-line continuation of the *Rose*. Guillaume left many things unsaid for the sake of discretion and stylistic indirection; Jean, a product of his scholastic education, aspires to 'know everything' (15184). Guillaume focuses primarily on description and narration; Jean prefers direct discourse. Guillaume's narrator is a courtly lover; Jean's is also a student, albeit one who often fails to grasp, or is indifferent to, the knowledge imparted to him. Finally, though the goal of the love quest remains the same, Jean's poem actually manages to achieve it, recounting the assault on the castle and plucking of the rose in a series of lurid, thinly veiled sexual metaphors. If Guillaume was reticent about depicting the last *gradus amoris*, Jean has no such scruples. His goal is to add whatever words are needed to Guillaume's poem, be they 'sages ou foles' (10568; 163: 'wise or foolish'), until Amant is able to take the rose from its branch.

That said, Jean also plainly grasped the constitutive ambiguities of Guillaume's allegory and sought to amplify them using *disputatio*: the scholastic method for pursuing knowledge through opposing propositions and authorities. Beyond completing the love quest, Jean is not terribly interested in advancing the plot. He emphasizes speeches instead – monologues and dialogues in which characters like Reson (Reason), Ami (Friend), Faus Semblant (False Seeming), La Vielle (the Old Woman), Nature, and Genius hold forth on a variety of issues, including, but not limited to, love. Whereas Guillaume sought to pluralize his poem's meaning by indefinitely deferring textual closure, Jean makes space for an even broader variety of discourses and perspectives, including overtly discrepant ones. Using the techniques of a *compilator* (who cites the work of others but disguises his own opinions), he transforms Guillaume's psychological romance into a massive polyphonic composition, one in which there are no sovereign voices, only dialectical tensions between incompatible ones.

Poirion observes that this 'blossoming of dialectic' in Jean's continuation is at the expense of 'faith in words', and indeed Jean repeatedly insists on the dislocation of truth and authority in language.[10] As we have seen, Guillaume's *Rose* casts doubt on poetry as a vehicle for truth by heralding a definitive meaning that never actually arrives. Jean insists that truth is not only lacking in his poem but is also difficult to distinguish from poetry. In the course of a digression about the composition and reception of the poem itself, the narrator urges:

> Notez ce que ci vois disant,
> d'amors avrez art souffisant.
> Et se vos i trovez riens trouble,
> g'esclarcirai ce qui vos trouble
> quant le songe m'orrez espondre.
> Bien savrez lors d'amors respondre,
> s'il est qui an sache opposer,
> quant le texte m'orrez gloser;
> et savrez lors par cel escrit
> quant que j'avrai devant escrit
> et quant que je bé a escrire. (15113–23)

(Take note of what I say now, and you will have art of love enough. If you have any difficulty, I will explain whatever is troubling you when you hear me interpret the dream. Then, when you hear me gloss the text, you will be able to reply on behalf of love if anyone raises objections; and you will be able to understand through this writing what I will have written previously, as well as what I wish to write.) (234, modified)

Jean here offers an unmistakeable echo of his predecessor's work: line 15117 is virtually identical to line 2073, cited above. Moreover, just as Guillaume fails to expound the hidden meaning of his dream, Jean's promise of a gloss remains unfulfilled: once the lover has plucked the rose, the poem concludes abruptly with the dreamer's awakening. However, Jean does not simply insist on the failure of allegory to reveal truth; he also suggests the impossibility of discovering *anything* beyond the imperfect realm of signs. The lack of an ulterior *escrit* to stabilize the present one is mirrored by a play of verbal tenses in the promise itself. Using the future and future perfect, Jean imagines a subsequent moment in which the reader *will know* the meaning of a text Jean *will have written* but has not yet. Since that text does not exist, Jean's *Rose* is caught in a temporal paradox: it imagines the eventual discovery of its meaning in an *escrit* that always will have been written but never has been. The allegory does not enclose or disclose its truth. Instead it constructs an infinite loop in which linear chronology collapses into temporal paradoxes and a signifying chain in which there are no stable or positive terms.

Jean returns to the notion of language as a purely relational system at the end of his poem. In the course of discussing the relative charms of young and old women, the narrator summarizes an argument from Aristotle whereby an entity can only be known through knowledge of its opposite:

> Ainsinc va des contreres choses,
> les unes sunt des autres gloses;
> et qui l'une an veust defenir,
> de l'autre li doit souvenir,
> ou ja, par nule antancion,
> n'i metra diffinicion;
> car qui des .II. n'a connoissance,
> ja n'i connoistra differance,
> san quoi ne peut venir en place
> diffinicion que l'an face. (21543–52)

(The nature of contrary things is that the one is the gloss of the other: if you want to define one, you must be mindful of the other, or else you will never achieve a definition, however good your intentions. Unless you know both, you will never understand the difference between them, without which no proper definition can be made.) (332, modified)

In Jean's hands, Aristotle's logical argument becomes a linguistic and literary one. There can be no knowledge and no determination of meaning without discrepancy. Things are texts ('gloses') that relate to one another as a signifier to a signified or a poem to its exegesis. There are no self-defining values, only contradictions that require the interpretive efforts of a reader in order to yield meaning. Put another way, the signified always functions as a signifier and cannot prevent slippages of meaning. This volatile relationship between figuration and signification is what Poirion calls the irony of Jean's *Rose*: the discrepancy between a figure of speech and the significance it bears or an irresolvable dispute between competing discourses, none of which is fully reliable.[11]

One might imagine that Reson, as the embodiment of the rational faculties, could resolve these contradictions and yield internally consistent forms of knowledge. Certainly, she claims to offer an alternative to Fortune's capriciousness and Amor's mutability. If Amant abandons the love quest and devotes himself to her, he will become, like Socrates, 'fors' ('firm') and 'estables' (5818; 90: 'strong'). Reson even suggests that she has mastery over allegory itself, that she can extract the 'secrez de philosophie' (7140; 109: 'secrets of philosophy') from 'geus' (games) and 'fables' (7145) through integumental reading. Tellingly, though, this theory arises within a discussion of a mythological exemplum (Jupiter's castration of Saturn and the resultant birth of Venus) that Reson *never* fully explicates and that she in fact uses to defend plain speaking and to elucidate the arbitrariness of language and the lack of inherent truths in signs. Amant priggishly denounces Reson for using a vulgarity, *coilles* (balls), in recounting the tale. She retorts that there is nothing sinful in the things themselves (which God created), nor in the names used to signify them. If, when she originally imposed names on things, Reson had called *coilles reliques* (relics) and *reliques coilles*, Amant would undoubtedly now find fault with the word *reliques*. A word is therefore not intrinsically obscene but becomes so through social convention. As Hult argues, Jean uses this episode to effect 'a direct figurative relationship between castration or bodily dismemberment and linguistic functions as they are predicated upon the tenuous yet commonly accepted bond between word and thing'.[12] Just as Saturn's *coilles* were severed from his body, so speech is dislocated from intention, signs from referents. And just as Saturn's castration leads to Venus's birth, so 'the loosening of ties between words and things betokens the possibility of figuration in a variety of dimensions'.[13] Of course, Reson, herself an allegory, is not exempt from alienation in signs but is replete with slippages and contradictions. She offers a passionate defence of plain speech and critique of intentionality, but simultaneously insists that her own discourse is deliberately obscure. And though she attempts to convince Amant to shun love, she also tries to convince him to take *her* as his 'amie' (5771; 89: 'beloved')'! Is Reson entirely reasonable and 'estable', then? Or is she instead passionate and 'muable'?

The unreasonableness of reason not only reflects Jean's fondness for irony and paradox but also his awareness that language is fundamentally incompatible with truth. Susan Stakel argues that the language of deceit is pervasive in Jean's *Rose* and that the character of Faus Semblant offers a paradigm for discursive representation generally.[14] Faus Semblant first appears in the poem as Amor rallies his armies for an attack on the castle. He swears to fight on Amant's behalf, but Amor, doubting that a character so-named could be a reliable ally, demands to know where Faus Semblant can be found when he is needed. The answer does little to reassure Amor, for Faus Semblant is apparently everywhere and nowhere at once. Though utterly ubiquitous, he generally passes unnoticed: 'Onques en vile / n'entrai ou fusse conneüz, / tant i fusse oïz ne veüz' (11154–6; 172: 'I have never been recognized in any town I have entered, however much I may have been heard and seen there'). And though his disguises are many, he is expert at deceiving through signs: 'Sai par queur trestouz langages' (11166; 172: 'I know all languages by heart'). Could Faus Semblant know the language of Reson and furtively speak to readers through her? As Stakel demonstrates, this is indeed the case: the lexical family and synonym group linked to deception (more than 600 words and expressions) pervade *all* the speeches in Jean's poem, including those of Ami and La Vielle, who openly advocate deceit, and Reson and Nature, who supposedly illuminate higher truths.

The unreliability and inextricability of language find their most radical expression in Jean's authorial signature, really a double signature in which Jean names Guillaume (who failed to name himself) as the original author of the *Rose* and himself as continuator. He does this obliquely, however, speaking through Amor. Addressing his army before the assault on Jealousy's castle, Amor introduces the previously nameless lover as Guillaume de Lorris and announces that Guillaume will begin 'le romant / ou seront mis tuit mi conmant' (10519–20; 162: 'the romance that will contain all my commandments'). To reaffirm his fealty, Amant has just repeated Amor's commandments, which he first learned in Guillaume's poem. The commandments will indeed be set down – or have been set down, since we have read them now twice. From the naming of Amant we can understand two things: first, that Amant is Guillaume, who will be/was the original author of the poem we have been reading; second, that the poem will have/had a second author. The poem *had* an author, otherwise it would not exist, but it also *will have* an author, since Amor prophesies that the poem in which he speaks remains to be written. Tracing another temporal loop and chain of *escrits*, the *Rose* incorporates into its narrative the written record of a prophecy of the writing down of that prophecy.

This chronology is rendered more intricate still when Jean identifies himself as the author of the continuation. After introducing Guillaume to his army, Amor cites what will be the last few lines of Guillaume's poem – words we have already read. He then predicts the death of Guillaume, who will leave his poem incomplete, and announces the birth, forty years afterward, of Jean de Meun, who will discover and complete Guillaume's fragment. In other words, this implicit authorial signature lies chronologically somewhere between Guillaume's death and Jean's birth. This temporal paradox is captured rather creatively in a sixteenth-century illuminated manuscript (Pierpont Morgan M948) in which Guillaume is depicted as a cadaver lying on a dissecting table with a book open on a shelf above him, while Amant waits outside for Jean to continue his story (see Figure 1). Through this tortuous account of the poem's genesis, Jean suggests that the author and his name are, like the poem itself, signifiers cut off from their origins. The signature does not contain the reality of what it names but is instead a fictional construct liable to the unpredictability of interpretation and the play of differences between 'contreres choses': being and nothingness, life and death. For Jean, subjectivity is constituted in, and fragmented by, language and temporality. It is not a conscious presence or a reliable recollection of the past, rather an evanescence of words and meanings in time.

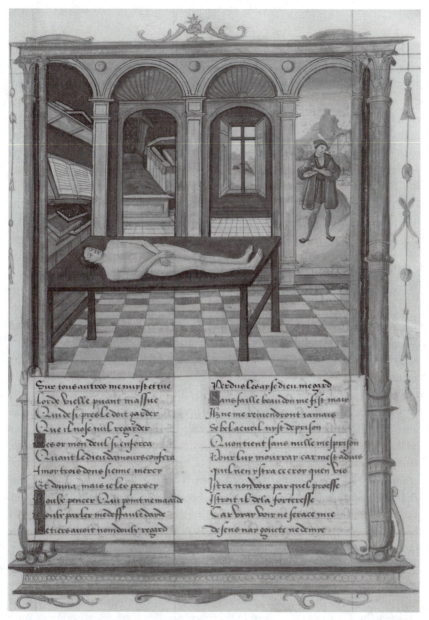

Figure 1. *Le Roman de la rose*, Pierpont Morgan M948, fo. 44r. This illumination (from a lavish manuscript produced in 1525 for François I, king of France) appears immediately after Guillaume de Lorris's poem has ended and Jean de Meun's has begun. It depicts Guillaume as a cadaver crowned with laurels and lying on a dissecting table. There is a book (perhaps the *Rose* itself) open on a shelf above Guillaume. Amant waits outside for Jean to continue the love story.

## Conclusion

If the authorship of the *Rose* is as elusive as its *senefiance*, could the authors ever be held responsible for the content of their work or its effects on readers? Jean's narrator explicitly addresses this question prior to the assault on the castle, seeking to forestall accusations of obscenity and misogyny. He claims to have done nothing but 'reciter' (15204: 'repeat') the writings of others, and indeed has done so only to advance knowledge. He ought not to be blamed, therefore; rather, 'aus aucteurs vos an prenez / qui an leur livres ont escrites / les paroles que g'en ai dites' (15188–90; 235: 'Do not call me a liar, but blame those authors who have written in their books what I have said').

Is this claim sincere, or yet another instance of imposture and false seeming? The question has been debated at least since the *Querelle de la Rose*, a late medieval polemic in which Christine de Pizan and Jean Gerson disputed the moral status of the *Rose* with Pierre and Gontier Col and Jean de Montreuil (see further Chapter 8). The former object to Jean's *Rose* as an offence against public morality, with Christine objecting in particular to passages that are libellous to women. The latter echo Jean himself, countering that characters speak for themselves, not the author, and that their words must conform to their natures, whether upright or dissolute. As has often been observed, there is unsound reasoning on both sides. Jean's detractors argue that the lack of overt moralization contributes to the delinquency of readers. However, if moral responsibility implies the capacity for choice, they in effect deny readers the necessary precondition for rectitude by insisting that all texts be morally unequivocal. Jean's defenders identified this contradiction and argued for a firm distinction between characters' words, authors' intentions, and the ethics of a text. Pierre Col praises Jean for granting readers the opportunity to learn from, and defend against, his characters' lubricity. Yet in the same breath he defines Jean's intentions and the morality of the *Rose* almost as narrowly and conventionally as his opponents do: '[Jean] teaches the defenders to guard the castle: and it was for this purpose that he wrote [the *Rose*].'[15]

What is most valuable about the *Querelle* is not, however, the inconsistencies of the opposing arguments, rather the insights it gives us into the difficulties faced by medieval readers as they sought to grasp the moral and political implications of a text in which authority, intention, and meaning have been radically destabilized. These are the same difficulties faced by critics today. Does Jean's rupturing of words and things, language and identity imply an analogous break with social constraints and sexual repression, as Poirion argues?[16] Or is Alastair Minnis right to claim that the *Rose* exposes 'paradoxes, tensions, and apparent absurdities' internal to elite clerical culture only to promote in turn its core beliefs and values?[17] To my mind, Minnis's argument is the more convincing of the two. If Jean points to rifts and contradictions within clerical ideology, this in turn requires a compensatory gesture: words and fictions that remind the clergy of their power by pointing to the forms of social distinction that constitute them as a ruling class, notably the exclusion and subordination of women.[18]

Strikingly, one of the clearest examples of misogyny in the *Rose* is also one of its most densely metaphorical passages: the assault on the castle and plucking of the rose. After Venus engulfs the castle in flames and razes it to the ground, Amant thrusts his staff into an aperture in the fortification, scatters seed from his sack onto the rosebush, and, finally, plucks the rose from its branch. Though the ulterior meaning of this scene is never revealed (as was once promised), it plainly represents an aggressive, even violent act of insemination, a sexual union that is anything but mutual, and a juxtaposition of 'contreres choses' in which one thing is known by the other but without reciprocation. Indeed, the rose remains utterly passive, mute, and inert even as she/it is literally and metaphorically inflamed by desire. The *Rose* here rehearses, without fully ironizing, a display of masculine bravado that depends upon the silencing of contrary discourses (the rose's speech has been nipped in the bud) and the objectification of women (the rose is not, properly speaking, a personification but a flower).

There are, of course, a range of perspectives on this and every other issue related to form, meaning, and ideology in the poem. The *Roman de la rose* is a paradigmatic example of the medieval predilection for open, active, inexhaustible texts, and full consensus on its meaning is neither possible nor desirable. If this massive, hybrid, recondite poem presents modern readers with formidable interpretive challenges, it amply rewards us by casting and recasting the very questions that fascinate and disturb us today: the relationship between language and meaning, representation and truth, gender and politics, social roles and moral values.

## Notes

1. See S. Huot, *The 'Romance of the Rose' and its Medieval Readers: Interpretation, Reception, Manuscript Transmission* (Cambridge University Press, 1993).
2. See H. M. Arden, *The 'Roman de la rose': an Annotated Bibliography* (New York, Garland, 1993).
3. J. L. Baird and J. R. Kane, trans., *La Querelle de la Rose: Letters and Documents* (Chapel Hill, University of North Carolina Press, 1978), p. 147.
4. References are to line numbers in Lecoy's edition, then page numbers (where relevant) in *The Romance of the Rose*, trans. F. Horgan (Oxford University Press, 1994).

5. D. F. Hult, *Self-fulfilling Prophecies: Readership and Authority in the First 'Roman de la rose'* (Cambridge University Press, 1986), p. 70.

6. S. Gaunt, 'Bel Acueil and the Improper Allegory of the *Romance of the Rose*', *New Medieval Literatures* 2 (1998), 65–93 (p. 75).

7. Hult, *Prophecies*, p. 261.

8. D. Poirion, *Le Roman de la rose* (Paris, Hatier, 1973), p. 98.

9. Poirion, *Roman*, p. 98.

10. Poirion, *Roman*, p. 142.

11. Poirion, *Roman*, pp. 145–73.

12. D. F. Hult, 'Language and Dismemberment: Abelard, Origen, and the *Romance of the Rose*', in K. Brownlee and S. Huot (eds.), *Rethinking the 'Romance of the Rose': Text, Image, Reception* (Philadelphia, University of Pennsylvania Press, 1992), p. 121.

13. Hult, 'Language', p. 122.

14. S. Stakel, *False Roses: Structures of Duality and Deceit in Jean de Meun's 'Roman de la rose'* (Stanford, ANMA Libri, 1991), esp. pp. 46–82.

15. Baird and Kane, *Querelle*, p. 109.

16. D. Poirion, 'Les mots et les choses selon Jean de Meun', *L'Information Littéraire* 26 (1974), 7–11.

17. A. Minnis, *Magister Amoris: the 'Roman de la rose' and Vernacular Hermeneutics* (Oxford University Press, 2001), p. 193

18. N. D. Guynn, *Allegory and Sexual Ethics in the High Middle Ages* (New York, Palgrave Macmillan, 2007).

# 4

ADRIAN ARMSTRONG

# The *Testament* of François Villon

Villon's *Testament* is a satirical will in which a first-person narrator, pur-
portedly on his death bed, leaves a series of burlesque bequests, among them
many specimens of Villon's own lyric poetry, intended to punish or reward
people he has known. Most critical studies of the *Testament* adopt one of
two main approaches. One, which we might call 'life-based', assumes that a
text is a record of its author's experience, to be understood in relation to the
real-world context in which it was composed. 'Life-based' studies privilege
the *Testament*'s relationship to historical contexts, to Villon's life – insofar as
this can be delineated from the very limited documentary evidence – or to
the Paris of the late 1450s and early 1460s. The other, which we might call
'art-based', assumes that a text and its meanings are products of linguistic
and aesthetic conventions, and can be understood only in relation to these.
'Art-based' analysis concentrates upon the ways in which the *Testament* both
uses and disrupts various kinds of conventions: those of the legal will, or of
different poetic genres, or of proverbial language.[1] The range of interpretations
of Villon's best-known work is hardly surprising, for particular features of the
*Testament* seem to appeal to one or other of these types of reading. It is crucial
to recognize, however, that the opposition between 'life-based' and 'art-based'
approaches is a false one. The two are in no sense mutually exclusive: adherents
of the former regard art as a product of experience, while adherents of the latter
regard experience as constructed through art. Indeed, neither view can be
upheld in pure form. No text can be a pure record of fact, as its language
always bears traces of other texts, whether literary or non-literary; nor can a
text consist of pure language, for it is always the product of a certain author
(whether individual or collective, identifiable or anonymous) in a certain
context. In the case of the *Testament*, different aspects of its content and
form superficially elicit either 'life-based' or 'art-based' readings, but prove
on closer examination to undermine any notion that the two are opposed.

Any examination of this kind must address the question of textual transmission, a question which is manifested on two levels. Most obvious is the

poem's own transmission: in the late fifteenth and early sixteenth centuries, manuscripts and printed books conveyed different versions of the *Testament*, accompanied by other texts of different kinds. These witnesses both indicate and influence the poem's reception, showing how scribes and printers perceived Villon's work and conveying those perceptions to other contemporary readers. But textual transmission is also a major preoccupation of the poem itself, where it informs a wide range of themes and techniques. Perhaps inevitable in a parodic testament – wills are, after all, centrally concerned with transmission, albeit of worldly rather than wordy goods – this preoccupation emerges most strikingly in a pervasive sense that texts are *fragile*. Fragility is physical: the vicissitudes of transmission threaten the material survival of Villon's poem, and indeed of any document. Equally, it is linguistic and aesthetic: language and cultural conventions change constantly, in ways which risk making the poem inaccessible to posterity. These different manifestations of fragility impact upon not only aesthetic but also biographical responses to the *Testament*, for a truncated, distorted, or otherwise incomprehensible poem threatens the survival in readers' memories of the characters and settings which Villon depicts. Focusing upon these questions of transmission and interpretation, the following study examines five key aspects of the *Testament*, illuminating such issues as the poem's thematic and formal coherence, its relationship to other texts, and its suggestive presentation of the creative intelligence which has produced it.

## Villon's persona

Numerous scholars have observed that Villon's testator (the usual term by which critics designate the *Testament's* first-person narrator) is an unstable persona, who adopts a series of roles rather than a consistent stance. At certain points he is a martyr to love (625–722, 910–69); at others he is a repentant sinner (89–112), a moralist reflecting on the transience of worldly affairs (305–444), or a dying invalid (729–31, 785–6). Each of these roles is familiar from amatory and didactic literature (see Chapters 6, 7, 8, and 10 for precedents and parallels), and thus invites an 'art-based' reading: the testator is characterized through his relationship with existing literary types. It is unprecedented in previous literature, however, for a single first-person voice to adopt so many different, indeed incompatible, roles. If readers assume that characters must be coherent, the multiplicity of the testator's roles encourages a more 'life-based' interpretation: since these temporary masks do not add up to a stable character, it is assumed that the testator's coherence must lie outside the poem, in an historical author who assumes and discards the masks at will. This effect is especially powerful when the testator draws attention to his role-playing: 'De viel porte voix et le ton, / et ne suis q'un jeune cocquart' (735–6: 'I put on an old man's voice, but I'm just a young twit'). Self-consciously revealing himself to be a performer, the testator suggests that his performance conceals a true self – a self which readers might assume coincides with the historical Villon.

A similar effect is produced by the allusiveness of references to named characters. The testator mentions Thibaud d'Aussigny, for instance, only obliquely and in fragments: readers cannot reconstruct a coherent narrative which would explain the testator's animosity towards him. For readers vainly seeking such a narrative, the very incompleteness of the references implies that Villon is withholding details of real events – details which could be completed if the circumstances of the *Testament*'s composition were fully grasped.[2] These unsatisfying allusions make the *Testament* appear all the more fragile, in a linguistic and aesthetic sense, as historical distance prevents readers from reliably interpreting names and places. The fragility is partly illusory: Villon's contemporaries were scarcely better able than modern readers to understand the allusions, precisely because they are couched in terms which *resist* complete comprehension. Nevertheless, Villon's technique of fragmentary exposition draws our attention to the way contexts of interpretation change over time, leading to an inevitable erosion of meaning.

A further element which might encourage 'life-based' readings of the testator is that he is not only a subject who perceives, experiences, and speaks; he explicitly presents himself as an author. He bequeaths poems to various recipients; he alludes to the composition of his own earlier testamentary poem, the *Lais*; in the *Ballade des femmes de Paris* (1515–42), he asks his audience whether his enumeration of women from other regions is long enough to demonstrate the superior verbosity of Parisian women: 'Ai ge beaucoup de lieu[x] compris?' (1536: 'have I included a lot of places?'). Since the testator is a poet, readers are all the more likely to conflate Villon's persona with the historical author. Similar processes are often apparent in Villon's near-contemporaries, the so-called *Rhétoriqueurs* (rhetoricians), political and didactic poets active from the mid fifteenth to the mid sixteenth century. A representative example is the prolific *Rhétoriqueur* Jean Molinet (1435–1507), whose work occasionally accompanies Villon's in manuscripts, and whose narratorial persona is sometimes characterized as an author who comments on the creative process.[3] However, Molinet's readers are much less likely than Villon's to interpret his poetry in 'life-based' terms, for Molinet's work is much less strongly marked by various features which, in the *Testament*, have elicited readings of this kind. One of these is the use of incomplete allusion mentioned above; in other words, a formal technique. The other features, which the rest of this study will examine, are likewise effects of form and language, analysis of which reveals how erroneous it is to oppose biographical and aesthetic approaches.

## Voice and writing

Throughout the *Testament*, there is an insistence upon the spoken word. The narrator, as we have just seen, ventriloquizes a polyphonic variety of voices. The poem's very composition is staged as dictation, through references to 'Fremin l'Estourdiz' (565: 'scatterbrained Firmin'), the secretary who transcribes the testator's words: 'Fremin, siez toy près de mon lit / ... pren ancre tost, plume, pappier!' (787–9: 'Firmin, sit down by my bed ... quickly, fetch a pen, paper, and ink!') More generally, Villon's syntax creates a strong impression of spontaneous oral composition: the testator frequently uses rhetorical questions and exclamations, interrupts or corrects himself, and fails to finish his sentences, thereby adopting patterns which appear characteristic of unpolished everyday speech rather than considered literary language. The tone is set in the first stanza, which begins by accumulating subordinate clauses that we expect will eventually coalesce around a main verb (1–6); no such verb appears, as the name of Thibaud d'Aussigny triggers a syntactically unrelated exclamation:

> Non obstant maintes peines eues,
> lesquelles j'ay toutes receues
> soubz la main Thibault d'Aucigny...
> s'esvesque il est, signant les rues,
> qu'il soit le mien, je le regny! (4–8)

(Notwithstanding numerous penalties I've received, all under the jurisdiction of Thibaud d'Aussigny ... If he's a bishop, blessing the crowds, I won't admit that he's mine!)

The prominence of voice, and its connotations of spontaneity and naturalness, might steer readers towards a 'life-based' interpretation of the *Testament* as a direct, sincere product of Villon's consciousness.

Nevertheless, the poem's oral qualities, however unpolished an effect they might create, are the products of artifice, an artifice which reflects a highly literate and literary compositional practice. The testator's address to Firmin has a fifteenth-century poetic precedent, in Pierre de Hauteville's comic work *La Confession et testament de l'amant trespassé de dueil*, where a lover writing his will speaks to his secretary. Villon seems to play upon this fiction, recasting it by making the will into an inappropriately public document: Firmin is instructed 'Ce que nomme escriptz vistement, / puis fay le partout coppïer' (790–1: 'Write down quickly what I dictate, then have it distributed everywhere').[4] As for the testator's 'speech patterns', these are anything but artless: they depend on rhetorical techniques taught in the medieval educational curriculum and familiar to educated readers, such as *correctio* (self-correction) and *aposiopesis* (the abandonment of a construction before it is syntactically complete).[5] Still more fundamentally, speech may be a striking surface feature of the *Testament*, but only writing can communicate the text to its audience. The fiction of dictation, indeed, draws attention to the materials essential to the poem's production: 'ancre . . ., plume, pappier'.

Materials, however, do not transcribe poems themselves – and by this point, we already know that Firmin is not a reliable scribe, at least according to the testator, who proclaims his intentions 'Devant mon clerc Fremin qui m'ot/ – s'il ne dort!' (779–80: 'in the presence of my secretary Firmin, who's listening – unless he's asleep!') The fiction is not only comic in itself; the testator's dependence upon a copyist of doubtful competence reaffirms the theme of textual fragility. Writing is uncontrollable; it is always a form of *re*writing, and as such constantly threatens the very survival of a text, which means only what its successive scribes set down, and what its readers understand and remember of those transcriptions. The testator frequently misquotes previous literary works, a tendency examined in the following section, which amply illustrates the fate that can befall written texts. Moreover, it becomes all too apparent that the *Testament* is likely to share this fate. Its forerunner, the *Lais*, has already undergone distortion, disseminated under an unauthorized title:

> je feiz à mon partement
> certains laiz, l'an cinquante six,
> qu'aucuns, sans mon consentement,
> voulurent nommer 'testament';
> leur plaisir fut, non pas le myen.                    (754–8)

(when I left in 1456 I made certain bequests, which some people, without my consent, decided to call 'testament'; that was their decision, not mine.)

In his closing pronouncements, the testator pre-emptively accommodates the prospect of similar rewriting for the *Testament*, as if clawing back a semblance of authorial control from posterity: the work will be travestied and misremembered whatever the poet's precautions, so why not create at least an illusion of authority, by explicitly permitting the inevitable? Thus Jean de Calais – a historical figure contemporary with Villon, the officer responsible for confirming the legitimacy of wills made by lay Parisians – is permitted to amend the entire will as he sees fit (1844–59). Thus, too, when the testator proposes an impossible tomb for himself – in the chapel of Sainte-Avoie (1868–9), that is on the upper floor of a building which housed a community of religious women – he dictates an evanescent inscription to accompany it:

> vueil qu'autour de ma fosse
> ce qui s'enssuit, sans autre histoire,
> soit escript en lectre assez grosse;
> qui n'auroit point d'escriptoüoire,
> de charbon ou de pierre noire,
> sans en rien entamer le plastre. (1876–81)

(I wish the following to be written around my grave, in fairly large lettering without further ornament; if the writing materials aren't available, let it be in charcoal or coal, but it mustn't damage the plaster in any way.)

The *Ballade de conclusion* (1996–2023) provides an appropriately final statement of the *Testament*'s fragile integrity, since its speaker, and hence its relationship to what precedes it, cannot be identified. As it refers to 'povre Villon' (1997: 'poor Villon') in the third person, and describes him as already dead (2013), its voice must logically be distinct from that of the testator, the first-person speaker who has delivered the preceding verses either directly or via assumed voices, and who identifies himself as François Villon (1887). This does not, of course, imply that the *ballade*'s historical author is necessarily distinct from the author of the rest of the *Testament* – but its voice gives us no clues as to its relationship with the testator. Are we to read the *ballade* as a fictitious postscript, added by Firmin or Jean de Calais? No conclusive answer can be supplied; more important is the principle which the *Ballade de conclusion* demonstrates, that a text can always be retrospectively amended after it has escaped its author's control. As the following section outlines, this is precisely what happens to a wide range of texts at Villon's hands.

### Intertextual echoes

The *Testament*'s very first line, 'En l'an de mon trentïesme aage' (1: 'when I was thirty years old'), signals to readers that the poem cannot be read without reference to other texts – in this instance the *Roman de la rose*, whose first line after its prologue, 'Au vuintieme an de mon aage' (21), Villon playfully reworks.[6] Such intertexts are present throughout, via quotations or allusions of different kinds. The use of Pierre de Hauteville's *Confession et testament* has already been mentioned; the title which the testator bestows (1458) on *Les Contredits Franc Gontier* (1473–1506) indicates that this *ballade* responds to a poem by Philippe de Vitry in praise of the pastoral life; the *rondeau* for Jacques Cardon (1784–95) is introduced with references to popular melodies to which it might, possibly incongruously, be set; the Book of Ecclesiastes is cited twice (209–16) amid the testator's reflections on his misspent youth. Other intertextual resonances involve particular motifs and forms, rather than discrete texts. The overall testamentary framework recalls both real and literary wills,[7] while on a much more specific level the opening lines of the *Ballade de la Grosse Margot* (1591–1627) and *Ballade pour prier Nostre Dame* (873–909) adopt the vocabularies of amatory and devotional poetry respectively. Much attention has been devoted to the affinity between one of Villon's most vividly realized characters, an ageing prostitute known as the Belle Heaulmiere, and its apparent literary source, La Vieille from the *Roman de la rose*.[8] There are even several allusions to Villon's own *Lais*, often in the form of oblique references to characters mentioned in it (for example 753–60, 1275, 1346–7). Intertextual allusion, then, is copious, diversely realized, and frequently overt – much more so, in all these respects, than in a great deal of late medieval poetry. Its sheer obviousness is apt to influence interpretation: we are constantly made aware (and if we forget, the notes in scholarly editions remind us) that the *Testament* relies for its meaning upon a universe of pre-existing texts. In short, the allusions direct us towards an 'art-based' conception of the text.

Yet Villon's citations and allusions cannot be adequately accounted for within this framework. They certainly produce meanings, but these meanings shift and clash. The Ecclesiastes citations, from successive verses (11: 9, 10), are misleadingly selective: by omitting the didactic material between them, the testator creates an apparent and puzzling opposition between two statements about youth.[9] Hence, far from helping readers to fix the sense of the *Testament*, the use of a biblical intertext complicates their task. Equally, *Les Contredits Franc Gontier* misrepresents the pastoral discourse to which it responds: whereas the literary tradition initiated by Philippe de Vitry used pastoral to castigate the physical and moral dangers of court life, Villon presents it as praising poverty in itself and, by shifting the ground of the debate, challenges received literary wisdom on poverty.[10] The Belle Heaulmiere is not straightforwardly modelled on La Vieille, but adopts an openly professional attitude towards sex which contrasts with the essentially deceptive pleasure-seeking advocated by her predecessor.[11] And the *Testament* as a whole does not simply supersede the *Lais*, as we might expect of a subsequent will; rather, it develops and nuances the earlier poem's themes, particularly the characterization of the testator as a martyr to love.[12] Meanings, then, cannot easily be deduced from comparisons between the *Testament* and its intertexts: they are rendered challengingly unstable. Similar instability is apparent in tone and genre: the *Ballade de la Grosse Margot* and *Ballade pour prier Nostre Dame* begin by signalling particular registers, but proceed to undercut these by the incongruity of the language which follows. This might suggest that the disruption of poetic norms is a systematic principle, but not even that interpretative route is open to us: the *ballade* for Robert d'Estouteville (1378–1405) adheres consistently to the codes of courtly occasional poetry. The *Testament*'s overt intertextuality resists readings which privilege the role of conventions. Notions of textuality as 'art-based' prove inadequate, yet a 'life-based' interpretation proves no more sustainable, for it is only through form and language – or, to be more precise, through unexpected uses of form and language – that the poem gives the impression of being a product of the historical Villon's experience. The *Testament* seems to trick its audience into oscillating between 'art-based' and 'life-based' readings, in a movement that can never be resolved because it takes place between poles which are not in fact opposed.

The movement is further complicated because the poem's intertextual allusions and quotations are all too often distorted or inaccurate. Villon's treatment of Ecclesiastes and Philippe de Vitry exemplifies this tendency, but the best-known instance is the testator's reference to the lessons of 'le noble *Rommant / de la Roze*' (113–14: 'the noble *Roman de la rose*'); lessons which, as the context makes clear, appear not in the *Rose*, but in *Le Testament de Jean de Meun*, a thirteenth-century poem well known to Villon's contemporaries.[13] Whatever their local significance might be, these misquotations have a crucial element in common: they illustrate the hazards of reception, the propensity for texts to be wrongly transcribed, or incompletely transmitted, or simply mis-remembered. On the one hand, these hazards reflect a wider theme in the *Testament*, the unreliability of memory: critics have often noted that, when enquiring after the whereabouts of various historical figures in three succes-sive *ballades* that render the conventional Latin theme 'Ubi sunt . . .' ('Where are . . .?', see 329–412), the testator has remembered these figures errone-ously.[14] On the other, they encapsulate the preoccupation with textual fragility, the risks to the survival of documents and discourses which are posed by, among other things, the unreliable memories of readers.

### Lyric insertions

One of the *Testament*'s most obvious formal features is the insertion of common late medieval lyric forms – sixteen *ballades* and three *rondeaux* – into a sequence of octosyllabic *huitains* familiar from such important fifteenth-century narrative poems as Martin Le Franc's *Champion des Dames* and Alain Chartier's *Belle Dame sans Mercy*. The technique of lyric insertion is frequent in medieval French verse narratives (see Chapters 6 and 10) and, by the mid fifteenth century, had begun to appear in a growing body of didactic prose writing. As such, it encourages an 'art-based' reading: Villon is not only following the compositional practice of illustrious poets such as Machaut, but also demonstrating his technical mastery of lyric genres, and giving the *Testament* a richer formal texture by varying stanza and line lengths. Yet these insertions do not seem to follow clear principles of differentiation from the rest of the poem. In respect of form, the lyrics often employ the octosyllables and *huitains* used elsewhere in the *Testament*. The *rondeaux*, based on a quatrain structure, are all octosyllabic. Three *ballades* are in decasyllabic *huitains*, and four in decasyllabic *dizains*; the other nine, including a *double ballade* comprising six stanzas rather than the usual three (625–72), use octosyllabic *huitains*, and can thus be formally distinguished from the non-lyric *huitains* only by the presence of refrains and *envois*. Though headings in the manuscript or printed witnesses sometimes signal these pieces as *ballades*, this is not always the case,[15] and in the absence of such clues contemporary readers could not unambiguously identify the lyric forms until the second occurrence of the refrain – over half-way through a normal *ballade*.

The contrast in function between the insertions and the surrounding *huitains* is often no stronger than the formal contrast. Most clearly differentiated in functional terms are the pieces which constitute distinct bequests by the testator. Yet even these are framed with different degrees of clarity. The *Ballade pour prier Nostre Dame* may be read as the direct object of 'donne à ma povre mere' (865: 'I give to my poor mother') in the preceding *huitain*, but the verb 'donne' may be understood without an object, as 'I give a gift'; it is semantic, not syntactic, coherence that requires us to read the *ballade* as a bequest to the testator's mother. Other bequests are signalled more explicitly – *rondeaux* for Ythier Marchant (978–89) and Jacques Cardon, a *ballade* for Robert d'Estouteville – though their significance is not always clear: the poem for Jacques Cardon, in particular, has sustained widely varying interpretations (ed. Rychner and Henry, II, 248–9). Some lyrics are not complete bequests in themselves, or are presented in terms which make it uncertain as to whether they are being genuinely bequeathed. The testator sends rather than gives *Les Contredits Franc Gontier* to Andry Couraud, using the verb 'mande' (1458: 'I address'), while the *Ballade de bonne doctrine* (1692–1719) is part of a larger bequest, a lesson for socially marginal young men. And some apparent bequests turn out, on closer examination, to be nothing of the kind: the testator does not properly bequeath the *Ballade à s'amie* (942–69) to his lady, but sends it to her to settle his accounts with love (926–7), and he bequeaths to its eponymous anti-heroine not the *Ballade de la Grosse Margot* itself, but a *recital* of the piece. The bequest, then, is a less common and less clear-cut function of the insertions than appears at first sight. Other insertions have a variety of functions, more or less distinct from those of the *huitains* around them. Some comment on the accompanying discourse: the *Ballade des femmes de Paris* expands upon the allusions to the disreputable garrulity of Parisian women in the surrounding *huitains*, while the *Ballade de la belle Heaulmiere aux filles de joie* (533–60) and *Double ballade* (625–72) each deliver disabused lessons which emerge from the preceding stanzas. The *Verset* (1892–1903) is a prayer which the testator's proposed epitaph exhorts readers to say for the deceased; the *Ballade de merci* (1968–95) is a plea for forgiveness, which follows and complements a sequence of clauses typical of historical wills, such as the nomination of executors and the selection of a place for burial; and the *Ballade de conclusion* plays a primarily narrative role, recounting the testator's final acts. The lack of consistent differentiation on the functional level between lyric forms and *huitains* is reflected on the level of enunciation: there is no systematic principle of either correspondence or contrast between the voice used in the insertions and the voice of the *huitains* around them. Some lyric pieces, such as the *Ballade pour prier Nostre Dame* and the *ballade* for Robert d'Estouteville, have a first-person voice of their own; others, such as the *ballades* on the *ubi sunt* theme, continue the discourse of the testator; the *Ballade de la belle Heaulmiere* is part of a 104-line block in that character's voice. The variation of voice in the lyric insertions, indeed, mirrors that in the *huitains*, where the testator adopts not only the voice of the Belle Heaulmiere, but also those of the pirate Diomedes (140–52), his own heart (283–8), and a hypothetical interlocutor (572–84), to name only the most prominent 'speakers'.

Hence neither the form, the function, nor the voice of the lyric pieces are consistently marked off from their context. In this respect, Villon contrasts with most earlier practitioners of lyric insertion. From the early fourteenth century onwards, lyric insertions tended to be formally distinct from the narrative discourse in which they were set, and to perform one or more of a rather limited repertoire of functions: providing moments of narrative stasis or affective intensity, acting as kernels from which the surrounding narrative is generated, or commenting on preceding events or arguments.[16] Villon's *ballades* and *rondeaux* all too often fall short of, or indeed go beyond, these traditional roles: frequently less formally distinct than might be expected, they sometimes functionally overlap with the adjacent *huitains* (or with each other, in the case of the *ballades* on the *ubi sunt* theme), and sometimes bear relationships with their context that cannot be accounted for in terms of the traditional roles of lyric insertions. Consequently, like Villon's citations and allusions, the insertions dismantle the opposition between 'art-based' and 'life-based' interpretation. It is clearly inadequate and reductive to assess them in formal terms, as elements which show Villon's technical prowess and enrich the *Testament*'s formal sophistication – but we cannot assume on those grounds that the insertions transparently express the author's thoughts and feelings, for that assumption itself depends on Villon's handling of compositional conventions.

## Physical presentation and transmission

The fragility of the *Testament*, and the ambivalent differentiation of the lyric insertions, are never more apparent than in the material contexts, the manuscripts and early editions, in which the poem was transmitted. No complete copy has survived, and the extant versions often evince a degree of textual variation which suggests that Jean de Calais has been at work. In one manuscript anthology (Stockholm, Royal Library, MS V.u.22), various *huitains* are shifted from their normal place in the sequence, and there are numerous omissions, including, in whole or in part, eight lyric insertions – three of which have been transcribed separately at an earlier point in the volume (ed. Rychner and Henry, I, 6–12). A sixteenth-century manuscript (Brussels, Bibliothèque royale Albert Ier, IV, 541) contains an even more truncated version, comprising two separate portions of the *Testament*; the lyric pieces are sometimes displaced, and no material before line 1070 is reproduced.[17] Readers are consequently presented with a *Testament* consisting essentially of bequests: the testator's opening reflections on age, death, and poverty are absent, as is much of Villon's more obvious play upon established poetic forms, while satirical allusions to specific Parisians are relatively more prominent. Numerous manuscripts reproduce the lyric insertions independently of the *Testament*: the *Ballade de la Grosse Margot* and *Ballade des langues ennuieuses* (1422–56) are especially popular, appearing in this guise in the Stockholm manuscript and in five and four other anthologies respectively (ed. Rychner and Henry, I, 21–2).[18] This pattern of transmission suggests that the *ballades* were regarded as rhetorical set-pieces, comprehensible without their narrative context as impressive examples of lyric art; it is surely no coincidence that both are in decasyllabic *dizains*, which of all the stanzas used in the insertions are least compatible with the main body of the *Testament*, and most prestigious according to contemporary norms of versification.[19] In some anthologies, insertions are copied alongside other lyric pieces by Villon, which scholars normally term his *poésies diverses*; this is the case in an anthology of the early sixteenth century (Bibliothèque Nationale de France, fr. 12490), where a string of insertions – including the *huitain* which introduces the *Verset* – is followed by several *poésies diverses*. Strikingly, a title introduces the whole set of poems as 'Balades extraictes du Testament et Codicille M^e François Villon' (fo. 84r: '*Ballades* extracted from the *Testament and Codicil* of Master François Villon'): there is no indication that the *poésies diverses* have a different provenance.

While the *Testament* is often subject to abridgement and extraction, it is never transmitted separately from other Villon material: the *Lais*, the *poésies diverses*, the *ballades en jargon* (underworld slang). Manuscripts and early editions often select and order these pieces in ways which invite readers to adopt a 'life-based' interpretation, by offering what appears to be a coherent biographical narrative involving Villon's imprisonment and the threat of execution.[20] But other aspects of these anthologies may promote different ways of reading. Unlike the printed editions, which focus squarely on Villon's work, the manuscripts of the *Testament* always contain material by other poets. One of the most important manuscripts (Paris, Bibliothèque de l'Arsenal, 3523) is a large collection of fifteenth-century poems, many of which evidently respond to, or have been influenced by, others which have been copied alongside them. It thereby promotes a view of poetry as a knowing, competitive game in which authors strive to outdo each other, and encourages us to read the *Testament* in 'art-based' terms, as a text which ingeniously plays with poetic tradition; indeed, it contains Pierre de Hauteville's *Confession et testament*, thus drawing attention to the contrasting ways in which this poem and the *Testament* employ the fiction of dictation.[21] Similar comparisons are facilitated by the Stockholm manuscript, which contains several well-known narrative poems from the earlier fifteenth century, by authors such as Alain Chartier and Michault Taillevent; the presence of Villon's work alongside these pieces makes apparent his play with the poetic conventions of an earlier generation.[22] Particularly revealing is the placing of the *Ballade de la Grosse Margot* amid a sequence of bawdy *ballades*, allowing readers to see how far Villon's piece excels these ostensibly similar poems in sophistication.[23] Similarly, the manuscript commonly regarded as the best witness of the *Testament* (Bibliothèque Nationale de France, fr. 20041) reproduces it, together with the *Lais* and four *poésies diverses*, after Coudrette's *Roman de Mélusine*, a relatively conventional verse romance alongside which the unusual qualities of Villon's poems stand out (ed. Rychner and Henry, I, 15–20). The *Testament*'s transmission indicates that it is a protean work, combining multiple thematic and formal elements which different witnesses can highlight selectively: its relationship to various traditions, its lyric insertions and their individual characteristics, its potential for biographical reading.

The ways in which the *Testament* undoes oppositions between 'art-based' and 'life-based' readings, and the related question of its transmission, play a crucial role in helping us understand the delicate, ambivalent relationship between the text and its author. Villon's poem teems with elements that encourage biographical reading, producing the illusion that the author is somehow present in the text. Yet these elements are ultimately conventional: they are effects of language, form, and intertextuality. They are, moreover, subject to variation in manuscripts and early editions, so that readers of different witnesses obtain different impressions of the *Testament* and its author according to the assumptions of scribes and printers. Reflecting the poem's own preoccupation with transmission and its implications, this variation embodies the fragility of the author–text relationship, the discrepancy between what someone writes and what someone else reads, understands, or remembers. Villon's testator neatly encapsulates the relationship, appropriately enough by citing proverbial wisdom which does not belong to him alone: 'Ung chacun n'est maistre du scien' (760: 'nobody's master of what's his').

## Notes

1. For recent examples of both approaches, see respectively M. Freeman, *François Villon in his Works: the Villain's Tale* (Amsterdam, Rodopi, 2000); T. Hunt, *Villon's Last Will: Language and Authority in the* Testament (Oxford University Press, 1996). Quotations from Villon's *Testament* are cited from the edition of C. Thiry.

2. See N. Freeman Regalado, '*Effet de réel, Effet du réel*: Representation and Reference in Villon's *Testament*', *Yale French Studies*, 70 (1986), 63–77.

3. See A. Armstrong, 'François Villon: rhétoriqueur?', in M. J. Freeman and J. H. M. Taylor (eds.), *Villon at Oxford: the Drama of the Text. Proceedings of the Conference Held at St Hilda's College Oxford, March 1996* (Amsterdam, Rodopi, 1999), pp. 51–84. On Molinet's narratorial persona, see A. Armstrong, *Technique and Technology: Script, Print, and Poetics in France, 1470–1550* (Oxford University Press, 2000), pp. 19–20.

4. See Hunt, *Last Will*, pp. 25–6.

5. See Hunt, *Last Will*, pp. 87–9, 94–5.

6. See Hunt, *Last Will*, pp. 34–8.

7. On the testamentary form, see A. J. A. van Zoest, *Structures de deux testaments fictionnels: le* Lais *et le* Testament *de François Villon* (The Hague, Mouton, 1974).

8. Most recently in J. H. M. Taylor, *The Poetry of François Villon: Text and Context* (Cambridge University Press, 2001), pp. 90–101.

9. Hunt, *Last Will*, pp. 17–18.

10. Taylor, *Poetry of François Villon*, pp. 114–38.

11. Taylor, *Poetry of François Villon*, pp. 86–113.

12. Taylor, *Poetry of François Villon*, pp. 34–57.

13. N. Freeman Regalado, 'Villon's Legacy from Le Testament of Jean de Meun: Misquotation, Memory, and the Wisdom of Fools', in Freeman and Taylor (eds.), *Villon at Oxford*, pp. 282–311.

14. See, for example, Taylor, *Poetry of François Villon*, p. 73.

15. For more details, see the variants in *Le Testament Villon*, ed. Rychner and Henry; subsequent references in the text.

16. See J. Cerquiglini, *'Ung engin si soutil': Guillaume de Machaut et l'écriture au XIVᵉ siècle* (Geneva, Droz, 1985), pp. 23–49; F. Rouy, *L'Esthétique du traité moral d'après les œuvres d'Alain Chartier* (Geneva, Droz, 1980), pp. 345–9.

17. J. Lemaire, 'Meschinot, Molinet, Villon: témoignages inédits. Etude du Bruxellensis IV 541, suivie de l'édition de quelques ballades' (*Archives et Bibliothèques de Belgique*, special issue, 20 (1979)), 17, 59–68.

18. See also *Quinze années d'acquisition: De la pose de la première pierre à l'inauguration officielle de la Bibliothèque* (Brussels, Bibliothèque royale Albert Ier, 1969), p. 108.

19. See D. Hüe, *La Poésie palinodique à Rouen (1486–1550)* (Paris, Champion, 2002), p. 893.

20. N. Freeman Regalado, 'Gathering the Works: the *Œuvres de Villon* and the Intergeneric Passage of the Medieval French Lyric into Single-Author Collections', *L'Esprit Créateur*, 33 (1993), 87–100 (pp. 97–8).

21. Taylor, *Poetry of François Villon*, pp. 25–7, 109–10.

22. On this manuscript's contents, see A. Piaget and E. Droz, 'Recherches sur la tradition manuscrite de Villon, I. Le Manuscrit de Stockholm', *Romania*, 58 (1932), 238–54.

23. Taylor, *Poetry of François Villon*, pp. 142–5.

# PART II

# What is a medieval French author?

# 5

MATILDA TOMARYN BRUCKNER

# Chrétien de Troyes

If Lancelot and the grail are names that anyone familiar with Arthurian literature recognizes without hesitation, the same cannot be said for the author who stands behind their invention. Yet asked to identify the most important romancer of the Middle Ages, any connoisseur, medieval or modern, would likely name Chrétien de Troyes, the writer who stepped beyond antique romances to offer models that energized and redirected romance from the twelfth century on, first in verse, later in prose. Through allusions and adaptations, translations, amplifications, parodies, and prosifications, Chrétien's five romances spawned a huge variety of offspring that span medieval Europe and spin anew in modern forms and media.

What do we know about the author 'Crestïens de Troies', as he identifies himself in his first romance, *Erec et Enide* (9)? Though historical identification eludes us, a number of possibilites emerge in the romances themselves. Similarities between the coronation scene at the end of *Erec* and Henry II's court at Nantes (Christmas 1169), when his son Geoffrey was recognized as the future duke of Brittany, suggest that Chrétien may have been associated with the Anglo-Norman court at that stage of his career.[1] Such a displacement might explain why the romancer adds a place name to his signature in *Erec*, thereafter simply signing 'Crestïens' in prologue or epilogue. Chrétien names two patrons, Marie de Champagne (wife of Henry the Liberal, count of Champagne) and Philippe d'Alsace, count of Flanders: they place him, *c.* 1160s–1191, at two important political and cultural centres of northern France, located along significant commercial axes connecting northern and southern Europe, England, and the Continent.

The court of Champagne was known for its literary patronage: two other names associated with Chrétien – Godefroi de Leigni, the writer who finished his *Chevalier de la charrette*, and Guiot, the scribe who copied all five romances in BnF, fr. 794 – are connected to places located in Henry's principality.[2] Nevertheless, no documents verify Chrétien's presence in Troyes or Flanders. It has been argued that Chrétien's name is rare and might designate a converted Jew, that he could be the canon Christianus of Saint-Maclou included in Henry's witness lists,[3] that he was connected with Islamic mysticism imported from northern Spain.[4] His name has been read as the Christian of Troy, combining the riches of pagan Antiquity with those of medieval Christian Europe.[5] Was *Crestïen* a pseudonym or an 'anonym' assumed by writers renouncing their individual identity, substituting a common name for their proper name to suggest a Christian viewpoint for evaluating textual play?[6]

What all these suggestions share is the unsolved enigma of Chrétien's identity and the sense that it entails an exotic 'other'. Compare speculation on the author of Shakespeare's plays: verifiably documented, Shakespeare the man seems insufficient to explain the depth of his work and is repeatedly pushed aside in favour of 'better' candidates for Shakespeare the author. In our case, uncertainties attend not only the man but also the wide-ranging body of works signed by *Crestïen*: which texts properly belong to Chrétien de Troyes? Decisions to include or exclude have largely been decided by how well a given text corresponds to the figure of the author/narrator extrapolated from his romances. The reasoning is circular and, though we cannot resolve the puzzle, we can investigate what is at stake in determining the nature and scope of Chrétien the author.

Images of authorship surface most especially through Chrétien's specific authorial practices, but also result from the role played by other writers, scribes, editors, and compilers. In the absence of any verifiable biography, the manuscript tradition itself serves as a double of the author, constantly mediating our perception of Chrétien. His projected public plays an equally crucial role. Twelfth-century readers are primarily listeners, present in a court setting, as Chrétien himself, with tongue tucked firmly in cheek, represents the scene in *Yvain* when the castellan's daughter reads a romance 'by I don't know whom' (5362) to her parents. Eschewing anonymity, this author expects readers to appreciate his ability to entertain and edify, so that his name will live, as he claims punningly in *Erec*, 'Tant con durra crestïentez' (25: 'as long as Christianity endures').

Multiple views of medieval authorship surface in a corpus whose boundaries demonstrate an unsettling tendency to remain fluid. Mapped by the contours and contents of five romances, this chapter will demonstrate that, for contemporary readers, Chrétien as author represents an invention constructed not only by what he wrote but what medieval writers and rubricators or modern scholars do or do not ascribe to him. Chrétien's authorial conundrum thus conjures up (1) the author/narrator in the fiction distinguished from the historical author in the real world of patrons; (2) the Latin *auctores*, the only 'authors' recognized as such in the twelfth century; (3) authoring (and thus endorsing or 'authorizing') a vernacular corpus, as highlighted in Chrétien's catalogue of works in his second romance; (4) authorship as treading a path between tradition and innovation, exemplified by the reinventions of Tristan in *Cligès*, *Lancelot*, and *Yvain*; (5) displaced authorship such as when the *Ovide moralisé* includes his *Philomena* in Book VI; (6) attributed authorship produced by references and rubrics, as in the *chansonniers* (song collections) that credit Chrétien with four lyrics; (7) disputed authorship as with *Guillaume d'Angleterre*; and finally (8) collective authorship constructed with the continuators of *Perceval*, Chrétien's unfinished grail romance.

The opening phrases of *Erec*'s prologue immediately plunge readers into a network of allusions, initiating the portrait of an artist who places the first Arthurian romance within the context of multiple Latin and vernacular traditions. Borrowing the opening maxim on the necessity of sharing one's knowledge, which the authors of *Thèbes* and *Troie* relate to classical and biblical *auctores*, Chrétien shifts to a different kind of 'scïance' (17) by invoking a proverb to justify a new choice of subject that may not appear at first glance to have great value in comparison with antique romance's prestigious Latin and Greek traditions, but will prove its worth in the hands of a writer who knows how to make 'a very beautiful composition' (14) out of 'an adventure story' (13) typically fragmented and corrupted by storytellers (19–22). Chrétien's mastery of exordial topics confirms his school training as *clerc* (cleric, clerk, intellectual, in twelfth-century usage), able to innovate within the 'already said', as taught by the art of rhetoric and the *auctores*.

We can begin to grasp this new 'art poétique' by focusing on four aspects of *Erec*: the Arthurian frame, narrative structure, the conjunction of love and combat, description – all cornerstones of Chrétien's corpus, as of romance in general. Drawing on oral Breton tales and written sources (transmitted by Geoffrey of Monmouth's influential *Historia*, composed c.1135–8, the earliest extensive account of Arthur's career in Latin, and its Anglo-Norman French adaptation of c.1155, the *Roman de Brut* by Wace), Chrétien establishes Arthur's court as the centre of his romance world. It furnishes names, typical and recurrent characters (Gauvain, Yvain, dwarves, giants, the fair unknown), conventional scenes and situations (judicial duels, hospitality, damsels in distress). In the first part of *Erec*, Celtic motifs structure two major events. Arthur decides to observe his father's custom of hunting the White Stag (the colour denotes a magic potential realized, for example, in Marie de France's *Guigemar*), which leads the hero to pursue a knight on his way to the Sparrowhawk Contest. The winner must defend the claim that his beloved is the most beautiful, just as the one who captures the White Stag bestows a kiss on the most beautiful lady. Both contests find a happy resolution when Erec meets Enide, defeats Yder's claim to the sparrowhawk, and brings his new lady back to Arthur's court.

Chrétien constructs his plot as a series of episodes centred on combat and adventure, connected by one or more quests. *Aventure* is a key term and signals through its etymology that 'what will happen' on the hero's route will put him to the test and form his identity. The narrator announces the end of the first part at line 1840 (in a romance of nearly 7000 verses, typical in Chrétien's corpus). He thus signals that readers should pay attention to the articulations of his narrative. Indeed, narrative structure as manipulated by the author (even more than direct narratorial intervention) conveys meaning to be decoded by alert readers, guided by the repetitions and variations operating at all levels. Chrétien's art of conjunctions becomes apparent when he moves from the short-story-like structures of his source material to the complex arrangement of a romance where multiple segments are layered together: an initial series of adventures ends in success (here marked by marriage), but a crisis puts into question the hero's identity and necessitates a second series of adventures, culminating in superior achievement and enhanced heroic status.

Erec's crisis is caused when love for his new wife so occupies him in post-nuptial passion that he fails to engage in feats of prowess. When Enide inadvertently awakens Erec and is forced to report the criticism that engulfs her husband and herself, Erec orders her to put on her best dress, keep quiet, and ride before him as the two set off with no apparent destination. At this point, the narrator denies us access to Erec's motivation, while making us privy to Enide's fears, as she repeatedly has to decide whether to speak out to warn Erec about impending disasters that proliferate on their path – thieving knights, deceptive host, and so on – or obey his order to remain silent. Gradually we learn that Erec is testing Enide's love for him while reconstructing his chivalric reputation, but what remains a matter of debate for readers today, as it was no doubt for the medieval public, is who is at fault in the couple and indeed exactly what error requires such *errance* to resolve it. By exploiting the gap between the third-person author (introduced in the prologue and responsible for the overall design of the narrative) and the first-person narrator (whose voice and point of view constantly filter the story narrated), Chrétien opens a space for irony, puzzles, and specular effects, as in the 'Joy of the Court' episode, the extraordinary adventure that caps Erec's second quest and furnishes in the story of Mabonagrain and his lady a mirror image that comments on the entire romance.

Description no less than narrative structure can be engineered to send interpretive signals to the readers. Just before the 'Joy of the Court' episode, Enide receives a new saddle carved with the story of how Eneas came to Carthage, fell in love with Dido, then left her for Rome and Lavinia (5330–40). The initiated reader recognizes in this summary of the *Roman d'Eneas* positive and negative models for Enide. Descriptions of luxury items are typical ingredients in the antique romances, and Chrétien makes use of them to rival with his predecessors, as in the closing scene when the elaborate description of Erec's coronation robe refers implicitly to similar descriptions in *Eneas* and *Troie*, while explicitly the narrator invokes Macrobius, the fifth-century *auctor* who teaches him the art of description (6730–5).

In *Cligès*, Chrétien continues to innovate by bringing the Arthurian world into contact with Byzantium. He innovates on the convention of describing the movement of learning and empire (or *translatio studii et imperii*, as this notion was called in the Middle Ages), when he claims in the prologue that learning and chivalry have moved from Greece to Rome to France (30–40). The historical trajectory described is linear, but in the romance plot, displacements between east and west multiply in the stories of father and son, as characters move back and forth, linking Greek imperial power and Arthurian chivalric glory to stories of love frustrated and fulfilled. *Cligès* is Chrétien's most 'artificial' romance, an intense combination of historical allusion, realistic topography, and fiction. Its points of reference include Arthurian history and contemporary events involving Byzantine–German alliances. Battle scenes recall *chansons de geste* and tend to unknit the romantic conjunction of love and prowess. *Cligès*'s highly rhetorical style and convoluted plot, in which a host of other stories and literary models are cannibalized, produce a romance that foregrounds artifice. Always lurking right behind the scene is the shadow of the author, the artificer in chief, who sends his doubles into action as narrator to tell the stories or characters to engineer the action. Before retiring backstage, however, Chrétien takes the spotlight: the prologue begins with a list of his previous works, a show bill for the author and his new romance. He boldly proclaims his authorship of *Erec et Enide*, then cites an assortment of Ovidian translations (the *Art of Love*, tales from the *Metamorphoses*), among which he drops in a work 'about King Mark and Iseut' (5). Chrétien has clearly cut his teeth on Ovid, the *auctor* par excellence of the twelfth century, but his passion for the love story of Tristan and Iseut runs equally deep.

Chrétien maps Thomas's two-generational story of Tristan across two generations of couples: in the first half, primarily through description, in the second, action. Thomas's famous triple pun on *la mer* (the sea), *l'amer* (loving), and *l'amer* (bitterness) resurfaces on shipboard when Queen Guenevere mistakes Alexander's and Soredamor's lovesickness for seasickness (548–63). The magic potion responsible for Tristan and Iseut's fatal love is displaced and doubled when Fenice requests her nurse Thessala's help:

first, a potion gives her husband (Cligès's uncle) the illusion that he is making love to his wife; later, another potion gives everyone (including her lover) the illusion that Fenice has died. Her martyrdom at the hands of three doctors allows Chrétien to borrow from folklore the story of Solomon's wife and her false death as a prelude to reinventing Tristan and Iseut's exile in the forest of Morrois (and Thomas's refuge in a crystal cave).

Medievalists have argued about how to read *Cligès*: is it an anti-*Tristan*, or a re-presentation of it? But the question of any moralization of the story pro or con is undercut by Chrétien's all pervasive irony and his evident pleasure in the game of invention itself, as he places his own mark on the common matter. Consider the plot's end followed by the epilogue: Alis dies just as Arthur is about to organize an invasion force to come to the aid of Cligès, the legitimate heir to Greece, and 'la guerre de Troie n'aura pas lieu', as Giraudoux might put it: the couple lives happily ever after but subsequent empresses are kept in prison to make sure the story does not repeat.

The Ovidian connection in *Cligès* signals Chrétien's interest throughout his corpus in all the modalities of love, as well as his fascination with the process of transformation that informs the writer's art as well as his characters' experience. In one of the happy accidents of history, Chrétien's *Philomena* was saved because it was included in the fourteenth-century *Ovide moralisé* and twice identified as Chrétien's translation to open and close the section. More enigmatically, at the midpoint of the narrative, Chrétien identifies himself (or is it still the anonymous translator/compiler referring to him?) as 'Crestïens li gois' (734). No satisfactory explanation of 'gois' (attribute? place?) explains this unusual signature, though scholars have generally agreed that this is indeed our Chrétien, still close to his school exercises but demonstrating the virtuoso rhetorical play found in his romances, in the many monologues and dialogues on love that bring his characters to life, whether they are just discovering the emotion or facing the difficulties of separation.

Chrétien learned the art of making love speak not only from Ovid but from the troubadours, whose lyric motifs furnish a repertoire for reinvention by the lovers. Although only two of the songs attributed to him are accepted by modern scholars, Chrétien's named presence in the *chansonniers* shows that he achieved recognition among the first generation of *trouvères* who disseminated Occitan lyric forms and themes in northern France (see Chapter 6).[7] 'D'Amors qui m'a tolu a moi' places him in a poetic exchange with Bernart de Ventadorn and Raimbaut d'Aurenga,[8] and may once again situate the historical Chrétien in relation to the court of Henry II and Eleanor of Aquitaine. The link passes through Tristan, used as *senhal* (secret code name) by Bernart and commandeered by Chrétien's poetic 'I' to prove the superiority of his love, not forced by the potion but 'voluntarily' assumed at the command of his eyes (28–36): even in his lyric persona, Chrétien plays ironically. In 'Amors tençon et bataille', he willingly pays the loss of reason as love's entry fee (stanzas II, V); in 'D'Amors', reason nevertheless articulates his complaint against the lady's failure to reward loyal service, though the lover expects his reward to be sweeter after a delay (43–5), just as Gauvain suggests to Yvain when persuading him to leave his new wife and go tourneying.

In *Yvain* and *Lancelot*, Chrétien not only uses troubadour material in the lyric voice of monologues but moves lyric motifs into narrative action. The 'Knight of the Cart' (the oxymoronic title Chrétien gives his romance and hero) acquires his pseudonym when he steps into a shameful cart in order to pursue Guenevere and her abductor Meleagant. His two-step hesitation translates the debate between Reason and Love, but Love, enclosed in his heart, easily wins (360–77). Whenever a conflict arises between shame and love, Lancelot chooses love which, paradoxically, redounds to his chivalric glory and heroic achievement (though not without moments of ridicule). Lancelot's love for Guenevere repeatedly enacts the lyric motifs of *fine amour* as veneration, as when he kneels before her bed, 'for in no saint's relic does he believe so much' (4653).

But lyric is not the only model shaping Lancelot's love. Like Tristan, Lancelot will leave in the queen's sheets blood-stains that betray the presence of her lover. Meleagant, already defeated in a combat whose outcome has been deferred (and will be again), misreads those signs, permitting Lancelot to defend Keu against the accusation of treasonous adultery. In Chrétien's most significant rewriting of the Tristan story, the queen's lover is no longer the king's nephew but remains his best knight, the one who acts when the king fails in his duty to defend the queen and rescue his people imprisoned in Gorre. Incognito for readers and characters, Lancelot encounters en route to Gorre a series of adventures that gradually reveal his heroic destiny. Chrétien makes good use of the Breton marvellous to show the extraordinary character of his hero: the flaming lance that attacks his bed nonchalantly extinguished, the future cemetery where Lancelot raises the stone identifying the prisoners' saviour, the Sword Bridge Lancelot crosses on bare hands and knees, the magic ring given to him by the Lady of the Lake. We may not know who Lancelot is until the queen reveals his name during the first combat with Meleagant, but we can already see that he is, as the tournament herald announces, 'the one who will give the measure'.

The paradoxical nature of Lancelot as hero is one of the many puzzles Chrétien invents in the *Chevalier de la charrette*. He is the impossible embodiment of a particular logic that lies at the heart of Chrétien's romance world: located where oppositions and contradictions accumulate, Lancelot says yes to each of the opposing terms. Yes, he will show mercy to the Orgueilleux; yes, he will cut off his head to grant Meleagant's sister her request. Yes, he is the queen's lover and yes, her love is what makes him both traitor to his lord and Arthur's best knight. Lancelot crystallizes an epistemological problem that pervades Chrétien's romances: how to interpret signs correctly when their meanings shift as our point of view changes? The split between author and narrator, fundamental in a written text, plays a crucial role in representing this problem, as the narrator focalizes what we see through the characters' eyes, limits what we can know, and complicates with conflicting perspectives any effort to totalize knowledge. Who is Lancelot? What is Lancelot?

Indeed, who is Chrétien? What is Chrétien? These are the questions we began with in trying to determine what Chrétien's authorship entails. The romancer has cleverly dramatized the parallels by constructing in the *Charrette* a series of echoes between prologue and narrative, echoes that seem to propose an enigma. Chrétien composes the romance at the command of his lady, who has furnished him with 'matter and *san* (meaning)' (26). She authorizes the romance; he brings only his toil and attention to arrange the work (27–9), and his *sans* (23: understanding). The duplication of *san(s)* suggests that Chrétien's humility is itself an exordial topic and should not disguise the power he wields as writer, even as he shares the authorial function with patrons, sources, maxims, proverbs, and so on. Most of the prologue is filled with Marie's praise (7–20), wittily and ironically hyperbolic in order to claim that the author/narrator is not indulging in mere hyperbole. He belongs totally to his lady (4), just as later he will describe Lancelot with the same words as totally Guenevere's (5656; cf. 1264, 4187, 5874–5).

Then why does Chrétien form a third analogous couple with Godefroi, who announces in the epilogue that he has written from Lancelot's imprisonment to the end with Chrétien's 'good will' (7106)? We do not know what circumstances motivated the shift. But this has not prevented speculation that his patroness's meaning – assumed to be adulterous love, based on Andreas Capellanus's representation of her in *De Amore* – must not have been to Chrétien's liking, so he abandoned the job to Godefroi. In my view, this is merely a fiction that fills a space where Chrétien has typically left a gap, a loose thread that tantalizes us. Here he has done so not only within the narrative but between the fiction and the real world outside it – or at least the image of that world invented in the prologue. And many readers have fallen into the trap, confusing history and fiction, whose relationship remains fraught throughout Chrétien's corpus. The ending of the *Charrette* thus seems problematic and, for some readers, doubled: Chrétien's 'ending' leaves Lancelot in the tower and the end to Godefroi's 'continuation' finally kills off Meleagant but leaves the love story between Lancelot and Guenevere with an uncertain future.

The beginning and ending of *Yvain* are equally problematic, as Chrétien composes a complementary experiment in fiction while writing *Lancelot*. This at least is the impression created when two characters in *Yvain* allude to events in the *Charrette*, thereby connecting the action of both romances. Did Chrétien have a deadline imposed by a patron, necessitating a second author to finish one while he worked on the other? Did he invent Godefroi to double his efforts? Possible scenarios multiply once we come under the spell of the master who authorizes fictions, but again we have only the texts to guide our interpretations. The title the romancer confers in the epilogue along with his name (6804–5: 'Chrétien thus finishes his romance on the Knight of the Lion'), echoes in its construction the identity problem of 'The Knight of the Cart', though this time the puzzle lies not in the joining of contradictory terms but in the replacement of the hero's name by the figure of the lion – and the delay of onomastic authorization through authorial signature until the end. An anticipatory process of displacement appears in the opening moves: *Le Chevalier au lion* begins without prologue as Arthur's court celebrates Pentecost. But narratorial reflections on love nowadays and then, along with other oppositions (truth/fable, *vilain/courtois*) deployed in conjunction with a narrative that undermines the claimed superiority of the past, surreptitiously outline a prologue that problematizes the nature of the Arthurian ideal. Chrétien's last three romances all posit that ideal as given while simultaneously demonstrating its faults. Illusion and disillusion inextricably combine: the particular mix may differ from Chrétien to Cervantes, but the tension remains in the heart of romance.

A linear reading from the beginning of *Yvain* implicitly asks, who authorizes this work? There is no patron, no book cited. In the absence of the author figure, a character steps forward: Calogrenant's prologue calls listeners to pay attention with their hearts and ears (149–74). His tale of misadventure models the whole romance: Calogrenant's shameful failure at the magic fountain will be corrected by his cousin's successful return; then Yvain's own failure to keep his promise to Laudine will require several more returns to the fountain, as the Knight of the Lion strives to rebuild his heroic identity. The narrator's single evocation of a source (2685: 'li contes') recalls Calogrenant's eyewitness account (59, 60: his 'conte') and at the same time provides blanket coverage for numerous models brought into play: the lady from lyric, the fairy of Breton tales, and the widow of misogynistic tradition who falls in love at her husband's grave stand behind Laudine; Yvain's leonine companion steps out of bestiary lore, biblical and classical traditions (for instance, his parody of Pyramus's suicide when he thinks Thisbe has been killed); Tristan's feigned folly becomes Yvain's real madness. When Chrétien finally provides his authorial endorsement in a short epilogue, he labels lies any further additions to his story, just as we begin to wonder if the reconciliation between Yvain and his wife, accomplished through the trick of Lunete's words, is really the last word on their future. We are thus returned to the problem of the (non)prologue and the question of how to read the dissonance between and within narratorial comment and romance action. Teasing invitations to allegorical interpretation introduced by the lion are similarly undermined and teach readers that any simple translation from matter to meaning is not what Chrétien's romances are about.

*Le Conte du graal* (The Story of the Grail, which is here a deep, wide serving dish!) takes to new heights Chrétien's gift for creating brainteasers that delight. The romance not only remains unfinished after 9000 plus verses; it multiplies enigmatic features: the unexpected doubling of heroes, the irregular interlacing of Perceval's and Gauvain's adventures, the introduction of unconventional materials (an adolescent hero, mothers, religion, a mysterious grail not yet the Holy Grail). Chrétien's patron, whose death on crusade in 1191 supplies a limit date for the text, has also furnished him with a book (65). Is it merely an exordial convention to authorize the story like Marie's *matiere*? Interestingly, William Lovel, the likely patron of *Guillaume d'Angleterre*, moved in the same patronage circles as the count of Flanders.[9] Arguments against identifying its author as our Chrétien tend to reflect stylistic judgements or object to the hybrid nature of the tale, combining saint's life and romance adventure story,[10] yet the mixing of religious and Breton elements is also one of the unusual features of *Perceval*.

Perhaps responding to Philip's religious zeal (and undoubtedly in his own self interest), Chrétien offers fulsome praise to a patron whose charity places him above Alexander, famed for his generosity. Mixing the parable of the sower with New Testament quotations, Chrétien offers a sample exegesis that has led some to suppose that allegorical interpretation is the correct mode for reading *Perceval*. But already in the prologue and later in the plot, Chrétien's rhetorical and narrative pyrotechnics undermine any programme of allegory even as they invite readers to discover figurative meanings in the play of the letter. Perceval's difficulties in understanding the advice he gets from his mother, his mentor Gornemant, or the seneschal Keu give ample testimony to the arduous apprenticeship required to operate successfully in this romance world.

Perceval himself is a new kind of hero: a young fool (*nice*) raised far from the Arthurian court, he aspires to knighthood and seems to achieve in his meeting with Gauvain the kind of heroic status sought by each of Chrétien's heroes, just at the moment when his greatest failing is announced at Arthur's court. Failure to ask questions about the grail and the bleeding lance that would heal the Fisher King leads Perceval on a quest to rectify his catastrophic error, at the same time that Gauvain is accused of murder and must justify himself in a judicial combat at Escavalon. Thus begins the story of a second hero whose adventures strangely mirror those of Perceval and require us to read across the interlace: both itineraries serve as commentaries of each other and even as alternating stages of development in a single superstructure. The Welsh youth and the exemplar of Arthurian chivalry start at opposite poles, yet are pulled into each other's orbit as resemblances between them emerge in the plot and complicate how we read their differences. Gauvain's mother and grandmother who appear in the last, unfinished episode, as if in response to Perceval's mother in the opening scenes, furnish only the most striking example of many provocative parallels.

Chrétien's talents as a great comic artist operate at full throttle in *Perceval* where the witty, ironic narrator who is his signature voice elaborates scenes that make readers smile, just as, at Arthur's court, Perceval himself lights up the prophetic 'maiden who laughs': the young naïf mistaking a tent for a church who, in a caricature of rape, climbs on top of the lady inside to wrestle her down for a kiss; the beleaguered Gauvain and the king's sister defending themselves with chess board and pieces against angry townspeople. If the laughs sometimes backfire, as they do for the Tent Maiden (cf. Guenevere's jokingly cold reception of Lancelot), they nevertheless take us to the heart of Chrétien's paradoxical romance world. In the *Conte du graal*, the turmoil of history is pressing in from the wings and knights resemble angels 'who kill all they encounter' (371–2), as violence explodes in every scene and even the heroes are perpetrators who must correct their mistakes.

Although Gauvain's triumph as the one who delivers the inhabitants of Roche de Champguin might presage Perceval's successful achievement, how Chrétien would have finished his romance remains a perplexing question, even though four verse continuations pick up the threads of Chrétien's narrative to complete Perceval's quest. The continuations have often struck modern readers as a heterogeneous collection, but the manuscript tradition shows that for a medieval public they form a whole, however changeable across successive accumulations. Indeed, interest generated by the continuing dialogue between Chrétien's *Conte* and the continuations may account for the large number of extant copies of *Perceval* among the forty some manuscripts that include Chrétien's romances. While *Erec*, *Cligès*, and *Yvain* each appear in twelve to fourteen copies or fragments, and *Lancelot* in only eight, *Perceval* survives in eighteen (only three of which do not include one or more continuations) and appears in the most varied manuscript contexts (author collections, romance or genre compilations, the cycle of verse

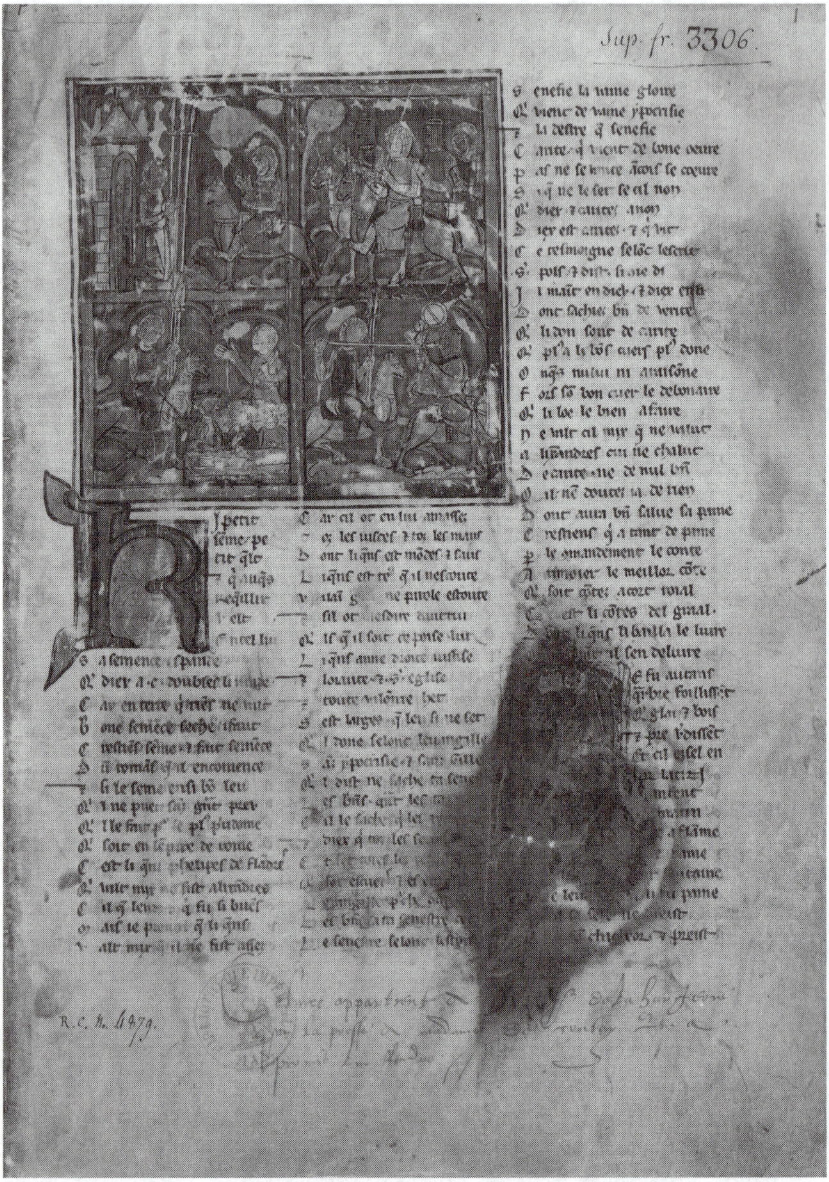

Figure 2. *Le Conte du graal* and four Continuations (MS T; second half thirteenth century),
BnF, fr. 12576, fo. 1r. The beginning of the *Conte* is marked with a four-part miniature
illustrating key scenes from Perceval's first adventures: his first encounter with knights (top,
right and left), arrival at Arthur's court (bottom, left), and Perceval throwing the javelin right
in the Red Knight's eye (bottom, right). The sixteenth-century inscription in the lower
margin reads: 'This book belongs to Monseigneur de la Hargerie who lent it to Madame de
Contay who promised to return it to him.'

continuations).[11] *Perceval* is also the most frequently illustrated among Chrétien's romances. In BnF, fr. 12576, the most cyclical of the *Perceval* manuscripts (including all four continuations), a four-part miniature that anticipates the main actions of the opening scenes marks the first folio (Figure 2): Perceval kneels before the first knight he has ever seen (whom he mistakenly believes to be God, so brilliantly does his armour gleam in the sunshine), while four more knights observe from the next frame. On the lower register, Perceval arrives at Arthur's court and asks the man holding a knife which one is the king (the illustrator represents even this small textual detail). On the lower right, Perceval has exited from court to demand the Red Knight's arms: while the latter holds the cup stolen from Arthur's table, Perceval sends a javelin straight into his eye (Perceval holds two more javelins in his other hand which, according to the narrator, his mother had already removed lest he look too Welsh). The full page shows the wear and tear of many readings, as well as hints of this thirteenth-century manuscript's long history. The sixteenth-century inscription in the lower margin reads: 'This book belongs to Monseigneur de la Hargerie who lent it to Madame de Contay who promised to return it to him.'[12] A lavishly decorated manuscript from the fourteenth century, BnF, fr. 12577 (which contains the more 'canonical' combination: *Perceval*, First, Second and Third Continuations), also opens with an illustration of Perceval meeting the five knights, then confronting the Red Knight, but adds two more scenes on the left side of the two-part miniature: on the top register, Perceval takes leave of his mother and her manor; on the bottom, we see her fallen, as Perceval rides off without realizing she lies dead (Figure 3).

Like these illustrators, whose visual representations offer a glimpse into the medieval reception of Chrétien's romance, all four continuators are careful readers of Chrétien's 'mother text' to which they return again and again for characters, episodes, and especially the basic questions engaged by the initiating romance: the relation between the two heroes, as between the grail quest and Perceval's love for Blancheflor, the role of religion in relation to chivalry and the problem of violence. Authorized by *Perceval*'s reappearance at the beginning of each manuscript compilation, the continuators institute a form of collective authorship with Chrétien whose name and mastery continue to play through their additions. His authorship gains in authority as it passes from production to authorization, even if the identity of *Crestïen* is not always warrantable: one version of the First Continuation cites his name twice to authorize descriptions, only one of which finds its source in the *Conte*, the other invented by a continuator. The vernacular author, like the Latin *auctor*, now recognizably encompasses for the medieval public the act of composition and a guarantee of authenticity.

Figure 3. *Le Conte du graal* and three Continuations, BnF, fr. 12577, fo. 1r. This deluxe manuscript from the fourteenth century opens with a two-part miniature showing Perceval's departure from his mother (left, top and bottom), and (right, top and bottom) his meeting with the five knights, followed by a confrontation with the Red Knight. The whole page is elaborately decorated with two foliate letters, leafy borders, and six roundels containing busts of knights.

Ironically, the great success of Chrétien's authorship first expands his influence in twelfth- and thirteenth-century romance, then contributes to his eclipse in later medieval tradition (as well as our renewed interest since the nineteenth century). For his immediate contemporaries, his romances furnish models to be reinvented for new heroes like Partonopeu or Fergus. His most successful stories and heroes, *Lancelot* and *Perceval*, supply the kernels for enormous romance cycles in prose, where they are completely absorbed and rewritten for readers whose voracious appetite for more leads to compilations like the Vulgate cycle, combining Arthurian and Grail history. If their first readers recognized Chrétien's intertexts, later readers found their realm of reference in the vast accumulation of the prose cycles themselves. Though Chrétien's romances continue to be copied till the mid fourteenth century, as his language ages and tastes turn from verse to prose narrative, as the ironic character of romance fades (until *Don Quixote* renews it for modern tastes), only occasional antiquarian interest returns directly to Chrétien, as when Pierre Sala updates *Yvain* for sixteenth-century readers. For the post-modern public today, the appeal of Chrétien's romances is found in their game-playing and hybridity, their self-conscious artistry and love of artifice. If the historical Chrétien is nowhere to be found, the author Chrétien lives on abundantly in his collected works, as they appear in proliferating numbers of editions, translations, bibliography, internet projects, and cinematic reinventions.

## Notes

1. B. Schmolke-Hasselmann, 'Henry II Plantagenêt, roi d'Angleterre, et la genèse d'*Erec et Enide*', *Cahiers de Civilisation Médiévale*, 24 (1981), 241–6.
2. A. Putter, 'Knights and Clerics at the Court of Champagne: Chrétien de Troyes's Romances in Context', in C. Harper-Bill and R. Harvey (eds.), *Ideals and Practices of Medieval Knighthood*, v (Woodbridge, Boydell and Brewer, 1995), pp. 243–66.
3. Putter, 'Knights', pp. 254–5.
4. M. Reichert, *Between Courtly Literature and Al-Andalus: 'Matière d'Orient' and the Importance of Spain in the Romances of the Twelfth-century Writer Chrétien de Troyes* (New York and London, Routledge, 2006). See especially the introduction.
5. R. Dragonetti. *La Vie de la lettre au moyen âge: Le Conte du graal* (Paris, Seuil, 1980), pp. 20–2.
6. S. Kay, 'Who Was Chrétien de Troyes?' *Arthurian Literature*, 15 (1997), 1–35.
7. Printed in *Cligès*, ed. Méla and Collet.
8. Kay, 'Who Was Chrétien', pp. 24–6.
9. M. D. Legge, 'The Dedication of *Guillaume d'Angleterre*', in F. Whitehead (ed.), *Medieval Miscellany presented to Eugène Vinaver* (Manchester University Press, 1965), p. 199.

10. E. J. Mickel, Jr, 'Studies and Reflections on *Guillaume d'Angleterre*', *Romance Quarterly*, 33 (1986), 393–406.

11. K. Busby, T. Nixon, A. Stones, and L. Walters (eds.), *The Manuscripts of Chrétien de Troyes*, 2 vols. (Amsterdam and Atlanta, Rodopi, 1993), I, 13–15. K. Busby, 'The Manuscripts of Chrétien's Romances', in N. J. Lacy and J. T. Grimbert (eds.), *A Companion to Chrétien de Troyes* (Cambridge, D. S. Brewer, 2005), pp. 69–72.

12. *The Manuscripts*, II, 117–18.

# 6

SIMON GAUNT

# The Châtelain de Couci

The Châtelain de Couci was one of the best-known *trouvères*, this being the term for lyric poets from the late twelfth through to the end of the thirteenth century. Although they composed in a variety of genres (some drawn from popular song), they are best known for their *grands chants courtois*, songs of unrequited *fine amour* ('pure love'), modelled on the Occitan troubadour lyric, and addressed to a haughty noble lady. These were originally performed to music, which is often transmitted in the manuscript anthologies that preserve them, known as *chansonniers*.

Unusually for a late twelfth- or thirteenth-century French author, we do know something about the Châtelain. Gui, castellan of Couci from at least 1186, was like most contemporary *trouvères* a high-ranking noble (which may account for why we can identify proportionally more *trouvères* than other twelfth-century writers); his death on the Fourth Crusade in 1203 is chronicled by Villehardouin's *Conquête de Constantinople*. Do we have, then, in his lyrics, a body of texts attributable with some certainty to a named and identifiable author, whom we can situate in time and space? And should we thereby think about them differently from the majority of contemporary texts, which are either anonymous or attributed to a name we cannot identify, particularly since courtly lyrics are written in the first person and purport to speak sincerely of the subject's experience of love? Finally, should these questions matter to the modern reader?

Asking such questions in relation to the Châtelain is not arbitrary, for his work and its legacy pose a number of problems relating to authorship. First, in the modern critical tradition the importance of the 'author' to any reading of courtly lyric has been called into question, since the whole tradition has been described as a *poésie formelle* that empties the first person of referential content. According to this view, each lyric is but a tissue of conventions, and the 'author' (in the sense of a writer who is the text's point of origin, who expresses his ideas, feelings, and experiences in it) has little importance: the tradition authorizes the lyric's meaning, not its relation to the writer's life or his experience. Secondly, if the *chansonniers* attribute unequivocally seven lyrics to the Châtelain, some twenty-six other lyrics are attributed to him in at least some manuscripts, some of which were certainly the work of other well-known contemporary poets with whom he had contact (Gace Brulé, Blondel de Nesle, Conon de Béthune). Thus, in a manuscript tradition in which, as we will see, attribution and authorship seem important, the authenticity of an attribution is less crucial than the ascription itself as certain kinds of texts seem to be attracted magnetically to certain names. Finally, the Châtelain is unique among *trouvères* in that he has an afterlife as a fictional character who in the first instance at least is based closely upon the lyrics ascribed to him: thus the first-person voice of his lyrics is transposed through reception and transmission into a narrative character, who is a product of a fictional world instantiated by the textual tradition itself.

The Châtelain's lyrics are often taken as paradigmatic of the *grand chant courtois*, and the first section of this chapter offers some general reflections on the genre. The second considers the presence of the author within this genre and the final section examines how the figure and lyrics of the Châtelain are incorporated into a later narrative tradition. The conclusion will return to the question of authorship and attribution in *trouvère* lyric, but viewed in the light of the Châtelain's narrative fame.

## The *grand chant courtois*

The *trouvères* have had a bad press in modern times. They are given short shrift in literary histories, which stress above all their debt to the highly regarded and more influential troubadours, particularly Jaufre Rudel (died c.1148) and Bernart de Ventadorn (mid twelfth century). If criticism on the *trouvères* was given intellectual bite by important studies stressing the complex formal and conventional properties of their lyrics, their debt to the troubadours remains a constant critical refrain, while the perception of their work as formal display contributes to an over-riding sense of this poetry as arid and lifeless. As Robert Guiette put it, 'in the 2000 songs there is nothing, as it were, but tradition and convention'.[1] This approach reaches its apogee in the work of Paul Zumthor, whose seminal work on *trouvère* lyric remains influential (though it has been frequently critiqued in troubadour scholarship). Using a lyric by the Châtelain as illustrative of the *grand chant*, Zumthor concluded his formal analysis: 'the song is ... its own subject, without a predicate ... the poem is its own mirror'.[2] He thus saw the *grand chant* as a self-referential poetic structure, in which the 'I' who speaks has a purely grammatical function, devoid of reference to anything other than the act of singing which it performs, records, re-enacts, and anticipates.

Zumthor's conclusions echo Guiette's premise that: 'the theme is but a pretext. The formal work itself is the subject.'[3] Here is the lyric in which he grounds his analysis (Lerond III, with some modifications to punctuation):

I   La douce voiz du louseignol sauvage
qu'oi nuit et jour contoier et tentir
m'adoucist si le cuer et rassouage
qu'or ai talent que chant pour esbaudir;
bien doi chanter puis qu'il vient a plaisir     5
cele qui j'ai fait de cuer lige homage;
si doi avoir grant joie en mon corage,
s'ele me veut a son oez retenir.

II   Onques vers li n'eu faus cuer ne volage
– si m'en devroit pour tant mieuz avenir –     10
ainz l'aim et serf et aour par usage,
maiz ne li os mon pensé descouvrir,
quar sa biautez me fait tant esbahir
que je ne sai devant li nul language;
nis reguarder n'os son simple visage,     15
tant en redout mes ieuz a departir.

III   tant ai en li ferm assis mon corage
qu'ailleurs ne pens, et Diez m'en lait joïr!
c'onques Tristanz, qui but le beverage,
plus loiaument n'ama sanz repentir,     20
quar g'i met tout, cuer et cors et desir,
force et pooir, ne sai se faiz folage:
encor me dout qu'en trestout mon eage
ne puisse assez li et s'amour servir.

IV   Je ne di pas que je face folage,     25
nis se pour li me devoie morir,
qu'el mont ne truis tant bele ne si sage,
ne nule rienz n'est tant a mon desir.
Mout aim mes ieuz qui me firent choisir:
lors que la vi, li laissai en hostage     30
mon cuer, qui puiz i a fait lonc estage,
ne ja nul jour ne l'en quier departir.

V   Chançon, va t'en pour faire mon message
la u je n'os trestourner ne guenchir,
quar tant redout la fole gent ombrage     35
qui devinent, ainz qu'il puist avenir,
les biens d'amours (Diex les puist maleïr!)
A maint amant ont fait ire et damage;

mais j'ai de ce mout cruel avantage
qu'il les m'estuet seur mon pois obeïr.                    40

(The sweet voice of the uncaged nightingale that I hear night and day chirping and trilling softens and soothes my heart so that now I wish to sing in order to rejoice; indeed I must sing since this pleases the one to whom I have given my heart in liege homage; and I should have great joy in my heart if she wishes to retain me.

Never have I had a false or fickle heart towards her – and great good should thereby come to me – rather I love and serve and adore her every day, but I do not dare reveal my thoughts to her, for her beauty so astonishes me that I do not know how to speak before her; nor do I even dare look upon her pure face, since I so fear tearing my eyes away.

I have set my heart on her so firmly that I think of nothing else, and may God give me joy of this! For never did Tristan, who drank the potion, love so loyally and unrepentantly, for I put everything into this, heart, body and desire, strength and power, and I don't know if this is foolish: yet I fear that in my entire life I may not be able to serve her and her love enough.

I do not say this is foolish, even if I had to die for her, for I find no more beautiful or wiser woman in the world, nor is there anything I desire more. I love my eyes greatly since they made me choose her: as soon as I saw her, I left her my heart as a hostage, and since then it has resided a long time with her, and I never wish to take it away.

Song, go off, deliver my message there where I dare not return nor tarry, since I so fear the stupid, crotchety ones who guess [who it is that gets] the pleasures of love before they even materialize, God curse them! They have annoyed and damaged many lovers, but I have one cruel advantage in this: I must obey them against my wishes.)

The conventional aspects of this song are legion. Though many *trouvère* (and troubadour) lyrics exploit varying line lengths, also experimenting with complex rhyme-schemes and/or difficult rhyme-sounds, thereby anticipating some of the formal gymnastics of later medieval practice (see Chapter 10), this song uses the common decasyllable uniformly and shares a rhyme-scheme (ababbaab) with hundreds of other troubadour and *trouvère* texts; it also uses common rhyme-sounds (-*ir* and -*age*). This simplicity of form may of course have been modulated by complex ornamentation of the melody, but it also encourages a certain focus on content. The poet begins by suggesting an analogy between his feelings and some pleasant element from nature, here the quintessentially conventional nightingale (often used to figure the lover/singer and, as here, his need to sing), before going on to deploy a panoply of *topoi* (common-places) that recur frequently throughout the tradition: the poet has given his heart to his lady, expressing their relation in feudal terms (stanza 1); he is faithful, serving her unconditionally, but is struck dumb in her presence, overwhelmed by her beauty (stanza II); he compares himself to Tristan, the archetypal ideal lover, aligning himself thereby with many of his predecessors and contemporaries (stanza III); this raises the spectre of dying for love, which he then articulates more clearly, binding himself and his heart to his lady, also evoking the mesmerizing power of gazing upon her (stanza IV); finally, he sends his poem off to a vague, unidentified place ('la', line 34) to transmit his message, suggesting that his reluctance to go there himself (perhaps also his vagueness) is due to *la fole gent ombrage*, easily identifiable as the *losengiers* (the *lauzengiers* of troubadour lyric), those wicked and sharp-tongued courtiers who conventionally seek to harm the lover and his lady (stanza V).

As Zumthor suggests, the meaningful unit of composition is the stanza. However, his implication that the stanza order is immaterial, since no logical progression is implied, begs the question.[4] He concedes that the position of the first and last stanzas is fixed, but here the sequence of the third and fourth is also important since line 25 echoes and glosses line 22, while line 26 depends on the reference to Tristan in stanza III; similarly, the insistence on the relation between love and service makes better sense if it follows directly the reference to liege homage in line 6. While stanza order is often mobile in transmission with some troubadour and *trouvère* lyrics, with others a fixed stanza order enables logical progression in an argument. Here all nine *chansonniers* to preserve the poem in its entirety agree on the stanza order. I would suggest, therefore, that this poem has semantic direction.

In his lengthy formal analysis, Zumthor stresses the deployment of variations on key semantic elements, particularly *chant/chanter/chançon, cuer/corage, amour/amer/amant, joie/joïr, douter/redouter, pensé/pens*. This creates, in his view, a 'signifying redundancy', with no necessary sequence, the point being simply the production of phonic and semantic echoes.[5] This stress on the phonic accords well with his remarks on the poem's rhymes, since he evaluates these exclusively in terms of timbre and tonality. But I would suggest that in lyrics such as these rhyme may have a semantic value that exceeds any contribution to phonic patterning.

Each of the two rhyme-sounds occurs twenty times. As is often the case with troubadour and *trouvère* lyric, the rhyme-sound determines the most likely part of speech for the rhyme-word. In this instance, fifteen of the twenty -*age* rhyme-words are nouns; seventeen of the -*ir* rhyme words are infinitives. In his analysis of tenses in the *grand chant*, Zumthor rightly stresses that the overwhelming temporal and spatial impression is always *je, ici, maintenant* due to the prevalence of first-person present indicative forms,[6] but he fails – oddly given the centrality of grammar and syntax to his analysis – to remark on a phenomenon previously noted by Roger

Dragonetti, namely the prevalence of infinitives at the rhyme in *grands chants*: as Dragonetti, notes 57.469 per cent of Gace Brulé's rhyme-words are infinitives, 51.767 per cent of Thibaut de Champagne's, 68.474 per cent of Blondel de Nesles's.[7] This dominance of the infinitive is easy to explain: *-er* is the easiest rhyme to use, followed by *-ir*, precisely because so many infinitives can be selected as rhyme-words and because they are easy to deploy syntactically. Nonetheless, the comfort factor for the poet should not blind us to a point Dragonetti makes eloquently, 'rhyme itself can even become ... the starting point for the creation of the poem'.[8] What Zumthor's analysis misses (despite his emphasis on sound and lexis) is that rhyme provides an alternative syntax to courtly lyrics, creating semantic connections between words that are not dependent on the grammar of individual sentences. An obvious example of this in 'La douce voiz' is the sequence of final rhyme-words in each stanza, which in performance might have had particular weight precisely because of their mnemonic final position: *retenir, departir, servir, departir, obeïr*. Consider how, with songs, we often remember the rhyme-words better than the body of the line. Then note the symmetry created by the repetition of *departir* (which few listeners or readers can fail to notice) and the emphasis this gives to the centrality of *servir* with two other feudal terms topping and tailing the lyric (*retenir, obeïr*). Now each of these infinitives in its syntactic context in the lyric relates in some way to the lover or the lady as subject or object, but set off in a sequence they take on an abstract, almost theoretical quality, since infinitives present action in a pure, conceptual form, devoid of tense or person, instantiating thereby a general reflection on love service and fear of separation. This tendency towards abstraction in courtly lyric can be enhanced by other techniques, such as personification allegory. But here the main device used to create an effect of abstract discourse, I suggest, is the prevalence of infinitives, which is enabled by the choice of rhyme.

## The author in the *grand chant*

Does this mean that the presence of the 'author' is negligible, that he disappears behind a foreground of formal structure, abstraction, and convention? This will depend largely on the mode of reception, but in most circumstances the presence of the author – or a surrogate – is crucial to a full understanding of the aesthetics of courtly lyric. First, let us consider the original context of performance. Consideration of the music unfortunately exceeds my competence, but it is nonetheless obvious that a singer – whether the poet himself or a minstrel – will *embody* the *je* of the poem, lending it an autobiographical or pseudo-autobiographical frame of references. If we then turn to the *chansonniers*, the earliest of these postdate the early *trouvères* by about a hundred years, so author and text have necessarily become disconnected. But as Sylvia Huot indicates, many *trouvère chansonniers* organize *grands chants courtois* according to authorial attribution (even if attributions sometimes conflict) and frequently each new author-section begins with a portrait, which 'even if fictional ... serves to endow the *trouvère* with a specific identity'.[9] In some instances it is possible to authenticate a *trouvère*'s coat of arms as historically accurate: thus, 'the combination of the heraldic image and the aristocratic title of the rubric points to an actual historic existence for these figures, grounding the lyric "*I*" in an extratextual reality'.[10] Ironically, the context in which the author seems least present is the modern critical edition, which packages the text in a critical apparatus and notes, as an object of study, no longer a poetic utterance, or a record of this utterance.

If we consider *trouvère* lyrics in these two medieval modes of reception, the crucial role of an identifiable singer in performance or of a supposedly identifiable historical author in the *chansonniers* encourages us to read the songs as attempts by individual poets to negotiate a position in relation to a conventional and abstract model of love, rather than dismissing their convention and abstraction as purely conventional and abstract. The *je* would not therefore be purely grammatical: as a grammatical position it may be occupied by individuals other than the original author, but it is always (in medieval contexts) occupied, or represented as occupied.

Furthermore, the aristocratic identity imputed to most early *trouvères* in the *chansonniers* points to another important feature of the tradition in the late twelfth century. When lyric poetry started to be composed in French (*c.*1160), initially the practice was limited to a small number of courts (mainly in North-Eastern France); it was almost exclusively the preserve of high-ranking nobles until *c.*1200, after which it was taken up by clerics and educated non-nobles in towns (for instance Adam de la Halle).[11] This parallels the development of the troubadour tradition, since initially (before *c.*1160) the number of Southern courts where troubadour poetry was composed and disseminated was very restricted (even though troubadour lyric was socially more heterogeneous from early on).[12] Maybe the *chansonniers* stress the aristocratic nature of early *trouvères* precisely because they were indeed highly aristocratic. And as with the early troubadours, the early *trouvères* were a small, refined group of initiates.

Indeed, the Châtelain was part of a tightly knit group of *trouvères*, in dialogue with each other as well as with contemporary troubadours. Thus, if 'La douce voiz' is modelled to some extent on Bernart de Ventadorn's 'La doussa votz', it is in fact more a reaction to this lyric than merely an imitation of it, since the Châtelain is considerably less irascible in his lyric than Bernart, indicating that his nightingale is conveyed in wholly positive terms, which is not necessarily the case with Bernart's.[13] Furthermore, the Châtelain's poem needs in addition to be read alongside a series of lyrics by contemporary *trouvères* – Gace Brulé, Blondel de Nesles, and Gilles de Viés-Maisons. As Jörn Gruber has shown 'La douce voiz' borrows formal elements (including melodic) from a Gace lyric ('Tant m'a mené force de seignorage'), while replying to a tetchy lyric by Gilles ('Chanter m'estuet'), in which he claims to sing not because he is moved by love, but on the contrary in order to attack love and by implication a faithless, recalcitrant lady.[14] Apart from thematic and phonic echoes, that 'La douce voiz' (then two lyrics by Gace, and one by Blondel) may be read as a reply to Gilles is suggested by a further lyric, in which Gilles reprises in the last line of each stanza the first line of well-known lyrics by his fellow poets:[15]

> I  Se per mon chant me deüsse aligier
> de l'ire grant ke j'ai en mon couraige,
> mestier m'avroit, car a moi leecier
> ni me valt riens, ne ne mi rasuaige
> fuelle ne flors, chans d'oixiaus per boscaige;
> plux seux iriés quant plux oi coentoier
> *la douce voiz dou roisignor savaige.*　　　　　(1–7)

(If through my song the great anger in my heart could be lightened, I would need this, for neither leaf nor flower, nor birdsong in the wood does anything to make me happy or soothe me; I am more angered the more I hear 'La douce voiz'.)

The precise sequence of these lyrics is unclear: Gilles goes on to cite Gace's 'De bone amour' and 'Tant m'a mené', also Blondel's 'Quant je pluz sui'. Our sense of how they originally related to each other is further complicated by there being two versions of 'Se per mon chant'. In what appears to be the earlier, Gilles expresses reservations about his lady before turning to his colleagues' lyrics for comfort or edification (with the exception of the Châtelain lyric, which seems simply to exacerbate his ire); in the second, he cites but two lyrics (the Châtelain's and one of Gace's) before going on to express at more length conventional and unconditional devotion to his lady, with an *envoi* that equally conventionally designates his *chançon* as his messenger. Fred Marshall confects complex biographical explanations for the existence of two different versions of 'Se per mon chant'.[16] However, the precise circumstances of its recasting (if indeed both versions are by Gilles), together with the order in which the various lyrics were composed, necessarily remain open to conjecture and the circumstantial details are less important than the fact that we are left with the traces of encoded messages which offer testimony to a dialogue between individual and individuated authors. That we can no longer decode these messages precisely should not lead us to assume they were devoid of referential content. Zumthor reads the Châtelain's injunction to his song to go off 'pour faire mon message' at the end of 'La douce voix' as the ultimate marker of the lyric's self-reflexivity,[17] but the very notion of a message inscribes the poem in an intertextual and social network, since a message, by definition, is putatively addressed to someone, and we need not assume – given the indeterminate *la* of the destination – that the only addressee here is the lady.

To see the early *trouvères* as engaged in a homosocial dialogue in which their songs are a vehicle for aesthetic competition and ethical debate, conducted by a group of educated, refined, and also – let's face it – precious men, again points to parallels with the troubadours.[18] But rather than seeing the *trouvères* merely as imitators of Occitan poetry, it is fairer to see them as a parallel, but related poetic community. If there is demonstrable contact between troubadours and *trouvères* in the late twelfth century, there is as much reference to *trouvère* poetry among contemporary troubadours as vice versa,[19] and whereas the work of two troubadours – Jaufre Rudel and Bernart de Ventadorn – was influential in the North, they were also frequently emulated by late twelfth-century troubadours and their German counterparts, the *Minnesänger*. In other words, their discernible influence on the *trouvères* is not necessarily evidence of the Northern poets' slavish devotion to Southern models, but rather part of a broader body of evidence for the pan-European popularity of Jaufre and Bernart.

### The Châtelain's literary afterlife

Though critics are quick to point out the early *trouvères*' debt to the troubadours, they often fail to comment on how a number of them, but particularly the Châtelain, gained a reputation as exemplary lovers among the next generation of poets. For example, Eustache le Peintre (early thirteenth-century) compares himself to the Châtelain, Blondel [de Nesles] and Tristan, and an anonymous *trouvère* draws attention to his imitation of the form of one of his songs ('A vous, amant', Lerond, 1):[20]

> Onques Tristan n'ama de tel maniere,
> li Chastelains ne Blondiaus autresi,
> come j'ai fet, tres douce dame chiere ...

(Never did Tristan love as I do, nor the Châtelain, nor Blondel, sweet dear lady ...)

Li Chastelains de Couci ama tant
qu'ainc por amors nus n'en ot dolor graindre;
por ce ferai ma complainte en son chant . . .

(The Châtelain de Couci loved so much that no one through love ever had greater pain, which is why I will compose my lament to his tune . . .)

This interest in the early *trouvères* as model lovers is attested throughout the thirteenth century, but not just in lyrics: there was also a minor vogue for the composition of romances citing well-known lyrics by early *trouvères*. Jean Renart's, *Roman de la rose* (1210/20s), Gerbert de Montreil's *Roman de la violette* (before 1250), the *Châtelaine de Vergy* (c.1270?), and Jakemes's *Castelain de Couci* (c.1280?) are among the most sophisticated and delightful of thirteenth-century narrative texts; they inaugurate a practice of lyric insertion in longer texts or sequences that was to thrive in the later Middle Ages (see Chapters 4 and 10). Furthermore, because most and perhaps all of these romances predate the surviving *chansonniers*, as Ardis Butterfield puts it 'narrative contexts represent some of the earliest stages by which lyric genres were recorded in writing'.[21] Within this corpus the Châtelain stands out on two counts: first, his are the only lyrics to be cited in *all* these texts, indicating he was thirteenth-century France's favourite twelfth-century poet; secondly, he is uniquely the subject of a poetic biography, in that Jakemes's *Castelain*, rather than citing lyrics by a range of poets and interpolating them into an extraneous narrative, uses only lyrics attributed to him, integrating them as circumstantial pieces into the supposed story of his life. In aligning the Châtelain with Tristan, a fictional character, Eustache le Peintre thus seems to have been prescient. To cite Butterfield again, quoting the Châtelain's '*chansons* developed into a topos in its own right'.[22]

One Châtelain lyric is cited in all these romances: 'A vous, amant'. Surviving as it does in eleven *chansonniers*, this was indeed a popular lyric, as Jakemes acknowledges when he introduces it, with interesting ambivalence about whether it is a 'song', to be learnt by heart, or a 'text', to be written down, since the verb *recorder* can mean both:

Et en ramembrance de li
fist il ce cant et dist ensi
c'on a recordé moult souvent:
A vous, amant, ains qu'a nule autre gent . . .

(Castelain, 7344–7)

(And in order to remember her, he composed this song and sang it thus, as it has been often learnt/written down: 'To all you lovers, rather than to anyone else . . .')

As with each of the cited lyrics, the first verse is rhymed with the previous line, thereby breaking the sequence of octosyllabic rhyming couplets but physically embedding the lyrics in the form of the romance. The lyrics are all also directly assimilated into the plot. Jakemes's stroke of genius, in the *Castelain*, was to combine a fairly banal tale of courtly adultery, entailing some pot-boiling twists and turns before the hero finally beds his lady (the Dame de Fayel), with the best-known element of the historical Châtelain's life (his death on crusade), then more importantly with the popular 'eaten heart' story, in which an adulterous wife is fed her lover's heart by her jealous husband, to die shortly afterwards from a mixture of grief and ecstasy. When the romance hero sings 'A vous, amant' ('To all you lovers') he has just been tricked by the Lord of Fayel, who has recently discovered his wife's affair, into an oath to go on crusade. If the canonical version of the lyric announces a departure ('Je m'an vois, Dame', 41), the romance has an *envoi* only otherwise preserved in one *chansonnier*:

> Nus n'a pité. Va, cancons, si t'en croie
> que je m'en vois siervir Nostre Seignour;
> si saciés bien, dame de grant valour,
> se je revieng, que pour vous siervir vais.          (7395–8)

(No one pities me. Song, go and bear witness that I go to serve Our Lord; and most worthy lady, know that if I return I go to serve you.)

It is possible this *envoi* was in Jakemes's source, but it is equally possible he composed it himself, *adapting* the famous lyric to narrative circumstances, not just citing them.[23]

The citation of 'A vous, amant' in the *Castelain* neatly demonstrates that Jakemes did not simply preserve the Châtelain's lyrics, he responded to them as texts that were still very much alive in the society for which his romance was destined. Of course he could have known that the historical Châtelain did indeed die *outremer*, but he could also have surmised his departure from the lyric 'Li nouviaux tanz' (Lerond, V, cited 7005–11). His assimilation of the Châtelain's story and lyrics to the 'eaten heart' legend, though on one level fanciful, may also be read as a response to the lyrics, since the Châtelain dwells insistently in a number of lyrics cited in the romance on his likely death from love and on the gift he makes of his heart to his lady: witness 'La douce voiz' (6–7, 19, 26, 30–1), but also 'A vous, amant', which as it occurs in the romance has lines such as 'S'ainc nus moru per avoir coer dolant' (7353: 'If anyone ever died from a suffering heart'), 'Comment me poet li coers el corps durer / Qu'il ne me part?' (7369–70: 'How can my heart survive in my body without leaving it?'), 'Ne je ne puis de li mon coer oster' (7377: 'Nor can I take my heart away from her'), and 'u que mes coers traie' (7391:

'wherever my heart may go'). In other words, Jakemes responds to what Eugene Vance – who like Zumthor takes the Châtelain as paradigmatic of *trouvère* lyric – has called the 'latent narrativity' of the *grand chant courtois*:[24] what writers of thirteenth-century romances with interpolated lyrics realized was not only that putting a song into a story makes for good entertainment, but also that good songs often already contain virtual stories. I will not dwell here on my reading of this particular story: the hero of the many versions of the 'eaten heart' story in medieval narrative is always a poet, whose ethical gift of himself to his lady in lyric – figured through the heart – is transposed into a narrative fantasy of incorporation, of a perfect union with the Other, leading to *jouissance*.[25] It is more important in the context of my argument here that this romance, like many of the contemporary *chansonniers* (troubadour and *trouvère*), grounds the lyrics it cites in a specific subject (albeit largely fictional), occupying an identifiable position in time and space. Jakemes's romance shows that the Châtelain's memory lived on after his death; later medieval citations and a fifteenth-century *mise en prose* indicate his fame continued to endure.[26] Interestingly the *mise en prose*, which is quite a close adaptation of Jakemes's romance, suppresses all the lyrics with just one exception, but nevertheless acknowledges that few surpassed its hero in 'singing, composing ballads, songs, and in other gracious activities' (36). The exception is 'La douce voiz', of which the first and last stanzas are quoted (50), indicating perhaps the longevity of some early medieval lyrics in terms of popularity.

## Conclusion

The combination of the popularity of his songs with the macabre lustre of the 'eaten heart' legend clearly lodged the Châtelain's name firmly in the minds of the lyric tradition's public, which may explain the number of lyrics apparently misattributed to him.[27] 'A la douçor du tens' (Lerond, XIV), for example, is anonymous in eight manuscripts, attributed to Blondel de Nesle in three, Gace Brulé in one, and the Châtelain in two: reference to the sovereignty of the poet's heart (20) and an insistent stanza on dying of love (29–35) might well have struck a chord with scribes who knew the romance, leading to an ascription to the Châtelain. The more famous lyric 'Ahi! Amours' (Lerond, XXVI), usually considered the work of Conon de Béthune, speaks of the pain of separation from one's beloved when leaving on crusade. Here the obvious parallel with aspects of 'A vous, amant' (particularly as transmitted in the romance) and particularly the lines 'Se li cors vait servir Nostre Seignour, / li cuers remaint du tout en sa baillie' (7–8: 'If my body goes to serve Our Lord, my heart remains here at her command') might have been sufficient to produce the attribution to the Châtelain in four manuscripts. Conversely, 'Au renouvel de la douçour d'esté' (Lerond, XXVII), generally attributed to Gace Brulé in the *chansonniers*, may have been assimilated to the Châtelain's corpus by Jakemes because of its references to the poet's heart (5957, 5976).

The memory of an author-figure haunts the reception of the Châtelain's lyrics to such an extent that his spectral presence invades the work of other writers and poets. I am not hereby pleading for a new mode of author-centred, biographical criticism of *trouvère* lyric. This would be reductive and naive, and what we know of the historical Châtelain's life in fact amounts to precious little. What I am suggesting, rather, is that we need to think about the power of the figure of the author in the genesis, transmission, and reception of *trouvère* lyrics and that we should not dismiss them as 'nothing … but tradition and convention'.

## Notes

1. R. Guiette, *D'une poésie formelle en France au moyen âge*, new edn (Paris, Nizet, 1972), p. 18.
2. P. Zumthor, *Essai de poétique médiévale* (Paris, Seuil, 1972), p. 218.
3. Guiette, *Poésie*, pp. 33–4.
4. Zumthor, *Essai*, p. 195.
5. Zumthor, *Essai*, p. 200.
6. Zumthor, *Essai*, p. 205.
7. R. Dragonetti, *La Technique poétique des trouvères dans la chanson courtoise* (Bruges, Tempel, 1960), p. 405.
8. Dragonetti, *Technique*, p. 416.
9. S. Huot, *From Song to Book: the Poetics of Writing in Old French Lyric and Lyrical Narrative Poetry* (Ithaca and London, Cornell University Press, 1987), p. 57.
10. Huot, *Song*, p. 57.
11. See G. Zaganelli, *Aimer, sofrir, joïr: i paradigmi della soggettività nella lirica francesa dei secoli XII e XIII* (Florence, La Nuova Italia, 1982), pp. 191–2.
12. See M. L. Meneghetti, *Il pubblico dei trovatori: ricezione, e riuso dei testi lirici cortesi fino al XIV secolo* (Modena, Mucchi, 1984).
13. See R. Rosenstein, 'La douce voix du Châtelain: le Châtelain de Couci et les troubadours, vingt ans après', in A. Touber (ed.), *Le Rayonnement des Troubadours: Actes du Colloque de l'AIEO (Amsterdam 16–18 octobre)* (Amsterdam, Rodopi, 1998), pp. 227–53 (pp. 231–3).
14. J. Gruber, *Die Dialektik des Trobar* (Tübingen, Niemeyer, 1983), pp. 242–55.
15. For the texts of these lyrics see F. Marshall, 'Blondel de Nesle and his Friends: the Early Tradition of the *Grand Chant*', *New Zealand Journal of French Studies*, 5 (1984), 5–32 (pp. 10–16).
16. Marshall, 'Blondel', pp. 26–9.
17. Zumthor, *Essai*, p. 209

18. Note that the Gui Gace Brulé addresses in five lyrics is generally identified with the Châtelain.

19. Rosenstein, 'La douce voix', pp. 241–2.

20. Eustache cited from A. Långfors, 'Mélanges de poésie lyrique française v', *Romania*, 58 (1932), 353–74 (p. 374), the anonymous *trouvère* from Lerond, p. 19.

21. A. Butterfield, *Poetry and Music in Medieval France: from Jean Renart to Guillaume de Machaut* (Cambridge University Press, 2002), p. 26.

22. Butterfield, *Poetry*, p. 36.

23. It is not possible to establish the relative chronology of the one *chansonnier* to preserve the *envoi* and Jakemes's romance. Jakemes is thought to have composed the shorter lyrics in the romance himself.

24. See E. Vance, *Mervelous Signals: Poetics and Sign Theory in the Middle Ages* (Lincoln and London: University of Nebraska Press, 1986), p. 88.

25. S. Gaunt, *Love and Death in Medieval French and Occitan Courtly Literature* (Oxford University Press, 2006), pp. 90–103. See also: A. Allen, 'La mélancolie du biographe: le *Roman du Castelain de Couci* et le deuil de la voix', *Neophilologus*, 85 (2001), 25–41; Huot, *Song*, pp. 117–31; H. Solterer, 'Dismembering, Remembering the Châtelain de Coucy', *Romance Philology*, 46 (1992), 103–24.

26. On later citations, see Butterfield, *Poetry*, pp. 38–9; for the *mise en prose*, *Le Livre des amours du Chastellain de Coucy et de la Dame de Fayel*, ed. A. Petit and F. Suard (Lille, Presses Universitaires de Lille, 1994).

27. The influence of Jakemes's romance on the *chansonniers* is attested by the later addition of the name Reignault in BL Egerton 274: this is the Châtelain's name in the romance, and Jakemes probably knew that several castellans of Couci bore this name in the thirteenth century.

# 7

## DEBORAH McGRADY

# Guillaume de Machaut

Armes, Amours, Dames, Chevalerie,
clers, musiciens, faititres en françois,
tous sophistes, toute poeterie,
tous ceuls qui ont melodieuse voix,
ceuls qui chantent en orgue aucune fois
et qui ont chier le doulz art de musique,
demenez dueil, plourez, car c'est bien drois,
la mort Machaut le noble rethorique.

(Eustache Deschamps, *ballade* 123, 1–8)

(Men of arms, lovers, ladies, knighthood, clerics, musicians, writers of French, all philosophers, all of poetry, all who have a melodious voice, those who sing with accompaniment on occasion and hold dear the sweet art of music, show your grief, cry, because it is true, the death of Machaut, the noble poet.)

Composed soon after the death of Guillaume de Machaut in 1377, Eustache Deschamps's lament attests to the tremendous legacy already afforded the master at the end of his life. As the author of over 400 poems, 117 songs, 23 motets, 13 *dits*, and the first full Mass cycle, the Machaut celebrated by Deschamps assumes legendary proportions as the master of lovers, knights, and ladies; musicians, poets, clerics, and philosophers. Subsequent generations rarely wavered in their celebration of Machaut. In the realm of music, Machaut is universally recognized as the last of the great poet-composers, the greatest practitioner of the musical style known as *ars nova* (characterized principally by a freer attitude towards rhythm than had been the case previously), the master of polyphony, and the first composer of a complete Mass. In literature, he is regarded as no less than the *pater familias* of French poetry. From René d'Anjou who considered Machaut second only to Ovid to Daniel Poirion who recognized him as a precursor of Malherbe, Machaut's legacy was to have masterfully united the *auctor* of classical literature and the vernacular author, music and poetry, the clerkly and the courtly world. Lest we believe that readers acted independently in attributing such lofty roles to the poet, a study of the skilful shaping of Machaut's authorial persona in his poetic corpus reveals to what extent his fame was orchestrated by himself and his bookmakers.[1] Drawing from established literary sources, traditional iconography, and advances in book technology, Machaut and his bookmakers typically worked in unison to present the unprecedented portrait of a vernacular author solely responsible for a wholly unique and unified corpus.

To appreciate Machaut's masterful use of literary sources, an overview of his treatment of four major canonical works – the *Roman de la rose*, the *Consolation of Philosophy*, Scripture, and Ovidian mythology – exposes the strategies used to usurp the authority previously conferred to these texts. Of these works, the *Roman de la rose* is by far the most influential source for his poetic compositions and, as such, it deserves particular attention.[2] Adapting a courtly discourse reminiscent of Guillaume de Lorris's portion of the *Rose*, Machaut punctuates the *Loange des dames*, an anthology of poems composed over the course of his career, with conventional courtly concepts: he compares his lady to a rose (35, 19), and presents himself as a *humble serf* (59, 2: 'humble servant') who suffers silently in Love's *prison joieuse* (88, 1: 'joyous prison'). The link to Guillaume's *Rose* is most apparent in Machaut's earliest *dit*, the *Dit dou vergier* (1330s). The tale opens with the narrator seeking solace in an enclosed garden, where he quickly falls into a catatonic stupor brought on by amorous suffering. Having thus entered the dream realm, the narrator encounters the God of Love and his twelve servants. This conventional frame, with its obvious indebtedness to the *Roman de la rose*, has led scholars to identify the *Dit dou vergier* as Machaut's most derivative work. Yet a closer examination reveals the poet challenging his literary source. Having set the stage by drawing on the *locus amoenus* of love and poetry and then populating it with the expected actors, Machaut presents a system dominated by an especially violent and indifferent master that even surpasses Jean de Meun's vision of the warring God of Love and a lover marked by fear, naïveté, and neglect. The *Vergier* narrator's first sight of Love fills him with 'frëour ... doubtance et paour' (195–6: 'terror, doubt and fear'),[3] and only after much hesitation does the narrator finally sum up the courage to approach the company without a guide. If the narrator is first delighted that Love greets him in a pleasing manner, he quickly discovers Love's more sinister side, as he boasts of his powers over rich men whom he holds in constant fear and misery (247–55). When the narrator attempts to redirect the conversation to address his personal dilemma, his own situation is pushed aside by the God of Love who continues to revel in the details of his authority. When he finally addresses the lover's complaint after a second request, Love provides only superficial advice, easily applicable to any lover: in proving his loyalty, the lover will have the power to alter the lady's heart (1105–40). Far from mirroring the pugnacious advice Jean de Meun eventually attributes to the God of Love, Machaut's God of Love counsels patience, silence, and passivity instead of seduction and conquest. Having received scarcely an offer of assistance, the *Vergier* lover finally resolves to nourish his own intimate dreams of love rather than take action and reveal his sentiments to his lady: 'Pour ce l'ameray loyaument / Et serviray celéement' (1263–4: 'For this reason I will love her loyally and will serve her secretly'). Breaking sharply once again with the final outcome of the *Rose*, the *Vergier* closes with a new courtly paradigm in which the lover practises submission over exploits, favours dreams over deeds, and privileges sublimation over conquest.

In later works Machaut pursues this disjunction between the successful lover of the *Rose* tradition and the faltering, cowardly, and cerebral men who populate his writings. These unlikely lovers must inevitably confront their failure to match up to the ideal, but Machaut offers them an alternative realm in which they may thrive. For example, in the *Remede de Fortune* (1350s), the intimidated narrator who runs from his lady has greater success with the allegorical figure of Lady Hope, who repeats the *Vergier* message, exalting love's anguish over the joy of reciprocation and celebrates the hope of love over its actual realization (2857–92).[4] In his lyric response to Hope's advice, the lover identifies as his true source of joy no longer his lady but hope:

> Cils dous espoirs en vie me soustient
> et me norrist en amoureus desir,
> et dedens moy met tout ce qui couvient
> pour conforter mon cuer et resjoïr . . .          (3021–4)

(This sweet hope keeps me alive and nourishes me with amorous desire and it fills me with all that is necessary to comfort and to bring joy to my heart.)

Having successfully sublimated his desire through poetry, the lover returns to court with the necessary confidence required to speak openly with his Lady and the two quickly agree to exchange rings as a symbol of their feelings. Yet, the relationship abruptly ends here when the lover chooses to take his leave. Rather than experiencing great sorrow because of the separation, the lover 'joyously' composes a *rondelet* on the subject and settles for observing court activities at a far remove from the crowd. Distancing himself to an even greater degree from actual events, the poet replaces his lady with Love, to whom he address a final convoluted oath of fidelity. His devotion hinges on a wish addressed to Love: unlike the typical lover who might desire a future meeting with his lady, our narrator requests only that Love assure a reading of his work by his lady (4284–96).

In other compositions, Machaut further defers the love interests of his poetic double by repeatedly sacrificing the poet–lover's story in the name of another's suffering. In the *Jugement dou roy de Behaigne* (1330), the narrator's daydreaming of his lady is waylaid so that he can record the sufferings of a knight and a lady who vie for the title of the most miserable in love. The narrator of the *Dit dou lyon* (1342) also abandons thoughts of his lady to give voice to the silent suffering of a lion. Although the narrator once again adopts the role of a cowardly lover and comic buffoon who evokes his lady's name as protection when he mistakes the suffering lion as a threat, it is the lion who truly assumes the role of the pathetic lover. As the story unfolds, the reader discovers a sheepish lion who languishes in silence at his lady's feet until the poet intervenes to give voice to his true feelings. Later in the *Fonteinne amoureuse* (1360–1), the poet lends his voice and skills to a prince who suffers so greatly that his painful nocturnal moans cause the poet to mistake him for a spectre, a thief, or a monster rather than a lover (69–76, 87–8, 96–9).[5] These examples reveal that it is not only the poet–lover in Machaut's writings who defies the established courtly model; in fact, lions, princes, and ladies equally suffer at the hands of love and fortune and in so doing, they challenge the amorous precepts developed in the *Roman de la rose* at the same time that they allow the poet to underscore his role as mediator.

As Machaut's treatment of the *Roman de la rose* challenges accepted views by presenting unconventional lovers, so too the poet recasts the *Consolation of Philosophy*, Scripture, and Ovidian mythology to propose a new vision of the relationship between the vernacular author and his audience. These classics provide a rich source of *exempla* that Machaut adapts to contemporary concerns and events. In the *Remede*, Boethius's Lady Fortune is identified as the cause of all amorous suffering. Then, inspired by Lady Philosophy's consolation of the imprisoned Boethius, Machaut writes the *Confort d'amy* (1356–7) to console King Charles of Navarre who was imprisoned by the king of France in 1356.[6] First modelling his advice on that of Boethius's Lady Philosophy, Machaut goes a step further in counselling the king to draw inspiration from the lives of Judaic kings and mythological heroes as well as the specific writings of Boethius and Solomon. Daniel's multiple adventures are a particularly rich resource in this work. Machaut moves from the expected reading of Daniel as a model for the prince to Daniel as a precursor of the vernacular poet. Describing how Daniel's words save Susannah from an unjust punishment and how his mediation assures the transmission of God's wishes to Nebuchadnezzar and Belshazzar, Machaut presents a scriptural precedent for his strongly worded advice to Charles. He further secures his authority in the *Confort* when he counsels Charles to study the books of Boethius (1904) and Solomon (1979–80), only to then provide a detailed summary of each book and their obvious relevance to Charles's current predicament. This appropriation of learned and prized texts evokes his own mastery of the materials at the same time that it reinforces his position as Charles's advisor. Following this lengthy reflection on biblical models of perseverance, Machaut turns to love. To overcome this final form of suffering that Charles must endure, the narrator again evokes hope as key to surviving trying times. Should Charles not fully understand the power of hope in love, Machaut counsels him to consult his very own *Remede de Fortune* (2248–9). Through this complex game of intertextuality, literary appropriation, and self-citation, Machaut transforms the vernacular love poet and the comic buffoon of his courtly works into a wise counsellor reminiscent of Daniel, Solomon, and Lady Philosophy. In the process, he elevates his courtly texts to the level of learned writings.

The *Fonteinne amoureuse* also depends on classical models to emphasize the vernacular writer's crucial role in the healing process. This second consolation piece addresses Jean de Berry, identified in a closing anagram, who was obliged to serve as a political prisoner during the Hundred Years' War in exchange for the conditional release of his father, King John II. In a veritable tour de force, the *dit* opens with a timorous narrator who, after getting over his initial fears of the moaning lover, will assume the role of poetic spokesperson for the prince. The narrator, now reborn as a poet and counsellor, comforts both the suffering lover and the political prisoner. So precious is the friendship and advice the young prince receives from the poet that the prince rewards the narrator for his writings and the great comfort he has provided by bequeathing to the poet the extraordinary gift of all his land and riches. This final gift has the startling effect of replacing the prince with the poet as the figure of authority, a transformation already anticipated within the dream world of the text.

In fact in the *Fonteinne amoureuse*, we find one of Machaut's most striking reinventions of canonical works in his retelling of the story of Paris and the golden apple. While medieval poets commonly turned to Paris to flesh out the courtly lover or to serve as a warning to princes, Machaut lends new meaning to the myth. In this version of the tale, Paris's negotiations with Venus and the other goddesses bring attention to his status as master of an artistic object that grants power to the gods (1633–2144). In so doing, Machaut shifts the perspective away from the love intrigue – of both Paris and the duke – to insist instead on artistic objects as essential to the securing and commemoration of power. The significance of this message for the poet and prince of the *Fonteinne* is monumental: like the golden apple, the narrator's poetic rendition of the prince's suffering secures for the latter his status as a great lover and a generous leader.

Whether referencing the *Roman de la rose*, Scripture, Boethius or Ovid, Machaut went beyond citation to establish a complex tapestry that joined his works to a recognized tradition. Once established, Machaut then wove his own textual legacy into the very fabric of the canon. As already mentioned, Machaut cites in the *Confort* his earlier work as a supplemental source of advice for the king. A similar strategy links Machaut's *Jugement dou roy de Navarre* (early 1350s), also dedicated to Charles of Navarre, to his first judgement poem, the *Jugement dou roy de Behaigne*, dedicated to the king of Bohemia.[7] The second work opens with a noble lady, Dame Bonnheurté, accusing the poet Guillaume of mishandling the earlier judgement and demanding a retraction. When the poet protests his innocence, Bonnheurté retorts that Guillaume should reread his complete works and take responsibility for his long history of treating women unfairly. Guillaume denies these accusations and adds that given the richness of his corpus, he lacks the time to read everything:

> J'ay bien de besoingnes escriptes
> devers moy, de pluseurs manieres,
> de moult de diverses matieres,
> dont l'une l'autre ne ressamble.
> Consideré toutes ensamble,
> de chascune bien mise a point,
> d'ordre en ordre et de point en point,
> dès le premier commencement
> jusques au darrein finement,
> se tout vouloie regarder
> – dont je me vorray bien garder –
> trop longuement y metteroie . . .                    (884–95)

(I have a surplus of writings before me that address many different subjects of which one does not resemble the other. To examine everything together and each one individually from one part to the next and from sentence to sentence, from the first beginning to the last ending, if I wanted to study it all closely (which I would prefer to avoid), it would take too much time.)

The pairing of the judgement poems demonstrates that Machaut's interest in inserting his writings into the larger narrative of canonical literature was matched by his concern for establishing internal linkage among his own works. The vast corpus Guillaume evokes in the *Jugement dou roy de Navarre* is held together by a prolific author-figure personally impressed by the breadth and depth of his corpus. This preoccupation with the unity of his corpus dominates his final years.

In the *Voir dit* (1363–5), Machaut goes beyond citation of his various compositions to establish a single unified figure capable of embracing the multiple authorial identities developed throughout his corpus. The *Voir dit* deftly unites the poet-lover, the comic buffoon, and the learned writer of earlier works to create a unique overarching authorial identity who lays claim to Machaut's entire corpus. The work allegedly represents a faithful record of a love affair between yet another unlikely lover, the aged Guillaume, and a paragon of youthful beauty, Toute-Belle. The relationship that emerges, however, exists almost exclusively as an intellectual rather than a physical coupling. Guillaume expresses a clear preference for writing over visiting his lady and for meditating on her portrait over contemplating her in person. Here the written word in the form of poetry, songs, and letters exchanged between lovers replaces all physical contact. Where traditional lovers hover on the brink of death because of a kiss denied, Guillaume wastes away on his deathbed until he receives a letter from Toute-Belle. Rather than inspire him to mount a horse and join his lady, her love note inspires a poem. Indeed the affair quickly appears as a pretext for writing. Guillaume proves to be highly self-conscious of writing a book and producing a corpus of materials, referencing on multiple occasions his own scribal preoccupations. Thus, following claims of his undying love, Guillaume writes primarily to Toute-Belle about his literary activities: he refers to copies of his works that have been sent to a scribe for musical notation; he documents his progress on the book in terms of the number of *cahiers* it fills; and, most intriguingly, he refers to the 'livre ou je mets toutes mes choses' that contains his other compositions (specifically the *Fonteinne amoureuse*), implying a 'master' copy of all his writings.

Reinforcing the notion of authorial control in the creation of his corpus is the poetic manifesto written as a preface to Machaut's corpus (*c*.1372). Versions of this Prologue figure in five extant copies, of which four contain the poet's complete works.[8] The Prologue opens with four interlocked *ballades* that document an imagined conversation regarding his literary obligations that transpires between Guillaume and Lady Nature and the God of Love. Nature first offers the author the necessary resources to compose poetry, represented here by her three children, *Sens*, *Retorique*, and *Musique* (Meaning, Rhetoric, and Music). She insists on the poet's predestined status as a creative genius:

> Je, Nature, par qui tout est fourmé,
> . . .
> vien ci a toy, Guillaume, qui fourmé
> t'ay a part, pour faire par toy former
> nouviaus dis amoureus plaisans. (1–5)

(I, Nature, by whom all is created ... come before you, Guillaume, whom I created specially so that by you would be created new and pleasing poems about love.)

The God of Love follows with the presentation of his three children, Dous Penser, Plaisance, and Esperance (Sweet Thoughts, Pleasure, and Hope), who will provide the poet with subject matter. The poet identified in rubrics as 'Guillem de Machaut' promises to obey their commands in two responding *ballades*. Then in a final fifth section, consisting of 183 lines, the poet reflects on his talents and the exhaustive corpus that testifies to his mastery of a great variety of lyric forms, principally distinguished by their formal properties, including

> Double hoquès et plaisans lais,
> motès, rondiaus et virelais
> qu'on claimme chansons baladées
> complaintes, balades entees.　　　　　　　　　　(13–16)

(Double hoquets and pleasing lays, motets, roundels and virelays (which are called *chansons baladées*), complaints, [and] *ballades* with refrains.)

The fifth section also includes references to the full thematic range of his corpus, from love poetry to sacred music. Modelling himself on two *poetes*, David and Orpheus (138), Machaut offers his strongest claim yet of his command of a biblical and classical heritage, a claim, as we have seen, he had already intimated in earlier compositions. This synthesis of form and content in the Prologue directs attention to the overarching author-figure identified as source and master of the entire corpus.

Machaut's extraordinary self-portrait as a vernacular author descending from the gods clearly influenced his bookmakers who underscored the presence of an overarching author-figure in the decoration, ordering, and layout of his manuscripts. In BnF, fr. 1584 (MS A), the earliest extant codex to include the Prologue, the Master of the Bible of Jean de Sy used two exquisite half-paged miniatures presented on separate folios to draw attention to the author-figure (Figures 4 and 5).[9] In both instances, the poet assumes the more commanding position before his illustrious guests. This two-part frontispiece draws from two familiar scenes of textual transmission to imagine the poet's fantastical encounter with his sources of power and inspiration. Drawing from donation scenes, the artist rejects the conventional submissive posture of the poet kneeling before the patron. Instead, in the first miniature, the poet stands at the foot of a throne-like structure at the entrance to his study, where he greets the slightly bowed but crowned Lady Nature. In the next illustration, rather than the conventional scene of the poet approaching his source of inspiration, whether an enthroned patron or an allegorical figure, the God of Love approaches the poet who occupies the seat of authority, here identified as a lectern replete with books. This uncommon display of authorial power is further strengthened in the God of Love scene by strong allusions to Annunciation iconography. Where the open book in

Figure 4. Nature introduces her children to the poet, BnF, fr. 1584, fo. E

Figure 5. The God of Love introduces his children to the poet, BnF, fr. 1584, fo. D

Annunciation scenes anticipates and testifies to Mary's predestined role that the Angel Gabriel will elucidate, so both the presence of the God of Love and the open book visually announce the poet's role as the founding father of vernacular poetry. Text and image play off one another as Machaut establishes his genealogy by identifying his poetry as the union of the sacred (David) and the classical (Orpheus). The bold claims evoked in the opening materials of MS A find textual reinforcement at the head of the table of contents, where Machaut's authority is extended to the material production of the codex: 'Vesci l'ordenance que G de Machau wet qu'il ait en son livre' ('Here is the order that Guillaume de Machaut wants his book to have'). Additional reinforcement of Machaut's authority comes from frequent rubrics inserted throughout the corpus that return attention to the poet through his constant naming. The MS A illustration programme maintains a focus on the poet throughout the codex. The 154 miniatures persist in countering the literary protestations of the naive lover, the bumbling observer, or the frightened poet of individual texts with portraits of the vernacular writer writing, reading, and counselling his audience.

While the material presence of the author-figure in MS A has garnered the greatest scholarly attention, other copies of Machaut's complete works place a similar emphasis on portraying the poet as writer. The two-volume collection, BnF, fr. 22545–6, generally believed to have also been composed before Machaut's death, similarly invites its audience to consider Machaut's involvement in book production through repeated scenes of the author-figure engaged in activities, such as reading, transcribing, and dictating texts. Even in BnF, fr. 1586, considered the earliest copy of Machaut's collected works (1350–6), the codex incorporates four illustrations in the *Remede de Fortune* alone that depict the poet with scroll and pen in hand. Whether working under Machaut's supervision or independently, bookmakers typically perpetuated the poet's unprecedented depiction of the vernacular author as master of both the poetic and material artefact.[10]

If Machaut sidesteps the issue of patronage in the Prologue by insisting on the author's individual genius and destiny as determined by Nature and Love, the important role patrons fulfilled in the construction and continuation of Machaut's authorial identity must not be ignored. While rarely identified as sole recipients and owners of the final work, they served as catalysts for poetic creation; as models for the poet's fictional lovers, knights, and ladies; as avid collectors of his writings; and as important contributors to the construction of his powerful authorial identity. Machaut's first patron, Jean de Luxembourg, king of Bohemia, played an especially important and long-lasting role in the poet's professional life. After having most likely completed university training, Machaut entered his service as his secretary in the 1320s. Machaut clearly felt a great affinity for Jean because in writings composed after the king's death, he liberally refers to their extended travels together and recalls the wisdom he acquired under the king's tutelage (see especially the *Fonteinne amoureuse*). Similarly Machaut frequently evoked his name as a paragon of heroism and largesse to be imitated by other princes (see the *Confort d'amy* and *Prise d'Alixandre*). Church records reveal that Machaut had every reason to be grateful to Jean de Luxembourg because as early as 1337, he secured for Machaut several benefices, including a canonicate at Reims cathedral. This position was a permanent appointment, affording a fixed income, lodging, as well as the freedom to pursue his musical and poetic interests. As a direct result of this canonicate, after 1337, Machaut needed neither patrons nor court positions to secure his livelihood.

In spite of the financial security he enjoyed after 1337, Machaut continued to present new patrons with original pieces and copies of his works. In most cases, his exact relationship with specific members of the nobility remains uncertain in spite of tantalizing allusions and enticing archival references. There is speculation that the king of Bohemia's daughter, Bonne de Luxembourg, played a key role in Machaut's career. If the poet did not expressly write the *Dit dou lyon*, the *Dit de l'alerion*, and the *Remede de Fortune* in her honour, it would seem that Ladies Esperance and Bonnheurté were strongly inspired by Bonne. In addition, it is possible that the earliest extant collection of Machaut's collected works, BnF, fr. 1586 (MS C), was intended for her, even though inventory and payment records link it solely with her husband, the future Jean II of France. Apart from the presence of MS C in the king's library, little additional evidence links Machaut with King Jean II, so-called 'the Good'. In fact, he openly opposed the king of France by composing the *Confort d'amy* for the imprisoned Charles of Navarre. In the final two decades of his life, the poet ostensibly offered original works and copies of his writings to numerous princes, including Jean le Bon's son, the future Charles V of France; the dukes of Berry and Burgundy; and Pierre de Lusignan, king of Cyprus.[11] While Machaut generally refrained from explicitly identifying patrons as recipients of his work, several of his alleged patrons make cameo appearances in the *Voir dit*, where, surprisingly, they are repeatedly criticized for their meddling and the detrimental effect they have on the poet's ability to write. When Machaut does name his patron, as when he associates his judgement poems with their intended privileged recipients, the *Fonteinne amoureuse* with the duke of Berry, or the *Confort d'amy* with Charles, he often downplays praise for them to favour instead self-congratulation. Besides the authorial bravado recorded in the *Jugement dou roy de Navarre*, the prince of the *Fonteinne amoureuse* praises the poet for both his wisdom in matters of the heart and his literary talents (1501–10) and, in the *Voir dit*, Toute-Belle frequently reminds Guillaume that his reputation as an accomplished composer and poet is well established.

This inscribed praise cannot be far from the sentiments held by Machaut's readers, as they sometimes went to great expense to acquire the poet's works. BnF, fr. 22545–6, often identified as the most faithful transcription of the poet's works and certainly among the most richly decorated, provides evidence of the pride the owner would have felt in possessing the master's work. The owner, who is as yet unidentified but most likely a member of the upper middle class, is represented in 28 of the 148 miniatures through the incorporation of his coat of arms. Such insistence on the manuscript patron's intimate relationship with Machaut's corpus makes abundantly clear the cultural worth attached to his writings. The duke of Berry also clearly held Machaut in high regard, for he purchased an elaborate copy of his works, distinguished by its dimensions, layout, and design, after the poet's death (BnF, fr. 9221, *c.*1390). Further testifying to the prestige associated with owning Machaut's manuscripts, the library inventories of Amadeus VI, the Green Count of Savoy; Robert d'Alençon, count of Perche; and Philip the Bold, duke of Burgundy, list several now lost copies of the poet's works. Finally, Yolande de Bar, queen of Aragon, was such an avid and devoted reader of Machaut that she sought out known versions of his manuscripts so as to confirm the authority and integrity of her own copy.[12] In these multiple examples, we see an audience not only desirous to acquire copies of Machaut's works, but 'authentic' copies that in content, layout, and decoration bear witness to the master's achievements.

It should not be ignored, however, that while copies of Machaut's manuscripts dating from his lifetime and in the first decades following often provide a coherent narrative of authorial dominance, later copies of his work reveal efforts to sever Machaut's corpus from authorial control. Already the duke of Berry's manuscript, completed one to two decades after Machaut's death, recasts the poet as a compliant subject. Not only is this codex identified as the property of the duke of Berry on the opening folio, but the Prologue is revised in text and image to insist further on the poet's subservience. First, this version of the text presents only the dialogue between the poet and the God of Love and Lady Nature, thereby completely eliminating the poet's detailed celebration in the fifth section of the rich contents of his corpus. Second and most strikingly, the opening frontispiece provides a dramatic reversal of the power-dynamics displayed in MS A and all other depictions of the Prologue. Here the author-figure is twice presented in a posture of subservience at the centre of a two-part register with his allegorical 'patrons' flanking each side of the illustration. In the left register, the poet kneels to face Nature on his right, and then, in the right register, his double appears on bended knee to face the God of Love who stands to his left (Figure 6).

Figure 6. Two-scene miniature, BnF, fr. 9221, fo. 1r. Left-hand scene: Nature presents her children to the kneeling poet; right-hand scene: the God of Love presents his children to the kneeling poet. Manuscript made for the duke de Berry *c.*1390.

In Pierpont Morgan M. 396, which dates from 1425–30, there is again evidence of efforts to downplay the image of Machaut as master of his corpus. Specifically, the collection presents a heavily mediated version of the *Voir dit* in which all references to Guillaume the narrator's involvement in book production are methodically erased.[13] Yet further evidence that Machaut's self-portrait as an author of a coherent corpus suffered at the hands of his later audiences appears in the numerous fifteenth-century anthologies that present only selections of his writings and often without correctly identifying the poet.[14] Machaut's modern editors have taken similar liberties with the master's text, from Paulin Paris's streamlining of the *Voir dit* and rewriting of the closing lines so that the anagram 'works' to later editors' decisions (most often dictated by publishing realities) to break up Machaut's corpus into individual works, to separate out music, and to exclude illustrations. And yet, even these blatant acts against the integrity of Machaut's corpus cannot completely overwrite the poet's inscribed comments that intertwine references to his other works and thus evoke a coherent whole, nor can they efface the vivid scenes of the poet at work. Whether reinforcing his message of authorial dominance or seeking to downplay his authority, generations of readers have ensured that Guillaume de Machaut stands tall as a pivotal figure in medieval literature, simultaneously representing the last troubadour and a prototype for the modern author.

## Notes

1. On the shaping of Machaut's poetic identity as a buffoon, see W. Calin, *A Poet at the Fountain: Essays on the Narrative Verse of Guillaume de Machaut* (Lexington, University Press of Kentucky, 1974); on his self-presentation as a learned figure, see K. Brownlee, *Poetic Identity in Guillaume de Machaut*

(Madison, WI, University of Wisconsin Press, 1984) and J. Cerquiglini-Toulet, *'Un Engin si soutil': Guillaume de Machaut et l'écriture au XIVe siècle* (Paris, Champion, 1985), esp. pp. 105–56; and on bookmakers' and readers' role in authorial construction, see my *Controlling Readers: Guillaume de Machaut and his Late Medieval Audience* (Toronto University Press, 2006).

2. See especially, S. Huot, *The* Romance of the Rose *and its Medieval Readers* (Cambridge University Press, 1993).
3. Cited from vol. I of *Œuvres de Guillaume de Machaut*, ed. Hoepffner.
4. Cited from *Œuvres*, ed. Hoepffner, vol. II. On the concept of sublimation used here, see D. Kelly, *Medieval Imagination, Rhetoric and the Poetry of Courtly Love* (Madison, WI, University of Wisconsin Press, 1978), pp. 122–50.
5. Cited from *Œuvres*, ed. Hoepffner, vol. III; see also *La Fontaine amoureuse*, ed. and trans. J. Cerquiglini-Toulet (Paris, Stock/Moyen Age, 1993).
6. Cited from *Œuvres*, ed. Hoepffner, vol. III.
7. The *Jugement dou roy de Navarre* is cited from *Œuvres*, ed. Hoepffner, vol. II.
8. Cited from *Œuvres*, ed. Hoepffner, vol. I.
9. F. Avril, 'Les Manuscrits enluminés de Guillaume de Machaut', in *Guillaume de Machaut: Poète et compositeur. Actes et colloques. Reims (19–22 avril 1978)* (Paris, Editions Klincksieck, 1982), pp. 117–33.
10. The degree of Machaut's involvement in the production of this manuscript and other collections has preoccupied scholars for decades. For dating details on copies of Machaut's collected works, see L. Earp, *Guillaume de Machaut: a Guide to Research* (New York and London: Garland, 1995), pp. 77–97. On Machaut's relationship to MS A, compare S. J. Williams, 'An Author's Role in Fourteenth-Century Book Production: Guillaume de Machaut's "livre où je met toutes mes choses"', *Romania*, 90 (1969), 433–54; L. Earp, 'Machaut's Role in the Production of Manuscripts of his Works', *Journal of the American Musicological Society*, 42 (1995), 461–502; McGrady, *Controlling Readers*, pp. 81–3.
11. Earp, *Guillaume de Machaut*, pp. 40–8.
12. Earp, *Guillaume de Machaut*, p. 60, 2.2.1.b.
13. See McGrady, *Controlling Readers*, pp. 190–210.
14. See Earp, *Guillaume de Machaut*, pp. 105–28.

# 8

MARILYNN DESMOND

# Christine de Pizan: gender, authorship and life-writing

The literary corpus of Christine de Pizan ($c.1363–c.1431$) enacts all aspects of authorship as a performance of gender: not only does Christine self-consciously construct a gendered voice within the rhetorical structures of late medieval literary cultures, but this construct changed and evolved during Christine's long and prolific career as a writer. Over the course of almost four decades, Christine produced more than twenty texts in verse and prose in a variety of literary genres, including *ballade* cycles, debate poetry, allegory, epistolary treatises and political tracts, as well as texts such as the *Epistre Othea* that defy generic classification. Her œuvre thus demonstrates not only her mastery but also her transformation of literary forms and traditions. In addition, Christine was extensively involved in the production of manu-scripts of her texts, even to the extent of supervising the layout and visual programmes (illustration, decoration) of her work. In the course of such intensive textual activity, Christine frequently invokes her personal circum-stances in order to situate her literary performances: in autobiographical vignettes and authorial intrusions inserted throughout her work, Christine connects her emergence as a poet in the 1390s to her widowhood. Such comments contextualize her performance as a writer in relation to her expe-riences as a woman. The Christine corpus is consequently animated by a discourse of life-writing that provides a link between her texts and through which she exposes the gendered structures of literary history. In addition, Christine's narrators repeatedly refer to the activities of reading and writing that enable as well as authorize literary production. In several of her longer works, as we shall see, she emphasizes the rhetorical foundations of authorship in order to claim for herself, a late medieval woman, the identity of author.

Though born in Venice, Christine was raised in Paris where her father, Tommaso de Pizzano, was an astrologer in the court of the French king Charles V. Christine was married at the age of fifteen to Etienne de Castel, a notary and royal secretary. By her account, her life and marriage were happy until the sudden death of her husband in 1390 left her solely responsible for her dependent children and her widowed mother. Left on her own at the age of twenty-five after ten years of marriage, she turned to the composition of poetry in fixed forms as a means of support as well as a vehicle for articulating her grief. Yet the conventions of love poetry did not include a language with which she could express her gender-specific experience as a widow. Her first cycle of *ballades*, the *Cent ballades*, juxtaposes the idealizing discourse of love as conventionally formulated in lyric traditions to the feelings of loss she experienced as a widow.[1] Christine transforms the traditional language of love when she speaks as a grieving widow seeking solace in the composition of verse. As she tells it later in the *Advision*, the novelty of her status as a female poet gained considerable attention for these early poems, which in turn brought her patronage. After her initial success with these *ballades*, Christine turned to epistolary rhetoric as a means of developing her voice and literary persona; the literary letter had a venerable history in Latin but was a new arrival, with strong humanist associations, in vernacular literature. In 1399, in the *Epistre au dieu d'amours*, she dramatically stages a critique of Ovid's *Ars amatoria* and Jean de Meun's *Roman de la rose*. The *Epistre au dieu d'amours* is playfully structured as a verse letter dictated by Cupid, the eponymous 'dieu d'amours', to a royal secretary who records Cupid's grievance on behalf of women who claim that they been defamed by these two texts. The *Epistre au dieu d'amours* illustrates Christine's familiarity with the notarial forms of late medieval French court culture while the exhortative mode of the epistle allows her to develop a critique of love and its discourse. Thus within the satiric framework of the *Epistre*, Christine comments on the reception of literary texts from a female perspective.

With the composition of the *Epistre Othea* in 1400, Christine interrogates classical mythography for its sexual politics and thereby acquires the authority of a humanist scholar. Christine invented the figure of Othea to personify wisdom, and the *Epistre Othea* is itself addressed to the Trojan prince Hector; the letter provides the sort of advice found in texts intended for the instruction for princes, the genre known as the *miroir de princes*. In each of the 100 chapters that constitute the *Epistre Othea*, the text of the epistle – a short verse in Othea's voice – is followed by two prose segments in Christine's authorial voice, each segment marked as *glose* and *allegorie*. The *Epistre Othea* is the most intensively illustrated of all of Christine's works, and the two luxury editions of the *Epistre Othea* produced in the early fifteenth century include a finely wrought image as the central component of each chapter. In these two manuscripts – BL, Harley 4431 and BnF, fr. 606 – the images carry a significant portion of the meaning of each unit of the mythological narrative. In Harley 4431, the visual programme includes an eloquent representation of Christine's authorial status in the *Othea*. Chapter 7, on the goddess Venus, forms part of a sequence on the 'children of the planets', a textual and visual representation of pagan deities and the nature of their power over mortals.[2] In the Harley image (Figure 7), Venus occupies the top portion of the miniature: she is seated on a cloud in the sky with a garland of hearts in her lap. Below her a group of mortals who are followers of Venus hold hearts in their hands as a manifestation of their dedication to the goddess of love. Christine herself stands in the foreground of the image just below the goddess; her figure is recognizable from the presentation miniature at the start of the *Othea*. While she gestures with her right hand towards the goddess above her, with her left hand she clasps a heart close to her chest, as though she refuses to dedicate herself to Venus and the amatory values embodied by the goddess. By contrast, most of the other mortals hold their hearts up towards Venus, as though they are completely enthralled by her. The *texte* reinforces such a cautionary approach to Venus when Othea directs Hector to avoid becoming indentured to Venus: 'De Venus ne fais ta deesse, / ne te chaille de sa promesse' (7. 6–7: 'Do not make Venus your goddess; have no thought for her promise'). The *glose* and the *allegorie* also warn Hector not to make Venus his goddess. This pictorial depiction of Christine in an expository rather than amorous role suggests that she saw the *Othea* as the text that marked her transition from love poet to vernacular humanist; indeed, this image of Christine offers a pictorial version of the various authorial intrusions found throughout her œuvre.

Soon after completing the *Othea*, Christine participated in an epistolary debate, the *Querelle de la Rose*, on the ethics of reading Jean de Meun's section of the *Roman de la rose*. Christine adopts a bureaucratic persona in the three prose letters she composed in the course of the *Querelle*. Unlike the playful use of epistolary rhetoric in the *Epistre au dieu d'amours*, the letters in the *Querelle* adopt a serious tone: each letter, signed by Christine, articulates a sustained critique of the issues posed by the *Roman de la rose*.[3] Christine entered the debate in the summer of 1401 when she wrote to Jean de Montrueil, provost of Lille, to criticize a treatise he had circulated in praise of Jean de Meun; in this letter she identifies several issues regarding the social implications of reading the *Rose*. She later expanded and developed these arguments in letters she sent to Gontier Col and Pierre Col, both of them royal secretaries. These letters specifically address the possibility that some individuals might read the *Rose* as a text that authorizes violence against women. The letters in the *Querelle* follow the rhetorical formulas of the *ars dictaminis* which require that a letter emphasize the rank and status of the letter writer in relation to the addressee. Given her late husband's career, Christine was familiar with the epistolographic practices of the day; as a woman, however, she was excluded by her gender from occupying any

Figure 7. Venus and her children, Harley 4431, fo. 100r.

clerical office. Epistolary rhetoric required that the salutation of each of her letters acknowledge her lack of position in relation to the authoritative status of her male interlocutors, all of whom were members of the clerical elite. Nevertheless, rhetoricians considered letter-writing to be an adversarial performance, and Christine's contributions to the *Querelle* are notable for their oppositional if not aggressive arguments, despite the social inequality between sender and addressee. In the course of the *Querelle*, Christine cultivates a voice that is simultaneously self-effacing yet highly confident in its pointed criticism of Jean de Meun's text. The rhetoric of critique that Christine developed in these letters proved to be formative for her performance as an author.

Having occupied such an adversarial role within the rhetorical structure of a literary debate, Christine proceeded to compose several dream allegories, initially in verse, then later in prose. The conventions of the dream allegory allowed Christine to articulate how the activities of reading and writing are shaped by – and responsive to – the experiences of gendered embodiment. In the *Livre du chemin de long estude* (1403), Christine-the-dreamer begins by voicing a detailed complaint against Fortune for the death of her husband which had plunged her into thirteen years of mourning. Given the solitary nature of grief, she describes how she withdrew to her study to search for a book which might speak to her emotional state. Towards the end of the day, she turns to Boethius's *Consolation of Philosophy*, a Latin dream vision from the sixth century in which Lady Philosophy appears to Boethius the dreamer/narrator and consoles him for having been expelled from the Roman senate and imprisoned under threat of death. Since the grammatical gender of Latin required that *philosophia*, an abstract noun, be personified as a woman, the *Consolation* enacts a gendered dynamic in which a wise woman instructs a disconsolate and dispossessed man. The *Consolation* had been widely read throughout the medieval period, and by Christine's day it had been repeatedly translated into the vernacular. By depicting herself as a reader of Boethius, whose 'book [she] loved very much' (203: 'Un livre que moult amay'), Christine aligns herself with the masculine philosophical tradition and the world of learning. When she had read the *Consolation* late into the night, Christine reports that she experienced some comfort for her own sorrows, but as she falls into a trance, she contemplates the prevalence of conflict, war, and corruption throughout the world. The Cumaean Sybil, a figure drawn from the classical tradition, appears to Christine and together they embark on a 'chemin de long estude', a path of long study, which takes Christine through the known world as far as the earthly paradise and into the celestial kingdom in search of the sort of wisdom that might answer the world's ills. The text concludes when Christine, having witnessed the decision that the court of France should select a world emperor, is awakened in the morning by her mother's knocking on her bedroom door.

Soon after completing the *Chemin de long estude*, Christine began the *Livre de la mutacion de Fortune* (1403), a long verse narrative on Fortune and historical transformation. In this text, Christine programmatically addresses issues of gender and authorship. At the start of the *Mutacion de Fortune*, Christine-the-narrator states that she speaks as a man:

> Mais, pour mieulx donner a entendre
> la fin du procés ou vueil tendre,
> vous diray qui je suis, qui parle,
> qui de femelle devins masle
> par Fortune, qu'ainsy le voult;
> si me mua et corps et voult
> en homme naturel parfaict;
> et jadis fus femme, de fait
> homme suis, je ne ment pas.                    (139–47)

(But in order to better explain the purpose of this process, I will tell you who I am, who speaks, who from female became male by Fortune, who willed it so; she changed me, both body and face into a perfect, natural man; while I was formerly a woman, I am in reality a man. I do not lie.)

Following this declaration, the first part of the *Mutacion de Fortune* narrates Christine's life from her birth through her upbringing and marriage until the death of her husband. Christine appeals to the notion of bodily transformations derived from Ovid's *Metamorphoses* in order to justify her emphasis on the corporeal effects of Fortune's changes.[4] Christine first complains that, having been born a daughter, she was not in a position to inherit her father's 'wealth' (knowledge and learning), and that Fortune instead sent her by ship to the court of Hymen. Christine then structures her account of her happy marriage through the metaphor of a ship at sea. She depicts her husband's death as his falling overboard; at the point that Christine has to take control of the ship, Fortune brings about her physical transformation and provides her with the body of a man. This transformation has all the corporeal emphasis of Ovid's *Metamorphoses* when she describes the changes that masculinity brought to her physical form: 'Estoit muee et enforcie / et ma voix forment engrossie / et corps plus dur et plus isnel' (1349–51: 'I was changed and become stronger, and my voice grew deeper, and my body harder and more agile'). Towards the end of this section, she notes that she has been a man for more than thirteen years. The rest of the *Mutacion* develops a long Boethian meditation on Fortune which envelops her account of her personal misfortunes within a larger paradigm of universal history and concludes with a commentary on contemporary events in her own time. The framework of universal history depends on genealogical narratives of lineage that organize a vision of the past in monumental terms. The *Mutacion de Fortune* implies that only a man would be fitted to such a task, yet Christine's status as a widow, through which she has acquired the strength of a man, has equipped her for the monumental task of historical writing.

The *Livre de la cité des dames* (1405) marks a distinct shift in the concept of authorship as developed in the *Mutacion de Fortune*. The role of the reader structures the *Cité des dames*, a prose allegory that depicts the construction of a walled city built to house and protect the mythical, historical and religious women excluded from conventional structures of history found in the *Mutacion de Fortune*. Unlike the authorial moment in the *Mutacion de Fortune* that prompts Christine to describe her transformation into a man, the *Cité des dames* opens with a scene of reading that emphasizes the bodily status of the author as a female. Christine describes how she searched among her books for some light reading that might offer some diversion at the end of a day spent in serious study. She picks up a book she identifies as Matheolus's *Lamentations*, a text she has heard to be favorable towards women. The *Lamentations*, however, is an especially virulent example of clerical misogyny, a Latin genre intended to discourage clerks from marriage by recounting stories that depict women as dangerous and evil. The Latin text of the *Lamentations* had been translated into French verse by Jean le Fèvre in the fourteenth century, and then further expanded by Jean into the *Livre de leesce*, a version of the *Lamentations* which juxtaposes Matheolus's anti-feminist *exempla* to counter-arguments in favour of women. From Christine's description of the text in question, it would appear that she has mistaken Jean le Fèvre's translation of the *Lamentations* for the *Livre de leesce*. Struck by the vicious tone of the *Lamentations*, Christine begins to question the prevalence of misogyny in textual traditions as a whole: 'Mais la veue de ycellui dit livre, tout soit il de nulle auctorité, ot engendré en moy nouvelle pensee … que tant de divers hommes, clercs et autres, ont esté et sont si enclins a dire de bouche et en leur traictiez et escrips tant de deableries et de vituperes de femmes et de leurs condicions' (42: 'But the sight of this book, even if it had no authority, made me wonder … why so many different sorts of men, clercs and others, have spoken and continue to hold forth and to write in treatises and texts so many diabolical things and slanders against women and their condition'). As a woman reading a text that depicts women as the root of all evil, Christine-the-narrator succumbs to depression and despair. Though she notes that her own experience does not coincide with the depiction of women in the mis-ogynist tradition represented by Matheolus's *Lamentations*, the narrator of the *Cité des dames* nonetheless finds herself enveloped by self-loathing, as though it is her experience as a reader that definitively constructs her as female: 'par ma foulour me tenoie tres malcontente de ce que en corps feminin m'ot fait Dieux estre au monde' (46: 'in my folly, I thought myself to be extremely discontented that God placed me in a female body in this world').

While the *Mutacion de Fortune* suggests that her social status as a widow allows Christine to assume masculine agency, the act of reading depicted in the *Cité des dames* inescapably returns her to a state of gendered embodiment, even when she questions the authority of the text she reads. If texts such as Matheolus's *Lamentations* argue that the female body is vile and monstrous, the allegory of the *Cité des dames* addresses itself to rewriting the discourse of the monstrous feminine so that the implied female reader of the *Cité des dames* might experience a less disabling form of female embodiment. To this end, Christine's text allegorically constructs a walled city that itself represents a contemporary ideal of urban protection, since the Hundred Years' War had forced extensive encastellation of cities in order to provide protection against the English invasions. In each of the three books of the *Cité des dames* Christine engages in dialogue with one of three female personifications – Raison, Droiture, and Justice (Reason, Rectitude, and Justice) – who retells the biographies of ancient, historical, and religious women. The first two books present the life stories of women from classical myth and history. These biographies are arranged and revised, often subtly, so that each woman's life exemplifies a positive trait that might be found in women, despite what misogynists such as Matheolus claim. In the course of the allegory, femininity becomes associated with virtues such as constancy, fidelity, and chastity, in direct contradiction to the misogynist conflation of femininity with vice. In the third book of the *Cité des dames*, Justice narrates a series of female saints' lives. These hagiographic anecdotes explicitly depict women in all their corporeal vulnerability since each saint's devotion to God allows her to endure and to triumph over torture and the threat of rape; the female body renders these women transcendent rather than monstrous. The *Cité des dames* exploits hagiography as a genre of life-writing that has the potential to model an enabling form of embodiment for its female readers. Since the saints will join the pre-Christian women in the city of ladies, the hagiographical discourse of the third book marks the culmination of the rhetorical aims of all three books.

The *Cité des dames* creates a vision of female embodiment beyond the constraints of the anti-feminist tradition. After completing the *Cité des dames*, Christine composed a conduct book for women, the *Livre des trois vertus* (1405), also known as the *Trésor de la cité des dames*. In the *Trois vertus*, Raison, Droiture, and Justice appear once again to Christine and demand that she record their instructions so that contemporary women might be able to cultivate the same virtues exhibited by the women invited into the *cité des dames*. As a didactic sequel to the *Cité des dames*, the *Trois vertus* assumes that women who read these allegories will be able to perform a socially and religiously sanctioned version of feminity. In the first book of the *Trois vertus*, Raison emphasizes that reading has ethical implications for women when she advises that a princess will only read 'livres d'enseignemens de bonnes meurs et aucunes fois de devocion, et ceulx de deshonnesteté et de lubrece herra perfaictement et ne les vouldra avoir a sa court' (45–6: 'books of instruction on good morals, and occasionally books of devotion; she will have a complete aversion to those about indecency and lewdness and not wish to have them in her court'). Unlike misogynous texts such as Matheolus's *Lamentations*, the books described here are potentially enabling for the female reader. Whereas the sequence of exemplary lives narrated in the *Cité des dames* might alleviate the paralysing depression that overcomes Christine-the-narrator when she encounters the misogynist tradition, the carefully detailed instructions in the *Trois vertus* are designed to elicit particular female bodily practices from its readership; women who perform their gender according to these precepts will disprove the anti-feminist rhetoric perpetrated by misogynist clerks.

The various allegorical and autobiographical threads that run throughout these works all culminate in the *Livre de l'advision Cristine*, a dream vision in prose completed in 1405. In the *Advision*, Christine succinctly juxtaposes a commentary on the contemporary political situation to her own biography. The first book of the *Advision* opens with 'Cristine's' dream that her spirit has left her body and encounters an apparition of Chaos; along with all other earthly bodies, 'Cristine' is swallowed into the belly of Chaos. During her descent she meets a crowned lady who describes the current political crises in France. In book 2 'Cristine' travels to Athens where she meets and speaks to Dame Opinion, and in the final book, 'Cristine' finds herself in the presence of Lady Philosophy, to whom she narrates her life story. The third book of the *Advision* offers the most developed account of life-writing to appear in the corpus of Christine de Pizan. As we have seen, Christine had already included an autobiographical outline in the *Mutacion de fortune* and the *Chemin de long estude*; the version in the *Advision*, however, includes more details and anecdotes that flesh out the basic facts of marriage, widowhood, and writing. The presence of Lady Philosophy in the *Advision* pointedly elicits a discourse of life-writing shaped by Boethian categories of biography, according to which the experience of misfortune is crucial, since it teaches human beings not to care for worldly affairs. In such a context, 'Cristine' dwells on her widowhood as the definitive misfortune of her life. Philosophy, however, tells 'Cristine' that she should not continue to blame Fortune for the direction of her life, since it was only through becoming a widow that she could have pursued a life of study. Indeed, Philosophy insists that the pursuit of letters offers consolation for the loss of her husband:

> A ton propos il n'est mie doubte que, se ton mary t'eust duré jusques a ore, l'estude tant comme tu as n'eusses frequenté, car occupacion de mainage ne le t'eust souffert ... Donc ne te dois tu pas tenir pour meseuree quant tu as entre les autres / biens une des choses du monde qui plus te delicte et te plaist a avoir, c'est assavoir le doulx goust de science.                    (3.18; p. 123)

> (By your account there is no doubt that, if your husband were still alive, you could not be as dedicated to study as you are, because your domestic duties would not allow it ... Thus you should not consider yourself unfortunate that you have among other goods one of the things in the world that it most delights you to possess, namely, the sweet taste of learning.)

Whereas in the *Consolation*, Philosophy ultimately persuades Boethius not to care for the things of this world – among them, the rewards he has received from the life of letters – so that he might reconcile the philosophical concepts of fate and predestination, 'Cristine' eventually eschews the abstract consolations offered by Philosophy in the *Consolation* and settles instead for the more mundane consolations represented by a life of letters. As a record of her achievements in the pursuit of learning, 'Cristine' states that she has produced fifteen major works filling seventy quires since she first took up her pen. By staging 'Cristine's' epiphany regarding her widowhood and writing in the *Advision*, Christine de Pizan claims an authorial identity that might transcend her gender: in the *Advision* she definitively achieves an authorial stature, and after completing the *Advision*, she does not engage in any further life-writing, although she frequently attends to issues of gender as a category. The trajectory of Christine's career thus suggests that life-writing was necessary for her to establish her credentials and authority as an author.

Over the course of the next decade, Christine produced a series of prose treatises and epistles intended to address the increasingly volatile political situation of her day. As the conflict with England began again to threaten life in Paris, and the disputes within the royal family began to erupt into civil war between the Burgundians and the Armagnacs, Christine's texts became more directly concerned with these ongoing crises. In the *Livre du corps de policie*, a prose treatise completed by 1407, Christine adopts the metaphor of the body politic from Plutarch to argue for good governance on the part of the ruling elite, strict observance of chivalric values on the part of the nobility, and loyal obedience on the part of the common people. While the *Cité des dames* evoked the walled city as a metaphorical space that might offer protection to women whose bodies made them particularly vulnerable, the *Corps de policie* relies on the notion of the polity as a 'living body' ('un droit corps vif')[5] whose health depends on all the classes functioning together. If the 'body politic' is not specifically gendered in the *Corps de policie*, the author's body is foregrounded when the narrator declares that she is speaking as a passionate woman ('bien me plaist en ceste partie estre passionnee comme femme') whose heart overflows with the desire for virtue ('fontaine interissable de mon couraige qui ne peut estancher de getter hors les desirs de vertu'). Christine adopts a similar rhetorical stance in the *Livre des fais d'armes et de chevalerie* (1410), a prose treatise on the ethics of warfare, when she invokes Minerva: 'Dame et haulte deesse, ne te desplaise ce que moy, simple femmelette ... ose presentement emprendre a parler de sy magnifie office comme est celuy des armes' ('Lady and high goddess, may it not displease you that I, a simple, little woman, dare now to undertake to speak about such a great office as that of arms').[6] In the *Fais d'armes*, Christine distils received wisdom on military strategy and the conduct of war from ancient and contemporary texts for the benefit of knights who might lack such learning. Although as a woman and a non-combatant she lacked any first-hand knowledge of war, she nonetheless speaks authoritatively on all aspects of military activity, so that the *Fais d'armes* demonstrates her conviction that through learning and study she is able to overcome the customary limitations on gender and authorship. While Christine continued to write lyric poetry on courtly themes as well as devotional poetry during this time, the tone of her prose treatises becomes increasingly urgent. In the *Lamentacion sur les maux de la guerre civile* (1410), she urges the women of France to cry out for reconciliation between the two sides of the civil conflict, since the 'swords that will make you widows and deprive you of your children and kin have already been sharpened!' ('ja sont aguisiez les glaives qui vous rendront veufves et desnuees d'enfans et de parens!').[7] In the *Livre de la paix* (1415), she is equally eloquent in calling for a truce between the Burgundians and the Armagnacs. However, after the French defeat at Agincourt in 1415, she appears to lose any hope for peace, and in her letter addressed to Marie de Berry, the *Epistre de la prison de vie humaine* (1418), she offers only words of consolation.[8] At this point, Christine withdrew from Paris and entered an abbey safely outside the city, probably at Poissy where her daughter was a nun.

Christine's retreat from urban life may have removed her from the dangers of war and civil strife, but it also appears to have removed her from the institutions and patrons that sustained her literary activity, and her textual output all but ceases at this point. In 1429, however, when Joan of Arc had managed to lift the siege at Orleans and have Charles VII crowned king, Christine composed a poem in honour of the occasion, the *Ditié de Jehanne d'Arc*. Christine situates herself in the first stanza by reference to the time she has spent in seclusion: 'I, Christine, who have wept for eleven years in a walled abbey' (1–2: 'Je, Christine, qui ay plouré / XI ans en abbaye close'). She extols Joan as a credit to women: 'Hee! quel honneur au femenin / sexe!'(265–6: 'Oh! What honour for the female sex'). She describes Joan as an embodiment of her view that through the cultivation and practice of virtue, women can achieve as much or more than their male counterparts: 'Jamais force ne fu si grant, / Soient ou à cens ou à miles!' (283–4: 'Never did anyone see greater strength, even in hundreds or thousands of men!'). The *Ditié de Jehanne d'Arc* is the final word from Christine, which suggests that she died soon after writing this poem and before she could witness Joan's downfall.

The rhetoric of gender and authorship frames every one of Christine's texts; her authorial performance, however, was equally enabled by the various technologies of textual production in late medieval Paris. Although Christine repeatedly refers to her widowhood as the precondition for her activities as a writer, her authorial self-fashioning depended just as much on access to books, libraries, and scriptoria. Although her gender excluded her from receiving a formal education, Christine apparently had some informal instruction, presumably from her father, since in the *Advision* she speaks of the remnants of Latin she retained from her education as a child. Christine's texts demonstrate that while she possessed some facility with Latin, she nonetheless worked closely with a large number of classical texts in French translation. During his reign (1364–80), Charles V had promoted the translation of Latin texts into French and commissioned a number of manuscripts for an extensive library that formed the basis for the vernacular humanism of late medieval Paris. The proliferation of vernacular versions of classical texts made it possible for a woman like Christine who lacked a formal education to participate fully in the literary cultures of the day. For instance, she knew Aristotle's *Ethics* and *Rhetoric* in Nicole Oresme's translations; Ovid's *Metamorphoses* in the anonymous *Ovide moralisé*; and Virgil's *Aeneid* in the prose compilation of universal history, the *Histoire ancienne jusqu'à César*. In addition, in order to manipulate the patronage system of early fifteenth-century Paris, Christine had to ensure that her texts were produced in luxury manuscripts made to her specifications. As a consequence, Christine was closely involved in the production of her work; such an entrepreneurial approach to book production was crucial to her ability to attract patrons.[9] At the end of the fourteenth century, when Paris was the centre of the European book trade, Parisian workshops appear to have been open to women. Indeed, Christine speaks as though she had direct experience with the book trade: in the *Cité des dames*, she refers to Anastasia, a female artist she had employed, who was known for the high quality of her work. Scholars have even suggested that Christine herself may have worked as a scribe in the first decade of her widowhood.[10] Throughout her work, Christine demonstrates an acute awareness of the visuality of literary texts and the material status of texts as artefacts, an awareness no doubt derived from her supervision of the layout and visual programmes in manuscripts of her work. Thus her success as a female author depended to some degree on the fact that all aspects of the book trade were open to female participation. Christine de Pizan's notable accomplishments as an author testify to the currency of vernacular humanism – which provided her access to texts – as well as the technologies of book production – which enabled her to attract patrons and thereby support herself as a widow. Perhaps because she was female, she appears to be exquisitely attuned to the conditions in the public sphere that allowed her to achieve recognition as an author. In its gendered attention to the material conditions as well as the rhetorical foundations of authorship, the œuvre of Christine de Pizan renders legible the construction of authorship as a cultural category.

## Notes

1. See T. Adams, 'Love as Metaphor in Christine de Pizan's Ballade Cycles', in B. K. Altmann and D. L. McGrady (eds.), *Christine de Pizan: a Casebook* (New York, Routledge, 2003), pp. 149–65.
2. A digitized copy of BL Harley 4431 is being prepared; see www.pizan.lib.ed. ac.uk. See also J. Laidlaw, 'Christine de Pizan: an Author's Progress', *Modern Language Review*, 78 (1983), 532–50.
3. See *Débat*, ed. Hicks.
4. J. L. Kellogg, 'Transforming Ovid: the Metamorphosis of Female Authority', in M. Desmond (ed.), *Christine de Pizan and the Categories of Difference* (Minneapolis, University of Minnesota Press, 1998), pp. 181–94.
5. *Le Corps de policie*, ed. Kennedy, p. 1.
6. *The Book of Fayttes of Armes and of Chyvalrye*, ed. Byles, p. 8.
7. Cited from *The Epistle of the Prison of Human Life*, ed. Wisman, pp. 86–7.
8. R. Blumenfeld-Kosinski, 'Christine de Pizan and the Political Life in Late Medieval France', in Altmann and McGrady (eds.), *Christine de Pizan: a Casebook*, pp. 9–24.
9. Deborah McGrady, 'What is a Patron? Benefactors and Authorship in Harley 4431, Christine de Pizan's Collected Works', in Desmond (ed.), *Christine de Pizan and the Categories of Difference*, pp. 195–214; J. Laidlaw, 'Christine de Pizan: a Publisher's Progress', *Modern Language Review*, 82 (1987), 35–75.
10. Willard, *Christine de Pizan*, pp. 44–7.

# PART III

# What is the value of genre for medieval French literature?

# 9

KEITH BUSBY

# Narrative genres

The anonymity of much medieval literature has encouraged and facilitated scholarly studies which posit the notional or actual existence of genres in the minds of medieval authors, audiences, and readers on the one hand, and of modern readers on the other. This chapter will not offer a survey of medieval narrative types but rather consider the validity and usefulness of the concept of genre by looking at a number of individual texts from a generic perspective and by weighing certain kinds of evidence regarding the medieval and modern perceptions of generic form. I will concentrate here on verse literature of the twelfth and thirteenth centuries, that is to say, the period traditionally considered Old, as opposed to Middle, French.

There is little doubt that the near-universality of reference to medieval narratives as, for example, epics, romances, *lais*, or *fabliaux*, corresponds both to a modern need to categorize as a means of accessing texts and to shared features that appear to signal generic distinctions. One question that has therefore received much attention is whether the modern perception of genres corresponds to a conscious effort on the part of medieval authors to compose texts their audiences would recognize as belonging to a category, and if so, how strictly defined those categories were. Without actually being a red herring, this question has sometimes proven as obstructive as constructive, and efforts to define genres have often obscured and even sacrificed the qualities of individual texts by attempting to impose conformity on a motley corpus. That said, the very existence of terms such as *geste, roman, lai, fablel (fabliau), dit, conte,* and so on, attests to an awareness on the part of medieval authors and audiences of both similarity and difference between types of narrative.[1] The problem is that the more precisely one defines such terms, the more resistant texts seem to the definition, while conversely, all-inclusive definitions tend to be so vague as to be of limited interest and use. The much used definition of the *fabliaux* as 'des contes à rire en vers' by one of the founding fathers of medieval studies, Joseph Bédier, is a case in point: incontrovertible, but unhelpful beyond a certain basic point.[2] The approaches to medieval narrative that have been most useful are those developed by Hans-Robert Jauss and Paul Zumthor (see Introduction for their concepts of 'horizon of expectation' and 'register'), but by situating each text in the wider context of an interlocking genre system they become essentially intertextual in nature.

It is important to stress that, whatever the status of the idea of genre in the Middle Ages, the kinds of narratives we refer to as, say, epic, romance, or saint's life, evolve across the medieval centuries. A late twelfth-century *chanson de geste* or Arthurian romance may be quite different to one written in 1250 or 1350. Moreover, the later medieval reception of early texts can be conditioned by the nature of more recent examples just as the latter build selectively on earlier traditions. A monolithic vision of 'the Middle Ages' carries with it the danger of distortion and should at least be treated with caution. While the Jauss–Zumthor model has become a handy and largely uncontroversial means of approaching the question of genres, subsequent decades have restored a human dimension. The horizon of expectation is manipulated by authors; texts do not just move, they are prodded and pushed.

Literary terminology in medieval texts themselves can be useful, but usage is inconsistent and the semantic fields of *roman* (originally meaning just 'vernacular') or *dit* ('a telling'), for example, are wide-ranging. Reliance on medieval terms works relatively well for the *lai* and the *fabliau*, provided account is taken of the constantly changing meanings of the Old French terms.[3] The meaning of '*fabliau*' is, however, complicated by the derivation of the word as a diminutive of the Latin *fabula*, which in both its Latin and Old French manifestations often means little more than a tale or fiction; significantly, the Aesopic fable collection is generally referred to in Old French as an *Ysopet*. Moreover the *lai* (discussed below) assumes several forms in the Middle Ages, from the *lai breton* strictly defined (which adapts Celtic material into French octosyllabic rhyming couplets) through the *lai lyrique* (mainly lyric pieces inserted in prose romances) of the later period. The most successful attempts to define genres have been, not surprisingly perhaps, those based on a shared subject matter: *chanson de geste*, Arthurian romance, and hagiography (with a long Latin tradition), for example. Such attempts have a late twelfth-century precedent in Jean Bodel's celebrated observations about the three *matières*, of Britain, Rome, and France, in his *Chanson des Saisnes*, where they are attributed specific purposes: to simplify, Arthurian entertainment, classical edification, and French history.[4] On the other hand, recent studies which define *dits* and *voies de l'au-delà* (in which a living person journeys into the world of the afterlife) as genres from the perspective of content fail to establish much more than some thematic links and subject matter shared by a disparate corpus of texts.[5]

Ultimately, the purpose of thinking about genre and questioning narrative texts as to their generic affiliation must be to enable modern readers to situate them in their medieval textual context and to make them reveal by comparison significant details about their form and meaning. Like the study of medieval vernacular literary terminology, genre study can be both synchronic and diachronic, and compare genres, not simply examples of what are deemed to belong to the same category. The *idée reçue* that epic is simply older than romance and that its audience is a predominantly masculine feudal one when compared with the mixed courtly audience of the other genre has been contested, for example.[6] Thus even if epic may have a chronological priority over romance, within a few decades, examples of both were being composed simultaneously and copied alongside each other in the same manuscripts, intended for the same audience and readership.

Thus preconceptions of genre can be misleading and obscure that which generic study ought to reveal. The elevation of a particular text as the paradigm of a particular genre is suspect and reveals as much about the aesthetics of literary and philological scholarship as it does about the medieval text itself. Some texts may be foundational, but they are not typical or representative. The paradigm of romance as learned from reading Chrétien can be a serious hindrance to an appreciation of other texts designated by scholars as romances, such as Béroul's *Tristan*, entitled variously as *Le Roman de Tristan* by Muret-Defourques and *The Romance of Tristran* by Alfred Ewert.[7] One looks in vain for many of the qualities prized in a Chrétien romance (say, quest structure or psychological character development), and the text can remain a puzzle until it is seen as a confluence of many kinds of narratives: romance, epic, and *fabliau* foremost among them.[8] For example, the love triangle of Mark–Tristan–Iseut, in some ways 'courtly', and the catalyst for most of the events in the narrative, is related in Béroul by a partisan narrator, familiar from the *chanson de geste*; the traitorous barons are also figures of the an epic cycle known as the *barons révoltés*. Repeated laments and frequent expressions of intense emotion add a lyric dimension, while the episode at the ford, with the leper's offer to take Iseut as a communal mistress for himself and his companions, is redolent of the *fabliau*; Tristan's encounter with the leper leader (curiously named 'Ivain') in this scene can be viewed as a parody of single combat from epic poetry. Consequently, the lexis of Béroul's poem shifts from the courtly to the popular in conformity with the various intertexts it evokes. It is remarkable that, until the appearance in 1980 of Beate Schmolke-Hasselmann's study of Arthurian verse romances composed in the wake of Chrétien de Troyes, works such as Raoul de Houdenc's *Meraugis de Portlesguez* were mainly read by odious comparison with Chrétien.[9] The same is true of the judgement of, say, *Renaut de Montauban*, by the standards of *La Chanson de Roland*.

In many ways, the Old French epic is more easily describable than romance, since the latter term is used to designate a more widely disparate range of texts. It is relatively easy to put together a broad description – rather than definition – of these poems based on a reading of the extant corpus. But even here, a broad-brush generic description is likely to contain elements that are not found in, or are contradicted by, individual *chansons de geste*. More can probably be learned by examining works traditionally deemed by scholars as difficult to classify than by confirming the affiliation of less problematic texts. Consequently, two works will now be considered which are generally discussed as *chansons de geste* but which raise interesting intertextual issues: *Ami et Amile* and *Huon de Bordeaux*.

The version of *Ami* considered here is preserved in Paris, BnF, fr. 860 (second half of the thirteenth century), where it is the third of five *chansons de geste*: *La Chanson de Roland*, *Gaydon*, *Ami et Amile*, *Jourdain de Blaye*, and *Auberi le Bourguignon*. The manuscript context is clear: by the middle of the thirteenth century, and probably earlier, these poems were seen as being of a kind. Modern scholarship, however, has not treated them with equal respect and attention. The Paris text of the *Roland* has suffered at the expense of the Oxford version, *Gaydon* has been consigned to the category of 'late and degenerate epic', *Jourdain de Blaye* seen as the sequel to *Ami et Amile* and second part of 'la petite geste de Blaye', and *Auberi le Bourguignon* almost entirely neglected, in part no doubt because of its length (about 26,000 lines). It is significant that while *Ami et Amile*'s most recent editor, Peter F. Dembowski, calls the poem a *chanson de geste* on his title page, his brief discussion of the literary aspects of the work distinguishes two basic versions of the story, one *romanesque* (that is to say romance-like), the other hagiographical. Despite the hagiographical elements indicated below, the version in BnF, fr. 860 belongs to Dembowski's *romanesque* group. Nowhere is the poem discussed as a *chanson de geste*, although its manuscript context, amongst other things, identifies it as such. In a sense, this terminological issue illustrates well the way in which a narrative text can move between recognized types and defy precise categorization.

The two eponymous heroes of *Ami et Amile* are members of the French aristocracy who enter Charlemagne's service. A traitor, Hardré, becomes jealous and conspires against them. A truce is established, as part of which Ami marries Hardré's niece, Lubias, from which union is born a son, Girart. The internecine struggles, a few scenes of single and collective combat, and the presence of Roland's sword, are all redolent of the *chanson de geste*. Yet it is the melding of these epic features with others more properly character-istic of, say, romance and hagiography, which defines *Ami et Amile*.

The simultaneous conception and birth of the two main protagonists have something of the prophetic about them, while the appearances of admonitory angels and the role of the Pope as godfather to both link the poem to hagiography and the miracle tale. An unusual element is the generally disastrous marriage of Ami and Lubias, in which the latter functions both as a female member of a lineage of traitors and as an obstacle to Ami and Amile's companionship. The *in flagrante* entrapment of Belissant and Amile by Hardré and the denunciation to Charlemagne appear as variants of episodes from the Tristan or Lancelot stories with overtones of the *fabliaux*; the sword Amile places between himself and his wife also recalls the Tristan romances. The physical resemblance between the two heroes permits the use of disguise and mistaken identity, more typical of romance than of epic, while the goblets given by the Pope enable Amile to recognize Ami, disfigured by leprosy. Ami's miraculous cure by bathing in the blood of Amile's sacrificed children (subsequently restored to life) is strongly redolent of hagiography, as are the heroes' final pilgrimage to Jerusalem and entombment at Mortara. Metrically and stylistically, the poem bears the characteristics of a *chanson de geste*, being written in *laisses* of assonating decasyllables with a hexasyllabic final line (or '*vers orphelin*') in each *laisse*; it favours parataxis, and frequent appeals to a listening audience anchor the poem in the Old French epic tradition, while its lexis corresponds to the shifting generic affiliations noted above. Thus does *Ami et Amile* move on the horizons of expectation of its audience.

The long *chanson de geste* of *Huon de Bordeaux* (10,553 assonating decasyllables), probably composed sometime between 1216 and 1229, shows generic intertextuality of another kind. Like *Ami et Amile*, *Huon de Bordeaux* is usually classed as an epic in histories of Old French literature, but its associations with romance, particularly by virtue of marked supernatural elements, are so clear as to be perhaps the one aspect upon which most scholars agree. Indeed, the opening *laisse* makes its hybridity evident:

> Segnour, oiiés – ke Jhesus bien vous fache,
> li glorieus ki nous fist a s'ymage ! –
> boine canchon estraite del lignaige
> de Charlemaine a l'aduré coraige,
> et de Huon ki tant ot vaselaige,
> et d'Auberon, le petit roi sauvaige
> que tout son tans conversa en boscage.
> Chil Auberons que tant ot segnoraige,
> sachiés k'il fu fieus Juliien Cesare
> qui tint Hungrie, une tere sauvaige,
> et Osteriche et trestout l'iretaige.
> Coustantinoble tint il tot son eaige;
> set lius grans fist faire de muraige

qui encor durent, desc'a le mer salvaige.
Jules ot feme, une dame moult sage;
Morge ot a non, moult ot cler le visaige;
cele fu mere Auberon le sauvaige,
si n'ot plus d'oirs en trestot son eaige.                    (1–18)

(Lords – may Jesus, the glorious one who made us in his image, treat you well –, listen to a good song of the lineage of brave Charlemagne, of Huon so valiant, and of Auberon the wild little king who always frequented the woods. You should know that this powerful Auberon was the son of that Julius Caesar who ruled over Hungary, an untamed country, and Austria and all its dependencies. He also held Constantinople during his lifetime; he had walls built which still exist, seven leagues long, as far as the wild sea. Julius had a wife, a very wise lady; her name was Morgan, radiant-faced; she was the mother of Auberon the wild. Caesar never had any other heirs.)

The fantastic lineage of Auberon, which supplants Calpurnia by Morgan Le Fey as wife of Caesar, would surely have provoked astonishment in the thirteenth century, and anchors the poem in both the classical and Arthurian traditions as well as in an early Austro-Hungarian empire and Byzantium. The Carolingian underpinnings and the identification of the hero as a son of Seguin, duke of Bordeaux, add (pseudo-)historical contexts which complete the covering of most narrative bases: indeed there were several dukes of Bordeaux named Seguin and curiously, the first assumed the title in 778, date of the battle of Roncevaux.

The types of secular narrative which coalesce in *Huon de Bordeaux* are distinguished one from another primarily by subject matter. It brings together Jean Bodel's three *matières*, showing that Bodel's words are not to be taken as gospel. Even before this, authors such as Chrétien de Troyes were using Arthurian legend for courtly didactic purposes; but *Huon* goes further in breaking down the barriers that Bodel was setting up. The struggle between the lineage of the dukes of Bordeaux and Charlemagne mark the poem as an epic of rebel vassals. Up to the point where Huon kills Amauri in judicial combat, the narrative indeed conforms to the pattern of the rebel epic, but it is with the expiatory tasks imposed on Huon by Charlemagne that the *chanson de geste* begins to move in other directions. Visiting the emir of Babylon, slitting the throat of the first dinner guest he meets, kissing three times the emir's daughter, Esclamonde, are all tasks reminiscent of the hero's deeds in a folktale, as is the obligation to demand the emir's moustaches and four of his teeth. The eastward travels of Huon, which take him to Rome, Brindisi, the Holy Land, and the reign of 'Femenie', are strongly evocative of pilgrimage literature, the Crusade cycle of epics, and *Le roman d'Alexandre*, among other genres, but the most striking and original feature of *Huon de Bordeaux* is the appearance of the diminutive fairy king, Auberon.

The phantasmagoric appearance and disappearance of Auberon, his unerring bow, magic horn and goblet, supernatural abilities, and fairy lineage, are the stuff of romance, although a token effort is made to give them a Christian colouring. Auberon's horn recalls *La Chanson de Roland*, while the storm it generates and the interdictions governing its use make it paradigmatic of the intersection between *chanson de geste* and Arthurian romance. The mysterious forest and castle setting of this central section of *Huon de Bordeaux* is also that of romance, even if the guide's parting of the river with a golden rod is obviously modelled on events from Exodus. Further examples from *Huon* could be multiplied: Caesar's castle of Dunostre with its copper guardians, forty headless corpses, a damsel held captive by a giant, Orgueilleux, a magic hauberk and gold ring; Malabron, the sea-monster, mounted on which Huon crosses the Red Sea; a fountain of youth guarded by a serpent.

The love relationship between Huon and Esclamonde and the idea that the former is atoning for his errors relates the text more to the kind of romance permeated by the courtly love ideal (say, Chrétien's *Erec et Enide* or *Yvain*, which the author of *Huon de Bordeaux* certainly knew) while the fast-paced series of combats, emprisonments, escapes, and rescues suggests an ill-defined category that scholars have dubbed *roman d'aventures*. All this, together with the supernatural, the Arthurian, and the classical is woven – rather successfully – into the framework of a *chanson de geste*, and specifically the local epic of rebellion and family disputes. For long sections of the poem the *merveilleux* is absent, but the conclusion is significant. Just as the author opened the poem with his statement about Charlemagne, Huon, Auberon, Caesar, and Morgan le Fey, so he ends by restating Auberon's parentage and completing the integration of epic and romance by making of Huon Auberon's heir apparent. The opening and closing passages of *Huon de Bordeaux* suggest a stronger authorial hand at work directing operations than in, say, *Ami et Amile*. If *Ami* has more of a typical epic narrator who hides behind his material, the author of *Huon de Bordeaux*, through the interventions of his narrator prods and pushes his poem in different directions, creating its rich intertextual links with the Old French genre system.

One other aspect of *Huon de Bordeaux* relevant to the perception of genres is the creation of a cycle by means of posterior additions or continuations which take their cue from the original work. Many *chansons de geste* occur in cyclical manuscripts (Guillaume d'Orange cycle, Loherain cycle, Crusade cycle) as do the Alexander romances. Whether a cycle is formed by posterior additions to a base work (sometimes unfinished) or by the accretion and reworking of already existing and originally independent poems, it has consequences for the reading of each constituent element. This is particularly important for the interpretation of characters' actions and for the analysis of narrative structure, as frequent intratextual allusions refer back and forth to the different parts of the cycle, duly expanding narrative time and space (cf. the evolution of the Vulgate cycle discussed in Chapter 2).

Romances demonstrate the same tendency to absorb elements from other narrative types. A clear example is *Eracle* by Gautier d'Arras (between 1176 and 1184), a romance of 6568 octosyllables dedicated to Count Thibaut of Blois. Gautier d'Arras is significant both in his own right and as a contemporary of Chrétien de Troyes, with whom he has often been contrasted as an author who seems to eschew the Arthurian *merveilleux* in favour of more realistic subject matter and treatment. This may be more evident in Gautier's other romance, *Ille et Galeron*, for *Eracle* can best be described as a 'hagiographical romance'. As such, it makes interesting comparative material for *Ami et Amile*. The opening of the poem builds curiously on both saint's life and *fabliau*. Initially, the angel's announcement to Mirïados and Cassine of the impending conception of Eracle, his birth, and prodigious childhood, is the material of hagiography. However, at his second appearance, the angel hands over a letter from God which explains that Eracle has been endowed with three gifts: the knowledge of precious stones, horses, and women. The potential for *fabliau*-type humour here is evident. Cassine sells her son to the emperor's seneschal and retires to a convent. The second part of the poem, clearly marked as such by a narrator's intervention, relates the infidelity of the Roman empress, Athanaïs, with her lover, Paridès. Her imprisonment in a tower by a jealous husband is a motif of lyric poetry, while the assignations in the old woman's cellar and discovery by Laïs once more evoke the *fabliaux*. The poem's final part, also clearly marked, turns back towards hagiographical legend with the story of Chosroès and the True Cross.

These texts which seem to resist or undermine classification by genre are perhaps extreme examples, but exemplary of the situation nonetheless. Neither *Ami et Amile*, nor *Huon de Bordeaux*, nor *Eracle* belong to the canon of Old French texts frequently prescribed and studied in universities although *Aucassin et Nicolette* (early thirteenth-century) has long been favoured by scholars and students because of its brevity, humour, and general accessibility. Unlike the three texts discussed above, however, *Aucassin et Nicolette* does not have a basic affiliation to a recognized genre such as *chanson de geste* or romance, being the unique example of a self-designated *chantefable*, and consequently free of generic 'clutter' (for definition and discussion see Chapter 11). *Aucassin et Nicolette* is thus formed by a confluence of elements scholars have deemed characteristic of various types of narrative and lyric literature. The other primary difference between *Aucassin et Nicolette* and the texts discussed so far in this chapter is that its dominant mode is parodic and burlesque. This makes it an excellent text for introducing the established major narrative and lyric genres. Its unique alternation of verse and prose raises issues of the use to which the two forms can be put, and its accompanying music can foster discussion of the relation between text and melody in lyric poetry. Both of these questions have far-reaching consequences for defining or describing genres.

The medieval perception of genres may also sometimes be discerned in the principles which seem to have governed the composition of manuscripts. Close examination of certain codices can reveal how those involved in their manufacture (planners, booksellers, and customers) regarded the relationships between types of narrative. Many epics and romances, particularly those in cyclical form, are transmitted by virtue of length in manuscripts containing nothing else, and their generic affiliations are thus defined by the confines of the codex, in other words, their covers. This is the case with the various epic cycles discussed above, Chrétien's *Perceval* and its continuations, and *Le Roman d'Alexandre* (whose manuscripts incorporate such later additions as *Les Vœux du paon*); it is also true of *Le Roman de Renart*.

Long narratives are not the only ones to be generically marked by the parameters of a manuscript. Collections of animal fables (*Ysopets*) and edifying tales in general may be long enough to form a book unto themselves. Often, these are defined as collections, either by their (putative) source or as the work of a particular author: for instance, *La Vie des pères*, a thirteenth-century series of tales, some translated from the *Vitae patrum* and other Latin sources, or Gautier de Coinci's *Miracles de Nostre Dame* (before 1236) or the Anglo-Norman *Gracial* of Adgar (end of the twelfth century). Occasionally, the *Vie des pères* and Gautier's *Miracles* are found, in part or in whole, in the same manuscripts, confirming generic affiliations, despite a certain degree of variation between the numerous tales. On occasions where, say, an *Ysopet* is found in the same manuscript with other works, its intertexuality with other genres is underlined. For example, Marie de France's *Ysopet* is adjacent to her *Lais* in London, BL, Harley 978 (Anglo-Norman, middle of the thirteenth century), stressing authorial identity, but adjacent to Guillaume le Clerc's *Bestiaire* in Oxford, Bodl., Douce 132 (Anglo-Norman, end thirteenth century), underlining the didactic use of animals in the stories. In other Anglo-Norman manuscripts of Marie's *Ysopet*, such as Cambridge, UL, Ee. 6. 11 (first half of the thirteenth century) or York, Minster Library, XVI K. 12 (second half of the thirteenth century), her fables are accompanied, respectively, by a life of St Margaret and an *Espurgatoire saint Patrice* (not Marie's), and *Le Voyage de saint Brandan*. The didactic and edifying context is evident. Continental manuscripts of the text, such as

Paris, Ars. 3142, Paris, BnF, 1593, 2168, 19152, and 25545 (all from between the second half of the thirteenth century and the first half of the fourteenth), contain a much wider range of secular and religious texts, arguing for a more expansive view of the animal fable as genre.

It is the collections or anthologies, the *recueils*, which are of particular interest from the point of view of genres. Selection and ordering of texts within a manuscript can tell us whether certain texts were regarded as of a kind, as contrasting with one another, or, on a basic level, codicologically compatible; and, of course, we are here dealing with perceptions current at the time of the manufacture of the manuscript, not at the time of composition of the texts themselves. In the final part of this chapter, I will briefly consider a few such anthology manuscripts before looking in a little more detail at the case of the *lai*.[10]

Almost by definition, any medieval manuscript is unique. Consequently, the range of manuscripts is wide and includes single-item codices and author collections, as well as those whose contents may have been determined and arranged in whole or in part by generic considerations. Manuscripts containing romances alone, for example, suggest that our view of the genre was shared to some extent in the Middle Ages. Chantilly, Musée Condé 472 (end of the thirteenth century), for example, is primarily a collection of Arthurian verse romances, including three by Chrétien de Troyes and some epigonal texts. It is significant that Chrétien is not given pride of place at the head of Chantilly 472, but rather *Les Merveilles de Rigomer*, one of the very latest Arthurian verse romances; Chrétien's *Erec et Enide*, *Yvain*, and *Lancelot* are interspersed among the other texts. It is possible to see the manuscript as a 'cycle' held together by the figure of Gauvain, while the inclusion of a branch of the *Roman de Renart* opens up possibilities for intertextual readings between Arthurian romance and the animal epic. Paris, BnF, fr. 794 (second quarter of the thirteenth century), copied by the scribe Guiot, also contains Chrétien's romances, but includes Wace's *Brut*, *Le Roman de Troie*, *Athis et Prophilias*, and *Les Empereurs de Rome* by Calendre. Ideas of universal history and *translatio studii et imperii* also seem to have determined the contents and ordering of Paris, BnF, fr. 1450 (second quarter of the thirteenth century), in which *Le Roman de Troie* and *Le Roman d'Eneas* precede Wace's *Brut*, into which Chrétien's romances are inserted at the point where Wace talks of minstrels telling the fables of the Britons, before concluding with the rest of the *Brut* and *Dolopathos*. The chronological structure is most evident in a later manuscript, Paris, BnF, fr. 60 (second quarter of the fourteenth century), which contains, in order, *Le Roman de Thèbes*, *Le Roman de Troie*, and *Le Roman d'Eneas*. In all of these manuscripts, subject matter (historical, pseudo-historical, mythological, legendary) and form (octosyllabic rhyming couplets) are the common 'generic' denominators.

Although long (and misleadingly) referred to in English as 'miscellanies', such manuscripts as Paris, BnF, fr. 837 and 19152 (both late thirteenth to early fourteenth century), are partly structured by genre. Pairs or small groups of *fabliaux* alternate, for example, with contrasting pairs or groups of religious or didactic poems; the grouping is also sometimes thematic within or between genres. These two manuscripts (sometimes known inaccurately as *fabliaux* manuscripts *A* and *D*) also contain a few longer works, but are predominantly of short narratives, and are practically libraries in themselves. Their relatively modest nature raises the question of whether they were owned by professional performers who could have performed from them, or by *scriptoria* who could have copied texts or series of texts into other manuscripts at the request of customers. Whatever their purpose, it is clear that the perception of genres, even if no more specific than 'short verse narrative', had a hand in their manufacture.

Saints' lives form a recognizable medieval narrative genre, the nature of which is partly defined by a long Latin tradition. Although hagiography is quite clearly delineated, in Old French as it is in Latin, the vernacular tradition influences perceptions of the genre and the codicological contexts in which saints' lives appear. The idea of the holy life transcends the difference between verse and prose in such manuscripts as Arras, Bibliothèque Municipale 307, Paris, BnF, fr. 19525 and 19531 (all second half of the thirteenth century), where both forms are represented. London, BL, Add. 70513 (Anglo-Norman, last quarter of the thirteenth century) is a collection of English lives in verse and assembled with a national as well as generic purpose. Oxford, Bodl., Canon Misc. 74 (early thirteenth century) includes versions of the legends of St Patrick's Purgatory and the Antichrist, as well as a poem on the Last Judgement alongside saints' lives proper in what could best be described as a relaxation or expansion of the genre beyond the hagiographical. Other manuscripts, however, locate saints' lives in a more worldly context, underlining the dangers of making too strict a scholarly separation between the sacred and the secular. After all, secular authors such as Wace, Jean Bodel, and Rutebeuf all wrote saints' lives as well as (pseudo-)chronicles, *fabliaux*, and (in Bodel's case) a *chanson de geste*, among other types of narrative.

With the possible exception of the saint's life, the Breton lay may be the most susceptible of all medieval narrative genres to the traditional kind of generic definition or description, yet even here such a characterization should not be used as a rigid model. The earliest *lais bretons* are certainly the twelve written before 1178 by a poet known to us as Marie de France, first preserved in London, BL, Harley 978 (cf. above, the discussion of the *Ysopet*), along with the same author's collection of animal fables. They are preceded by a prologue in which Marie names herself, expounds her poetics, and mentions a dedicatee. What is significant for the present purposes is that in later manuscripts, none of which contain all twelve *lais* from the Harley manuscript, the prologue is not present and the poems are to all intents and purposes anonymous. Equally significant is that alongside some of Marie's *lais* in these later manuscripts are a number of anonymous poems of the same kind, clearly written in response to her 'originals', in some ways similar to the so-called epigonal romances written in the wake of Chrétien de Troyes.[11]

If the first stage in the post-Marie evolution of the *lai* is emulation, first straightforward, and then parodic in the case of *Ignauré* and the *Lai du lecheor*, the second stage is marked by the application of the term *lai* to short narratives of different kinds which may not appear to have very much in common with the *lai breton*. Texts such as the Ovidian tale of *Narcisse*, Jean Renart's courtly *Lai de l'ombre* and the *fabliau*-like *Lai d'Aristote* (by Henri d'Andeli?) are brought into the orbit of the *lai breton* in manuscripts which essentially drop the Breton element from the definition, along with the kind of *merveilleux* and supernatural which characterizes it. The chronology of this process is difficult to pin down but it appears to have taken place during the last quarter of the twelfth century (that is in the aftermath of Marie's *Lais*) and the first half of the thirteenth. In the end, only relative brevity, love interest, and a certain courtliness remain as common denominators, although the courtly *fabliaux* are excluded.

The contents of some manuscripts, in order, will illustrate this observation:

BnF, fr. 2168 (second half of the thirteenth century), ff. 47ra-70rb: *Yonec, Guigemar, Lanval, Narcisse, Graelent*

Cologny, Bibliotheca Bodmeriana, Bodmer 82 (end of the thirteenth century): Raoul de Houdenc, *Le Roman des eles, Le Donnei des amants, Haveloc, Désiré, Nabaret*

BnF, nouv. acq. fr. 1104 (end of the thirteenth century): *Guigemar, Lanval, Désiré, Tyolet, Yonec, Guingamor, Espine, Espervier, Chievrefoil, Doon, Les deus amans, Bisclavret, Milun, Fresne, Lecheor, Equitan, Tydorel, Cort mantel*, Jean Renart, *Lai de l'ombre, Conseil, Amours, Aristote, Graelent, Oiselet*

In BnF, fr. 2168, *Narcisse* is situated between Marie's *Lanval* and the anonymous *lai breton*, and headed 'De Narciso li lais'. Raoul de Houdenc's *Le Roman des eles* is a didactic courtesy poem referred to in another manuscript as 'Li lais des .vii. eles', while *Le Donnei des amants* (1244 lines and fragmentary) uses language reminiscent of the *lai* and contains a version of *Le Lai de l'oiselet*; *Haveloc*, although strictly speaking part of the Matter of England, is framed by the usual attribution to the Bretons and statement of commemorative function; *Désiré* is a version of the fairy-mistress story (cf. *Lanval*) and *Nabaret*, parodic. Despite including several texts (*Epervier*, *Ombre*, *Conseil*, *Amours*, *Aristote*, *Oiselet*) which have few or no Breton elements, BnF, nouv. acq. fr. 1104 has an *incipit* on fo. 1r ('Ci commencent les lays de Breteigne') and an *explicit* on fo. 79r ('Explicit les lays de Breteigne') which appears to include all poems in the manuscript. One final observation concerns the application of the term *lai* in the development of the so-called *lai lyrique* in the second quarter of the thirteenth century, where courtly poems of a fixed form are accompanied by music. These *lais lyriques* are sometimes embedded, appropriately enough, in the late Arthurian prose *Tristan* and related texts. The list of lays found in Shrewsbury School, MS 7 (about 1270) contains classic Breton lays (by Marie de France and anonymous), non-Breton lays, and lyric lays. Thus does a 'genre' appear to redefine itself in the course of approximately a hundred years.

Such evidence from manuscripts is instructive insofar as it suggests that medieval readers and listeners, and that those who made the books they read or read from, had a much more flexible view of genre than modern scholars do. Taken together with traditional textual analysis and theoretical consideration of the meaning and usefulness of generic study applied to medieval literature, manuscripts constitute an authentic witness to the medieval awareness of genres. The real lesson in the end is surely not to be obsessive about genre definitions, to admit their elasticity, and to appreciate the interplay between the many varieties of Old French narrative.

### Notes

1. See U. Mölk (ed.), *Französische Literarästhetik des 12. und 13. Jahrhunderts* (Tübingen, Niemeyer, 1969).
2. J. Bédier, *Les Fabliaux: études de littérature populaire et d'histoire littéraire du moyen âge* (Paris, Bouillon, 1893), p. 37.
3. See O. Jodogne, *Le Fabliau* (Turnhout, Brepols, 1975), published together with J.-Ch. Payen, *Le Lai narratif*.
4. Bodel, *La Chanson des Saisnes*, lines 6–11.
5. M. Léonard, *Le Dit et sa technique littéraire, des origines à 1340* (Paris, Champion, 1996); F. Pomel, *Les Voies de l'au-delà et l'essor de l'allégorie au Moyen Age* (Paris, Champion, 2001).
6. S. Kay, *The Chansons de geste in the Age of Romance: Political Fictions* (Oxford University Press, 1995).
7. In the series Classiques Français du Moyen Age and Blackwell's French Texts respectively.
8. See K. Busby, 'Le *Tristan* de Béroul en tant qu'intertexte', in N. J. Lacy and G. Torrini-Roblin (eds.), *Continuations: Essays on Medieval French Literature*

*and Language in Honour of John L. Grigsby* (Birmingham, AL, Summa Publications, Inc., 1989), pp. 19–37.

9. B. Schmolke-Hasselmann, transl. as *The Evolution of Arthurian Romance: the Verse Tradition from Chrétien to Froissart* (Cambridge University Press, 1998).

10. All of the manuscripts mentioned below are discussed in my *Codex and Context*, 2 vols. (Amsterdam, Rodopi, 2002).

11. *Lais anonymes des XIIe et XIIIe siècles*, ed. P. M. O'Hara Tobin (Geneva, Droz, 1976). This contains only the anonymous Breton lays, not those such as *Narcisse*, *Ombre*, and *Aristote* referred to below.

# 10

## JANE H. M. TAYLOR

# Lyric poetry of the later Middle Ages

On 25 November 1392, Eustache Deschamps, indefatigable versifier, completed what he calls an *Art de dictier* – a treatise on the art of composing verse.[1] It may have been intended for Louis, duke of Orléans, and as such directed primarily at the amateur, courtly, poet rather than at the sort of professional who frequented what are called *Puys d'amour* (poetic competitions, often for hugely elaborate *serventois* expressing devoted service to the Virgin rather than secular love poems);[2] Deschamps does not, he says, intend to prescribe rules for such verse forms, because 'it has not been the custom for noble men to compose [them]' (82). This, the earliest known treatise in French on the subject, starts rather ponderously with a discussion of the seven liberal arts, and comes finally to the seventh, music, 'the medicine of the seven arts' (61); it is on this last section that I want to concentrate.

Deschamps is distinctly convoluted. There are, he says, two sorts of music, the *artificiele* and the *naturele* (60). *Musique artificiele* – 'artificial' because it demands 'art' – need not detain us: it embraces the music of instruments and the music of song, and it requires the trained ability to understand, if not read, music. What is interesting here is what Deschamps calls *musique naturele*, 'an oral music producing words in metre' (63). By contrast with artificial music, it cannot in essence be taught, or rather, it cannot be taught to anyone who is not naturally gifted. Certainly, anyone can learn the mechanics of verse – how to produce a competent *ballade* or a decent *rondeau* – but natural music stems from innate ability, and, spontaneously, from inspiration: from love, for instance, 'amorous desire in the praise of women' (63). Proficiency in *musique naturele* has no necessary connection with *musique artificiele* (Deschamps is clear that poetry, *musique naturele*, is entirely separable from music proper) but it is so called because although the poets are generally ignorant of *musique artificiele*, nevertheless their *dits* and *chançons* 'can also be uttered and recited by one man alone aloud; or any book of these pleasing things can be read before a sick person' (62–4).

Now, there are a number of things which are interesting here. First, of course, is the separation of poetry (*musique naturele*) from music proper (*musique artificiele*): the lyric–song relationship that has been a given for poets such as the Châtelain de Couci and his like is, it seems, thereby largely dissolved. Deschamps is asking his readers to recognize – and this is the crucial point – the melodic power of language-without-music: the voice may not be *chantable* (it does not sing), but mere speech, the lyric read aloud, produces *douces paroles*, sweet words, which, he continues, are 'pronounced and made distinct by the sweetness of the voice and the opening of the mouth' (64). What he proposes to teach his readers is modest. It is the skills, the building blocks, to compose *musique naturele*: strophic patterns, principles of rhyme, which vowels 'are euphonious together' (66). Deschamps, in other words, will concentrate on craft, that is, on word skills that can be learnt, and on the ways in which inspired, or born, poets can improve the medium whereby they voice their inspiration.

These points – the conviction that words-without-music are melodic, the importance of vocalizing lyric by performing it or reading it aloud, the emphasis on craft and skill – will inform this chapter, but first let me expand on the crucial premise, what I called the dissolution of the lyric–song relationship. I do not, of course, mean to suggest that song and music are radically and universally separated in the later Middle Ages (nor indeed, as Chapter 6 points out, that all earlier lyric is indissolubly musical); Deschamps himself finds it difficult to make the distinction consistent, and continues to pay lip-service, at least, to the idea that poetry is song by referring to his distinctly prosaic *ballades* as *chansons*:

> Grace et Octroy, Maniere et Contenance . . .
> veuillés pour moy a ma dame *parler*,
> ou il me fault mes dolens jours finer,
> se ne reçoit mon offre et ma *chançon*.[3]

(Please *speak* to my lady of my desire for mercy, my thoughts and feelings; I must end my days if she does not accept my offering and my *song*.)

And it is important to remember that the fact that there may be no accompanying music for lyrics in particular manuscripts need not mean that they were not sung: the practice of fitting words to already existing melodies (*contrafacta*) is widespread.[4] But poets, even musician-poets, seem increasingly to recognize that artistic merit and audience pleasure can attach to the lyric itself divorced from music.

The case of the poet-musician Guillaume de Machaut is instructive here. His *Livre du Voir dit* (1363–5), the true subject of which is the composing of poetry, does seem to make it clear that the greatest prestige attaches to the lyric with music: Guillaume himself is occasionally apologetic because he has not yet had time to set a particular lyric to music; Toute-Belle, Guillaume's correspondent in this epistolary romance, is most eager to have her copies of his lyrics not just copied verbatim, but *notés*, set to music.[5] Yet even here, Machaut recognizes the sheer enjoyment that words alone can give: the first *rondeau* that he receives from Toute-Belle, and which has no music, is, he says, careful and sophisticated, composed according to the rules (52: 'n'estoit pas rudes ne let, / n'il n'estoit mie contrefais'), refined and discreet (54: 'ne fu villaine ne fole'). More spectacularly, take the group of some two hundred of Machaut's fixed-form lyrics which is usually entitled the *Loange des dames*. In Machaut's complete-works manuscripts, this sequence is usually rubricated with variations on the phrase *Les balades ou il n'a point de chant*,[6] that is, the *ballades* for which there is no music. The rubric is revelatory, first because it makes it plain that for readers, lack of music may be remarkable, but secondly because it implies that even for a musician-poet like Machaut, the artful arrangement of mere words, *musique naturele*, is thought to be sufficiently pleasurable. Where *trouvère* song relied for its appeal very much not just on the stanza but also on the technical complexities of music, Machaut, it seems, envisages the fixed-form lyric – the *ballade*, the *rondeau*, the *chant royal*, the *virelai* – as affording its own aesthetic pleasure; certainly, the manuscript anthologies that contain the *Loange* make it clear that there is no expectation that the lyrics will be sung, nor any attempt, *a priori*, to marry words and music.

Scraps of evidence, throughout the later Middle Ages, would seem to endorse this: Deschamps again, who was Machaut's friend and perhaps pupil, tells us that in *c*.1370 he took a manuscript of the *Voir dit* with him to Bruges to the court of Louis de Mâle, count of Flanders, and that there he read (not sang) one of the *ballades* from the romance, to great acclaim;[7] Jean Froissart claims, in one of his pseudo-autobiographical *dits*, *L'Espinette amoureuse*, to have read (not sung) a *virelai* aloud to a lady to solicit permission to leave her country.[8] The implication, here, is that verbal virtuosity, ease even, was a response to the requirements and preferences and practices of an informed and sophisticated audience, and that it was rewarded accordingly. What I shall concentrate on, in the present chapter, are some of the consequences of that shift from the poem-as-partner-to-music to the poem-as-verbal-artifact: how did the poets of the later Middle Ages learn the technical complexities that, in the *trouvère* lyric, were often reserved largely for the accompanying music, and how did audiences acquire the prosodic and melodic discrimination to appreciate them?

But first, what is meant by the phrase verbal virtuosity? Some of the assumptions about the literary process articulated in their work by the poets of the later Middle Ages are instructive: Machaut himself, for instance, in his *Fonteinne amoureuse*, invites his audience's awed appreciation of his virtuoso feat in confecting no fewer than one hundred rhymes, all different (*despareilles*);⁹ Froissart, to return to the *Espinette amoureuse*, is also determined to ensure that his pseudo-autobiographical lady (and, presumably, his real audience) recognize his having managed one hundred different rhymes in her honour: 'Dame, cent clauses desparelles, / pour vostre amour, – n'est pas mervelles –, / ai mis en rime' (2340–2: Lady, I have rhymed one hundred different verses for your love: is that not remarkable?); so too is Christine de Pizan, puffing the fact that she has achieved the admittedly remarkable exploit of writing some 3500 lines in demanding *rimes léonines* (rhyme across two or more syllables), and stressing the sheer effort (*labour*) and skill (*science*) that this has demanded.¹⁰ The artistic preoccupations voiced here by professional poets like Machaut and Froissart and Christine need to be taken seriously: modern readers may find such achievements rather tiresome, but this verbal self-consciousness, these cultivated verbal games requiring a high degree of sophistication and compositional skill, play to the demands of an expanding literate audience which can recognize rhetorical and prosodic fireworks and which does not expect or wish them to be enhanced, or masked, by musical accompaniment.

It is surely no coincidence, moreover, that the fourteenth and fifteenth centuries are also the heyday of what are called *Arts de seconde rhétorique*, treatises written in the vernacular and designed precisely to inculcate the word-craft of poetry: what I called the skills that can be learned. One of them, Deschamps's *Art de dictier*, we have already met; there are a further eight or nine, often existing in single manuscripts.¹¹ There is debate as to their intended audiences: were they instruction manuals for the 'professionals' who might need coruscating rhymes and elaborate strophic models to impress patrons and *puys*, or were they recipe books for lyric designed for the occasional amateur of a princely and aristocratic court and who was less concerned with flamboyancy than with simple competence?¹² True, the treatises do not, as Olson says repressively, and rightly, give us 'a complete view of literature';¹³ but the distinct poetic practices that they profess, the complex verbal and prosodic strategies that they endorse, their redefinition of the poetic process, make them an eloquent showcase for the ambition of the late medieval lyric. What they stress, above all, is the mechanics of composition: stylistic expertise and control of form. Certain technicalities are a constant, whatever the intended audience: all of the treatises, for instance, lay out the prosodic rules that govern the canonical verse forms of the late Middle Ages, the *ballade* and the *rondeau*; all of them explain, in greater or lesser detail, the range of rhyme strategies available, from the commonplace *rime pauvre* (simple vowel rhyme) to the spectacular pyrotechnics of *rime annexee* ('Ainsi se fait rime *annexee, / annexant* vers a autre en*vers, / vers*ifiee . . .') or *vers enchainez* ('Ainssi sont enchainez *vers, / vers* les vifz engines . . .'), or *vers entrelacé* ('Entrelassez vers plaisans graci*eux, / eulx* se forment en telle forme ain*si, / si* sont plaisant . . . .'), which are probably the preserve of what I have called the professional poet (*Instructif de seconde rethorique*, fo. C$_i$v). Some, providently, parade lists of exotic rhymes, rhymes in *-bé*, or *-ulle*, or *-onde*, or *-ac*: the list in Langlois's treatise VII (*Recueil*, 323–426), which occupies 100 pages, four columns to a page, is a spectacular example; some, like Langlois's treatise II, give convenient handlists of mythological characters (*Recueil*, 65–72); a few of the later treatises, like the *Instructif*, prescribe certain rhetorical figures, the more histrionic the better (so there is a particular preference, for instance, for devices like synonymy, or syncope, or *equivoque* with its potential for ostentatious rhyme: *puissance*, say, rhymed with *ne puis sans ce*; *Instructif*, fo. a$_v$r). I shall return later to the wilder and more showy varieties of prosody which were to distinguish some of the poets of the late fifteenth century; I want first, however, to concentrate on more unassuming poets, and, returning to the *musique naturele* with which we began this chapter, to suggest that this is a community, whether amateur or professional, powerfully aware of the manner, not the matter, of verse, of its prosodic and melodic resources, conscious of the techniques and devices at its command, and confident in using them.

This contention will surprise some of the readers of late medieval *rondeaux* and *ballades*, which, because their sentiments seem commonplace and their lexicon limited, are all too often dismissed as repetitious and banal. But poems which may seem slight and unadventurous at first glance in fact yield dividends to close analysis. Take, for instance, the first, refrain line of a deceptively unaffected *rondeau* by Christine de Pizan, one of those I have called professional poets; I give the first stanza only:

> *Je suis vesve, seulete, et noir vestue*:
> a triste vis, simplement affullée,
> en grant courrous et maniere adoulée
> porte le dueil très amer qui me tue.
>
> > (*Œuvres*, ed. Roy, I, 148–9)

(I am a widow, alone and dressed in black, sad of face, simple of dress; grief-stricken, I wear bitter mourning.)

This *rondeau* is one of a group written between 1393 and 1399 and which focus on Christine's widowhood. These poems, because they seem to give us privileged and unmediated access to Christine's own subjectivity, have usually been regarded as her most successful – but what I want to stress here, on the contrary, is their artifice, the ways in which Christine makes lyric capital of the formal constraints of the *rondeau*, and in particular, from the refrain which is always, of course, the semantic key to the *rondeau*.[14] For its artlessness is only superficial. It centres, of course, rhythmically and semantically, on the loaded adjective, the diminutive *seulete*. I say 'loaded' because Christine has made it her emblem: it opens one of her *ballades* ('*Seulette* m'a laissée en grant martire . . .', 'I have been left *alone* in martyrdom'), gives the rhyme word for another *rondeau* ('Com turtre suis, sans per, toute *seulete* . . .', 'I am like the turtledove, with no mate, all *alone*'); most spectacularly, it opens every line of Christine's best-known *ballade*, '*Seulete* sui, et *seulete* vueil estre' ('I am *alone*, and want to stay *alone*') (*Œuvres*, ed. Roy, I, 15, 147, and 12 respectively). Here, however, Christine's state is entirely encapsulated in the refrain line: semantically again by the word *vesve*, which explains her solitude; visually, by the phrase *noir vestue*, highlighting her widow's weeds; phonetically, by the alliteration on the fricative *v* ('*vesve* . . . noir *v*estue') which brackets and reinforces the key adjective. This innocuous line, in other words, is in fact a sophisticated restatement of Christine's public persona – and proof that she was confident in exploiting the resources of prosody and the expressive value of sound.

It is this same studied sobriety which marks, say, Charles d'Orléans's verse half a century or so later; Charles was, of course, one of those I have called *amateurs*. Take his *rondeau*, of which again I give only the first stanza:

> Dedens mon Livre de Pensee,
> j'ay trouvé escripvant mon cueur
> la vraye histoire de douleur,
> de larmes toute enluminee.[15]

(In my Book of Thoughts, I found my heart writing the true history of grief, all illuminated with tears.)

Here, what is remarkable is Charles's nonchalant, adept exploitation of the resources provided both by late medieval personification and by prosody. Charles himself is, of course, rationally the *je*, the 'writer' – indeed quite literally so: the *rondeau* is copied into Charles's own personal manuscript, Paris, BnF, fr. 25458, in his own hand.[16] But here, as so often in his verse, Charles, the poet-I, stands at a safe and ironic distance, emotionally (and semantically) detached from his own reality, as his *cueur* fixes that reality in the locus of record and memory, the *livre*, which sets the poem's image and its lexicon: hence *escripvant, vraye histoire, enluminee*. What is striking is the way in which Charles, as expertly as Christine, employs his technical mastery of late medieval prosody to make the *rondeau* interestingly unemphatic and conversational: the enjambment between the second and third lines minimizes the rhyme and ensures that the phrase *vraye histoire* carries maximal rhythmic weight; the alliteration '*larmes / enluminees*' draws attention to what is actually a significant reflection on, and estrangement from, writing-as-enactment. Again, in other words, and again like Christine, Charles integrates technique and content, and surface limpidity is a disguise for considerable poetic sophistication.

I have several times used expressions like 'studied artlessness' because lyric poets like Christine and Charles and their contemporaries specialize in a well-practised naturalness which only a careful reading can deconstruct; they prefer to present the lyric as something effortless, redolent of what Baldasar Castiglione was to call *sprezzatura*, the sort of rehearsed spontaneity which conceals art. Fictionally at least, they like to describe the *rondeau* in particular as an activity for an idle moment: thus Froissart, in his *Meliador*, has one of his heroes compose not just words, but music, off-the-cuff (9782–5: 'And then he sang a single *rondeau* aloud, and I believe that he made it up as he sang, for it was very short'). All the evidence suggests that anyone with the remotest pretensions to social standing – anyone, that is, who aspired to being thought of as *joly* and *gracieux* (cheerful and gracious company) – was expected effortlessly to be able to turn a graceful *rondeau* or a witty *ballade*. One of the most admired warriors of the fifteenth century, Boucicaut, was trained in the art of composing *ballades* and *rondeaux d'amoureux sentement*; Charles d'Orléans, on Saint Valentine's day, calls his court to the composition of rhymes in French or Latin with every confidence that they can respond; when the Duke of Suffolk was sick in Paris, the best remedy was for his courtiers to compose *diz amoureux*; Queen Margaret of Scotland would spend nights composing *rondeaux*; and a couple of bourgeois, having competed in a comically *louche* seduction, 'mesmes firent de tres bons *rondeaulx*' ('even managed very good *rondeaux*').[17] These are, then, supposedly guileless compositions, imagined, to use Cerquiglini-Toulet's expression, as a 'light and graceful activity', a 'game that amateur and professional poets could play on equal terms'.[18] Fictional witnesses sometimes play to this stereotype, like an account of a *rondeau* competition in an anonymous fifteenth-century political allegory, *Le Pastoralet*,[19] where the poets are members of the French court thinly disguised, like Marie-Antoinette's courtiers, as shepherds and shepherdesses; they are charged with composing, and then reciting, *rondeaux* 'in praise of their ladies' (442–3). They retire into the shade of a may tree, to concentrate (447: 'pour . . . estre quois'), then emerge, triumphantly, minutes later, with poems more or less accomplished, but technically perfectly correct.

But were poets really so nonchalantly and effortlessly spontaneous? Another account of a poetry competition, in an odd little fourteenth-century romance called *Le Parfait du paon* (1340–8) by a certain Jean de Le Mote,[20] should make us wary. It is loosely attached to the Alexander the Great cycle, and includes – at some length – an account of a competition involving Alexander himself and seven members of his elegant and sophisticated court. The 'poets' are self-deprecating, but ultimately each of them produces a *ballade*, and performs it for the judgement of the rest of the court. What is interesting is the sharp critical acumen of the courtiers. They are dauntingly well informed: one poem is, says a courtier, marred by a hypermetric line (that is, one that is too long, 1412); another has used a false rhyme (1414); others have fillers (1415, 1425), or are, like Alexander's own, rather commonplace (1419: 'point tres hautement parlant'). The ultimate winner has produced the *ballade* that is by far the most highly worked: lexically clever, syntactically complex. The implication is that the courtier may well perform nonchalance, but not without scrupulous rehearsal.

If indeed games of this subtly competitive sort had the value I am suggesting, if poetry was indeed a social, and socially valued, occupation, this might in part account for the way in which what seem to us otherwise incomprehensibly unrelieved torrents of rather banal *rondeaux* and *ballades* are preserved with such scrupulous (and expensive) care in late medieval manuscript collections. A manuscript like Lille, Bibliothèque Municipale, 402, for instance, which dates from the very early Renaissance, has some 600 relentless lyrics, as does Antoine Vérard's *Jardin de Plaisance* of 1501; there are 500 or so dashed down in Paris, BnF, fr. 1719, 200 elegantly copied on good parchment into BnF, fr. 9223, another 100 just as elegant in BnF, nouv. acq. fr. 15771.[21] A straw in the wind: each of these is marked by the sort of strings of echo-poems and answer-poems, appeals to shared attitudes, and fondnesses for dialogue, which are characteristic of the coterie manuscript which acts as a channel of social communication. The most notable manuscript of this type is Charles d'Orléans's personal album to which I have already alluded, and which is worth examining because it is no doubt the nearest thing we have to a living document of social life at a highly cultured court in the 1450s and 1460s, and because it stresses the interactive and interchangeable roles of poet and audience.[22] It consists in part of Charles's own *ballades* and other poems, but otherwise, and spectacularly, of quires containing a wild proliferation of *rondeaux*, by Charles himself, by members of his household and by visitors, scrupulously attributed, entered on the pages in different hands and on what are plainly different occasions. The *rondeaux* are often copied in little groups related by a single refrain line, so that it is legitimate to suppose that Charles himself may have set themes for an evening. The courtiers perform more or less effectively: some are pedestrian, some are gifted-amateur, others again are visiting professionals. But what is striking, ultimately, is the mere fact that the poems are recorded: recorded not on stray slips of paper soon lost, but on quires of parchment ordered by Charles's household, often recorded in what we may assume to be the poets' own hands, and then scrupulously preserved and bound. Charles, we cannot but assume, derived pleasure from gathering a stable of poets; the poets, perhaps, blessed their good fortune in having their *rondeaux* housed in his no doubt prestigious collection (François Villon, one of the visiting professionals, calls it a *saint livre*).[23] The manuscript, in other words, is an index of how far the lyric, and the word skills that created it, were a social currency, and how much poetic exchanges may have confirmed social bonds, reinforced social standing.

It may also do something to explain a paradox of the late medieval lyric: the studious concern with which poets professional and amateur address the preservation of the poems they pretend to have tossed off, so carelessly, for mere amusement. Where the poetic experience, for the Châtelain de Couci and his circle, is invested in performance, the poets of the later Middle Ages are crucially concerned with poetic appearance, and there is a tension between their pretended carelessness, *sprezzatura*, and what it is surely proper to call an anxiety of authorship.[24] The arch example here is of course Machaut, fretting uneasily, in his *Voir dit*, lest the loose sheets he and his Toute-Belle exchange be mislaid, or misplaced, or bound out of order.[25] But in fact many of the professional poets of the late Middle Ages evince the same mindfulness: Froissart, for instance, congratulates himself on having presented a sumptuously bound, elegantly copied and illustrated volume of love poetry to Richard II of England,[26] and what purport to be the statutes of an authentic *cour d'amour*, poetic coterie, in Paris in 1402, make elaborate arrangements for the presentation and preservation of the poems: all entries are to be presented for the judges in an elegant white silk pouch, and the winning ones will be copied, elaborately, into *amoureux registres* to be preserved for posterity in one of the abbeys of the kingdom of France.[27] Poets also, as Sylvia Huot and others have argued,[28] go to considerable and creative lengths to ensure that their poems are preserved in an approved form and order: Villon again is an arch example, setting his *rondeaux* and *ballades* like jewels in the *Testament*, but Christine de Pizan too, in her *Cent Ballades d'amant et de dame*, notoriously, wove a hundred of her *ballades* into a complex story of love, betrayal, and despair, following a fashion established twenty years or so earlier, in 1389, by a little group of notables of the court of France who had, they claim, composed a narrative on the ethics of love over a hundred *ballades*[29] – and Froissart, either at commission or hoping to please, devised his vast Arthurian romance *Meliador* as a flattering showcase for the lyrics of his patron Wenceslas of Bohemia.[30] Poets of the late Middle Ages, in other words, valued their 'artless' *rondeaux* sufficiently to 'manage' their reception and preservation systematically and to stamp their identities on their lyrics via acrostics (in which the initial letters of lines spell the author's name or that of his addressee), author-portraits, ringing claims to poetic pre-eminence, and sumptuous presentation copies.

In highlighting *sprezzatura*, and 'artlessness', moreover, I risk misrepresenting late medieval verse. Anyone who has spent time on the rhetorical treatises (*Arts de seconde rhétorique*) of this period will have been struck by the labyrinthine prosodic complexities which many of them recommend to their readers. Certainly, all of them make recommendations as to the structure and patterning of the *rondeau* and the *ballade*, the workhorse genres favoured by a Charles d'Orléans or a François Villon and which are therefore the staple of the poetic communities of the later Middle Ages. But what most of them revel in is the pursuit of generic complexities in which elegant stylists like Charles and Villon never indulge. Deschamps himself may well have claimed only to offer models of the *ballade* and the *rondeau* for 'noble men', but he cannot resist cataloguing highly sophisticated word games, 'les plus fors balades qui se puissant faire' (74: 'the hardest *ballades* that can be written'): *ballades* with spectacularly punning rhymes (such as *equivoque*, *leonime*), *ballades* built for wilful artifice and not meaning, with rhymes 'retrograde' and *enchainez*:

> Lasse, lasse, maleureuse et do*lente*!
> *lente* me voy, fors de souspirs et *plains*.
> *Plains* sont mes jours d'ennuy et de tour*mente*;
> *mente* qui veult . . . .               (*Art de dictier*, 76)

(Alas, alas, unhappy and mournful, weary I see myself, burdened by sighs and complaints. My days are full of ennui and torment. Lie who will . . . .)

Even Deschamps, then, has composed an inventory which already, at the end of the fourteenth century, betrays an acute and inescapable consciousness of poetic variety.

I say 'even Deschamps' because it is precisely that consciousness of variety, that attention to genre, which will come to characterize the poets and the arts of rhetoric of the end of the fifteenth century. Take yet again the sober *rondeau* and *ballade*. They naturally figure large in Jean Molinet's *Art de Rhétorique* (*c*.1490), which he has, he claims rather implausibly, composed for his *très honnouré seigneur* (most honoured lord) so that the latter can learn to compose verses which will win a *victore glorieuse* over his lady.[31] I say *implausible* because Molinet pays very little attention to the *rondeau* as it seems to have predominated in Charles's and the other coteries I referred to earlier: the artless little octosyllabic poems turned around a refrain. Molinet's *rondeaux* – *rondeaux simples*, he calls them – are considerably more demanding, and much more spectacular. They can, he says, have any number of *dictions et sillabes* (words and syllables); each line can consist of one, or two, or three, or five, or more syllables; they can be single or double, or *jumeaulx* (twinned); in the right hands – surely not those of the amateur – they can be almost unbearably complex:

| | | |
|---|---|---|
| Souffrons a point | Soyons bons | Bourgoingnons |
| Bourgois loyaux | Serviteurs | De noblesse |
| Barons en point | Prosperons | De noblesse |
| Souffrons a point | Soyons bons | Bourgoingnons[32] |

The particularity of this *rondeau* – of which I give only the first four lines and which I am too craven even to try to translate – is that it can be read in no fewer than seven ways ('Sept rondeaulx en ce rondeau Sont tissues et cordelez', 'Seven separate *rondeaux* are woven and knit in this *rondeau*'). It can be read 'straight': that is, as a decasyllabic *rondeau* ('Souffrons a point: soyons bons Bourgoingnons', 'Let us suffer together; let us be good Burgundians'); on the other hand, each vertical segment, as I print them here, can be read independently:

> Souffons a point,
> bourgois loyaux!
> Barons en point,
> souffrons a point!

(Let us suffer together, loyal bourgeois! Barons, let us suffer together!)

And so on, and so forth. It is difficult for a modern reader to imagine what can possibly have been the pleasure of these playfully challenging exercises – the zest of competition? the excitement of verbal licentiousness? – but what is striking here is the writer's fascination with prosodic genre: a fascination shared, to a greater or lesser degree, with all the writers of late medieval arts of rhetoric, including, as we have seen, Deschamps.

Does this attention to types and genres simply reflect a late medieval liking for the encyclopaedic? Did the theorists see these verbal complexities as compensation for the disappearance of the musico-verbal complexity which lay behind the far less prosodically challenging lyrics of the *trouvères*? After all, when music and poetry were conjoined, the rhythmical organization of the poem came not only from words but also from an external musical structure (so that poems require, for full understanding and appreciation, the musical dimension within which they were first conceived); now that poetry can be conceived of independently from music, then *musique naturele* must find its structure in the tight organization of word sound; is it coincidence that an early fourteenth-century *chansonnier*, Oxford, Bodl., Douce 308,[33] which has no music, is also sedulously and meticulously arranged on generic lines?

It is perhaps significant that, as the advent of printing came to threaten the social embeddedness of verse and the immediate social value attached to it, the prosodic intricacies became more and more flamboyant and startling, and the strategies of self-presentation favoured by poets became more and more complex, more and more recondite, more and more designed to dazzle the coterie audience for which any poem in manuscript might be devised. The so-called Grands Rhétoriqueurs, of whom Jean Molinet was one and who were attached largely to the hot-house court of Burgundy at the turn of the fifteenth and sixteenth centuries, use what I called the wilder varieties of prosody to draw strident attention to their verse as performative and ges-tural,[34] the ritualized cultural site no doubt making displays of pleasurably recondite wittiness – rebus poems, acrostich poems, formal virtuosities of all sorts – a valuable instrument in the forging or maintaining of the poet's social identity. Just as the poets of the fourteenth century, divorced from music, seem to have craved the discipline of form, so poets whose work was escaping the personal control of the manuscript environment seem to have felt the need to draw attention to the artifice that characterized their poems, by contrast with a Charles or a Christine who prefer largely to deflect it, or indeed with privileged, refined initiates like the Châtelain de Couci and his circle. Unable in this new world to rely on a poem's being received by what John Donne calls 'right readers', the poet can no longer afford the languid luxury of poetic *sprezzatura*, and the intense verbal activity of the Grands Rhétoriqueurs makes *musique naturele* profoundly artificial – although not, of course, *artificiele* . . .

## Notes

1. Cited from Sinnreich-Levi's edition (page references in the text); see also Deschamps, *Œuvres complètes*, VII, 266–92.
2. On 'professional' versus 'amateur', see M. Tietz, 'Die französische Lyrik des 14. und 15. Jahrhunderts', in Dieter Janik (ed.), *Die französische Lyrik* (Darmstadt, Wissenschaftliche Buchgesellschaft, 1987), pp. 109–77.
3. *Œuvres complètes*, III, 368.
4. See A. Butterfield, *Poetry and Music in Medieval France: from Jean Renart to Guillaume de Machaut* (Cambridge University Press, 2002), pp. 103–21.

5. Ed. P. Imbs *et al.*, p. 72.
6. See *Louange*, ed. N. Wilkins, and L. Earp, *Guillaume de Machaut: a Guide to Research* (New York, Garland, 1995), pp. 237–71.
7. Deschamps, *Œuvres complètes*, I, 248–9.
8. Ed. Fourrier, p. 140.
9. Ed. Cerquiglini-Toulet, lines 1021–2, 1052.
10. Christine de Pizan, *Livre du Duc des vrais amans*, ed. Fenster, p. 198.
11. See E. Langlois (ed.), *Recueil d'arts de seconde rhétorique* (Paris, Imprimerie Nationale, 1902; repr. Geneva, Slatkine, 1974); *Instructif de seconde rhétorique*, in E. Droz and A. Piaget (eds.), *Le Jardin de Plaisance et Fleur de Rhétorique par Antoine Vérard vers 1501*, SATF, 2 vols. (Paris, Firmin-Didot, 1910–25), I, fos. a$_{ii}$v-c$_{iii}$r.
12. See D. Poirion, *Le Poète et le prince: l'évolution du lyrisme courtois de Guillaume de Machaut à Charles d'Orléans* (Paris, PUF, 1965), pp. 457–80, and more recently C. Thiry, 'Prospections et prospectives sur la Rhétorique seconde', *Le Moyen français*, 46–7 (2000), 541–62; cf. also my *The Making of Poetry: French Poetic Anthologies at the End of the Middle Ages* (Turnhout, Brepols, 2007).
13. 'Deschamps' *Art de Dictier* and Chaucer's Literary Environment', *Speculum*, 48 (1973), 714–23 (p. 721), and more sympathetically E. Méchoulan, 'Les arts de rhétorique du XVe siècle: la théorie, masque de la *theoria*', in M.-L. Ollier (ed.), *Masques et déguisements dans la littérature médiévale* (Presses de l'Université de Montréal, 1988), pp. 213–21.
14. See M. Zink, 'Le lyrisme en rond. Esthétique et séduction des poèmes à forme fixe au Moyen Age', in *Les voix de la conscience: parole du poète et parole de Dieu dans la littérature médiévale* (Caen, Paradigme, 1992), pp. 71–90.
15. Charles d'Orléans, *Poésies*, ed. Champion, II, 308, *rondeau* XXXIII. Charles's *rondeaux* span the years 1444–65.
16. See P. Champion, *Le Manuscrit autographe des poésies de Charles d'Orléans* (Paris, Champion, 1907; repr. Geneva, Slatkine, 1975); M.-J. Arn, *The Order of Composition in Charles d'Orléans' Personal Manuscript (Paris, Bibl. Nat. MS fr. 25458)* (Turnhout, Brepols, forthcoming).
17. For references, see my *The Making of Poetry*, introduction.
18. 'Le rondeau', in Poirion (ed.), *Grundriss*, p. 55.
19. Joël Blanchard (ed.) (Paris, PUF, 1983).
20. Richard J. Carey (ed.) (Chapel Hill, University of North Carolina Press, 1972).
21. On all these, see my *The Making of Poetry*, ch. 1.
22. This will be reinforced by Arn's *The Order of Composition*.
23. Charles d'Orléans, *Poésies*, ed. Champion, I, 196.
24. See S. Huot, *From Song to Book: the Poetics of Writing in Old French Lyric and Lyrical Narrative Poetry* (Ithaca and London, Cornell University Press, 1987).
25. Imbs *et al.* (ed.), p. 450; cf. J. Cerquiglini-Toulet, *La Couleur de la mélancolie: la fréquentation des livres au XIVe siècle, 1300–1415* (Paris, Hatier, 1993), pp. 49–56.
26. Kervyn de Lettenhove (ed.), Jean Froissart, *Chroniques*, XV, 167.
27. Carla Bozzolo and Hélène Loyau (eds), *La Cour amoureuse dite de Charles VI* (Paris, Le Léopard d'Or, 1982).
28. S. Huot, 'From Life to Art: the Lyric Anthology of Villon's *Testament*', in D. Fenoaltea and D. L. Rubin (eds.), *The Ladder of High Designs: Structure and Interpretation of the French Lyric Sequence* (Charlottesville, University Press

of Virginia, 1991), pp. 26–40, and N. F. Regalado, 'Gathering the Works: the "Œuvres de Villon" and the Intergeneric Passage of the Medieval French Lyric into Single-Author Collections', *L'Esprit Créateur*, 33 (1993), 87–100.

29. G. Raynaud (ed.), Jean le Seneschal, *Livre des cent ballades*, SATF (Paris, Firmin-Didot, 1905).

30. See S. Luce *et al.* (eds.), *Chronique*, 15 vols. (Paris, Renouard, 1869–1975), XII, 75–6.

31. Langlois (ed.), *Recueil*, pp. 214–52.

32. Langlois (ed.), *Recueil*, p. 229.

33. See M. Atchison, *The* Chansonnier *of Oxford Bodleian MS Douce 308: Essays and Complete Edition of Texts* (Aldershot, Ashgate, 2005).

34. See P. Zumthor, *Le Masque et la lumière: la poétique des grands rhétoriqueurs* (Paris, Seuil, 1978); L. W. Johnson, *Poets as Players: Theme and Variation in Late Medieval French Poetry* (Stanford University Press, 1990).

# I I

SARAH KAY

# Genre, parody, and spectacle in *Aucassin et Nicolette* and other short comic tales

It may seem strange to yoke the concepts of genre and parody to that of spectacle. Prevailing definitions of genre for medieval French literature are based on form and style as much as (or even more than) content; alternatives to the concept of genre also identify expression, or rather 'register' as Zumthor terms it (see Introduction), as differentiating between various kinds of literary production. Parody is typically seen as exaggerating, distorting, or inverting other texts, and since the comic tales (diversely labelled *contes*, *fabliaux*, and *nouvelles*, and the one-off *chantefable* of *Aucassin et Nicolette*) that are discussed in this chapter have often been seen as 'parodic' of other works or genres, critics have paid especially close attention to their formal and stylistic traits.[1] Indeed, some of the best criticism on the work that I shall be centrally concerned with, *Aucassin et Nicolette*, analyses the role within it of discourse, and the *fabliaux* have been brilliantly illumined from this angle too.[2] And yet discussions of genre, parody, and the comic tale have always drawn heavily on terms such as 'perspective' and 'distance' that imply a visual field. Witness for example Caroline Jewers's statement about *Aucassin*: 'its deviation from the form of romance allows for a privileged vantage point from which to view convention and constitutes another form of generic distance from the body of texts it comically reflects'.[3] In this chapter I propose to develop this visual image, but turn it around. That is, instead of envisaging a text such as *Aucassin* as a vantage point from which to view other things, I will consider it as engineering positions from which it itself is to be viewed. If we simply adopt the perspectives it creates for us we risk being oblivious to how they were created. However, if we analyse them we glean, among other advantages, a fresh purchase on the nature of genre and parody in medieval French literature.

## Aucassin et Nicolette

Preserved in a single manuscript, and difficult to date any more closely than the thirteenth century, *Aucassin et Nicolette* is the story of two love-struck adolescents: Aucassin, son of the count of Beaucaire, and Nicolette, a slave girl of Saracen (pagan) origin who has been baptized by his underling, the viscount. Despite their social difference they look identical, but because of it Aucassin's father opposes their union and insists that the viscount lock Nicolette away. Aucassin retaliates by refusing to help defend Beaucaire when it is attacked, except when he realizes he might get his head cut off, an outcome he is desperate to avoid since it would prevent him ever kissing Nicolette. His father punishes Aucassin for his recalcitrance by locking him up too. Resourceful Nicolette abseils from her tower and finds him; recognizing they can never be united she bids him goodbye. On news of her departure, Aucassin's father releases him. After a spell of tearful apathy, Aucassin obeys a knight's advice to leave Beaucaire. This generates more comic episodes, involving shepherds and an ox-drover, as Aucassin blunders around in a forest and eventually stumbles across Nicolette: literally so, since he unheroically falls off his horse and dislocates his shoulder, which she then resets. Together they take ship and are cast by a storm on the shores of a topsy-turvy kingdom called Torelore, where the king is lying in bed after childbirth while the queen fights a war in the form of a food-fight. Here Aucassin displays unexpectedly macho behaviour, to general disapproval, but Nicolette, who had been despised in Beaucaire, is universally admired. Captured by pirate raiders, then separated by another storm, Nicolette arrives in Carthagena which she instantly recognizes as her childhood home and 'remembers' that its king is her father; Aucassin lands back in Beaucaire, where his father has died, and becomes count in his place. Ever the more active of the two, Nicolette disguises herself as a travelling minstrel (*jongleur*) and seeks out Aucassin, singing to him of the loves of Aucassin and Nicolette. This rouses him from his passivity sufficiently to ask the *jongleur* to bring Nicolette to Beaucaire to join him. And so, after she has washed off her blacking and resumed feminine dress, they are finally united for the traditional happily-ever-after ending.

There are good grounds for considering *Aucassin et Nicolette* as a spectacle. Although not a play – it is a narrative in alternating sections of verse and prose – it is conceived as a performance, with music and singing, and lots of direct speech; critics have commented on its kinship with drama.[4] In addition, the theme of looking is itself very insistent in it, which in turn solicits an imaginary gaze from the audience. The culminating episode of Nicolette as *jongleur* epitomizes this tendency. But it is apparent from the beginning, as in this early episode after Aucassin's imprisonment by his father where he laments as follows:

> Nicolette, flors de lis,
> douce amie o le cler vis,

plus es douce que roisins
ne que soupe en maserin.
L'autr'ier vi un pelerin,
nes estoit de Limosin,
malades de l'esvertin
si gisoit ens en un lit,
mout par estoit entrepris,
de grant mal amaladis;
tu passas devant son lit,
si soulevas ton traïn
et ton peliçon ermin,
la cemisse de blanc lin,
tant que ta ganbete vit:
garis fu li pelerins
et tos sains, ainc ne fu si;
si se leva de son lit,
si rala en son païs
sains et saus et tos garis.
Doce amie, flors de lis...          (§ XI, 12–32)

(Oh Nicolette, lily flower, my bright-faced sweet love, you are sweeter than a grape or than sops in a wooden bowl. The other day I saw a pilgrim, a native of the Limousin, suffering from bouts of madness, lying in his bed, made ill by his illness. You walked by in front of his bed and lifted the train of your skirt, your fur-lined coat and your linen undershirt, so that he could see your little leg. The pilgrim was cured, completely well, more than he'd ever been before; he got up from his bed and went back home well and healthy and cured. Sweet love, lily flower ...).

It is clear from this passage that Aucassin is lexically challenged and instead appears to think in pictures, a trait he shares with the anonymous narrator. Here his thoughts are of seeing Nicolette, and of seeing her being seen by the pilgrim; the reader or audience of the text is thereby invited to gaze at Nicolette as well. The sight is worth it, by all accounts, since it works a miracle on the pilgrim who has presumably undertaken his journey to be cured of his craziness and is, but not at the expected shrine. So we are all engaged here – to put it bluntly – in looking up Nicolette's skirts. How far, and what we see, is up to us. The pilgrim sees something miraculous that stimulates him back into health. All Aucassin admits to seeing is her 'little leg'. But although he first describes Nicolette 'raising the train of her skirt', which doesn't indicate anything very revealing, when he goes on to talk of her raising her undershirt the scene gets a good deal more *risqué*. The spectacle proposed by the text is identified as a miracle, announced as innocent, but also tangled up in undeclared sexual fantasy.

A traditional definition of parody would lead us to read this episode in terms of the way it interacts textually with its model, most obviously here a saint's life (such as Wace's *Vie de saint Nicolas*) relating miraculous powers. Without denying the potential of this approach, my point is that the passage quite explicitly creates positions from which to *look back at it*. Whether or not it is read as parody, it solicits our gaze. The text here acts as a lifted hem that invites us to look up it. And the way it does so usefully reminds us that there is more to the gaze, literally, than meets the eye. What this passage arouses is what the Bible calls 'the lust of the eye': a desire or urge to see that goes beyond the merely visual, if by 'visual' is meant 'what is there to be seen'; the point is precisely that we don't know quite *how much* we see. The proffered spectacle relies on duplicity: piety and naivety combine with potential lasciviousness and profanity in a confusion of motives that corresponds directly, of course, with the text's evasions over what is seen.

Although this is just an excerpt, the mixed signals it gives out help explain critical responses to the text as a whole. One approach, the most long-standing, groups *Aucassin et Nicolette* with other narratives centred on childhood love, categorized as 'idyllic romances'; on this account the *chantefable* is praised as charming, naive, and possibly folkloric. A second, quite different approach reads it as a knowing parody and/or satire, and admires it for its mordancy, wit and sophistication.[5] The first approach invites readers to view the text with indulgence or nostalgia; the second to engage with it as critique. In the first, idyllic reading we allow the story to be nimbed with a halo of innocence; in the second we assume a self-conscious appraisal in which that innocence is reinterpreted as disingenuousness in the face of a complex literary environment and adult worldly concerns. *Aucassin* generates both these positions, however dissonant. Unless we recognize how we are thus contradictorily positioned to view what it stages for us, we will not appreciate its mechanisms as a comic spectacle.

A major problem in the way of interpreting *Aucassin et Nicolette* as parody has been that of deciding what it is parodic *of*.[6] It seems to want to square up to every available genre (lyric, romance, short story, heroic poetry) from a range of languages: French, Occitan, and even Latin models have all been proposed. Is the alternation of verse and prose a response to the learned *prosimetrum* (a Latin form, used in philosophical works), to romances that incorporate inset lyrics, or to the *chansons de geste* which provide the closest metrical model for the verse passages? If the text of *Aucassin et Nicolette* is taken as a vantage point for looking at other texts (in Jewers's phrase), then it appears to spin around manically, pointing in all directions.

A single episode can open up an entire literary panorama, such as the one in which Aucassin, in prison, pleads with Nicolette through a hole in the wall not to leave. The thought of her being with any other man would make him rush headlong against a rock and dash his brains out, he says. It is inconceivable she could be faithful because:

> Femme ne puet tant amer l'oume con li hom fait la fenme; car li amors de le fenme est en son oeul et en son la cateron de sa mamele et en son l'orteil del pié; mais li amors de l'oume est ens el cué plantee, dont ele ne puet iscir.
>
> (§ XIV, 17–210)

> (A woman cannot love a man as much as a man loves a woman. For a woman's love is in her eye and at the tip of the nipple on her breast and at the tip of her toe; but a man's love is planted deep in his heart from which it cannot be removed.)

Following their conversation, Nicolette is warned by the night watch that the guards are approaching and so makes her escape. The scene has been seen as a riff on the Ovidian tale of *Piramus et Thisbe*,[7] likewise about childhood sweethearts forcibly separated by their parents' opposition to their love and who communicate through a hole in the wall before dying as a result of tragic misunderstandings. It has also been read as recasting the genre of the *aube*, a poem where a knight is alerted by the watchman to leave his lady at dawn. Aucassin's suicidal impulse parodies the desperation to which Pyramus succumbs and which is shared by other romance heroes driven mad by the loss of their beloved, like Lancelot in Chrétien's *Charrette*, or Iseut's in the prose *Tristan*. It may additionally evoke the scene in *Yvain*, already edging towards parody, where Yvain's lion tries to kill itself by running onto a sword it has propped on the ground. Aucassin is in such a rush that he decides not to waste time with the sword and trusts to the rocks alone to do the trick.

This episode points to a seemingly random set of other texts, inviting readers to measure the distance between them and it. The tragic frame offered by the tale of Pyramus reinforces the view of *Aucassin* as a utopian idyll that blithely ignores adult realities. Other romance models increase the comic pathos of a hero incapable of any action except that of self-destruction. And comparison with the *aube* reinforces this pathos as passivity, by ascribing to Nicolette the active role of the knight who comes and goes, while Aucassin stays in his prison like a lady in her castle. In all cases, seeing the text as parodic invites us not only to identify a model, but also to assume it as a recognisable norm.[8] This process is especially insidious where gender roles are concerned. The more we see Aucassin's behaviour as 'exaggerated' the more we are tempted to suppose some norm of masculinity from which it departs; the more we interpret Nicolette's behaviour as a 'reversal' of expectation, the greater the temptation to institutionalize feminine 'passivity'. Once it is read as parodic, *Aucassin*, a text of no established genre (it announces itself as a *chantefable*, but there is no other example), becomes a major tool for codifying the genre of other works. The perception that parody affirms norms and conventions has been explored in an influential book by Linda Hutcheon, who writes: 'parody posits, as a prerequisite to its very existence, a certain aesthetic institutionalization which entails the acknowledgement of stable forms and conventions'.[9] In *Aucassin*, where parodic allusiveness leads in so many directions, it is not a single model that is normatized so much as the idea of *norm as such*, a position proposed in conflicting terms by several different generic models, and thus difficult to locate. The tale offers itself as a comic spectacle to a reader from the perspective of this imagined 'normality'.

As in Aucassin's 'pilgrim' speech, one of the contradictions in the position from which we view the lovers in this episode is that between innocence and lasciviousness. How should one respond to Aucassin's childish essay on the physiology of sexual difference? The visual lure of his words may be greater than their explanatory power, since it fosters the belief that difference is visible, at least in women. Aucassin's join-the-dots formulation of feminine desire – eyes, nipples, toes – conjures a body incongruously shaped by know-ingness and ignorance. We may concur that breasts are erotic markers, but who would seriously locate sexual difference in toes? As with the miraculous gaze up Nicolette's skirt, the combination of naivety and libidinal curiosity creates uncertainty over what is seen. Thanks to Aucassin's conviction that men and women desire differently, readers are enjoined to look from a normative position, but insufficiently informed as to where it is.

A counterpart to this passage is the work's closing sequence where Nicolette dresses as a *jongleur*, since it offers the by now familiar combina-tion of uncertainty as to whether there is such a thing as sexual difference, and titillation at the prospect of looking into it. This time, there is a clash between Aucassin's blithe inability to penetrate Nicolette's disguise – a standard feature of such scenes in medieval French literature, where no one seems capable of seeing beyond a contrived appearance – and the audience's satisfaction at possessing superior knowledge. Again, the scene is con-structed as a spectacle that we are invited to view from a position constructed by the diverse generic models which it posits. Some, like the various episodes of the Tristan legend where Tristan disguises himself, imply a gender reversal (with Nicolette taking the male role) while others, like *Beuve de Hantone* where the heroine Josiane likewise plays the minstrel to be reunited with Beuve, confirm the gender-appropriateness of Nicolette's behaviour. The practice of travesty (or transvestism) here links both content and form, pre-senting not only Nicolette in *jongleur*'s dress, but the text adopting the (contra-dictory) trappings of earlier texts.

The exhortation to adopt a normative gaze, and thus cement generic identities, is most clamorous in the Torelore episode (§§ 28–32), which likewise positively courts being looked at *as* spectacle. Insofar as this mind-boggling sequence is a parody *of* something else, its most obvious target is *chansons de geste* like the *Roland*, with their focus on male warfare and relegation of women to food, home, and the reproduction of warriors-to-be. The episode encourages us to judge as deviant and absurd the way people behave in Torelore relative to a position that is, by implication, 'normal'. The invocation of epic poetry introduces standards of behaviour in war and government which the text falls lamentably short of. However, as in other episodes, the *chanson de geste*'s adult, aristocratic world is oddly combined with childish sniggers. Just as elsewhere we look up Nicolette's skirt, ogle her breasts, or conjecture about the body under her clothes, now we are invited to look under the king's bedclothes as they are dramatically ripped off his bed. Has he really given birth to a son and if so how? Or does this episode, as some have suggested, represent an instance of male *couvade*, the practice observed among some primitive peoples in which men symbolically enact the experience of childbirth so as to appropriate it for themselves?[10] Once again, it is up to the gaze turned upon this scene by the reader or audience to take responsibility for what is 'seen'. But in contrast to the episodes discussed earlier, there is a threat of punishment if we look amiss. Parody is often conceived as not only reliant on some kind of institution, but also as policing or punitive, and these associations are both thematized and mocked in this episode. Aucassin acts on behalf of what he sees as 'normality' when he berates the king, hauls him out of bed, beats him, and forces him to promise that men in Torelore will never lie in childbirth again. His uncouth behaviour is in turn reprimanded by the king. The perspective of the *chansons de geste* may lead us to expect men to fight among themselves, but the grounds for aggression here create doubt whether the term 'men' means what we thought it did!

This episode's self-mockery regarding 'normality' can be used to shed further light on parody and genre. I have argued that *Aucassin* posits a position for the reader, passing it off as a 'norm' (generic, sexual, or otherwise) from which the text appears as a comic spectacle. By inducing us to adopt such models as our vantage point for looking at it, the text effectively stops us examining *them*. How genuine is this perspective, on what is it founded? *Aucassin* may indeed parody earlier works, but they only become important to the reader insofar as they are an *effect* of the text: it is enough that we are persuaded they exist. Thus parody, although giving the impression that its model is earlier than it is, may actually be what *founds* its model. Indeed, in the Middle Ages, there are sometimes texts that strike us as parodic whose closest available model dates from *after* they were written. And even where earlier models do exist our sense of what they 'really are' may be determined by the way the parody represents them! One can thus say of parody that it is both founding and anti-foundational, that it both relies on a model and fictionalizes it, and this is also Hutcheon's view when she says of literary works that 'they have sought to incorporate critical commentary within their own structures in a kind of self-legitimizing short-circuit of the normal critical dialogue'.[11] Comic spectacle in *Aucassin*, while normalizing the codes of other texts, retains licence to cast doubt on their veracity; and the same is true of the other assumptions it assigns its readers. As well as combining naivety and knowingness, the retrospective gaze that it trains on itself is anarchic as much as it is regulatory.

## *Fabliaux* and the *Cent Nouvelles nouvelles*

Other medieval French short comic tales construct this kind of retrospective gaze in varying ways. The *fabliaux*, short comic verse tales often on a bawdy theme whose currency is roughly contemporary with *Aucassin* (several are transmitted in the same manuscript),[12] have, like it, given rise to controversy about whether or not they are parodic. And as with *Aucassin*, various models have been proposed: courtly romance, *chansons de geste*, clerical texts of one kind or another (*exempla*, miracles, allegory).[13] Variant versions of some of these *fabliaux* are more or less naive or knowing, courtly or coarse, visual or verbal; in some the plot hinges entirely on linguistic misconstruals, and these are clearly not amenable to the approach deployed here.[14] In many, however, the gaze and what it sees or fails to see is an explicit theme within the story itself. The possibility that the text constitutes a comic spectacle is thus admitted in the texts themselves. A priest persuades his mistress's husband to look through a keyhole which, he is assured, is magic because it conjures into sight a couple making love; what the husband sees is indeed the priest with his wife, but he lets himself be persuaded that they are only eating dinner.[15] Another husband is induced to kill a series of priests (in a variant it is a series of hunchbacks) in the belief that the 'one' he has just killed has come back to life, and misunderstandings over the identity of an object that the characters fail properly to 'see' is a characteristic of another group of tales.[16] The *fabliaux* throng with characters who are apparently willing to believe they see what they are told that they see (even if they patently don't). Their gaze, positioned within the story, parallels the gaze which the story directs upon itself, and warns the reader not to fall into the same trap.

I'll take just one example, the *fabliau* 'Berengier au lonc cul'.[17] It concerns a rich peasant who marries the daughter of an impoverished castellan who owes him money. The high-born wife taunts her lazy food-swilling husband with constant reminders of her chivalric ancestors. Piqued, he resolves to demonstrate that he is as good a knight as them. So he puts on armour, goes into the forest, hitches his shield to a tree and belabours it with his sword until it looks suitably battle-scarred; then takes it home to show her and boast of his adventures. The wife, who is no dupe, seethes inwardly and decides to punish him for this cowardly pantomime. So one day, disguised in armour, she follows him to the forest and catches him in the act of hacking at his shield. The terms in which she accosts him have been identified as a comic deformation of Chrétien's *Yvain*, when Calogrenant is rebuked by Esclados for destroying his woodland (*Berengier*, 196–9; cf. *Yvain*, 489–500).[18] The peasant, horrified to find himself up against a real adversary, offers to make amends on any terms; and when his wife gives him the choice between fighting or kissing her backside he is too cowardly to hesitate. But as he approaches for the kiss he is mystified by the sight of her crack ('cil regarde la crevace / du cul et du con', 244–5) and thinks to himself that he has never seen such a long arse ('oncques si lonc cul ne vit', 248). The encounter concludes with a return to the conventions of courtly romance, with the defeated party asking the victor's name. As if reading his thoughts, she replies that her name is 'Berengier au lonc cul / qui a toz les coarz fait honte' (260–1: 'Long-Arse Berengier who brings disgrace on all cowards'). When he arrives home and finds her with her lover, his protests are vain. If he so much as breathes a word of complaint, she tells him, she will get 'Berengier au lonc cul' to intervene.

As in *Aucassin*, the lure of another genre – chivalric romance – creates a perspective from which to enter into the *fabliau*'s carefully constructed visual space. Also as in *Aucassin*, one pole of the gaze that is turned on its comic spectacle is ignorance of the purported 'reality' of sexual difference – the result here not of childhood innocence but lower-class imbecility. The peasant's inability to recognize his wife's behind is directly equated with his inability to control her sexually. The annexing of romance as a position from which to view the *fabliau* also proposes a perspective on chivalric norms. If hanging your shield up on a tree and hacking it is hardly a 'proper' use of knightly weapons, still less is styling yourself 'Berengier au long cul' an appropriate knightly surname, while baring your backside for a kiss is a far from chivalric form of conquest. The reference to *Yvain* may draw attention to the ethically dubious behaviour of its own hero in the forest. The position from which we view the *fabliau*'s spectacle creates a comic distance between reader and both its principal characters, inviting derision towards them, which we might then also 'see' as the construction that it is. In this *fabliau* (as in many others), the emphasis is more on licence than on regulation.

A later group of comic tales that also rely on stage-managing the gaze is the *Cent Nouvelles nouvelles*. This story collection from the 1450s is frequently bawdy or libertine; many *nouvelles*, like *fabliaux*, rely on what can or cannot be seen, and on discrepancies between what people think they see and what we are led to believe is really there (such as *nouvelles* XXVI and LXV, both involving cross-dressing). There is a lot of eager spying, especially by men on women, countered by much retaliatory concealment, often of men by women.[19] And as in the *fabliaux*, things that are quite openly visible are often not seen for what they are, with hilarious consequences (see example below). The collection is conceived as a recasting of Boccaccio's *Decameron*, known in French as the *Cent Nouvelles*. A prologue states that its tales are more recent and local than Boccaccio's, and while there isn't a frame narrative as such, rubrics represent the stories as being exchanged between the duke of Burgundy and members of his court. The collection thus sets up the *Decameron* as a position from which Philippe le Bon's wealth and power is admired or envied. The inscribed presence of Burgundian courtiers also creates an aristocratic perspective on the tales. The *nouvelles* parody less recognizable texts than generic forms (especially the *exemplum*, for example, *nouvelles* XXIX and LV) and discourses (those of courtly love, warfare, learning, or the church); the latter are often used in deliberately inappropriate contexts, often as a source of sexual metaphors (for example *nouvelles* XXIII, LXXI, LXXXV, and LXXXVI). The courtiers' assumed social superiority towards most of their characters parallels the literary distance between the noble genres and their burlesqued counterpart.

Again I give just one example, the opening tale in the collection. It is said to be narrated by the duke who thus inaugurates the collection and creates a model position for how the stories might be viewed. It tells of a well-to-do bourgeois who, attracted by his neighbour's wife, assiduously cultivates his neighbour's company. Eventually she agrees to see him when next her husband is absent. The husband duly announces a business trip; alerted to this window of opportunity, the bourgeois arranges a copious dinner with food and wine and hot baths: all the trimmings of seduction medieval style. He and the wife bathe and feast and go to bed, when there is a knock at the door. After a panicky delay, during which the bourgeois tells the wife to stay in bed and keep her head out of sight, the servants let the visitor in. Predictably it is the husband who is all suspicion at the sight that meets his eyes. What naughtiness is his neighbour up to, and with whom? In a fever of jealousy he makes to pull the bedclothes off the bed. After some resistance, the neighbour relents to the point of asking his servants to lift the sheets so as to reveal the backside of the woman in his bed. The bourgeois shows it off for his neighbour's approval and asks, would he say it was his wife's? The husband is perplexed. He agrees that it is an extremely fine backside, and that it might indeed be his wife's, but he isn't sure and is inclined to believe that it isn't. The bourgeois presses him to stay and enjoy the plentiful remains of the food and drink; meanwhile in the bed the bourgeois and the wife enjoy themselves. Some time later, the husband, very much the worse for wear, decides he really must go home. He asks to be let out through the little postern gate that gives directly onto his own house, but the bourgeois makes some excuse about it being too difficult to open and instead he lets him out of the front door so he has to walk round the block. The wife meanwhile is bundled out through the postern straight into her own house so she is back inside when her husband returns. At first she refuses to let him in, pretending not to believe that it is he. When eventually she relents she gives him a bad time for returning in such a state and at such a late hour. He is obliged to confess what he has been doing, including his suspicions about her, for which he is forced to make a grovelling apology.

As in the case of *Berengier* this tale hinges on a husband's inability to recognize and hence control his wife's body. In *Berengier*, this view was set up from a perspective based in chivalric romance. In the *nouvelle*, the ducal court provides an analogous context from which to 'see' the lower classes as unable to control their own lives and thus as meriting the court's derision; there is no answering mockery of the court. The tone of the *Cent Nouvelles* is thus very different from the *fabliaux*: less playful or anarchic, more regulatory and punitive.

The sole surviving manuscript sets out to solicit its readers' gaze in a way that may enable them to resist this perspective, however. It prefaces each *nouvelle* with a small picture which, in this case, presents us with a choice view of the woman's bottom (Figure 8). As we read this initial tale, our 'view' of what the picture means is gradually brought into focus as we realize what we have seen in this opening image, and what the husband fails to see. This pattern is repeated throughout the collection: the reader first sees a somewhat mystifying illustration, then watches a plot unfold in which someone within the story fails 'to get the picture' while, to the reader, it becomes hilariously clear. The gaze, occasionally invoked in *Aucassin*, regularly thematized in the fabliaux, becomes a material element in the transmission of the *Cent Nouvelles nouvelles*. Although told as 'seen' by the Burgundian court, the tales are a spectacle offered to the eye of all future readers.

## Conclusion

The argument presented in this chapter has taken a deliberately limited view of genre and parody. Sidestepping the field of intertextuality, whose

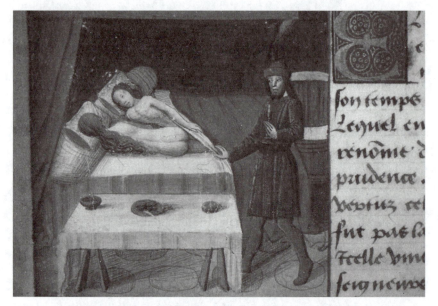

Figure 8. *Cent Nouvelles nouvelles*, Glasgow, Hunter 252, fo. 3r. This miniature prefacing
the first *nouvelle* depicts the neighbour looking at his wife's rear but unable to recognize
her; his uncomprehending gaze contrasts with the mastery of that of the tale's narrator,
the duke of Burgundy.

importance I would not for a moment deny, my efforts have been limited to
identifying a point of contact between parody as an intertextual relation,
and the visual provocation of medieval comic tales. I have argued that the
*chantefable* and other comic tales position readers in such a way as to
provide them with particular ways of looking back at these works as
instances of comic spectacle. Parody is a major device that all employ in
creating this position, for rather than leading away from the comic text to a
model, it posits that model as a position from which to view the comic text.
In the works I have discussed here, it leads the reader into an imaginary
complicity with another text or, more commonly, another genre, as instantiating norms for behaviour or identity. However, it also exposes the process
whereby such norms are fabricated. Different works (and no doubt different
readers) respond differently to the dissonance between naivety and know-
ingness, anarchy and institutionalism. What seems to me undeniable and
historically significant is the progressive internalization and institutionalization of the gaze within the comic tale itself, so that by the time of the
*nouvelle* it has become, as well as a motor of the plot, a feature of its *mise en
page*. If the short comic tale interacts with other genres to normalize or

undermine them, eventually it seems to find its own generic norm as a comic spectacle.

## Notes

1. A. E. Cobby, *Ambivalent Conventions: Formula and Parody in Old French* (Amsterdam, Rodopi, 1995), discusses both *Aucassin* and *fabliaux*.
2. K. Brownlee, 'Discourse as Proueces in *Aucassin et Nicolette*', *Yale French Studies*, 70 (1986), 167–82; E. Vance, '*Aucassin et Nicolette* and the Poetics of Discourse', in *Mervelous Signals: Poetics and Sign Theory in the Middle Ages* (Lincoln, NB, and London, University of Nebraska Press, 2006), pp. 152–83; R. H. Bloch, *The Scandal of the Fabliaux* (Chicago University Press, 1986).
3. C. A. Jewers, *Chivalric Fiction and the History of the Novel* (Gainesville, FL, University Press of Florida, 2000), p. 45; J. Tattersall, 'Shifting Perspectives and the Illusion of Reality in *Aucassin et Nicolette*', *French Studies*, 38 (1984), 257–67.
4. M. Roques described it as a 'mime' in his edition, *Aucassin et Nicolette: chantefable du XIIIe siècle*, CFMA (Paris, Champion, 1927), p. v.
5. Jewers, *Chivalric Fiction*, pp. 45–53; for earlier criticism, see B. N. Sargent-Bauer and R. F. Cook, *Aucassin et Nicolette: a Critical Bibliography* (London, Grant and Cutler, 1982). T. Hunt, 'La Parodie médiévale: le cas d'*Aucassin et Nicolette*', *Romania*, 100 (1979), 341–81, criticizes parodic readings.
6. R. S. Spraycar, 'Genre and Convention in *Aucassin et Nicolette*', *Romanic Review*, 76 (1985), 94–115.
7. See *Pyrame et Thisbé*, ed. E. Baumgartner.
8. This process of normalization is very marked in J. H. Martin's *Love's Fools: Aucassin, Troilus, Calisto, and the Parody of the Courtly Lover* (London, Tamesis, 1972).
9. L. Hutcheon, *A Theory of Parody: the Teachings of Twentieth-century Art Forms* (New York and London, Methuen, 1985, pp. 74–5). Her thinking is influenced by Bakhtin.
10. J. Gilbert, 'The Practice of Gender in *Aucassin et Nicolette*', *Forum for Modern Language Studies*, 33 (1997), 217–28 (pp. 218–22).
11. Hutcheon, *A Theory of Parody*, p. 1.
12. Paris, BnF, fr. 2168, known to *fabliau* editors as *H*. It contains versions of *fabliaux* 18, 35, 37, 62, and 74 (= *Le Sacristain*, see below) in the *Nouveau Recueil complet des fabliaux*, ed. Noomen and van de Boogaard (henceforth *NRCF*).
13. Cobby, *Ambivalent Conventions*, pp. 24–6.
14. e.g. *Estula* (NRCF 38), or *La Male Honte* (NRCF 43).
15. *Le Prestre qui abevete* (NRCF 98).
16. *Les Quatre Prestres* (NRCF 85), *Les Trois Boçus* (NRCF 47), *Le Sacristain* (NRCF 74, see note 13).
17. NRCF 34, cited from *Fabliaux érotiques*, ed. Rossi and Straub. Discussed in Gaunt, *Gender and Genre*, pp. 253–6, 277–80, and E. J. Burns, *Bodytalk: When Women Talk in Old French Literature* (Philadelphia, University of Pennsylvania Press, 1993), pp. 39–43; for earlier studies, see NRCF, IV, p. 251.
18. K. Busby, 'Fabliau et roman breton: le cas de *Berengier au lonc cul*', in *Epopée animale, fable, fabliau. Actes du IVe colloque de la Société Internationale*

*Renardienne*, ed. G. Bianciotto and M. Salvat, *Cahiers d'Etudes Médiévales* 2–3 (Paris, PUF, 1984), pp. 121–32 (pp. 127–8).

19. E.g. *nouvelles* XXXIII and LXIX (men spying on women) and XXVII, LXI, LXXII, LXXIII, and LXXXVIII (women concealing men); see D. A. Fein, *Displacements of Power: Readings of the Cent Nouvelles nouvelles* (Lanham, MD, University Press of America, 2003).

# 12

HELEN SOLTERER

# Theatre and theatricality

'Speak firmly and in an orderly rhythm.' 'Make appropriate gestures ... manifesting sorrow by falling down on the ground ... or showing joy through the face.'[1] These were the instructions given to people playing the first man and woman in the biblical *Jeu d'Adam* (late twelfth century). Talking in another voice and mimicking another person were the key body languages to master, the skills necessary to acting before others. They defined a practice that did not correspond to any formal conception of genre and extended far beyond what we recognize as theatre today. In a world where culture was transacted orally as much as through hand-written texts or manuscripts and the earliest printed books, such theatrical action informed the way texts were read aloud, the styles of celebrating religious and political occasions, as well as physical play, noise-making. As Paul Zumthor began to argue in the late 1960s, such action animated so many different forms of communication and expression that it is more telling to ask what was not characterized theatrically than to identify what was theatre.[2]

The Parisian schoolman, Hugh of St Victor (died 1141) captured this array of activity when he described in a Latin treatise the 'science called theatrics'. 'Epics were presented either by recitals or by acting out dramatic roles or using masks or puppets; choral processions and dances were held in the porches. In gymnasia, they wrestled, at banquets they made music with songs and instruments. In the temples they sang the praises of God.'[3] Hugh adapted a model that had come from imperial Rome to describe the rituals, sports, and verbal fictions of public life in twelfth-century Europe. He gives us a sense of the many different sites for theatrical action, and the people implicated.

At the heart of all this action the players stood. Even if these thousands of men and women remain largely unknown, they theatricalized action through their trained voices and deliberately shaped movements. They gave it palpable and impressive life. To inquire into medieval theatrical action is to follow their lead, imagining them reciting and singing in French dialects, processing across town squares, cavorting in open fields, and intoning Latin prayers in monasteries.

Players also help us to account for the different parties involved: from the composer of verbal and musical texts, through the personae created, to the audiences who participated in the action. Those responsible for enlivening the texts brought all these people together. Sometimes the player could well have been the composer, as in the controversial case of twelfth-century troubadours. Or the players stepped out of and receded back into the crowds attending the mass spectacles of religious drama in the fifteenth century. Indeed, sometimes player, persona, composer, and public seemed indistinguishable, as thirteenth-century poets Adam de la Halle from the city of Arras and Rutebeuf from Paris suggest. Whichever the case, the medieval player epitomized the communal dimension of theatrical action.

Today, actor–playwright Dario Fo impersonates the medieval player brilliantly, showing the influence of this tradition on contemporary arts. His work *Mistero Buffo* (*Comic Mysteries*) is steeped in fourteenth-century Franco-Italian religious drama and farce as it was rediscovered in part by modern-day theatre people in France. He improvised it to the provocation and pleasure of millions across Europe, Asia, and the Americas. Fo acknowledged his debt to the anonymous creators of medieval theatrical culture when he accepted the 1997 Nobel Prize in literature in the name of 'a multitude of mummers, jesters, and storytellers'.[4]

## In the beginning was dialogue

The Benedictine monastery of Saint Martial in Limoges gives us an early twelfth-century script of theatrical action, the first known example in France. The *Sponsus* reveals a kernel of dialogue between Christ, the bridegroom or *Sponsus*, and the church, *Ecclesia*, his virginal wife-to-be, between a heroic figure speaking the authoritative Latin language and a woman speaking in a juicy Franco-Provençal idiom.[5]

Composer and players remain unidentifiable yet they were most likely monks working to make the Christian liturgy more accessible to wider congregations. Like their Jewish peers during the eleventh century, they experimented with the call-and-response form, making it bilingual.[6] Through the two liturgical parts, they attempted to articulate the voice of the sacred, to incarnate the divine persona of Christ, and to humanize him in the guise of a husband-to-be. They turned to troubadour song; *Ecclesia*'s voice resonates strongly with that same poetic longing between lover and beloved. The two players were to do all this before a public including laypeople from the surrounding Poitou countryside. Could their action 'inculcate' the audience with pious behaviour as another twelfth-century churchman instructed?[7] It is difficult to fix the relation between their theatrical action and the liturgy. Did their playing complement the liturgical event or rival it in the minds of the public? This fundamental tension would temper religious drama and the church's attitude to all playing for centuries.

Several generations later in the Anglo-Norman territories further north, the *Jeu d'Adam* developed the first biblical scenario for a small group of nameless actors. The work, also known as the Latin *Ordo representacionis Ade*, the *Rite of Representing Adam*, was situated in a religious setting. Taking the office from the Book of Genesis spoken and sung on holy days during Lent, it transformed the responsorial texts: the first act of creation happened through dialogue.[8] The man playing God called out, '*Adam!*' and the response came back in French, '*Sire?*' Out of this bilingual exchange comes the story of Christian history, from its innocent beginnings to the loss of paradise, from the struggles between husband and wife and between brothers to the prophecies of redemption, all spoken in a rhythmic colloquial vernacular.

The *Jeu d'Adam* included a stagecraft manual of sorts in Latin. Players were trained how to walk and dance. They were advised about props: an artfully constructed serpent, the emblems of rod and book for Moses and Isaiah, pots to bang and clang together in a devilish cacophony. For the scene of fratricide of Cain and Abel, they were instructed how to act as if killing and being killed. The theatrical action that resulted seems to have exploited a greater degree of self-consciousness about acting a role, not only in the rapport between player and public, but also in the visceral connection between player and role. If indeed they performed in front of the sculpted facades of churches, their role-playing was intensified by the stone figures surrounding them. The choral song accompanying the play added to the awesome effect. Yet the Anglo-Norman dialogue, as critic Erich Auerbach noticed, domesticated these personae with simple comic tones; the actors thereby brought their story closer to audiences.[9]

## Acting in the city

During much the same period, the cities of Northern France gave rise to a form of theatrical action that broke free from liturgical celebration. The *Jeu de Saint Nicolas* (*c.*1200) capitalized on the wealth of saints' legends, the *lingua franca* of a lay religious imagination. But its miraculous story had less to do with inspiring piety than with tackling satirically the sapping of Europe by the Crusades. Gone was the biblical Eden, and in its place, 'Arabie', the land of the Saracen enemies. With a call-to-arms straight out of a *chanson de geste*, this play presents emirs mobilizing against Christians and massacring them. Out of this debacle emerges the saintly star, first as a figurine who gives the captive Christians courage, then as a larger-than-life saviour who avenges them by forcing the Saracens to convert. This is a holy war story with mock heroism, violence, and illusions of virtuous victory.

Jean Bodel was the composer identified with the *Jeu de Nicolas*, and for the first time we can associate theatrical action with a known poet and music-maker also attributed with a diversity of epic, lyric, and *fabliau*. Bodel was from Arras, an economic hub in Picardy. He chose to situate the story of this east/west confrontation at the heart of his community and turned to other townspeople to help dramatize its sorry impact on their world. Arras had one of the earliest corporations of workers that gave poet–performers an important civic status. Part fraternity, part trade union, the nascent *Confrérie des Jongleurs et Bourgeois d'Arras* most likely provided the social framework for Bodel's work. His scenario dramatized their common experience of religious war invading their daily life. It put the ideals of triumphant Christianity to the test, challenging them through the rowdy games of the city tavern. Several of his personae were home grown, and those playing the rogues of Arras were creating characters that were recognizable types coming out of their own circles. In the process, they were integrating this theatrical action more fully into the life of the town. Bodel's actors incited their community to face up to images of themselves.

Following Bodel's lead, Adam de la Halle further exploited this theatricalization of city life.[10] Around 1276, he composed and performed the *Jeu de la feuillée*, a parody of the foibles of Arras. His anti-hero is 'Adam', alter ego to the biblical persona, and a young fellow who epitomizes the dream of living the high life of clerics in Paris, but never makes it out of town. The other citizens, doctors, monks peddling relics, prostitutes, burghers are each exposed in turn for failing to realize their professional ambitions. Not even the magical character is spared disenchantment, the fairy queen suffering heartbreak in her *feuillée* (green bower). This comedy offers one characteristic alternative to despair: the tavern – a halfway house between paradise and hell, and a favourite meeting place for any urban milieu.

With the poet–performer Adam de la Halle, the art of theatrical impersonation was becoming more personal. His 'Adam' was also a poetic mask, and it is probable that the first audiences of the play in Arras would have recognized it as such. The names Master Henri, Riquier, and Hane le Mercier identified stock characters with known individuals. This linking of persona and person has the flavour of insider joking and no doubt was specific to a particular group at one time but suggests how role-play continued to develop innovatively.

Much of the local wit of the *Feuillée* escapes us, but its social function is no less clear. Acting theatrically was an increasingly vital dynamic of urban culture. With the greater prominence of the *Confrérie*, it began to be recognized as a type of work or what we might call community activism. Local archives show that numbers of the men involved in Adam de la Halle's play were influential members of this guild. But acting theatrically was equally important as a political medium. It enabled townspeople to externalize and debate the problems besetting them: religious hypocrisy, economic fraud, emotional deception. It did so via the actual men and women involved.

Paris, the largest French-speaking city, royal seat and intellectual centre, offered another major site for inventing personae in response to different social situations. Rutebeuf was a clerical composer working in the Latin Quarter, among disciples who, unlike Adam de la Halle's persona, had arrived in the capital. His repertory spanned Crusader songs, debate poems on the latest university scandal with the friars, and *dits*, satirical sketches akin to the pieces of modern vaudeville performers. For his *Miracle de Théophile* (mid thirteenth century), he drew a hapless character out of popular Marian tales. 'Caught between poverty and need', Rutebeuf's Théophile consorts with evil in the guise of an exotic sorcerer, the Semitic Salatin, and is saved by Mary's divine intervention. With a turnaround plot typical of miracle plays, Rutebeuf reinstates his character in the world of priests, making him once again true to his name: lover of God.

He was fashioning theatrical personae for the social caste who understood themselves as guardians and models of public morality. This was a particularly fraught attempt since Rutebeuf was showing the failings of the very group on whom he depended for a living. Yet all of Rutebeuf's compositions were animated by ordinary personae who spoke with self-deprecating humour. Whether it was his Théophile or the travelling salesman of the *Dit de l'herberie* they all 'complained joyously'. Their voices hardly suggested subjects in our psychological understanding, but they did convey some internal questioning.[11] In a series of *dits* given the poet's name, *La Pauvreté*, *Le Mariage*, *La Complainte* and *La Repentance*, the single speaker enacts the ups and downs of a personal story, one that resembles closely that of the Parisian cleric. Were 'Théophile' and 'Rutebeuf' alternating masks for the same person? Scribes copying down the compositions confused them. But with no evidence of theatrical action, we will never know for sure. Nor are we ever likely to ascertain if the man using these names could have performed all of these compositions. Still, the growing focus on the persona as personal mask signals the fundamentally theatrical nature of the human person in early European culture, as anthropologist Marcel Mauss argued.[12]

In another quarter of Paris across the Seine on the Right Bank, other groups worked at improvising Marian miracles on a much larger scale. Throughout the second half of the fourteenth century, the influential guild of goldsmiths gathered every year to do business and honour their patron saint, and their assembly was celebrated lavishly with banquets and over forty plays. *Les Miracles de Nostre Dame par personnages* was a cycle of drama charting the extraordinary travails of ordinary people like Rutebeuf's Théophile: children kidnapped by the devil, husbands and wives at each other's throats, bourgeois possessed to steal, clerics driven to jump into bed with their parishioners. The compassionate figure of Mary stood ever ready to rescue the weak at heart and remedy their desperate situations. Such scenes made for delightful *entremets* or intervals in the feasting, helping to confirm generosity and solidarity, principles dear to goldsmiths.

Enacting these miracles required large numbers of people. The confraternity's meeting occasioned an unprecedented degree of theatrical collaboration. Members of the cast were never singled out by name, but the phrase *par personnages* in their title, most likely referring to performing roles, points to a growing distinction of the players. During the late fourteenth century the term *personnage* appeared in the account books of the royal entourage, as well as in legal records of the municipal archive, signalling that more lay actors were recognized officially and paid for their work.[13] The activities of the Parisian goldsmiths were symptomatic of other urban festivities, in Amiens, for example, or Lille in the northeast, where citizens of various castes and ages were getting involved theatrically.[14] Bourgeois commitment to theatricality was building momentum. Performances of the *Miracles de Nostre Dame* on the Right Bank resembled or even rivalled the pageantry surrounding the entrances of monarchs into the city, the set pieces of *tableaux vivants*, or scenes from religious drama that syncopated the arrival of Queen Isabeau of Bavaria and the processions to her residence.

The festivities put on by the goldsmiths were also significant because they were put down in writing. The fourteenth-century Cangé manuscript, with its hundreds of folios, and bookish rubrication, poses the question of theatre as literature, as *civic* literature. How could theatrical action function through the medium of hand-written and illustrated texts? Why would this confraternity have chosen to give their *Miracles* this form as well? Researchers have squinted over the Cangé to decipher its rubbed-out rubrics. 'Joue au puy des orfevres a paris' (played at the goldsmiths' assembly in Paris): it is as if a byline noting performance had been erased to give precedence to a written rendition of the drama. On the one hand, we hypothesize players and live audiences enacting the *Miracles* and on the other, scribes and readers. During the high Middle Ages, blurred images in other manuscripts bear witness to their readers' physical give and take with the page: so many signs of what we describe in theatrical terms as 'identification'.[15] Like the Cangé smudge, these images challenge us to take *all* parties into account as we seek to understand the complementary function of manuscript and theatrical action in late medieval culture, and the key investment of the laity.

## The mass spectacle of mystery plays

Starting in the late fourteenth century, cities all across French-speaking Europe began organizing the grandest of theatrical actions known as *mystères* (mystery plays). Their religious scenarios traced the history of the cosmos; the productions undertaken were so ambitious as to involve thousands of people; and the social conflict they personified was played out against the backdrop of popular uprisings and the Hundred Years' War.[16] *Le Mystère de la Passion* was the paradigmatic drama. Building on the story of individual lives transformed in miracle plays, it encompassed Genesis and the entire Christian biblical story right up to the Last Judgement. At its centre, a story of betrayal and sacrifice, with the heroic figure of Jesus Christ, interrogated, tortured and put to death. It had all the makings of tragedy, yet it did not leave comedy out. Scenes of farce punctuated the play with the antics of devils and the buffoonery of workers. The laughter helped to make the expected outcome of violent death livable. The final act of Christ's Resurrection was intended to be 'hilarious', and open-ended.

The two principal versions, composed by clerics Arnoul Gréban (*c.*1450) and Jean Michel (*c.*1480) demanded the massive labour that only urban confraternities and corporations could muster. The *Confrérie de la Passion* was authorized by the French King Charles VI to take on just this mission in Paris in 1402, at a point when the phenomenon was already well under way in various regions.[17] With numerous individuals mobilized, their productions began to acquire a professional quality. A *fatiste* or compiler was commissioned to draw up a written version of the composer's text. An *entrepreneur de jeu* (director) was chosen, such as Jean Gorion in Vienne in 1400. Hundreds of actors began working together, including women like the daughter of the furrier in the 1468 mystery in Metz, and even children. Craftsmen constructed elaborate stage sets that traversed the central squares of their towns, paying particular attention to décor: the 'paradise' in Angers 1456 with its pomegranates, figs, and other artificially made fruit, far surpassed that of the *Jeu d'Adam*. Technicians devised rudimentary special effects, known as 'secrets': the illusion machines that made demons fly in Aix in 1444, and the tortured bleed to death. Even the huge audiences were taken into consideration, as in Reims in 1490, where they were provided with wine to keep them engaged. The operation of the mystery play was so complex as to monopolize a population for months on end, and when it finally came to performance, the city was often locked shut, as in Angers in 1486, as everyone gave themselves over to the spectacle.

Such grandiose theatrical action energized social rivalry and violence. With huge revenues expended, tensions between different classes were exacerbated, setting bourgeois against churchmen. Even the distribution of roles was fought over. The symbolic image of community forged by performing the *Mystère* did not translate easily into good working relations or solidarity but instead often gave rise to gruesome events. Convicted criminals were enlisted as players, and their executions threatened to become part of the notorious, sanctioned bloodletting of the play. The scenes of massacre and crucifixion were also known sometimes to incite anti-Semitic reactions.[18] All this happened in a world constantly alerted to the rumour of war, to the protracted struggle between the Armagnacs, the faction allied with the French throne, and the Burgundians allied with the English. It is not surprising then that the model of the mystery play was used to dramatize momentous current events. *Le Mystère du siège d'Orléans* presented Joan of Arc's climactic battle for this city, enacting many scenes in the very places where they happened, with citizens playing the roles of their contemporaries, including the extraordinary woman warrior.[19] By presenting their here and now theatrically in this manner, they made it part of cosmic, Christian history.

Mystery plays remained the most influential and enduring case of theatrical action, as the numbers of written versions also attest. Today research continues as manuscripts are rediscovered: the versions of the *fatiste* (composer or compiler), those intended for the *meneur de jeu* (director) such as the *Livre de conduite du régisseur* from Mons (1501), or those that read as lavish records of performances. The rarest and most unfamiliar manuscripts are the *rolets* that transcribe the actors' individual roles. Several from the late fifteenth century give us a crucial glimpse of the growing prominence of the player as the pivotal figure for theatrical action.[20]

At much the same time, the *Mystère de la passion* was also beginning to make its mark in the experimental realm of vernacular printed books. The earliest printing presses in Paris and Lyon around 1470 reproduced hundreds of copies, catering to the new communities of lay readers for whom this play was a favourite.[21] By the early sixteenth century, with tens of thousands of copies in circulation, there were as many people imagining the play through what they heard read as there were who saw it performed.

## The dangerous freedom of farce

Farce was always an indispensable part of the high theatrical action of mysteries. The noisy gesticulations of devils, *diableries*, as well as the rough-and-ready humour of shepherds, the *bergeries*, ran through these plays like currents of laughter and relief. Far from antagonistic to the tone of religious drama, they were integral to its effect. Farcical scenes accentuated what was fundamentally a comic vision of human life in the cosmos, as epitomized in Dante's *Divina Comedia*.

Comedy flourished throughout the fifteenth century, taking many rambunctious forms of action.[22] There were several hundred small pieces fondly ridiculing the usual suspects in urban and rural milieus: the gullible bourgeois husband, the pretentious cleric, the blind leading the blind, and of course, the crafty peasant who plays dumb. The *Farce de Maître Pathelin* (c.1460) presents a showdown between a legal conman and his client, the countryman, who outwits him by only ever saying *Bée!*[23] This anarchic verbal comedy was by far the favourite play; it still resonates today in idiomatic spoken French: *pathelin* meaning 'trickster' and *bouche-bée* 'dumbfounded'. Side-by-side with this farce were the *sotties*, short sketches or manic bursts of tomfoolery that often revolved around the single persona of the fool or *sot*. This persona had already made a cameo appearance in Adam de la Halle's *Feuillée*, but he transmuted explosively into a major figure in the courts and on the squares of late medieval Europe. With his ass's ears, and colourful cap and clothes, he stands for a jester *avant la lettre*, the figure who focalizes the lunacy and disarming frankness of society, and projects them back.

It was farce that gave rise to a category of actor who was more easily identifiable than his predecessors, more organized, and more controversial.[24] In Paris, groups of law students active in the Parliament banded together to put on comic pieces. The *Basochiens* were the archetypal young professionals running amok: invariably in trouble with municipal and church officials, and yet responsible for various performances that regaled their neighbourhoods. In other parts of the French-speaking world, there were groups known as *enfants sans soucis, sociétés joyeuses*, whom we could call comically 'the carefree kids, the joyboys'. These associations gave young people a framework for shameless playacting. Together with them, we also find individual actors who made a name for themselves. Jehan Descamp, or 'Watelet', was a well-known player around Saint Omer who performed farce, *sotties*, mixing them with *moralités* or short religious sketches. The court of René d'Anjou, a major patron of the performing arts, was entertained by one Triboulet, a *farceur* so accomplished that he has inspired great scholarly speculation.[25] Could he also have composed *Pathelin*? Could he typify the late medieval performer–playwright?

One way or another, such comic actors were gaining autonomy as the fifteenth century progressed. They were professionalizing, with the consequence that they were not only attracting followers but harsh judges. It is commonplace to note how the church stepped up its attack on large-scale theatrical actions mounted by lay players. Through the late fifteenth and early sixteenth centuries the criticism grew until, in 1548, a ban was proclaimed by the Parliament of Paris. One of the key targets was none other than the players of farce. Their performances of 'salacious farce and mummeries', especially at the beginning and ends of mystery plays, were responsible for all manner of moral problems, so the interdiction went. Comic actors were stigmatized as purveyors of immorality: 'Mass attendance was down, almsgiving too, mockery, adultery, fornication on the rise,' the Parliament ban continued to claim.[26] The charge was as ancient as the philosopher Augustine's railing against the seductions of theatrics in late antique Carthage. But its conditions were new, particular to the battle for political power in the cities of the French kingdom. The composers and players of farce were singled out because they appeared free to personify humorously *any* citizen, including nobles and religious men. They took increasing liberties with religious drama. Most worrisome of all, these players had enormous appeal to audiences, city- and countrywide, the 'ignorant fishmongers and weavers' whom the church disdained and still needed for their parish work.

Rather than consider this ban an end to medieval theatrical action, it is helpful to think of it as a symptom of its continually rousing effects. Farce and mystery together gave people the wherewithal to imagine their lives otherwise, to see a heavenly utopia, to laugh through the idiotic plights of working, to face death. These plays enabled them to place themselves differently, both in their locales and the wider cosmos. Imaginatively speaking, then, their theatrical action offered a livelihood – a way of understanding and changing their experience of the world. And in a number of cases as well, the plays provided the livelihood of a subsistence wage, as the Northern poet Jean Bouchet confirmed.[27] Much of this theatrical action hung on the voices and bodies of players who stood before the crowd. Their acting engaged audiences in what was a volatile exercise in extroverting the ambitions and frustrations of people, including the lowliest. From Adam de la Halle's persona *Li Kemuns* who bellows moo!, to the thousands of spectators whose chaotic presence at the *Mystère de Saint Martin* is set down in fifteenth-century Burgundian registers, the common people are implicated progressively and massively. Signs of performances in other centres testify that this kind of theatre could never have been regulated or curbed absolutely, even in the darkening atmosphere of sixteenth-century religious wars.

Many of the major creators in early modern France also point to the vitality of medieval theatricality. François Rabelais is hardly considered a writer of drama, yet his mock-epic prose is shot through with the raucous voices of earlier comic personae. Mikhail Bakhtin made the convincing case that Rabelais's writing capitalized on *farceurs* and their verve.[28] The carnivalesque style in his *Gargantua* and his *Pantagruel* unleashes the theatrical energy of *sotties* and religious-inspired 'feasts of fools'. In François I's circle, his sister Marguerite de Navarre was revered not only as a poet, but as an avid composer of *comédies bibliques*. Critics have dubbed them 'little mystery plays' because Marguerite drew ingeniously on the nativity tradition to improvise the dialogue between her characters of Joseph and Mary or between the 'enchanting' Satan and the shepherds.[29] While Marguerite's *Nativité*, *Trois Rois*, and *Innocents* clearly contributed to a vein of devotional literature, they adopt the structure and vocal play of religious drama that she may well have enjoyed 'live'. It was Jean Bouchet, however, who tells us in 1557, with a whiff of nostalgia, how much he still 'desires to see the Acts of the Apostles performed ... the mind is more satisfied by seeing than by hearing'.[30]

## Medieval play for modern times

To take the full measure of medieval theatricality, it is important to explore how we come to it by way of much avant-garde experimentation in the twentieth century. Between *jeux, dits, sotties*, and us stands a long line of creators and critics who rediscovered it and reconceived it under the aegis of modernity.[31]

When architect Viollet le Duc published his collection *Ancien théâtre François* in 1854, he made the tradition of farce a matter of national patrimony. Alongside the gothic cathedral of Notre Dame in Paris and the fortified castle of Carcassonne, he restored this corpus of plays with a mind to establishing and secularizing the textual foundations of France. Philologists Gaston Paris and Baron James de Rothschild produced the first modern texts of the *Mystère de la Passion* (1878) and a matching *Mystère du Viel Testament* (1878–91) in much the same spirit. An ensemble of scenes from their work became part of the school curriculum, available again to thousands of students. This was the surprising scholarly source that inspired new generations of composers and players to improvise with medieval personae.

The modern fashion of mystery plays in France was fuelled later by the Catholic revival of the *fin de siècle*. Charles Péguy was the impeccable example, the socialist militant who composed *Le Mystère de la charité de Jeanne d'Arc* (1911) and *Le Mystère des Saint Innocents* (1912) in a fervent rush as he converted to Catholicism. Yet there was an equally powerful fascination with medieval theatricality among iconoclasts who rejected its religious significance and sought instead its primitive creative force. The Russian man of theatre Nikolai Evreinov was among the first professionals to revive Adam de la Halle, Rutebeuf, and a cycle of miracle plays in St Petersburg in 1908. He aimed to re-theatricalize naturalistic drama by tapping into what he considered primordial scenarios of play. His experimental model for theatrical modernity was none other than the medieval player, and Evreinov took it with him when he fled to Paris in the wake of Stalinist oppression. During the tumultuous thirties and forties, there were other creators who used mystery plays as the raw material for inventing spectacles of brutality and mystical love. When Antonin Artaud proclaimed in the early thirties that the only real revolution in theatre depended on reclaiming the mentality and habits of the Middle Ages, he was working through his notorious Theatre of Cruelty.[32] Its ritualistic form with its purging spasms of violence was his medieval legacy. What Artaud created clearly did not correspond to the performances of mystery plays in fifteenth-century Paris or Valenciennes. But he nonetheless drew from them an alternative cosmic vision. Among the surrealists too, we find those drawn to the Passion as to Pathelin. The young poet Henri Pichette composed his *Epiphanies, mystère profane* frenetically in 1946 as the hopes of a new free world had grown desperate. In his imagination, the 'Adam' persona becomes a poet of free love who, from the 'first pulsations of the world', is confronted with Mr Devil declaring the final cataclysm of world war. Pichette transmuted the medieval mystery to grapple with the enormous scale of betrayal and destruction his generation had suffered. When *Epiphanies* was performed in 1947, it touched a raw nerve among Parisian spectators because it acted out a medieval myth for the Occupation and the arduous reconstruction facing them.[33]

It is our contemporary Dario Fo who demonstrates how medieval theatricality continues to feed avant-garde creativity. With his irreverent verve, he captures its quintessential combination of sacred mystery with buffoonery. His *Mistero buffo* uses it to set into action a social confrontation between high-minded authorities and ordinary men and women, one as familiar to us as it was apparent to communities in medieval Europe. To do so he animates multiple personae simultaneously. Impersonating a medieval everyman who goes to see Lazarus rise up from the dead, he's also a wage-earner who falls victim today to pickpockets. Spitting and cursing as a *sot*, he impersonates a construction worker denouncing Mafia kickbacks. For the player Fo, medieval personae are the antithesis of anachronism. They offer a potent imaginative resource that belongs to Europeans, but is available to all. What was medieval can be renewed every time audiences are open to players and the critical theatrical process of transforming their perceptions of the world, then and now.

## Notes

1. D. Bevington (ed.), *The Medieval Drama* (Boston, Houghton-Mifflin, 1975), pp. 81, 90, 102; 'firmiter, seriatim ....; gestum facientes competendum; vehementi dolore percussi prosternent se in terra ... dolorem gestu fatentes; laetu vultu', *Jeu d'Adam*, ed. Noomen, pp. 17, 26, 50.
2. P. Zumthor, *Essai de poétique médiévale* (Paris, Seuil, 1972), pp. 37–9.
3. *The Didascalion of Hugh of St Victor: a Medieval Guide to the Arts*, trans. Jerome Taylor (New York, Columbia University Press, 1961), II, 27.
4. Dario Fo, 'Contra Jogulatores Obloquentes', Nobel Lecture, 7 December, 1997. www.nobelprize.org/nobel_prizes/literature/laureates/1997.
5. *Sponsus: the Bridegroom, from Limoges*, in *Nine Medieval Latin Plays*, ed. and trans. P. Dronke (Cambridge University Press, 1994), pp. 3–23.
6. For the Hebrew/French texts, see S. L. Einbinder, *Beautiful Death: Jewish Poetry and Martyrdom in Medieval France* (Princeton University Press, 2002), p. 4.
7. Honorius of Autun, *de Tragediis* [*On Tragedies*], in Bevington (ed.), *Medieval Drama*, p. 9.
8. C. T. Downey, '*Ad Imaginem Suam*: Regional Chant Variants and the Origins of the *Jeu d'Adam*', *Comparative Drama*, 36 (2002), p. 359.
9. E. Auerbach, *Mimesis* (New York, Doubleday, 1953), pp. 143–73.
10. C. Symes, 'Appearance of Early Vernacular Plays: Forms, Functions, and the Future of Medieval Theater', *Speculum*, 77 (2002), 778–831, and her book, *A Common Stage: Theater and Public Life in Medieval Arras* (Ithaca, NY, Cornell University Press, 2007).
11. A. Corbellari, *Voix des clercs: littérature et savoir universitaire autour des dits du XIIIe siècle* (Geneva, Droz, 2005), pp. 235–50; Rutebeuf, *Œuvres complètes*, ed. Zink, pp. 27–45.
12. M. Mauss, 'Une catégorie de l'esprit humain: la notion de personne, celle de "moi"', in *Sociologie et anthropologie* (Paris, PUF, 1950), pp. 332–62.
13. E. Lalou, 'Réflexions sur cérémonie, cérémonial, et jeu', in J.-P. Bordier (ed.), *Le Jeu théâtral, ses marges, ses frontières* (Paris, Champion, 1999), pp. 115–24; G. A. Runnalls, 'Trade Guilds and the Miracles de Nostre Dame par personnages', *Medium Aevum*, 39 (1970), 257–87.
14. E. A. Knight, 'Beyond Misrule: Theater and the Socialization of Youth in Lille', *Research Opportunities in Renaissance Drama*, 35 (1996), 73–84.
15. G. Bartholeyns, P.-O. Dittmar, and V. Jolivet, 'Des raisons de détruire une image', in D. Donadieu-Rigaut (ed.), 'L'Image abîmée', *Images Re-vues*, 2 (2006). www.imagesre-vues.org.
16. J.-P. Bordier, *Le Jeu de la passion: le message chrétien et le théâtre français du XIII–XVIe siècles* (Paris, Champion, 1998).

17. Ed. W. Tydeman, *Theatre in Europe: a Documentary History, the Medieval European Stage, 500–1550* (Cambridge University Press, 2001), pp. 287, 299, 315, 347; E. Lalou and D. Smith, 'Pour une typologie des manuscrits du théâtre médiéval', *Fifteenth-Century Studies*, 13 (1988), 569–79.

18. J. Enders, *Death by Drama and Other Medieval Legends* (Chicago University Press, 2002), pp. 116–30, and *The Medieval Theater of Cruelty* (Ithaca and London, Cornell University Press, 1999), pp. 180–83; Miri Rubin, *Gentile Tales: the Narrative Assault on Late Medieval Jews* (New Haven, CT, Yale University Press, 1999), 169–73.

19. V. Hamblin, 'Le *Siège d'Orléans*: procession, simulacra, mystère', in Bordier (ed.), *Jeu théâtral*, pp. 165–78.

20. G. A. Runnells, 'The Medieval Actors' Roles Found in the Fribourg Archives', *Pluteus*, 4–5 (1986–7), 5–67.

21. G. A. Runnalls, *Les Mystères français imprimés* (Paris, Champion, 1999).

22. M. Rousse, *La Scène et les tréteaux: le théâtre de la farce au moyen âge* (Orleans, Paradigme, 2004); J. Koopmans, *Le Théâtre des exclus* (Paris, Imago, 1997).

23. '*Maistre Pierre Pathelin*': *le miroir d'orgueil*, ed. D. Smith (Saint-Benoît-du-Sault, Tarabuste, 2002); '*Maistre Pierre Pathelin*': *lectures et contexts*, ed. D. Huë and D. Smith (Presses Universitaires de Rennes, 2000).

24. A. Hindley, 'Acting Companies in Late Medieval France: Triboulet and his Troupe', in A. Hindley (ed.), *Drama and Community: People and Plays in Medieval Europe* (Turnhout, Brepols, 1999), pp. 78–98; M. Rousse, 'L'Acteur au moyen âge', in D. Souiller and P. Baron (eds.), *L'Acteur et son métier* (Editions de l'Université de Dijon, 1997), pp. 41–57.

25. B. Roy, 'Triboulet, Josseaulme et Pathelin à la cour de René d'Anjou', *Le Moyen Français*, 7 (1980), 7–56.

26. Tydeman, *Theatre in Europe*, p. 291.

27. Tydeman, *Theatre in Europe*, p. 334.

28. M. Bakhtin, *L'Œuvre de François Rabelais et la culture populaire au moyen âge et sous la Renaissance* (Paris, Gallimard, 1970).

29. Marguerite de Navarre, *Les Comédies bibliques*, ed. Barbara Marczuk with Beata Skrzeszewska and Piotr Tylus (Geneva, Droz, 2000).

30. *Theater in Europe*, p. 328.

31. H. Solterer, *Medieval Roles for Modern Times: Theater and the Battle for the Third French Republic* (forthcoming).

32. Enders, *Medieval Theater of Cruelty*, pp. 2, 95; H. Solterer, 'The Waking of Medieval Theatricality, Paris 1935–1995', *New Literary History*, 27 (1996), 357–90.

33. H. Pichette, *Les Epiphanies, mystère profane* (Paris, Gallimard, 1969 [original 1948]); A. Monnier, 'Lecture des "Epiphanies"', *Mercure de France*, September–December, (1948), 649–65.

# PART IV

# How can we read medieval French literature historically?

# 13

JAMES R. SIMPSON

# Feudalism and kingship

The aim of this section dealing with historical themes is to consider how medieval French texts invite historical or historicizing readings and in this chapter the focus will be on feudalism and kingship. Indeed, the question of what kind of histories can be written from the literary evidence seems especially acute when we look to representations of political and social structures. After all, a society's sense of its preoccupations does not invariably offer a secure guide to actual practices. Another difficulty with medieval French texts, especially those dating from the earlier period (on which this chapter will focus), is that their presentation of events is very often either partial or critical. Texts do not merely advance claims or accounts of events, they also question the ways in which such claims are made and legitimized.

Although they are often dealt with as separate themes, feudalism and kingship are both fundamental to conceptions of French identity, whether in relation to its myths of class structure, state formation, or legal and political institutions. This is especially true where the principles underpinning the two systems are seen to be in conflict. Terms associated with feudalism appear frequently in literary works, providing a language for exploring relations between the rights and dues owing to high-status individuals and for mapping out the consequences of actions in a dramatically compelling manner. Literary treatment of kings provides insight into how collective identities are founded and shaped, into the strains and conflicts created by the desire for, or imposition of, unity. One central example is the term *franc*, which, in that it means both 'Frankish' and 'free-born', combines both status and ethnicity.[1] Thus, in the text known as the *Pseudo-Turpin Chronicle*, the great emperor Charlemagne offers 'freedom' to all those who aid him in the fight against the Muslims in Spain. By the same token, in the thirteenth-century *chanson de geste Gui de Bourgogne* he allows those tired of the war in Spain to leave on the condition that they forsake their free-born status and become serfs. The images and myths elaborated are not simply entertaining fictions but advance claims about the world, situating local and national concerns on a grand historical stage, locating them through a rich and wide-ranging language of historical archetypes and patterns drawing on Frankish, antique, and biblical traditions.

## Background debates

'Feudalism' is presented by historians such as F. L. Ganshof as a structure 'proper to the states born of the break-up of the Carolingian empire'.[2] Through a graded system governing the gifting and claim of land rights in exchange for military service it created 'a system of reciprocal personal relations among members of the military elite', of rights to the gifted land of the 'fief' and personal loyalty often summed up under the later term 'fealty'.[3] Members of the warrior elite give up absolutely free status to act as the 'vassals' (*vassallus* from Celtic *gwas*, meaning 'lad'/'boy servant' and the adjective *gwassawl*, 'serving') of a man they serve as their lord in return for land privileges and enhanced standing, such as higher blood price or wergild.[4] Yet while that 'service' involves concessions regarding standing, it does not imply the servility associated with peasant serfs. Although the term 'vassal' is clearly used pejoratively in challenges and hostile greetings in medieval French literary works (for example Chrétien de Troyes's *Erec et Enide*, 840 and 851), it also refers to a value system wherein status is safeguarded through the emphasis on reciprocity, where valuable military support is acknowledged and recompensed by favour expressed in both economic and symbolic terms.

We know there was something called 'le régime féodal' if only because the Assemblée Nationale abolished it on the night of 4 August 1789, yet feudalism is a very problematic notion for historians. For example, to suggest that it fills the void left by the collapse of Rome may lead us to overlook administrative and governmental continuities or to make false assumptions about how structured the space was before.[5] Critics have argued that the codified versions of feudal practice contained in the laws of Henry I and in English common law have skewed our understanding of the feudalism of the high Middle Ages. Interestingly, the assault on feudalism has come mainly from anglophone historians, pragmatically quizzical about both the rush to system-building sometimes associated with Germanic-style institutional history (for example, Ganshof) or the potential for woolliness in *Annales* school claims about *mentalité* (for instance, Georges Duby). It was for such reasons that Elizabeth Brown notably described the continuing focus on feudalism as the 'tyranny of a construct'.[6] In particular, Susan Reynolds's highly sceptical *Fiefs and Vassals* has led many historians to question their assumptions about the prevalence and systematic nature of feudalism as a practice.[7]

As Frederic Cheyette comments in a review of Reynolds's work, it seems far from clear what understanding of early 'feudalism' we actually have or whether we can even assume we understand the same by such apparently familiar terms as 'buy' and 'sell' as did the authors of these sources.[8] That said, the continued use of 'feudalism' in discussions of medieval social structure is defended by William Jordan:

> Why then retain the term? It is because in the high Middle Ages the fief emerged as a form of landed property that symbolized the landed power of many aristocracies ... A vast juridical literature emerged to describe and categorise fiefs in the Middle Ages, and the vernacular literature of adventure written for the upper class and which seems to have expressed its mentality is obsessively concerned with the extent of fiefs, the inheritance of fiefs and the relations of people holding fiefs from one another.[9]

As Jordan argues, literary texts of the period suggest that notions and values associated with feudalism were accorded considerable importance as discursive bargaining tools, even if it would be unwise to construct any early picture of a densely administered system. The persuasiveness of some accounts based on such evidence suggests that absolute scepticism is a step too far.[10] Charter evidence indicates that documents were indeed important, although their importance not uncommonly lay in their symbolic function as objects rather than in the specific legal details they contained and preserved.[11]

Often allied with concerns with historical mission and with principles of justice, kingship also holds considerable sway over the cultural imagination of the Middle Ages, even where other noble houses and princely courts appear resentful of claims to royal status, especially those of the Capetians.[12] Texts romanticize and idealize Arthur or Charlemagne, with both reigns presented as golden ages of the French nobility. The 'matter of France' identified by Jean Bodel in *Les Saisnes* (see also Chapter 9) refers back to Merovingian kings (notably Clovis), Carolingians (notably Charles Martel, Pepin 'the Short', Charlemagne, and Louis IV), and the early Capetian dynasty (notably Hugh Capet). The 'matter of Britain' centres on Arthur, but also takes in other kings such as Mark of Cornwall. Tales of the ancient world praise leaders such as Aeneas, Julius Caesar, Brutus, Caesar Augustus, and Alexander as part of the grand narrative of the shifting of power known as *translatio imperii*, encompassing a sweep from the fall of Troy to the rise of Greece and Rome and then on to their medieval successors. From the biblical world we have figures such as Joshua, David, Solomon, and Jesse, not to mention Christ himself.[13] Such evocations mirror the practice of aristocrats who recurrently patterned gestures, speeches, actions, and spectacles after ancient models, commissioning artistic works of all kinds to create backdrops to mirror and amplify the deeds of the present. Genealogies and historical accounts were strategically reworked to invest the present with drama and authority. Kings were presented as the mimetic representative of Christ or God on earth. Saints' cults played their part in such affirmations, notably of the Capetians at the abbey of St Denis. Another key mission of the monarchy was that of defender of the faith, whether through promotion of crusade or support for the papacy. Royal figures also laid claims to monopolies on either justice or violence, and kings allied themselves with the interests of other groups, such as peace movements, a useful tactic enabling them to claim jurisdiction in contexts where they otherwise had no particular territorial claim. Finally, claims of kings to exceptional status were bolstered by the role of courts as prestigious cultural centres noted for their wealth and sophistication.

## Charlemagne and after

Charlemagne appears as the great hero of much of the *matière de France*. The Oxford *Roland* paints a picture of an earnest and benevolent leader, a warrior–patriarch favoured with miracles in the mould of Old Testament typologies drawing on a palette of ponderous gestures and imperial attitudes.[14] His charisma and heroism have earned him the devotion of an elite group of vassals, the peers of France, supporting him in a divinely ordained mission to free Spain from the Saracens. Materially, the Oxford *Roland* depicts a paradigmatic feudal system where conquered wealth is redistributed by the king in return for service, monarchy here playing a policing role in fiscal policy. The clinching argument in the trial – that Roland's service of the emperor ought to have ruled out any thought of vendetta by his traitorous stepfather Ganelon (3826–8) – seems a key element in the poem's assertion of a collective cause that transcends the narrow interests of the clan. This assertion is reinforced by Roland's death, the hero's dying attitudes incorporating feudal gestures that present his life and soul as a fief for which he is beholden to God (2389–92). Charles's authority may be threatened in the trial as his counsellors, cowed by fear, ask him to consider pardoning Ganelon, but the outcome of the ordeal between their respective champions, Thierry and Pinabel, reaffirms the rightness of his position, and, although weakened both politically and personally by the loss of Roland, his divine mission continues.

However, the *Roland*'s affirmation of royal right combined with the imperious nature of the crusading mission runs the risk of replacing any sense of reciprocal contract with a one-sided relation. The traitor Ganelon, initially presented as a valuable member of the court, is a focal figure in the articulation of the problems created by the work's absolutist claims: his attempts to put the case for the lesser vassal seem systematically undermined. His betrayal of the rearguard for bribes goes against the ideal transparency of exchange that obtains among the Franks. Moreover, this wealth – deriving from clandestine Saracen bribes rather than openly won through conquest or acquired in public gift-exchange – overshadows whatever Charlemagne might give him and thus makes a mockery of the system of judicial compensation. Accordingly, the final blackening of material wealth appears in Ganelon's desperate claim that Roland wronged him 'en or e en aveir' (3758). This vision of the traitor as an economic problem that threatens the feudal system with collapse is then echoed in sequels to the *Roland*, such as *Gaydon*, where the wealth of the traitors allows them to bribe their way back into favour.[15] This motif is also echoed in the *Roman de Renart*, where the court looks on aghast in one episode as the fox's kin secure his release through bribes (Branch 1a, 2059–84).

Ganelon's refusal to endorse the *Roland*'s vision of the feudal game may amount to treachery but it also finds an echo in the alienation and exhaustion expressed not merely in the machinations of the traitors but also in Charles's own grief, weariness and disquiet at the future (*Roland*, 4000–1). Whether their events are set before or after the battle of Roncevaux, the dark side of his personal loss and his single-minded defiance of his courtiers mark his presentation in later poems: for example, his determination is transformed into despotic vengefulness in *Renaut de Montauban*, leading to shows of bloodcurdling fury against enemies and supporters alike (see, for example, 11751–840). The tarnishing of his image echoes other negative representations of Carolingian royal figures, such as the weak and ungrateful Louis, Charlemagne's unworthy successor in *Raoul de Cambrai* or the William epics, or the sly and untrustworthy Charles Martel of the Loherain cycle. This sense of a political fall in the transition from Charlemagne to Louis is clearly signalled in the patriarch's walk-on appearance in *Le Couronnement de Louis*, where Louis's hesitation to take the crown leads Charles to dismiss him publicly as a worthless bastard fit only to be tonsured and put in a monastery (89–98).[16] However, the element of comedy here finds an echo in other texts that present Charles in still more unflattering light. In *Le Voyage de Charlemagne*, Charles's motivation for his expedition to Jerusalem and then on to Constantinople, where the emperor Hugh takes Charles and his peers up on their drunken boasts of vandalism and sexual prowess, is that Charles's wife casually implied that he in his crown is shorter than Hugh. In an age where critical voices in the West expressed doubts about the justness of the crusading cause, this poem's lambasting of such ideals in the form of an intercultural vanity contest appears striking and extreme. Indeed, the image of Charles and the peers in Jerusalem being miraculously showered with relics at the table of the Last Supper reads as a bitter satirical reflection on the use of crusading mythology.

In charting a decline from a golden age to one controlled by an excessively interventionist and autocratic crown, narratives from the *matière de France* often defend the rights of feudal subordinates, offering grim lessons in the consequences of failing to honour followers. In *Raoul de Cambrai*, following the death of Raoul's father Taillefer, Louis gives his widow, the lady Alice, to Giboin of le Mans and foolishly grants him temporary possession of the fief of the Cambrésis on condition that young Raoul should not be deprived of his 'eritaige' (123–8). A recipe for trouble, Louis's pretensions to savvy micromanagement of a non-hereditary feudal meritocracy look like a bungled game of musical chairs. However, the poem also suggests that expecting a finite system of territorial resources to offer the wherewithal to keep everyone happy all the time by rewarding *both* past service and present excellence might be unrealistic. In any event, the destructive power latent in the system explodes following the king's equally disastrous later decision to grant Raoul the land of the Vermandois (730–45). In the domino-effect wars that ensue it seems almost inevitable that someone will find it their regrettable duty to burn Paris in protest against the controlling activity of an ineffective centre. *Raoul* is also cited as an example of how literary works offer contesting visions of political situations: by reason of its date, the poem is often read as a reflection on the reign of Philippe Auguste.[17] Yet *Raoul*'s picture of Louis seems far removed from the reality of Philippe, whose capacity to control and call on increasing numbers of vassals from areas outside his immediate personal domain rested on a secure administrative base and grew throughout his reign.[18] Of course, other works explore the problems of heredity in a more light-hearted manner, as is the case with *Aucassin et Nicolette*'s vision of a mischievous pack of particularly bloody-minded shepherds refusing to obey Aucassin, arguing that they are his father's men, not his (*Aucassin*, §22), a moment that makes clear the problems inherent in a radically atomized feudal universe where no continuity is assumed.[19]

## Kings in translation: *Le Roman d'Eneas*

Evoking the ideas and achievements of the ancient world and foreshadowing aspects of medieval political organization, the Troy narrative becomes a key myth for medieval authors. The *Roman d'Eneas* provides a useful illustration of how classical sources articulating the concerns of Augustan Rome are recast in terms relevant and familiar to medieval aristocratic audiences.[20]

One key question is how Eneas assumes leadership over his men. Following the destruction of Trojan social structures through the razing of the city by Menelaus, a new social order has to be instituted rapidly. At this point Eneas's overtures to his men are distinctly cautious, referring to them as 'seignor' and 'francs chevaliers' (220). This contrasts with the impressively engineered city of Carthage, where Dido rules as an exemplary feudal lord (264–9). The description of the city emphasizes both physical layout and political organization: its towers and gates are manned by barons and knights organized in a feudal hierarchy whose duties and dues are elaborated with exemplary clarity (336–51). More impressive still is the political organization, which has reached such a pinnacle that the Carthaginians have 'already' developed the Capitol and Senate as judiciary and legislative bodies (506–9). In this respect, the *Roman d'Eneas* appears as a multi-layered political science fiction in which, as part of the narrative of *translatio imperii*, the past anticipates the (Roman) future. For the surviving Trojans, Carthage serves as an important tutelary interlude, serving to crystallize organization and allegiance: Ilïonus's greeting to Dido refers to 'Lord Eneas, our king' (552: 'danz Eneas ... nostre roys'), an epithet echoed regularly thereafter by the narrator. The Trojans likewise praise Dido for the loyal service she exacts from high-status retainers, which fits her to hold land: 'Mout est la dame preus et saige / qui se deduit a tel barnaige! ... / Bien doit celle terre tenir / qui tel gent a a son servir' (700–5: 'The lady who commands such a group of barons is indeed worthy and wise ... deserving to hold such land when she has such men in her service').

Of course, impressive though the initial presentation of Carthage may be, the text goes on to emphasize that its prosperity and order are built on the unstable sand of female lordship rather than the rock of patriarchal authority (for example, 1434–5). The text explores at length the fragile grounds of both identity and authority. In particular Eneas's own identity seems in doubt. Although Ilïonus and his fellows embrace the Enean project and insist on their leader's status as lord and king, such affirmations are contested from various quarters. The spurned Dido claims that Eneas is not even human (1880–9). Lavine's mother likewise makes a detailed and at least potentially plausible case for the Trojans being little more than cowardly, faithless interlopers (3366–411), criticisms later echoed in Turnus's counsels of war. In that context, Trojan claims to Lombardy as the land of their ancestor Dardanus (3283–7), although sanctioned by Anchise's prophecy of the line of kings that will descend from his son (2970–3077), take their place in a war of spin and counter-spin. One might even see a reflexive commentary on the useful pliability of the Trojan myth in Anchise's prophecy, which names Eneas's Roman descendants such as Julius Caesar and Caesar Augustus

(3040–9), but leaves the question of medieval futures handily open in the manner of a blank cheque.

The *Roman d'Eneas*'s narrative of expropriation and exile looks to feudal values as a source of stability, while suggesting that misbehaviour and impropriety are inevitable. Feudal keywords play a major role here, notably the recurring use of the term 'honnor', whether concretely to denote lordship over land ('fief': for instance, 267, 1435, 1445, 1514, 3540, 4258) or more generally as a value ('honour': 228 and 10265). The term is contrasted with the many words for shameful or transgressive behaviour, such as 'folie' (for example, 4072: 'folly'), 'putaige' (1655, 7184: 'whoring'), 'honte' / 'hontage' (1412, 1612: 'disgrace'), 'fellonie' (1618: 'felony'). In its repetitions, key territorial and ethical claims in the Old French text are implicitly, but tellingly, yoked to Aeneas's famed *pietas*, the term Virgil uses repeatedly to emphasize his sense of love and duty to kin and compatriots. This value is most prominently invoked in Anchise's praise of Eneas's love and courage when he seeks out his father in the underworld: 'Filz Eneas, or say et voy / … / que pïetés vainqui paor (2920–2: 'Eneas my son, now I know and see that piety vanquishes fear'), a fairly close rendering of the greeting Virgil attributes to Anchises in *Aeneid*, book 6: 'vicit iter durum pietas?' (688. 'So your faithfulness has overcome the hard journey?'). Eneas is likewise concerned to make due sacrifice to the gods of specific places, however infernal in appearance, and always to honour the lords of a given place through gift-giving (for example, 3357).

Lordly generosity and systems of reciprocity are presented as key to the reinforcement of bonds in spite of the sinister associations of some objects and the transgressive nature of some relationships. A good example is the cup Eneas sends with his message of greeting to Latinus, originally given to him by Menelaus (3221–3), or the numerous items he receives from Dido and passes on in subsequent exchanges. Although the associations attached to objects can be poignant or even sinister, eventually the question of historical baggage favours the Trojans: Eneas's sight of the ring Turnus took from the finger of the dead Pallas, a gift to the latter from Eneas (5842–7), provokes him to revenge, ending the war between the Lombards and the Trojans (9833–56).

The *Roman d'Eneas*'s treatment of passions has attracted considerable attention, notably in its reworking and policing of representation of gender and sexuality found in the classical sources.[21] The medieval *remanieurs* purge and punish, but also exploit the energies associated with same-sex affections and other transgressive impulses presented elsewhere as the vices of courtiers. Nisus's intense loving bond with his male companion Eurialus leads to the death of both of them on a night raid when the latter lingers too long because he wishes to steal a helmet (5161–3). Similarly, Camille the Amazon, although praised for her virtue, is killed as a result of failing to control her Dido-like lust for trophies in battle (7243–6). Eneas's affections also wander. Such desires for objects and persons are harnessed in turbulent cycles of loss and revenge that build to a climax in Eneas's revenge killing of Turnus. Eneas's impulsive act is then presented as a final exorcism of any kinship under the skin with Paris, the abductor of Helen, allowing him to assume the mantle of exemplary feudal sovereign.

This purging of libidinal energies marks the text's final modulation in a cycle of improprieties that began with the cause of the Trojan war. Accordingly, the resolution of emotional and political uncertainties is expressed in a solid language of feudal orthodoxy. Lavine, doubtful of Eneas's affections, states that Eneas cannot be accepted by the lords of 'ceste honnor' if he does not take her as his love (9933–47). When finally persuaded of Eneas's sincerity and moved by the gift of the ring, her acceptance is couched in feudal terms and she bows to the will of her lord (10240: 'a mon segnor toute m'encline'). This final gift of woman and city (at least temporarily) settles the dialectical forces characteristic of Eneas's wanderings:

> Quant pris ot la pucelle gente
> li baron de terre latine
> qui estoit au pere Lavine
> s'acorderent, grant et menor,
> a lui recevoir a seignor
> aprez le deces de lor roy.
> Eneas qui fu sanz desroy,
> amesurez, cortois et saiges,
> par son senz, par ses vasselajes
> conquist il des barons l'amor,
> qu'aprez la mort de lor seignor
> paisiblement la terre tint
> et les honnors totes maintint.          (10308–20)

(When he had taken the noble maiden, both the greater and lesser nobles of the lands of Latium, which were the domain of Lavine's father, agreed to take him as their lord after the death of their king. Through good sense and worthy deeds, Eneas, who was free of ignoble impulses, moderate, courteous, and wise, conquered the barons' love so that after the death of their lord he held the land, kept it in peace and maintained all the lordships.)

Thus the question of loyalty and service has been settled in a manner that allows for the order of patriarchal feudalism to truly begin. Where we were presented with a complex, conflict-ridden world Eneas could not negotiate without causing trouble, he now has the ability to reconcile the claims of *all* lordships. Future 'seductions' operate only in the domain of the ordered affections that should unite husband and wife or king and nobles.

## Feudalism and kingship in the age of the court

A theme common to the treatments of feudal rights and the role of kings in the literature of the central Middle Ages is the frequent concern with the increasing power of the court as a political and administrative centre. Court life was being radically transformed by the influx of a breed of 'new men', the lettered *clercs* called on to deal with the burgeoning administrative duties of a bureaucratic technocracy such as the minutiae of legislation and the maximization of revenue through taxation.[22] Nostalgic evocations of feudal reciprocity are also contrasted with anxieties about the rise of the money economy, seen as the preserve of *vilains* no longer confined to the fields but increasingly numerous and influential in court circles. In that regard, a number of *fabliaux* can be read as visions of aristocratic values either withering or reasserting themselves. In *Le Chevalier qui fist parler les cons*, a knight, impoverished through the decline in wars and tournaments, diversifies his economic activity thanks to an encounter with three fairies which leaves him with the lucrative, but socially lowering ability to make genitalia and anuses speak. By contrast, in *Berengier au lonc cul* the pretensions of a wealthy peasant husband to noble status and superiority over his wife, daughter of an impoverished nobleman, are cut down to size by her fearsome alter-ego, Long-Arse Berengier. A surreal but energetic compilation of *fabliau* and trickster motifs, *Trubert* is arguably one of the most interesting and nightmarish visions of the effects of money and trade on a world dominated by aristocratic values.[23] A country simpleton, initially innocent enough of the ways of the market to sell the family cow for the price of a goat, goes on to prove a quick student, and, in increasing improbability, disguises himself as all manner of guildsmen, a mercenary knight, and finally a young maiden in order to beguile, persecute, and ruin the family of a hapless duke. Many texts speak of loyal retainers of good stock passed over in favour of new arrivals of questionable birth and intentions. These people are often characterized as peasants or traitors, and the tales that deal with them either lament the passing of the old world or imagine some sort of restoration. In the *Charroi de Nîmes*, William kills Louis's counsellor, the treacherous slanderer, Aymes (729–52). More comprehensively, the hero of Jean Renart's *L'Escoufle* stages what amounts to a refounding of the Roman empire in the mode of Charlemagne, with the entire race of *vilain* counsellors driven into exile (1468–1651). Such narratives attest to a sense of disquiet at a court no longer the province of worthy retainers, where access to power and influence is replaced by opacity and arbitrary despotism, and whose values are unfamiliar or contrary to the principles of justice.

Another recurring theme symptomatic of the moral and political strangeness of the court is royal adultery, which, by combining secrecy, jealousy, desire, and division resumes many of the ills more generally associated with court politics as well as their sometimes counterintuitive attractions. In the various versions of the Tristan tale, King Mark's failure to punish the lovers hints at something rotten in the state of Cornwall. Although in the earlier Béroul version the barons appear as boo-hiss villains (to the point that one of them is called Ganelon), the concerns they voice are serious ones: if a man cannot govern his domestic sphere, what useful authority can he exert over the wider world? Nonetheless, such objections are consistently set aside in favour of a higher good that resides solely in Mark's personal judgement and sense of bond affirmed in even the most ambiguous of situations, such as the finding of the lovers in the forest, a scene in which Mark's personal interpretation of the postures of the sleeping lovers leads him to set aside his right to vengeance and instead leave tokens of his presence in a coded message of sympathy and reconciliation (2039–50).[24] The sense of the feudal age being supplanted by a new and puzzling world is apparent in episodes such as the account of Tristan's initial encounter with Mark's huntsmen and his demonstration of the division of the carcass and the arrangement of the hunt procession. (This episode does not figure in the surviving portion of the Thomas *Tristan*, but the fact that it figures in the *Tristrams saga* and Gottfried's Middle High German translation indicates a version was contained in the French original.) Previously, Mark's huntsmen had simply quartered the carcass, a crude but fundamentally egalitarian distribution that symbolically acknowledges the rightful needs of the four corners of the realm. In Tristan's method, everything is accounted for and nothing goes to waste: the hounds are fed the lungs and guts, while the backbone and attached parts are charitably given away. He also addresses the issue of cultural capital, emphasizing that proper bearing in the procession will enhance the standing of the courtiers. But even as the *fourchie*'s sophistication astounds the huntsmen, we seem invited to wonder whether this is a prudent maximization or cunning subterfuge. Crucially, Tristan's display directs attention away from potentially uncomfortable parallels between the body of the quarry and of the condemned: it is not inconceivable that his fate – if his adultery with the queen were proven – would have been that of Ganelon in the *Roland*. Thus his supplanting of the old model appears both as cultural imperialism and a prescient serving of his own interests.

Sexual and political intrigue also go hand-in-hand in *La Mort le roi Artu*, in which the incomprehension of loyal insiders such as Gauvain and

Agravain at Arthur's continued affection for both the queen and Lancelot speaks of a more general sense of bafflement at the counterintuitive workings of court diplomacy. However, even early Arthurian romances present problematic portraits. Although Chrétien de Troyes is fulsome in his praise of Philippe d'Alsace in the prologue to *Le Conte du graal*, in *Erec* we have an Arthur apparently careless of sowing division at court, while *Le Chevalier au lion* shows Yvain driven practically mad by backbiting and insults. In Marie de France's *lai* of *Lanval*, Arthur simply overlooks the eponymous hero. Fortunately, Lanval is then lavished with love and wealth by a fairy mistress and, heartened and enriched, distinguishes himself at court. Unfortunately, this new splendour attracts the attentions of the queen, who, when her adulterous advances are rebuffed, makes false accusations against him with a view to engineering his disgrace and death. The fairy lady intervenes in the trial in the nick of time and Lanval is taken away to Avalon. Feudal equality is thus replaced by courtly injustice in a work that seems to suggest that loyal service can go unrewarded or that excellence will attract malice and envy. The male-dominated public sphere seems at the mercy of a female-controlled shadow-world characterized by invisible and suspect means or straightforward betrayal. But then, in his relation with the fairy lady, Lanval is also already potentially as suspect a figure as Ganelon, the wealth of both characters enhanced by gifts from non-declarable sources.

## Conclusions

Feudalism is sometimes represented in the period we are interested in here as a sort of fractious but Edenic moment of social justice, but it can also appear as part of anxious reflections on the forces threatening its vision of tradition-based legalistic 'common sense'. Likewise, the sometimes nostalgic portraits of ancient kings can imply shrewd or jaundiced commentaries on the ambitions of their descendants, indicating that French nobles thought kingship a good thing in the abstract, but were very wary of making unexamined concessions to actual royal power. In any event, readings of these works and many others testify to a medieval literary culture fertile in vibrant, thoughtful, and contradictory explorations of the pasts, presents, and futures of the social and governmental structures.

## Notes

1. P. Freedman, *Images of the Medieval Peasant* (Stanford University Press, 1999), pp. 110–12.

2. F. L. Ganshof, *Feudalism*, new edn (London, Longman, 1964 [1979 printing]), p. xvii.

3. Ganshof, *Feudalism*, pp. 75–8.

4. Ganshof, *Feudalism*, p. 5.

5. See J. M. H. Smith, *Europe After Rome: a New Cultural History 500–1000* (Oxford University Press, 2006), pp. 28–31.

6. E. A. R. Brown, 'The Tyranny of a Construct: Feudalism and Historians of Medieval Europe', *The American Historical Review*, 79 (1974), 1063–88.

7. S. Reynolds, *Fiefs and Vassals: the Medieval Evidence Reinterpreted* (Oxford University Press, 1994).

8. F. L. Cheyette, review of Reynolds, *Fiefs and Vassals*, *Speculum*, 71 (1996), 998–1006.

9. W. Chester Jordan, *The Penguin History of Europe: Europe in the High Middle Ages* (London, Penguin, 2002), p. 15.

10. For a historicizing reading of literary evidence see D. Boutet, 'Les Chansons de geste et l'affermissement du pouvoir royal (1100–1250)', *Annales*, 37 (1982), 3–14.

11. M. Clanchy, *From Memory to Written Record: England 1066–1307*, 2nd edn (Oxford, Blackwell, 1993), pp. 254–60.

12. See G. M. Spiegel, *Romancing the Past: the Rise of Vernacular Prose Historiography in Thirteenth Century France* (Berkeley and Oxford, University of California Press, 1993).

13. On images of the Tree of Jesse, see R. H. Bloch, *Etymologies and Genealogies: a Literary Anthropology of the French Middle Ages* (Chicago University Press, 1983), pp. 87–91.

14. Cited from *Roland*, ed. Short. Much pertinent commentary can be found in *The Song of Roland: an Analytical Edition*, ed. G. J. Brault, 2 vols. (University Park and London, Pennsylvania State University Press, 1978).

15. On traitors, see especially S. Kay, *The Chansons de geste in the Age of Romance: Political Fictions* (Oxford University Press, 1995), chapter 7. On *Gaydon*, see my *Fantasy, Identity and Misrecognition in Medieval French Narrative* (Bern, Peter Lang, 2000), pp. 15–88.

16. Ed. Lepage, AB version.

17. P. Matarasso, *Recherches historiques et littéraires sur 'Raoul de Cambrai'* (Paris, Nizet, 1962), pp. 105–58.

18. J. Bradbury, *Philip Augustus: King of France, 1180–1223* (London, Longman, 1998), pp. 245–6.

19. *Aucassin et Nicolette*, 632–701, §22.

20. See J.-Ch. Huchet, *Le Roman médiéval* (Paris, PUF, 1984).

21. See W. Burgwinkle, 'Knighting the Classical Hero: Homo/Hetero Affectivity in *Eneas*', *Exemplaria*, 5 (1993), 1–43 and S. Gaunt, *Gender and Genre in Medieval French Literature* (Cambridge University Press, 1995), pp. 75–85.

22. See for example S. Kay, 'Courts, Clerks and Courtly Love', in R. L. Krueger (ed.), *The Cambridge Companion to Medieval Romance* (Cambridge University Press, 2000), pp. 81–96.

23. Both *fabliaux* and *Trubert* are in *Fabliaux érotiques*, ed. Rossi and Straub.

24. Cited from *Tristan et Iseult*, ed. Lacroix and Walter; see Bloch, *Etymologies*, pp. 182–3.

# 14

EMMA CAMPBELL

# Clerks and laity

The distinction between clergy and laity in the Middle Ages has traditionally provided a convenient description of a social divide that influenced literary production in this period. As we shall see, this distinction encompasses not only medieval social differences but also the ideological structures built upon them. Yet, for all that, the clerical/lay divide is by no means reducible to a set of mutually exclusive terms and, in this respect, poses certain challenges for modern readers of medieval texts that will be explored in what follows.

While attempting to give a sense of the scope and import of scholarly debate surrounding the interaction between clerical and lay in medieval French literature – in itself a vast topic – this chapter will focus particularly on religious and didactic literature, and will concentrate on the eleventh and twelfth centuries. I will begin by exploring the difference between clergy and laity and the ways this social division might affect vernacular literature. Focusing on the *Vie de saint Alexis*, the chapter will then consider how lay and clerical concerns might operate in religious literature. The final section will look at the illuminations to the *Vie* in the St Albans Psalter – a sequence of miniatures probably intended for the English recluse Christina of Markyate – with a view to exploring questions of gender and response.

## The social divide

'Clergy' and 'laity' referred to different social groups or 'orders' in the high and late Middle Ages that were distinguished to a large extent by education. Although not necessarily an individual in holy orders who identified strongly with the church and its teachings, the clerk – or cleric – was educated within the church and therefore knew how to read, write, and interpret texts.[1] Though the nature and depth of instruction could vary, clerical education focused on Latin and the literature and culture of classical antiquity. The association of the cleric with the ability to read Latin is reflected by the fact that the Old French term *clergie* could be used to mean knowledge of Latin, as well as referring to the social order associated with such learning.[2] Insofar as they constituted the literate elite, the clergy were responsible for written documents of all kinds, from record-keeping and the redaction of legal documents to the production of literary texts. Clerics were thus behind much of the literary output that has come down to us from the Middle Ages in both Latin and the vernacular.

By contrast, a layman was someone who had no such education – which is not to say that the laity were illiterate in the modern sense of the term. Although *laicus* (layman) and *illitteratus* (illiterate) are sometimes used synonymously in medieval documents, being illiterate can describe a state of being unlearned or illiterate in Latin, rather than a total inability to read or write. Laymen of the upper classes in particular may have had a degree of practical literacy and some may have read quite fluently. The distinction to be made here therefore has less to do with reading ability than with education and the individual's relationship to written texts. While the layman may have been able to decipher certain texts or parts of texts, he would not usually have been responsible for writing them out. Moreover, the cleric's Latin education meant he was responsible for mediating access to texts composed in this language, especially once French had evolved to the point where it no longer resembled its Latin ancestor. The laity's contact with written texts would therefore have been arbitrated largely through clerics.

Besides education, the distinction between clergy and laity had other social dimensions. For one, members of each order came under separate legal jurisdictions: whereas the clergy were subject to canon law and tried by ecclesiastical courts, the laity were judged in secular courts. The difference between clergy and laity was further reinforced by the programme of ecclesiastical reform instituted by Pope Gregory VII (1073–85) and by the enforcement of clerical celibacy in the first half of the twelfth century, when definitive legislation of priestly celibacy took place. Henceforth, those members of the clergy in orders were defined by their celibate lifestyle as well as the literate culture of which they were custodians.[3] The laity, by contrast, were defined by their non-adherence to such a lifestyle, though lay marriage, like clerical celibacy, was increasingly regulated by the church from the twelfth century. These dividing lines were not absolute: not all clerics were in orders and, in these cases, celibacy was not an essential requirement. Similarly, although not always approved of by church authorities, it was possible for members of the laity to undertake celibate marriages.[4] Nonetheless, the imposition of clerical celibacy went some way towards further distinguishing between social orders that were already differentiated by education.

From this very superficial outline, two initial observations emerge. First, it should be noted that clerical and lay do not map directly onto medieval class divisions. As of the eleventh century, the clergy were likely to have come from a range of different backgrounds; a layman could equally be anyone from the king of France to a sheep farmer in Montaillou. Second, though the clerical/lay divide might cut across class to some extent, this is not the case for gender. Men could, in theory, belong to either the clergy or the laity; women, however, could never join the clergy, even if they were in orders. This is not to say that women did not write texts or that they lacked Latin literacy: female authors such as Clemence of Barking and Marie de France are proof of this. Although women could possess the trappings of *clergie* they nonetheless remained excluded from this category in the strict sense.

Although the above definitions of clerical and lay orders might seem mutually exclusive, the two often occupied the same cultural and physical spaces. Clergy who were part of the official infrastructure of the church had a particular responsibility for the instruction of the laity and often lived among lay communities (as priests, bishops, and so on). Clerics who were not ordained frequently occupied medieval urban spaces. Clerics also lived at court and were incorporated into their everyday workings. For example, John of Salisbury, Walter Map, and Gerald of Barri were associated with the Anglo-Norman court of the Plantagenet king Henry II. Andreas Capellanus – another well-known, if enigmatic, clerical writer – can be associated with Marie de Champagne's court and possibly also that of France. Finally, one of the most famous medieval authors – Chrétien de Troyes – was in all likelihood a cleric associated with the courts of Marie de Champagne and Philippe d'Alsace.

This sharing of physical and cultural space had an effect on the literature of this period. As mentioned earlier, the clergy were to a large extent the producers of literature in Latin and the vernacular; in this capacity, they were responsible for writing courtly texts as well as religious literature.[5] Consequently, we see an interweaving of what are often characterized as 'lay' and 'clerical' motifs in both religious and courtly works, suggesting that the social oppositions that distinguished clerical and lay orders in medieval communities do not translate into two distinct literary traditions. In non-religious literature, modes of discourse drawn from clerical culture recur in vernacular texts belonging to what might be described as the courtly sphere. For example, the *chastoiement* – a discourse rooted in medieval pedagogy – finds its way into works such as Chrétien de Troyes's *Perceval*, the *Roman d'Alexandre* and, in ironic guise, Jean de Meun's *Roman de la rose*.[6] On the side of religious literature, we find similar evidence of borrowing and remodelling of courtly discourse. For example, this speech from the pagan tyrant Maxentius in Clemence of Barking's Life of St Catherine draws upon the conventions of courtly romance:

Reine, u averai ge confort
aprés ta doleruse mort.
Laissier ne pois que ne t'ocie;
assez m'ert pur mort puis ma vie.
Coment viveras tu sanz mei,
et ge coment viverai sanz tei?
Tu esteies sule ma cure
de desirer bone aventure,
et pur tei suleie duter
mal aventure et eschiver,
mes malement l'ai eschivee,
kant de tei l'ai encuntree.
Las, que me valt ore m'amur,
quant n'i receif el que dulur.
En grant tristur demenrai ma vie,
quant jo vus perdrai, bele amie.
Kar sule esteies mun delit,
et jeo le ten, si cum jeo quit.                    (2171–88)

(Queen, where shall I find comfort after your painful death? I cannot avoid
having you put to death, but thereafter my life will be a living death. How will
you live without me and how shall I live without you? You were my sole reason
for desiring good fortune and it is for your sake that I used to fear misfortune
and avoid it. But I have indeed avoided it badly, since I have encountered it at
your hands. Alas, what good is my love to me now when I receive nothing from
it but pain? I shall live out my life in great sadness once I have lost you, my fair
friend. For you alone were my delight and I yours, I believe.)[7]

The use of courtly conventions here is clearly strategic.[8] It is the pagan
persecutor of the Christians who launches into a courtly monologue lamenting his fate, not the saint herself. Conventional references to the pain of
betrayal and desire for death take on a new meaning in this context.
Maxentius's claims that he is condemned to a living death echo the more
brutal reality of the martyrdoms of Catherine and the queen while also
commenting on his spiritual state as a pagan who refuses the eternal life
promised by the Christian faith. Moreover, the situation that causes
Maxentius so much grief is entirely of his own making: he laments the
impending loss of his *amie* as he is preparing to have her brutally killed – a
fact that considerably mitigates our sympathy for his plight. The deployment
of courtly discourse here consequently exposes the emptiness of its rhetoric
in this instance, aligning courtly language and the sentiments it expresses
with the misguided position of the pagan tyrant.

Thus, whereas the clerical/lay divide might operate relatively clearly on the
level of individuals, this divide does not translate into two modes of writing.

Clerical and lay perspectives might be seen as hermetically sealed in certain cases but, as the examples just mentioned suggest, the division of lay and clerical interests can also be blurred or unstable in the texts themselves. In order to develop some of these points, for the rest of this chapter I will examine how lay and clerical interests are brought together in religious writing, most especially in saints' lives.

## Religious and didactic literature

Though less studied today than the so-called 'secular' genres of medieval French literature, religious and didactic works constitute one of the most important corpora of texts alongside romance. Apart from translations of the Bible, prayers, and liturgical texts, there is a large tradition of hagiography – or writing about saints – and literature with an instructive moral purpose written in French. Producing such texts was no marginal activity in the Middle Ages. A number of well-known medieval authors wrote religious literature: Wace was the author of Lives of St Margaret and St Nicholas as well as a *Conception Nostre Dame*; Marie de France composed an *Espurgatoire seint Patrice*; Guillaume le Clerc produced a Life of Mary Magdalene and Rutebeuf penned a number of religious works, including the *Miracle de Théophile*. The cult of the Virgin, which inspired a large volume of literary production, also induced accomplished writers like Gautier de Coinci – an author who also wrote a *Vie de sainte Cristine* – to compose his collection of *Miracles de Nostre Dame*. Didactic literature, which was not entirely separable from other kinds of religious writing, took various forms, depending on its function. Instructive literature such as Pierre de Peckham's *Lumiere as lais* or William Waddington's *Manuel des péchés* could be aimed at both religious and lay communities, whereas other educational texts, like the *Doctrinal Sauvage*, *L'Ornement des dames* or the *Chastiement des dames* were more concerned with the moral education of the laity.

The didactic function of medieval religious literature necessitated some engagement with the concerns of its audiences. That these texts were written in French dialects, while often translating (more or less faithfully) Latin sources, already suggests an effort on the part of clerical authors to appeal to an audience who may have struggled to understand Latin. Moreover, as writers like Clemence of Barking indicate, this engagement with the changing demands of the audience operates on the level of style as well as content and language. This is implicit in the example from the Life of St Catherine discussed above, but Clemence also explicitly mentions questions of style in her prologue to the *Vie*. Outlining why she has retranslated a previous, vernacular version of the story,[9] Clemence explains that a text more pleasing to contemporary listeners was required: although the previous version was 'sulunc le tens bien ordené' ('well set out according to the standards of the time'), men have since become more picky and the poem is consequently held in low esteem. Clemence therefore corrects the poem in order that the story might move with the times and people's changing tastes (Clemence, *Catherine*, 29–46).

If medieval religious texts like this had to 'move with the times' to get their message across, this does not mean they unproblematically represented the interests of lay audiences. Though an inability to understand Latin was likely to have particularly disadvantaged those without a clerical education, it is possible that the linguistic and stylistic changes that religious literature underwent responded to the changing demands of a variety of listeners, not just those of the laity. Moreover, where religious literature does engage with issues affecting the laity, the motivation for such an engagement makes it difficult to determine how far these issues accurately reflect the concerns of the lay community (as opposed to the way the church wished to shape those concerns). In many, if not most, cases this engagement with lay perspectives is ideologically unequal: the secular world is invoked in order to be corrected, reoriented or superseded along lines always dictated by the church. The dialogue that religious literature entertains with its lay audiences can therefore be seen as part of an ideological enterprise that aims more effectively to impose the world-view promoted by the church. Lay interests certainly have an impact on questions of representation, but these interests are remodelled at the same time.

To appreciate how some of these representational features might operate in practice, we can take the example of one of the best-known saints' lives in Old French: the *Vie de saint Alexis*. The legend upon which the various medieval redactions of Alexis's life are based was clearly popular in the Middle Ages. Apart from the oldest copy contained in the St Albans Psalter (also known as the Hildesheim text), thirteen versions of Alexis's Life in French have survived and even this figure is likely to represent only a fraction of those in circulation in the Middle Ages.[10] The earliest vernacular version of the legend was probably written in the mid to late eleventh century and, as such, ranks among the earliest extant examples of literature in the French language. In this version (ed. Storey), Alexis is the pious son of a nobleman called Eufemien. Wishing to ensure the continuation of his line, Eufemien marries Alexis to a well-connected girl of noble rank but, although the saint goes through with the marriage, he flees on his wedding night after realizing that his devotion to God is incompatible with family ties. Alexis leads a saintly existence for seventeen years until recognition as a holy man threatens to reconnect him once again to the world. Fearing worldly renown, Alexis returns home, where his changed appearance ensures that his family do not recognize him; he is thus able to sleep incognito under his parents' stairs for seventeen years. Having proved himself as a saint, Alexis then dies, leaving an explanatory letter that posthumously reveals his identity to the world; his body is discovered by the pope, who is led to him by God, and the saint is declared as such. Meanwhile, the saint's wife and parents are reconciled to their grief and eventually reunited with Alexis in heaven.

As this synopsis suggests, questions of family and heredity play an important role in the poem. Not only does Alexis flee his family and a marriage that would bind him to the dynastic ambitions of that family, he also returns to the home he abandoned in order to inhabit it in a radically different way. Rather than reintegrating him into the secular family, Alexis's return emphasizes his status as an outsider for whom the only relationship that matters is that between himself and God:

> Soz le degrét ou il gist sur sa nate,
> iluec paist l'um del relef de la tabla.
> A grant poverte deduit sun grant parage;
> ço ne volt il que sa mere le sacet:
> plus aimet Deu que trestut sun linage.   (*Alexis*, 246–50)

(There, beneath the stairs where he lies on his mattress, the [holy] man subsists on the scraps from the table. [Alexis] leads his great pedigree into great poverty but he does not wish his mother to know this; he loved God more than all his lineage.)

Alexis's situation at this stage of the poem emphasizes both proximity to and exclusion from the family. On one level, he is physically close to his human family, while also being peripheral to it – something that is emphasized by his habit of eating the scraps from the family table, rather than participating in the meal itself. Alexis's physical situation mirrors his spiritual location in this respect: the saint's love of God surpasses that which he might have for his lineage, indicating that Alexis is on the margins of the family in an ideological as well as a physical sense.

Lay concerns regarding family and heredity are thus placed in a new perspective that subordinates secular kinship to the saint's relationship to God. This, indeed, is a perspective that Alexis's family is encouraged to adopt after his death, when his identity is revealed. The family's lament for a lost son and husband is chastized by the pope in a passage of direct speech where he asks them what they are doing making such a kerfuffle:

> 'Seignors, que faites?' ço dist li apostolie.
> 'Que valt cist crit, cist dols ne cesta noise?

Chi chi se doilet, a nostr'os est il goie,
quar par cestui avrum boen adjutorie;
si li preiuns que de tuz mals nos tolget.'     (*Alexis*, 501–5)

('Sirs, what are you doing?' said the pope, 'What's the use of all this crying, grieving and noise? Whatever you feel upset about, to our people it is cause for celebration, for through this [saint] we shall have great help; let us ask him to guard us from all evils.')

The elevation and translation of the saint that follows this speech runs parallel to the emotional and spiritual renegotiation of the family's relationship to Alexis: they overcome their grief, achieve salvation through Alexis and are finally reunited with him in heaven. This section of the poem thus initially opposes the positions of the saint's family and the clerical delegation headed by the pope, but it does so in order to demonstrate how the family's (very human) reactions to Alexis's death might be brought into line with a more orthodox celebration of the saint. At the end of the poem we find a transformed model of the family that makes kinship a matter of spiritual communion rather than marriage or descent, a model that invites the Christian community to follow in the family's footsteps to achieve a place in heaven.

The development of this model in later versions illustrates how the negotiation between clerical and lay concerns in hagiography was part of an ongoing process that influenced the shape of the text. I confine my remarks here to two, later versions (known as 'S' and 'M²') edited and discussed by Alison Goddard Elliott.[11] Both of these texts elaborate the story as it appears in the St Albans Psalter and, in doing so, place greater emphasis on the saint's family and his abandoned bride. In S, for example, the poet expands several scenes from the Hildesheim version and introduces passages of dialogue: features that are particularly noticeable in the wedding-night scene and in Alexis's interactions with his family on his return to Rome. M² similarly expands the wedding-night scene and Alexis's conversations with his family during his time under the staircase. As in the Hildesheim version, the family's point of view contrasts with that of the saint and the church, but later versions articulate this point of view at some length prior to the saint's death as well as immediately following it. Two effects of these modifications are therefore to address more explicitly the concerns of the family that Alexis leaves behind and to allow the saint himself to participate in the spiritual reorientation of his human kin.

A striking feature of these reworkings in this respect is the focus on the bride and her instruction at the hands of the saint. In M², Alexis prefaces his departure by explaining the scriptures ('les escritures') to his new wife and by teaching her the path to heavenly glory ('l'autre voie de glore li aprent') (*Alexis*, M², 128–34). It is the bride who speaks to the saint on his deathbed and who is honoured after his demise when the letter he has written prior to his death miraculously flies to her breast – the significance of which, it is claimed, is that that men should honour their wives and that women should remain faithful to their husbands (*Alexis*, M², 938–47). In S, the newly married saint enters into a lengthy conversation with his bride and offers her religious instruction on their wedding night that is reported directly to the reader or listener as a form of sermon (*Alexis*, S, 267–84). As in M², the bride in the S version speaks to the saint on his deathbed and miraculously receives his letter after death as a mark of special privilege. Equally, although Alexis is reunited with his whole family in heaven, the bride is again singled out for particular attention:[12]

> Bele pucele, dont il se fist estrange,
> Or sont privé, emsamble sont lor ames.
> Or sont en glore sans nule repetance;
> Illuec conversent et si lisent lor salmes.
> Ne vous sai dire comme lor joie est grande.
>
> (*Alexis*, S, 1320–4)

([As for the] fair maiden from whom [Alexis] was separated, they are now close to one another and their souls are together. They are now in glory with nothing to repent; there they converse with each other and read their psalms. I cannot tell you how great their happiness is.)

Alexis's marriage is here translated into a posthumous spiritual bond that continues the couple's pedagogical relationship while replacing sexual pleasure with a form of ecstatic union based on conversation and devotional reading. The secular domestic bliss that the saint abandoned is thus consummated in the couple's relationship in heaven, a relationship that depends on spiritual education as well as physical proximity.

The reorientation of a world-view associated with the secular family is thus common to all versions, but this is achieved in subtly different ways in each case. The engagement with concerns surrounding heredity and marriage in various versions of the poem marks one of the ways in which such literature tried to interpellate and instruct its audiences. Yet, although this is on one level undoubtedly part of an ongoing dialogue between clergy and laity, this engagement is more complicated than a simple encounter between clerical and lay world-views. It is, for instance, unlikely to be accidental that the later versions of the *Vie de saint Alexis* focus on the saint's marriage and his abandoned bride; these poems were being produced at around the same time as the church was promoting a model of marriage that placed such unions within its jurisdiction and that insisted upon its religious as well as its social value.[13] Even if marriage and the family are particularly associated with the laity, we are thus not dealing with straightforward oppositions between clerical and lay concerns. Added to this is the extent to which what are traditionally flagged as 'lay' concerns might have also appealed to clerical audiences. Elliott suggests on the basis of textual evidence that S and $M^2$ have separate audiences in mind, arguing that whereas S represents a popular elaboration of the poem in line with epic poetry, $M^2$ represents more clerical, academic interests.[14] Although Elliott's conclusions concerning audience and composition may be correct, it should also be noted that both versions share an interest in family and marriage that is more developed than in the Hildesheim version. Clerical interests might thus intersect with those of secular society, rather than being thought of as entirely separate from them.

## Gender

Such questions of reception are complicated further when one considers the possible influence of gender. Women were important consumers and patrons of religious literature in the Middle Ages; they also, in some cases, produced such literature as scribes or authors. Yet, as intimated above, women illustrate the fragility of the clerical/lay divide I have been exploring: even if in religious orders, women were barred from ecclesiastical office and were unlikely to have had the same instruction as male clerics. In representational terms, it was common practice to define women primarily in terms of their gender in both literary and religious texts. These considerations suggest that women's participation in a clerically dominated literary culture was far from simple.

The illuminations to the Hildesheim text provide a means of addressing questions of gender and reception particularly as they concern female readership. The Hildesheim version of the *Vie de saint Alexis* is contained in a larger codex – the St Albans Psalter – that was, in all likelihood, intended for the female recluse Christina of Markyate (died 1155?).[15] The illuminations accompanying this version of the poem are unusual insofar as most illustrations of Alexis's life depict scenes from the later stages of the narrative, such as the family's failure to recognize the saint on his return or Alexis's life under the stairs. By contrast, the Hildesheim illuminations represent a sequence of images depicting the saint's departure on his wedding night (Figure 9). It has been suggested that the Life of Alexis may have been included in this codex on account of parallels between the saint's spiritual career and Christina of Markyate's experiences of early devotion to God and refusal of marriage, a

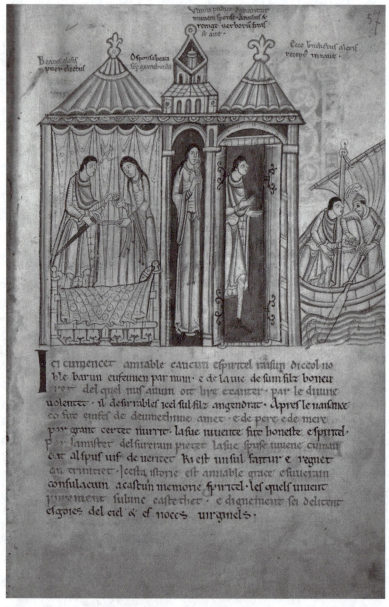

Figure 9. The St Albans Psalter (Alexis Quire), Hildesheim Dombibliothek, St Godehard, fo. 57r. This set of images prefaces the *Chanson de saint Alexis* in the St Albans Psalter. The sequence depicts Alexis's wedding night escape: on the far left, the saint offers a sword belt and ring to his wife prior to his departure; in the centre frame, the bride gazes at Alexis as he steps out of the door; and, on the far right, the saint boards a boat to Edessa.

possibility that might explain the choice of the wedding-night scene as the focus for the illuminations.[16] More recently, this view has been challenged on the grounds that the Alexis quire's insertion into the manuscript was the idea of Christina's spiritual advisor, Abbot Geoffrey. The more likely reference point for the images may therefore have been Christina's chaste relationship with Abbott Geoffrey, rather than the marriage from which she escaped.[17]

Though it is impossible to know how Christina would have responded to these images, the vocation that led her to abandon secular society and the relationships she entered subsequent to her escape may have resonated with the visual gloss given to the *Vie* in a number of ways. Even if it was not the primary motivation for the choice of subject, the scene of Alexis's wedding-night departure echoes Christina's own attempts to redefine her relationship with her fiancé in a way that would not conflict with her devotion to God. Although Christina was betrothed rather than married when her parents let her fiancé Burthred into her chamber, she, like Alexis, attempted to educate her future husband and persuade him to live chastely. While not originally intending to abscond after their conversation, Christina was also, in the end, forced to flee her family and future spouse when the response was not the one she was looking for.[18] The circumstances leading up to this scene also strike a chord with the situation that led Alexis to abandon his home. Like the saint, Christina found herself forced by her parents into a marriage that compromised her childhood vow to Christ: a fact that she mentioned explicitly when forced to justify her actions to the local prior. At the same meeting, Christina cited in her defence the biblical injunction to abandon one's home, family, and possessions to follow Christ – an injunction that is not only exemplified by Alexis's Life but that also, unusually, provides a focal point for the illuminations.[19]

Christina may have identified with the bride as well as Alexis in this set of illuminations. One possible context for the production of these images was Christina's resistance to two trips to Rome planned by Abbot Geoffrey, who may have chosen the scene as a consolation for Christina and a reminder to her to place less pressure on him when it came to the performance of his duties.[20] Quite apart from this, Christina may also have identified with the bride as a figure who follows the saint's example. The illuminations underline the interplay between proximity and distance, contact and separation that makes the bride a strategic figure in this respect. Alexis's wife is depicted as quite literally on the threshold between the secular society the saint leaves behind and the world that he enters by virtue of his sanctity. There are also suggestions here of the later devotion to Christ that will earn the bride a place in heaven with her husband: whereas in the first frame of the image, the bride

faces inwards, towards her husband, the central frame has her facing out-
wards, in the same direction as Alexis as he steps through the door to begin
his new life. Insofar as they highlight the bride's role alongside that of Alexis,
it is notable that these images anticipate later rewritings of the legend, which,
as we have seen, similarly emphasize the bride's significance. The prologue
that prefaces the *Vie* in the St Albans Psalter presents a summary of the story
that culminates in Alexis's commendation of his wife to God, suggesting that
the saint's abandonment of his wife and her subsequent marriage to Christ are
both seen as crucial to the poem's meaning even at this early stage of its
development. In this respect, the images and prologue work together to underline a feature of the story already implicit in the text: namely, the bride's role as
a point of contact with the saint and a spiritual model in her own right.

Christina's possible response to these illuminations – and to the text that
they accompany – draws attention to two important points. First, it should
not be assumed that women and men identified only with figures of the same
sex. Second, it is equally important to consider the role of auxiliary figures
(such as the bride) in reflecting on how these texts may have operated on their
readers or audiences. Even if the saint remains the focus of the text, his is not
the only example that audiences may have chosen to follow.

Both of these points extend to male as well as female responses. Consider
once more the bride as a figure with whom audiences of different kinds may
have identified. In addition to offering Christina a unique visual gloss of the
story that might connect with her own experiences and relationships, these
illuminations also present a way into the text that reflects the strategies that a
range of readers may have used in relating to the poem. In terms of the wider
audience of the Life of Alexis, it is feasible that the bride – rather than the
saint – may have provided a model of religious devotion particularly adapted
to the lay community insofar as she achieves salvation not as part of a divine
calling but as the result of that of Alexis, a process that involves redefining
her secular relationships and, in later versions, heeding the spiritual instruction of the saint himself. The bride's role as a privileged recipient of the
saint's teachings in later versions may also have made her a figure to whom
clerical as well as lay audiences could easily relate.

The illuminations to the Hildesheim text are thus a useful example of the
complexities of reception. When contemplating these images, Christina may
have seen parallels between her relationship with Abbott Geoffrey and
Alexis's with his wife; she may equally have identified with Alexis as an
individual who renounced marriage to pursue a life devoted to God. If we
consider the bride as a model for the Christian community, Christina may
have taken example from the bride as a figure who follows the saint in
devoting herself to Christ, providing a model of religious devotion that

might be more easily emulated than that of the saint. Rather than viewing these as mutually exclusive hermeneutic strategies, these different options should be seen as complementary and overlapping possibilities in which gender may be one of any number of factors in play. These illuminations thus provide an illustration of how individual and collective modes of response might converge in medieval religious literature, as well as exposing the complexities of women's inclusion in the dialogue between clergy and laity that this literature represents.

## Notes

1. On the *clerc* in twentieth-century criticism, see A. Corbellari, *La Voix des clercs: littérature et savoir universitaire autour des dits du XIIIe siècle* (Geneva, Droz, 2005), pp. 11–17.
2. On the meaning of *clericus* see M. Clanchy, *From Memory to Written Record: England 1066–1307*, 2nd edn (Oxford, Blackwell, 1993), pp. 226–30.
3. J. Brundage, 'Sexuality, Marriage and the Reform of Christian Society in the Thought of Gregory VII', *Studi Gregoriani*, 14 (1991), 69–73; J. Goody, *The Development of the Family and Marriage in Europe* (Cambridge University Press, 1983).
4. D. Elliott, *Spiritual Marriage: Sexual Abstinence in Medieval Wedlock* (Princeton University Press, 1993).
5. S. Kay, 'Courts, Clerks, and Courtly Love', in R. L. Krueger (ed.), *The Cambridge Companion to Medieval Romance* (Cambridge University Press, 2000), pp. 81–96.
6. D. Maddox, 'Avatars courtois d'un genre du discours clerical: le *chastoiement*', in C. Huber and H. Lähnemann (eds.), *Courtly Literature and Clerical Culture: Selected Papers from the Tenth Triennial Congress of the International Courtly Literature Society* (Tübingen, Attempto, 2001), pp. 161–73.
7. Translation from G. Burgess and J. Wogan-Browne, *Virgin Lives and Holy Deaths: Two Exemplary Biographies for Anglo-Norman Women* (London, Everyman, 1996), pp. 35–6.
8. See J. Wogan-Browne, *Saints' Lives and Women's Literary Culture c.1150–1300: Virginity and its Authorizations* (Oxford University Press, 2001), pp. 117 and 227–45.
9. This text may be a dramatized version extant in fragmentary form. See E. C. Fawtier-Jones, 'Les Vies de sainte Catherine d'Alexandrie en ancien français', *Romania*, 56 (1930), 80–104 (pp. 100–3).
10. A. Goddard Elliott, *The Vie de saint Alexis*, p. 16.
11. Elliott, *Alexis*. S and M² have been dated as late twelfth century and thirteenth century respectively.
12. No comparison with M² is possible here, as passages of text are missing.
13. G. Duby, *Le Chevalier, la femme et le prêtre: le Mariage dans la France féodale* (Paris, Hachette, 1981); C. N. L. Brooke, *The Medieval Idea of Marriage* (Oxford University Press, 1989); J. Brundage, *Medieval Canon Law* (London, Longman, 1995), pp. 70–97.

14. Elliott argues that M²'s attention to the saint's ascetic regime and references to learning and the liberal arts argue in favour of a clerical audience (*Alexis*, pp. 43–50).

15. O. Pächt, C.R. Dodwell, and F. Wormald, *The St Albans Psalter* (London, Warburg Institute, 1960), pp. 23–31; J. Geddes, *The St Albans Psalter: A Book for Christina of Markyate* (London, British Library, 2005), pp. 89–122.

16. *The St Albans Psalter*, pp. 136–44.

17. Geddes, *St Albans Psalter*, pp. 115–16; www.abdn.ac.uk/stalbanspsalter/english/essays/alexisquire.shtml.

18. C.H. Talbot (ed. and trans.), *The Life of Christina of Markyate: a Twelfth-Century Recluse* (Oxford University Press, repr. 1987), pp. 51–5.

19. *The Life of Christina of Markyate*, pp. 59–63. Christina is referring to Matt. 19.29.

20. See note 19.

# 15

WILLIAM BURGWINKLE

# The marital and the sexual

Though there are evident differences between medieval and modern notions of marriage and sexuality, there is really no way to contrast a set of beliefs labelled 'modern' with another called 'medieval'. Not only do the concepts themselves evolve through time within broad historical periods, but the way that they are understood can differ markedly from one community or individual to another. Most of the texts that are usually cited by historians as evidence of medieval thought are homilies and penitentials, theological treatises and records of legal proceedings, texts that shine with the lustre of authenticity and truth and may appear to be speaking in a unified voice but were often inspired by very particular concerns. They were also composed, almost exclusively, by an elite group of unmarried men whose job it was to defend church thought and local practice.[1] The fact that much of the extant vernacular literature of the period belies and contradicts these texts indicates that even if church policy denigrated all sexual expression when divorced from reproduction, such commandments were probably not foremost in people's minds as they went about their daily lives. I will therefore begin this chapter by looking at some of the structures within which marriage and sexuality were configured in the Middle Ages, church doctrine being one amongst them, then look at a selection of literary texts that offer typical but also surprising portraits of how that material was interpreted, undermined, twisted, and abused.

Both marriage and sexuality are terms that vary across time and space, best defined through specific cultural connotations. Though every culture and era has a system of norms and a vocabulary to signify recognized unions and sexual desire, the meanings attributed to those unions and desires can vary wildly. Western Christian marriage, both modern and medieval, is essentially a legal contract that determines or solidifies (a) gender relations (as in who gets to marry whom, who initiates what); (b) family structure (patriarchal or matriarchal, two parent or multigenerational); (c) community and religious models of governance (structured on a family model in which positions of authority and caregiving are differentiated); (d) economic exchange (as in how dowries function in alliances, truces, and the attribution of prestige); (e) inheritance law (women's rights to their dowry, primogeniture or equal division of goods); and (f) sexual behaviour (exclusively heterosexual or more inclusive, active and passive roles as gendered masculine and feminine). One is born into marriage as a pre-existing ideological system that opens and then limits one's horizons of expectations while also determining the sundry roles on offer – as caregiver, parent, hunter, and earner.

Yet marriage is particular as well as universal. Children are seen as the genetic carriers of a specific coupling, with all its attendant economic and legal rights and duties. Let us look at an exemplary medieval case – Perceval, the Welsh prototype of the universal subject from Chrétien de Troyes's *Conte du graal*. Born in seclusion, living alone with his mother after the deaths of his father and brothers, he is tricked by an illusion of splendour in the forest when he glimpses his first Arthurian knights. Pursuing them as models of what he hopes to be, he is subsequently lured into taking up a quest to solve the mystery of his identity. His mother's move to the forest to raise her child was based on a contention that one can escape fate, create a new ethical system free from the linking of law, genetics, and coupling that underwrites western marriage. Her ultimately unsuccessful attempt to raise her son with no name or history in the utopian forest is a parable *par excellence* about the tensions that exist between the public and the private. Her example proves, if nothing else, that one could challenge custom in the twelfth century and that the contours of marriage and sexuality were hot topics for debate. Young Perceval may learn who he is from learning where he comes from, albeit from suspicious sources, but the door to his identity is never shut completely. In the cracks remaining (especially visible in the grail *Continuations*), medieval authors intimate that the solid wall of law and custom, all that is presumably genetic and pre-inscribed, is itself an effect of the law that it claims as instantiating. The imperative that appears to stem from the law is actually what sustains that law, more a means of closing off other options than an iteration of fact.

The same could be said for sexuality: it is hard to conceive of it as a concept without reference to the ways it has been governed. The Middle Ages may not have had any inclusive term to indicate how we name and organize gender identification, desires, and norms – the word 'sexuality' did not enter the language until 1845 – but this does not mean that they lacked concepts.[2] Medieval French societies had a rich lexicon at their disposal to signify sexual tastes, many of which we probably still do not understand, and not all of these words were necessarily linked to fixed sexual identities. This might not mean that there was any more freedom to define oneself outside cultural norms in the Middle Ages, but it certainly does mean that one could perform certain sexual acts without necessarily seeing oneself as part of a larger group or category. Many who engaged in same-sex acts, for example, might never have seen themselves as 'sodomites', simply because these acts were performed actively rather than passively or did not show up in their confessors' discussions of sin.[3] Some whom we might call sadists or masochists might never have seen their behaviour as anything other than sanctioned devotional practice; and many adulterers could rightfully claim that this term did not actually encompass or define their behaviour. If they had never consented to the marriage to which they submitted, or the coupling within which they found themselves imprisoned, they could claim immunity from sin. Tristan, that master sophist, explains to the hermit in Béroul's version of the tale that he and Iseut have not sinned because they drank the love potion unknowingly. This argument allows him to skirt the mundane strictures of marriage and feudal codes and to redefine love as a fateful and fatal encounter outside social control. Though they may not have been any more successful than Perceval's mother in occasioning a complete readjustment of the symbolic order, this ardent defence proves again that such issues were ripe for discussion in the late twelfth century.

This is hardly surprising. One facet of the Gregorian reforms of the late eleventh century involved the church's attempt to wrest control of important social ceremonies like marriage from secular hands and redefine it. Over the course of the period 1100–1400, the definition of marriage evolved from being a contract between men, requiring no religious blessing or priestly presence, in which a woman was transferred (and paid for) from one family group to another, to a ceremony conducted by a priest, in which two individuals declared their willing assent to a contract before witnesses. Gratian's *Decretum* (*c.*1140) required that sexual intercourse accompany the spoken vow in order to establish the bond as legitimate; but just a decade later, Peter Lombard, in his *Sentences*, argued that consent alone was enough to sanction and sanctify a marriage.[4] The church's new role in presiding over the ceremony and certifying the requisite conditions established as well their right to intervene between a father and his child or a lord and his subject. They did not, however, succeed in reconfiguring marriage as an entirely voluntary, as opposed to abusive or forced, bond; nor did they succeed in refashioning it as an institution that placed love and contentment above economic concerns. Literary texts from the period provide sufficient examples of unwanted marriages (Marie de France's *Guigemar*, *Yonec*), extramarital sex (*Milon*, *Fresne*), and rape (*Roman de Renart*, the grail *Continuations*) to claim that these matters were ever definitively settled. Gradually, however, important changes were accepted into common practice and these changes had serious repercussions. Clerical marriages were banned, though the practice continued for at least another century; sexual abuse was regulated by both secular and ecclesiastical bodies; and sexual behaviour within religious orders came under ever-closer scrutiny. Concurrently, this move to regulate sexuality had another important, though probably unintended effect: sex in all its varieties and the travesty of marriage became major themes of vernacular literature.

The attempt to control sexuality and marriage through legislation and the interpretation of scripture brought into better focus the competing systems of law and language that operated throughout this period. Canon law was composed in Latin and reflected official, orthodox positions, while the growing body of secular law had to establish its own ground of authenticity and often in a vernacular language that was necessary for daily transactions but lacked the grounding of tradition. The status of law itself was thus called into question. Was it to be seen as a prior authority that foresees all eventualities, as in religious thought, or as a response to change, a second-wave body of knowledge based on common practice and precedent? Furthermore, as St Paul argued in Romans (7.7), law can create the very transgression that it seeks to legislate:

> Is the Law identical with sin? Of course not. But except through the law I should never have become acquainted with sin. For example, I should never have known what it was to covet, if the Law had not said, 'Thou shalt not covet.' *Through that commandment sin found its opportunity, and produced in me all kinds of wrong desires.*

Paul's admission that law actually produces sin, that sin without law, without external correction, is not transgression – not thrilling, not guilt-producing, not productive – is another way of saying that law and transgression are conterminous.[5] Following this logic, the legislative flurry of medieval theologians might actually have produced the very sins they were condemning. St Augustine, commenting on this Pauline imagery, described in *The City of God* (14:26) a prelapsarian (i.e. pre-law) Eden in which Adam's penis was completely under his conscious control and could be used as any other limb, without any concurrent loss of reason or experience of pleasure.[6] Augustine concurs that it is law that institutes subjectivity and a sense of sin, but he cannot accommodate within his vision opposing laws, laws that contest law and call into question the nature of law itself. The rise of 'heresies' in the twelfth and thirteenth centuries, with opposing variations on those laws, indicate that no one impregnable edifice of law obtained throughout this period. Political and doctrinal differences led to interpretive differences and vernacular literary texts tend to highlight just these cracks in the foundation.

One obvious effect of this highlighting was that the breadth of positions available to those subject to these sometimes contradictory laws expanded. Our relatively straightforward modern sexual categories of gay, straight, transsexual, etc., give way in the Middle Ages to a wider range of over-lapping positions that did not necessarily encase the subject in any one of these categories. Such positions would include approximations of desire that we might now call heterosexual, before any such term reified the supposed simplicity of that taste, or homosexual, which translates very imprecisely a variety of salacious derogations such as *sodomite*, *bougre*, *erite*, etc.; but other sexual categories as well emerged, including those of virgin and celibate. The Middle Ages was not a period 'before sexuality', in the sense that that implies a lack of self-realization, of subjectivity itself, and an ignorance of the joys of transgression; but neither was it a period of all-encompassing authoritarian monitoring of marital and sexual behaviour.

The category of 'virgin' is worth a discussion in itself. It appears to describe a simple lack of sexual experience, a state to which all are born, but how does it end? With the first experience of sexual pleasure, with masturbation, orgasm, the breaking of the hymen, oral sex?[7] Virginity in the modern West lacks the potentially disruptive quality that it once had when the choice of virginity as a sexual identity could be read as an act of rebellion. Rejection of sex could mean rejection of family and privilege, even of requisite gender roles, by expressing a preference for strong emotional and even erotic ties with God over a permanent union with another human subject. While 'celibate' today implies a state of sexual inactivity set by vow, in the Middle Ages to be celibate meant only to be single and unmarried rather than chaste.[8] A clerical vow of celibacy meant a vow not to marry, not a vow to renounce sex, and required a supplemental vow of chastity to match our contemporary expectations. Virginity, as distinct from celibacy and chastity, was an option open even to married couples (as in the *Vie de saint Alexis*, on which see Chapter 14), and many married female saints and mothers would later claim a reconstructed virginity that reflected spiritual rather than physical wholeness.[9]

What gets you into any one of these sexual categories, and what makes you ineligible to remain there, can vary enormously. Sodomy, for instance, was even then hopelessly confused. To a legalistic medieval cleric it might mean engaging in any sexual practice that could never lead to procreation. Oral or anal sex, birth control, or even, if some sources are taken literally, inter-course in any position other than the missionary, regardless of the gender of the partner, and especially if the position was chosen to increase pleasure, would all be culpable.[10] A married man who had sodomitical relations with his wife was only marginally less guilty of mortal sin than a man who did it with another male; and if this married man, especially if he were noble and played the 'active' role (the penetrator), also had sex with his wife and produced the requisite children, then his extra-marital sodomitical relations would probably not even have attracted much attention. A man who has sexual relations only with men, on the other hand, and in the 'passive' position, would be referred to as a prostitute and was subject to ridicule and anathema.

These examples illustrate how the shape sexuality takes is modelled by the freedoms and restrictions imposed on it. When sexual acts escape categorization altogether or their classification is unclear, it is difficult to imagine how guilt or transgression would operate. Take, for example, acts that are categorized as sinful when performed passively and less sinful when performed actively. How, in these cases, is culpability negotiated? Which party is 'active' in a same-sex act of oral sex? Does kissing and hugging, the only vaguely sexual act alluded to in most medieval romance ('accoler e baiser') come gendered or are both parties active? Are nocturnal emissions sexual acts?[11] Women, who were generally unsupervised in their relations with other women, might have escaped censorship entirely and never questioned their own 'sexuality' when they expressed affection sexually, provided that they also accomplished their 'marital duty' and bore the requisite children.

Questions of marriage and sexuality clearly do intersect then but they do not always travel hand in hand. In a romance such as *Eneas* (c.1155), for example, the exiled heir of Troy and his betrothed, Lavine, follow what seems a well-trodden narrative path: incitement of heterosexual desire leads to a tumultuous courtship and ends in triumphant marriage. But romance marriages can be deceptive. Said to celebrate love, they often legitimate instead dynastic coupling whose union of bodies allegorizes political alliances, territorial claims, and grafted ethnicity. The Saracen princess *topos*, a favourite of romance and epic, in which the western Christian conqueror marries the 'converted' Saracen lady and founds a new world order is probably the clearest and most familiar illustration of this textual imperialism (*La Prise d'Orange*) but *Eneas* complicates it by confounding every element along the way: the birth of sexual desire arises from imitation and same-sex attraction; duty and political imperative rather than love serve as the motivational drivers.[12] The love story and the climactic marriage thus appear to spring from completely different sources and follow different trajectories, intersecting only when social and narrative pressures require closure through the resolution of conflict. This is not to say that all passionate love affairs in vernacular literature are similarly and necessarily subverted to political and propagandistic agendas, but when marriage emerges as the only end to which such affairs can lead then you can be sure that the passion will be less than scalding and the biological urges more strategic than instinctive.

Other famous love stories, such as Chrétien de Troyes's *Erec et Enide*, feature marriage only as a narrative blip, a pseudo-climax that occurs early in the narrative and introduces more complications than it solves. Rather than serving as the ultimate sign of consummation – sexual, social, and familial – marriage paradoxically marks the first moment at which, a major obstacle having been disposed of, passionate sexual love becomes a possibility. With social stability and respectability won and virginity no longer an obstacle, marriage throws the door open to its many alternatives: loveless partnerships give way to erotic pairings (*Tristan et Iseut*); male enslavement of younger brides gives way to fantasy lovers (the *mal mariées* of Marie de France); homosocial bonding takes precedence over heterosexual pairing once the threat of sodomy charges is erased (Yvain and Gauvain in Chrétien's *Chevalier au lion*); magic herbs save women from unwanted sex with husbands while still guaranteeing them social status and the favour of their lovers (Chrétien de Troyes's *Cligès*). Marriage in these cases legitimizes, enables, and masks forms of transgressive behaviour that would otherwise remain proscribed: what nineteenth-century critics called 'courtly love' rears its head with the alluring promise of sin.

Let us look more closely at a few of Marie de France's *lais*, *Fresne* and *Guigemar*. Both deal with sexual error and both end with what seems to be a long-delayed marriage.[13] *Fresne* is the story of twin baby daughters, separated at birth by their slanderous mother. The cast-out baby has been raised by an abbess but is courted at adolescence by a wealthy local lord. When he wants to convince her to join him in his castle, he does so by warning her that her abbess/benefactor will be angry if her charge should end up pregnant (*Fresne*, 282–3). Passion and sexual congress clearly move at their own speed in this *lai*, with no mention of sin, guilt, or marriage. The domestic arrangement – lord living with concubine – does not, however, quite fit with what the local gentry expect of their overlord and they turn on him with threats. Fresne finds herself squeezed from her lover's bed by that enemy of true love, that ally of social convention – marriage. She is replaced by her sister in a wedding ceremony and demoted to serving as the couple's handmaiden until her mother, in town for the ceremony, recognizes Fresne as her own abandoned child and justice is done. The marriage is richly celebrated and establishes legitimacy in the eyes of the feudal court but what, if any, is its salutary effect on the lovers?

In *Guigemar*, the young noble hero suffers from his society's intolerance of anyone who lacks heterosexual desire. He is thus put through a ritual of sacrifice and identity-building that leads directly into the arms of his saviour, a lonely young woman across the sea, victim of her much older husband's jealousy. Once again, the young lovers act (lots of *acoler e baiser*; 531–2) with no thought of marriage until the husband gets wind of it and Guigemar is forced to flee. Back at home, he pines for his former happiness and remains unmarried, foiling his family's plans. When finally the two lovers meet again, Guigemar fails to recognize her and both must undergo a humiliating ritual in which suitors line up to untie a knotted shirt and chastity belt that each has fashioned for the other (651–4; 741–2). A war later, and his rival dead, the lovers are reunited but no mention is made of the marriage that must inevitably follow. The narrative interest of these marriages, one might conclude, arises not from the marriage itself or the celebration surrounding it, but from the fact that it has been strictly excluded as an option from the beginning of the narrative. Deemed impossible, either by reasons of social rank and class (*Fresne*), or previous marriage and lack of desire (*Guigemar*), the reunion that is finally celebrated is presented as the only possible way to ease tensions in the community, the only appropriate way to repair the social and personal wrongs suffered by the protagonists. The restorative function of marriage as the climax of such processes of wrongdoing thus signifies reintegration into the community: marriage as social unguent, interpellating subjects into recognizable categories.

This is a bit trickier when dealing with same-sex partners. While most references in vernacular literature are resolutely negative, this does not mean that the Middle Ages necessarily condemned and abhorred sexual activity that did not feature a man and a woman.[14] Reproduction was the key to a church blessing and this policy is both parodied and parroted in popular texts such as the *Roman de la rose*, texts that flirt with sodomy while denouncing it.[15] Same-sex activity in such texts is as often grist for humour and satire as it is for denunciation. *Eneas*, for example, makes open reference to married men who have sex with other men and Etienne de Fougères's *Livre des manières* to women who do it with women. While both are derogatory, using arguments familiar to contemporary marriage debates, they are also comical, stretching metaphors to the breaking point. In *Eneas*, the mother of the young Lavine tells her daughter when she learns of her attraction to a Trojan that such men are always inclined to prefer 'on garcon que toy ne autre acoler' (8626–7: 'his boyfriend over cuddling with you or any other woman'). He will use you to attract his prey, she says, then demand to mount him just as he mounted you (8642–8: 's'il les pooit par toy atraire … bien le laira sor toy monter / s'il le repuet soz soy torner'). In the *Livre des manières* (*c.*1170) Etienne de Fougères claims, in an elaborately rhetorical passage, that women who have sex with other women:

sarqueu hurtent contre sarqueu,
sanz focil escoent lor feu.
Ne joent pas a piquenpance,
a pleins escuz joignent sanz lance.
...
l'un[e] fet coc et l'autre polle.                    (1107–24)

(they bang coffin against coffin, / and without a poker they stir up their fire. /
They don't play at jousting / but join shield to shield without a lance ... one
plays the cock and the other the hen.)[16]

The *fabliaux*, one of the richest sources of descriptions of sexual activity
and coupling, are dismissive of fools and duplicity but never quite imply
that this extends to a condemnation of marriage or sex. Both are mocked
mercilessly but both are also, by tale's end, subject to pious and protec-
tionist commentary. The *fabliaux* might ridicule husbands as ineffectual and
incompetent, and wives as conniving and duplicitous, but this does not
mean that one should throw in the hat or join the nearest monastery. At
fault are those protagonists who fail to maintain the requisite balance of
socially defined power, men who let sexual desire blind them to the authority they should be exerting. These are men who listen too much to women,
who let them have things their way, who are too old or too proud to
satisfy them sexually. Their female partners, on the other hand, are declared
depraved, sometimes ironically, but their being so is unavoidable, driven as
they are by what medieval medicine considered excessive moistness and
bodily appetites. Their cleverness in manipulating men and juggling marriage with sex, two almost antithetical concepts, earn them envy as well as
disdain.

Marriages could end as well, and not always to pious protestation. In the
*Lais* of Marie de France, women subject to abusive marriages could find
other ways of evading the social scripts they had been handed. In *Eliduc*, the
wife and girlfriend of an adulterous knight end up retiring together to a
convent as a response to their lover's deception, where they offer their love to
God instead of any mortal man since 'mut est fole ki humme creit' (1084:
'any woman who trusts a man is mad'). Even women who had married, born
children, or lived on the value of their sexual favours, were able to give up
the world and embrace sexual abstinence in the name of a higher power.
Rutebeuf's *Vie de sainte Marie l'Egyptienne* offers a wonderful version in
which the body that was once Marie's means of sustenance becomes the
surest way of eradicating that past. Marie predicts that her sin will one day be
written on her forehead (226–9: 'Mes pechiez m'iert el front escriz ...'), but
the reader understands that that has always been the case. The stains of her

beauty can only be obliterated when virginity replaces and eradicates her former sin.

By the late Middle Ages, as societies recovered from plague and war, marriage was celebrated more frequently in literature as a Christian way of life – an institution offering a nurturing, productive, and supportive framework that mirrors God's relation to man. Much of this writing was produced, however, in reaction to, or in dialogue with, the late thirteenth-century continuation of the *Roman de la rose*. Jean de Meun's 'Genius' might well advocate procreative sexuality but he does so without insisting upon marriage, supposedly the only arena within which such sexual relations could take place. The prologue to the *Quinze Joies de mariage* (*c.*1400) takes up this reasoning, portraying marriage as an institution based on folly and suffering:

> ung homme n'a pas son bon sens, qui est en joyes et delices du monde comme de jeunesse garnie, et de sa franche voulenté et de son propre mouvement, sans necessité, trouve l'entrée d'une estroicte chartre douleureuse, plaine de larmes, de gemissemens et d'angoisses, et se boute dedens. (Prologue, 1–5)

> (any man who enjoys youth and the joys and delights of the world and who, of his own free will and impulse and without compulsion finds a narrow and sorrowful prison cell, full of tears, anguish, and lamenting, and throws himself into it, has lost his mind.)

Two brief examples illustrate the deleterious effects that marriage is said to have on promising young men. In *La Complainte Rutebeuf*, the poet/narrator presents his sad plight as the direct result of having taken a wife:

> Ne covient pas je vos raconte
> coument je me sui mis a hunte,
> quar bien aveiz oï le conte
> en queil meniere
> je pris ma fame darreniere,
> qui bele ne gente nen iere.
> Lors nasqui painne
> qui dura plus d'une semainne. (*Complainte*, 1–8)

> Tart sui meüz.
> A tart me sui aparceüz
> quant je sui en mes laz cheüz
> ce premier an. (*Complainte*, 46–9)

(I really shouldn't be telling you how I brought shame upon myself. You have all heard by now how I recently took a wife, a woman neither beautiful nor charming. From that came such pain that lasted more than a week ... I came late to my senses, realizing that I had fallen into my own trap that first year.)

Adam de la Halle has a similar complaint to make at the start of his *Jeu de la feuillée*. Nowhere is the description of love as a force that surrounds you and inflects every other perception more clearly exposed. At the beginning of the play, Adam decides to return to his studies in Paris, leaving his young wife behind in Arras in the care of his father. His friends object that that just cannot be since he was lawfully married in the church, but Adam responds, using rape imagery that could as well have been written by a woman, that his age and powerlessness before the force of Love are to blame:

> Amours me prist en itel point
> ou li amans .II. fois se point
> s'il se veut contre li deffendre.
> Car pris fu ou premier boullon,
> tout droit en le varde saison
> et en l'aspreche de jouvent,
> ou li cose a plus grant saveur,
> car nus n'i cache sen meilleur
> fors chou qui li vient a talent.   (*Li jus Adam*, 54–62)

(Love took hold of me just at the point when the lover is wounded twice if he wishes to defend himself against the attack. For I was taken right in the first budding of adolescence, in the most vulnerable moment of youth, when things still taste their sweetest. No one at that point is looking for what's good for him – only what he most desires.)

The weather, the adornments of nature, the birdsong are all to blame as they colour his first glimpse of the woman he will marry. She seems 'rians, amoreuse et deugie' ('gay, loveable, and svelte') and he finds her irresistible. Only later does he realize that she is in fact 'crasse, mautaillie / triste et trenchant' (72–3: 'filthy, misshapen, ill-tempered, cantankerous'). When he decides to leave her, his friends accuse him of being 'muavles' ('fickle'), an insult usually directed to women in misogynist commentary. Adam defends himself nonetheless saying that he had better leave now: he has no further interest in her and had best clear out before she is pregnant (172–4). His friend Rikier can only explain this change of heart by blaming the woman: she was too free with her sexual favours. This argument again relies on a misogynistic market view of sexuality, in which women control the supply and thus the demand: 'Ele a fait envers vous / Trop grant marchié de ses denrees' (79–80: 'she put too many of her goods on the market'). Adam claims that husbands' and wives' sexual appetites are out of sync: while he is sick of her, she hasn't nearly had her fill. The only way he can think of to kill that desire is to put mustard on his dick (43–4: 'Pour li espanir meterai / De le moustarde seur men[vit]')!

Yet there are happy marriages, or better yet, happy unions, though we usually only hear of them at the point of their dissolution or death. Christine de Pizan's lamentations over the death of her husband remain moving (*Cent Ballades*); Nisus and Euryalus's perfect same-sex love in the *Eneas* is one of the most praised unions in medieval literature; and Tristan and Iseut remain the prototypes of a perfect, if doomed, love. The medieval period may have denigrated and ridiculed sexual pleasure but it celebrated true love as almost no other. Marriage does not spring to mind as the best place to look for it – chivalric knighthood and religious houses would surely offer more fertile grounds – but that does not mean that we can discount its importance. Many a romance heroine needs marriage in order to ensure the protection of her property and family and will often stoop to seduction, even offering her body to the hero (Blanchefleur and Laudine in Chrétien's *Conte du graal* and *Yvain*), in order to get it. Marriage is unquestionably an institution that uses you – defining and enclosing you within a set of expectations; but it is also an institution that can be used to get what you need. Wedding bells may not be what every girl dreams of in medieval literature, but the financial security, title, property and respectability it brings can open doors to new conquests. At once contested and inevitable, desired and anxiety provoking, it remains the rock upon (and against) which medieval society defined itself – the rhetorical topos you can most count on to fuel fiction by inciting conflict, settling wars, enabling and celebrating transgression.[17]

## Notes

1. C. McCarthy (ed.), *Love, Sex and Marriage in the Middle Ages: a Sourcebook* (London and New York, Routledge, 2004), provides a good selection of sources and also illustrates their failure to reach unanimous or monologic conclusions. The works of J. A. Brundage are essential, especially *Law, Sex, and Christian Society in Medieval Europe* (Chicago University Press, 1987).
2. *Petit Robert*, ed. A. Rey (Paris, Société du Nouveau Littré, 1969), p. 1643.
3. Many penitentials and homilies actually counsel priests not to mention sodomy as a category of sin, for fear it might alert people to forbidden pleasure they might otherwise have missed. A study of insults from the period would indicate, however, that people were indeed classified by behaviour into sexual compartments, though such compartments were not necessarily exclusive or permanent.
4. Gratian, *Decretum, DD. 1–20: The Treatise on Laws*, trans. A. Thompson, J. Gordley, intro. K. Christensen (Washington, DC, Catholic University of America Press, 1993). See also J. A. Brundage, *Sex, Law, and Marriage in the Middle Ages* (Aldershot, Variorum, 1993).

5. See A. Badiou, *Saint Paul: la fondation de l'universalisme* (Paris, PUF, 1997).
6. St Augustine, *The City of God*, intro. E. Gilson (New York, Image Books, 1958), book XIV, chapters 18–25.
7. For further discussion, and different perspectives, see R. H. Bloch, *Medieval Misogyny* (Chicago University Press, 1991) and D. Elliot, *Spiritual Marriage: Sexual Abstinence in Medieval Wedlock* (Princeton University Press, 1993).
8. See R. M. Karras, *Sexuality in Medieval Europe: Doing unto Others* (New York and London, Routledge, 2005), p. 29.
9. See Karras, *Sexuality*, p. 48; also J. Wogan-Browne, *Saints' Lives and Women's Literary Culture c. 1150–1300: Virginity and its Authorizations* (Oxford University Press, 2001), pp. 47–8. Saints Paula and Elizabeth both provide examples of mothers moving beyond their families into a second state of virginity, incompatible with children and marriage.
10. See J. A. Brundage, 'Let me Count the Ways: Canonists and Theologians Contemplate Coital Positions', *Journal of Medieval History*, 10 (1984), 81–93; and 'Sex and Canon Law', in V. L. Bullough and J. A. Brundage (eds.), *Handbook of Medieval Sexuality* (New York, Garland, 2000), pp. 33–50.
11. Elliot, *Spiritual Marriage*.
12. See S. Kinoshita, *Medieval Boundaries: Rethinking Difference in Old French Literature* (Philadelphia, University of Pennsylvania Press, 2006).
13. 'Error' is another possible translation for the medieval French word *pechie*, though it is usually translated as 'sin', i.e. transgression against divine law. See Lacroix and Walter's note 25 in Béroul's *Tristan*, p. 87.
14. See, for further discussion, W. Burgwinkle, *Sodomy, Masculinity and Law in Medieval Literature* (Cambridge University Press, 2004) and the anthology of essays edited by C. Freccero and L. O. Fradenburg, *Premodern Sexualities* (New York and London, Routledge, 1996).
15. The famous diatribe of Genius in Jean de Meun's continuation of the romance has its roots in the eleventh-century clerical writings of Alan of Lille. See S. Gaunt, 'Bel Acueil and the Improper Allegory of the *Roman de la Rose*', *New Medieval Literatures*, 2 (1998), 65–93.
16. Translation based on R. L. A. Clark's in F. Canadé Sautman and P. Sheingorn (eds.), *Same Sex Love and Desire among Women in the Middle Ages* (New York, St Martin's Press, 2001), p. 166.
17. For a more historical approach to this topic, see Karras, *Sexuality*; J. Baldwin, *The Language of Sex: Five Voices from Northern France around 1200* (Chicago University Press, 1994); J. Boswell, *Christianity, Social Tolerance, and Homosexuality* (Chicago University Press, 1980); J. Murray and K. Eisenbichler (eds.), *Desire and Discipline: Sex and Sexuality in the Premodern West* (Toronto University Press, 1996).

# 16

SYLVIA HUOT

# Others and alterity

Medieval French literature is replete with alien and exotic beings: magical creatures, such as fairies and werewolves; marvellous or savage beings, such as giants and wild men; and ethnically or culturally different humans, such as Saracens. While there might seem initially to be a great difference between ordinary humans of a different culture, and marvellous creatures of an entirely different order of being, in fact this difference is often elided in medieval texts. In the *Pseudo-Turpin Chronicle*, for example, the Saracen champion that Roland fights is a Syrian Muslim who calls upon 'Mahomet' at the moment of his death; he is also a giant with the strength of twenty men and skin so tough that it cannot be pierced with a sword.[1] This chapter will examine selected examples of Old French texts involving fairies, giants, and Saracens. And while the aura of otherness surrounding magical beings may be more exciting, more exotic, and more dangerous, in the end all of these stories serve a common purpose, that of probing both the dangers and the delights of cross-cultural and inter-ethnic contact.

Attempted unions between humans and fairies figure in numerous medieval French texts, and are always presented as both alluring and problematic. Early examples can be found in the twelfth-century *Lais* of Marie de France. In *Lanval*, for example, the eponymous knight, a bit of a loner at Arthur's court, is summoned by a fairy who offers him her love on condition that the relationship remain completely secret. This arrangement is successful for a time, though it has the effect of isolating Lanval, who constantly seeks opportunities to evade his companions so that he can enjoy the company of the fairy. The conflict comes to a head when Lanval gets into an altercation with the queen, who has attempted to seduce him, and tells her that she is less beautiful than his lady, or indeed, than his beloved's least servant. Though the fairy initially punishes Lanval by witholding her presence, she eventually reveals herself and her servants at court, thereby absolving him of the charge of having falsely insulted the queen. When she leaves, Lanval goes with her, and is never seen again. Though the bond between human and fairy triumphs in the end, it is, in a sense, at the expense of Lanval's humanity: he cannot both participate in court society and maintain his relationship with a magical partner.

A similar message emerges from Marie's *lai* of *Yonec*. Muldumarec, the shape-shifting king of a mysterious subterranean kingdom, enters into an adulterous love relationship with the young wife of the elderly advocate of Caerwent in South Wales. Her husband discovers their love and sets a trap that kills Muldumarec, but by this time the woman is pregnant with their son, Yonec. She bides her time until, years later, she and her husband and son visit an abbey in Caerleon where they are shown the tomb of a king who died because of his love for a lady. Revealing that this king was her lover and the father of her son, the lady dies on the spot; Yonec kills his step-father and assumes the throne of his real father's kingdom. In this story, contact between the human and the magical realms is fatal for both sides. And although the half-blood son survives, he is integrated into the magical kingdom only, decisively rejecting his human heritage. Both *lais* can be read with reference to Plantagenet colonial activity in Wales.[2] They exploit the tensions surrounding Anglo-Welsh marriages, the dangers of a knight being lured away from the Norman castles and into the Celtic hinterlands, and the subversive potential of mixed-blood offspring, who might identify with their Celtic rather than their English lineage. As Sharon Kinoshita notes, *Yonec* 'is at once an erotic fantasy and an allegory of native resistance to colonial rule'.[3] Associating the indigenous Celtic culture with the mysterious domain of fairies is a way of expressing its potential both for alluring charm and for dangerous alienation from the centres of Anglo-Norman power.

More than two hundred years later, the theme of love and marriage across the human–fairy divide was still alive. It receives extended treatment in the romance of *Melusine*, which survives in both prose and verse redactions from the turn of the fifteenth century; my discussion here will be based on the prose version by Jean d'Arras (*c.*1399), which slightly predates the verse version by Coudrette.[4] This tale, which purports to explain the origins of the House of Lusignan, examines the difficult, and ultimately unsuccessful, process by which a fairy might attempt to be integrated into human society. The story begins with Melusine's mother, Presine, who marries King Elinas of Scotland. Though initially harmonious, the marriage ends disastrously with the birth of the couple's three daughters. Forgetting his wife's stipulation that he must not enter the room of childbirth during her period of confinement, Elinas rushes in to see the new babies, causing her to flee. At this, Elinas is so distraught that he loses his mind. Melusine and her sisters, Melior and Palestine, grow up in fairyland, hearing from their mother about their father's treachery. But when they punish him by imprisoning him inside a mountain, Presine is enraged, saying that Elinas was her only joy. For the first time, apparently, she reveals to Melusine and her sisters that their paternal lineage could have released them from the condition of fairyhood:

> La vertu du germe de ton pere, toy et les autres, eust attrait a sa nature humaine et eussiés esté briefment hors des meurs nimphes et faees sans y retourner. (134)

> (The power of your father's seed would have attracted you and your sisters to his human nature, and you would soon have been released from the realm of nymphs and fairies, never to return.)

By turning against their father, however, the sisters have squandered this chance at humanity. Denouncing them as 'faulses et mauvaises, et tresameres et dures de cuer' (134: 'false and wicked, very bitter and hardhearted'), Presine lays a curse on each of them. Melusine will now turn into a serpent from the waist down every Saturday. If she marries a man who never asks about her whereabouts on Saturday and never reveals her secret, she can become a mortal woman and die a natural death; but if he does denounce her, she will be trapped in her magical, serpentine body until the Last Judgement. Melior is sent to a castle in Armenia, where she too will remain until the Last Judgement; any knight who goes there and maintains a vigil for three days and three nights, at the Feast of St John the Baptist, can ask her for any gift of wealth or land. But he cannot ask for her body or for her love, whether in marriage or outside it; if he does, he will lose his wealth and his lands and his fortunes will decline, as will those of his descendants for nine generations to follow. Palestine, finally, is imprisoned in Mount Canigou in Catalonia; she can expect to be rescued some day by a knight who will also conquer the Holy Land.

The main focus of the romance is on Melusine, who marries the knight Remondin and founds the castle of Lusignan, and their descendants. For many years her husband respects her secret; even when he is finally driven to spy on her one Saturday night, seeing her in her half-serpentine form in the bathtub, he keeps quiet about this, so that all is still well. The couple have ten sons, each marked with some strange feature: huge ears, multicoloured eyes, tusk-like teeth. Thus Melusine does almost succeed in losing her magical identity and becoming fully human, but in the end her husband cannot put aside his fears, and publicly denounces her as inhuman, crying out: 'Hee, tresfaulse serpente, par Dieu, ne toy ne tes fais ne sont que fantosme ne ja hoir que tu ayes porté ne vendra a bon chief en la fin' (692: 'Oh, very false serpent, by God, both you and your deeds are an illusion, nor will any heir that you have borne ever come to a good end'). Though he repents almost at once and, consumed with remorse, devotes the rest of his life to the penitential rigours of a hermitage, it is all for naught. After a dramatic farewell, Melusine metamorphoses into something truly alien, a flying serpent, whose reappearances around the tower of Lusignan, throughout history, signal the imminent death of its lord. Though she remains connected to Lusignan, she is now always an outsider, unable to interact with the human inhabitants. In addition, one of her sons, Oruble, is so evil and so violent that he has to be put to death at the age of seven; his murder, in fact, is the last instruction that she gives before flying away. Most of the other sons, however, intermarry with the nobility of Europe. Though Melusine herself is expelled from society and remains a liminal figure, her blood is diffused throughout the noble families of Europe, from Britain to Armenia.

Much of the action in *Melusine* involves the sons, fierce warriors whose military adventuring wins them brides in a wide range of locations. Their kinship, and the strangeness of their unusual bodily features, unites them, so that although each is established in a different place, they end up creating a pan-European army that stands firm against threats both from within – marauding or unscrupulous barons – and without: Saracens. The Lusignan brothers, that is, create their own hegemony, recognized throughout Europe as a force that cannot be stopped. As their enemies comment at one point, 'Comment... a le deable apporté tant de ceulx de Lusegnen en ce paÿs? Il n'est nouvelle que de eulx ne entre Sarrasins ne crestiens' (760: 'How has the devil brought so many Lusignanians to this land? All the talk is of them, both among Saracens and among Christians'). By the late fourteenth century, the noble families who claimed descent from the House of Lusignan were many and far-flung. Summing up the positions of Melusine's surviving sons, the narrator enumerates her many descendants:

Et dist l'ystoire que le roy Uriien regna moult puissaument en Chippre et ses hoirs aprés lui, et Guion en Armenie, et Regnault en Bahaigne, et ses hoirs ont regné puissaument aprés lui, et Anthoine en Lussembourc et ses hoirs apréz lui, et Oeudes en la Marche, et Remond en Forests et Gieffroy a Lusegnen, et Thierry a Parthenay... Et encores en sont yssus ceulx de Pembroc en Angleterre et ceulx de Cabrieres en Arragon, comme j'ay dessus dit, et ceulx de Cassenages du Daulphiné, et La Rochefoucaut, et ceulx de Cadillac, si comme on le treuve es anciennes croniques. (780)

(And the history says that the king Urien reigned powerfully in Cyprus and his heirs after him, and Guy in Armenia, and Renaud in Bohemia, and his heirs reigned powerfully after him, and Antoine in Luxembourg and his heirs after him, and Eudes in La Marche, and Raymond in Forez and Geoffroy in Lusignan, and Thierry in Parthenay... And also from them are descended those of

Pembroke in England and those of Cabrera in Aragon, as I said above, and those
of Sassenage in the Dauphiné, and La Rouchefoucauld and those of Cadillac, as
is found in the ancient chronicles.)

Tracing their ancestry back to a half-blood fairy who lingers around the
edges of human society, herself the daughter of a fairy who fled human
contact, creates a kind of absolute origin, a genealogical 'ground zero'
beyond which it would be impossible to probe. In *Melusine* we literally see
the House of Lusignan emerge from the inhuman beyond, establishing
themselves as a European Christian bulwark against Islamic expansionism.

Though it is with Melusine that the text is principally concerned, we
do hear one anecdote relating to her sister Melior. We recall that as a
result of the spell cast by Presine, Melior can fulfill male desires, no matter
how extravagant; but she herself can never be the object of desire. Those who
attempt her vigil and fall asleep, moreover, are forced to spend the rest of
their lives at her court. Melior, that is, remains completely apart, like
Melusine, while at the same time exerting a dangerous attraction. Contact
with fairies – even half-breed fairies – is risky and, if not for extreme
vigilance, can result in the fate of Lanval: being subsumed into the magical
world. Allowing oneself to desire a fairy may lead to madness, grief, death, or
other disaster, as is shown not only by the examples in Marie de France's
*Lais*, but also by those in *Melusine*: Elinas, Remondin, and a king of Armenia
whose encounter with Melior proves very costly indeed. In a further twist to
this story of hybrid daughters caught between fairyhood and humanity, we
find that a being who seems utterly alien and exotic may turn out to be
uncomfortably familiar. A king of Armenia, overpowered by an ill-advised
love, keeps the vigil at Melior's castle and, when asked what he desires,
requests her hand in marriage. After attempting to dissuade him, Melior
repudiates her would-be suitor with a dramatic revelation:

> Povre fol, n'es tu pas descendu de la lignie du roy Guion, qui fu filz Melusigne,
> ma seur, et je suis ta tante. Et tu es si prez de mon lignaige, posé que je me
> voulzisse assentir a toy avoir, que l'eglise ne s'i vouldroit pas accorder. (804)

> (Poor fool, aren't you descended from the lineage of King Guy, who was the son
> of my sister Melusine, and I your aunt? And you are so closely related to me
> that, even if I wanted to take you, the church would never agree to it.)

It is hard to say which is more disorienting in Melior's words: that this
immortal fairy, capable of magically granting any wish pertaining to material enrichment, is a close blood relative of the king, or that she is a Christian
unwilling to go against the law of the church.

If Melusine is the intimate wife and mother who turns out to be terrifyingly, irrevocably other, Melior is seemingly exotic but turns out not to be 'other' at all. The maternal body, the mother's sister: these are sources of great good, but also surrounded by taboo. Melusine remains forever alien, yet in that very guise, she is also the guarantor of Lusignan identity and kinship across the European and Mediterranean world. Melior too is resolutely inaccessible, an alien resource to be mined and exploited, but never possessed or domesticated. But like Melusine she is also intimately close, indeed excessively so. Only Palestine can be conquered, rehabilitated, and readmitted to human society; and that resolution of traumatic difference is associated with the conquest and redemption of the Holy Land, whose name she bears. The narrator cites examples of people who have seen the mysterious lady of the Canigou, as reported by the 'roy d'Arragon et autres pluseurs de son royaume' (138: 'king of Aragon and many others of his kingdom'). Clearly, at the time of writing, Palestine has not yet been liberated – just as the place called Palestine has not. But eventually, both will be freed from their demonic and heretical possessors, and integrated back into Christendom.

The three half-fairy sisters therefore embody different kinds of alterity as well as proximity and familiarity. Each is both accessible and inaccessible, and each is associated with larger issues of religious, political, and hereditary sameness and difference. The story does not systematize these forms of difference, but it does invite the reader on a journey through an endlessly shifting landscape of alliance, repulsion, alterity, identity.

In addition to fairies, medieval romance is replete with another kind of inhuman being: giants. Giants do not have magic powers, nor are they immortal; and in that sense, they are more similar to humans than fairies are. They embody a primal savagery, however, that makes them the living remnants of that which must be excluded in order for civilization to take hold. In *Melusine*, Presine installs a giant as guard on her husband's subterranean tomb; his predations torment the people of the region until he is finally killed by one of Melusine's sons. Presine, the maternal ancestor lying behind the original maternal ancestor of Lusignan, stands outside the human world. And just as contact with her was lethal for Elinas, so an ongoing legacy of that marriage is devastation for an entire population.

Interestingly, though giants usually figure in medieval texts only so that they can be killed by the hero, it is occasionally possible for them to be rehabilitated. An interesting example occurs in the mid-fourteenth-century *Perceforest*, a vast prose romance set in pre-Arthurian Britain.[5] Here the young giantess Galotine is rescued by the British knight Lyonnel and his squire, Clamides, from the predations of her incestuous father, the Golden-Haired

Giant. Once the father has been killed, Lyonnel returns to Scotland, taking the giant's head as a gift for the young Scottish princess. But Clamides, knighted by Lyonnel after the combat, remains and marries the young Galotine, whom he seduced while Lyonnel was busy plotting his attack. As in so many medieval texts, the male giant is a ferocious being that threatens civilization, not only through murderous rampaging but also in his violent sexual aggression. The female giant, however, is his victim just as ordinary human women are, and as such can be rescued and recuperated. Galotine's sexual encounter with Clamides, though clearly transgressive – she is only nine years old, and even the giant was waiting for her to come of age before he married her – has the effect of deflecting her desire from an improper object, her father, to a proper one: an exogamous marriage partner. Though apparently the young giantess expressed no prior objections to her father's marriage plans, after her encounter with Clamides she informs her father that she has had a change of heart: 'Sire, je ne vueil plus estre vostre amie, car j'en ay trouvé ung plus bel et plus petit que vous' (*Perceforest*, 352: 'Sir, I no longer want to be your beloved, for I have found another man more hand-some and smaller than you'). And indeed after the marriage, Clamides successfully transforms his wife into a model of courtly femininity that is almost indistinguishable from the real thing:

> Mais le gentil chevalier nourry et enseigna en telle maniere sa jenne mariee ... qu'elle fut tenue la meilleure, la plus doulce et debonnaire, la plus charitable et de meilleure vie et la plus belle et la plus plaisant et la plus feminine selon sa grandeur que l'on sceust. (*Perceforest*, 363)

> (But the noble knight raised his young wife and taught her in such a way that she was considered the best lady, the sweetest and most debonnaire, the most charitable and best behaved and the most beautiful and the most agreeable and the most feminine, for someone her size, that anyone knew.)

Only Galotine's gigantic size – she was two feet taller than her husband – remains as a marker of her extraordinary lineage.

The underlying political agenda of this episode is clear: the isolationist ruler of an island kingdom, his resistance to external contact expressed in his incestuous designs, is eliminated. Though the Isle of the Giant is not precisely identified, we are told that it lies some distance beyond the Isle of the Serpent, which later becomes the seat of the kingdom of Orkney. Most likely, then, the kingdom of the Golden-Haired Giant is to be identified with the Shetland Isles, territory that was disputed between Scotland and Norway during the medieval period. Lyonnel's combat and Clamides's marriage wrest the island away from its ruler, a giant of Scandinavian origin, and place it in the hands of a British knight who owes allegiance to the kings of both Scotland and

England. As with the motif of the Saracen princess who converts to Christianity out of love for Crusader knights, the maiden's love for the knight who has conquered her people is an obvious trope of cultural conquest.[6] The fairy who longs to be human, the giantess who prefers a human husband, the Saracen willing to sacrifice her kingdom out of love for a European knight: these women embody the comforting myth that foreign people want to be liberated from false religions and oppressive regimes, and that they will instinctively desire assimilation to European culture if only they are given the chance.

An even more complex treatment of a foreign knight occurs in the mid-thirteenth-century prose *Tristan*.[7] Palamedes, a Saracen who associates with Arthur's knights but remains independent of the Round Table, is Tristan's chief rival for Iseut. Many knights love Iseut, but Palamedes is the most persistent and the most aggressive. He also has the distinction of having been in love with Iseut every bit as long as Tristan has – indeed, slightly longer, since it is when Tristan notices Palamedes's interest in Iseut, while both are visitors at the Irish court, that Tristan himself vows to win her love. Though up to that point Tristan had admired Iseut's beauty, 'son cuer n'i avoit pas mis dusqu'a l'amer granment' (Curtis, I, 165: 'his heart had not begun to love her very much'). But within days of Palamedes's arrival at the Irish court, the two knights have entered into a ferocious rivalry for the love of Iseut that will continue unabated until Tristan and Iseut are dead.

At that time Tristan's identity is unknown to Iseut, whose mother is only just completing his cure from Morholt's poisoned sword. He has not even recovered his strength enough to have demonstrated his prowess. He and Palamedes are both foreigners at court, known only for their respective qualities: Palamedes for his prowess and Tristan for his beauty. And when Brangain asks Iseut whether she would rather give her love to Palamedes or to 'our knight' – the incognito Tristan – the reply is interesting:

> je cuit que je m'acorderoie avant a Palamedes por sa bone chevalerie. Mes se nostres chevaliers fust de sa bonté et de sa proesce, et il fust si gentils hom com il semble, l'en s'i devroit mieuz acorder a ce qu'il seroit sanz faille, s'il estoit tres bien gariz, li plus biax chevaliers dou monde. (Curtis, I, 165)

> (I think I would rather choose Palamedes because of his great chivalry. But if our knight had his goodness and his prowess, and he was as noble as he seems, then it would be better to choose him, since, if he was fully recovered, he would surely be the most handsome knight in the world.)

The Saracen can be capable of marvellous feats of chivalry, and may earn the admiration of men, ladies, and maidens alike. When it comes to beauty, however, he cannot compare to Tristan. Iseut's assessment hints at an ethnic bias: the Saracen body, though powerful and highly skilled, lacks the beauty and the 'sex appeal' of a British knight.

Palamedes's resistance to Christianity is an essential part of his character, highlighted by the narrator at his first appearance in the text:

> Onques n'avoit esté crestiens, et si cuidoient li preudome entor qui il reperoit qu'il fust crestiens. (Curtis, I, 164)

> (He had never been a Christian, but the noblemen he associated with thought he was Christian.)

Palamedes, then, is potentially a dangerous figure, a covert Muslim masquerading as a Christian in order to win glory in the western kingdoms. Although his father and brothers embrace Christianity, he holds out. As long as he maintains this position, he is a lone figure, participating in countless tournaments and court festivities but always somewhat apart. He cannot join the Round Table, being excluded from its oaths and its culture of militant Christian knighthood. Nor can he be integrated through marriage to a Christian lady – one or the other would have to convert, since there was no law of marriage conceivable to medieval culture that could dispense with religious affiliation. Palamedes does consider that Iseut might be worth converting for. When he sees her for the first time, he is struck by her beauty:

> Si li chiet ou cuer, et tant li plest et atalente qu'il n'est riens ou monde qu'il ne feïst por li avoir, nes sa loi guerpi. Et ce estoit la riens ou monde que il feïst plus a enviz, mes totevoies la gerpiroit il por avoir Yselt, s'il poïst estre. (Curtis, I, 164)

> (She went straight to his heart, and so pleased and excited him that there is nothing on earth he would not do to have her, even giving up his religion. And that was the last thing he would ever want to do, but still he would do it in order to have Iseut, if that could be.)

Yet if Palamedes considers abandoning his faith for Iseut, he does not actually do so. As a result, there is always some blurring as to just what the real obstacle is that keeps him from Iseut. Ostensibly, it is Tristan that prevents her from loving Palamedes, while Mark is the obstacle to marriage. Yet the question of religious identity can never be forgotten. Palamedes's refusal to convert might allow for the comforting illusion that this, in fact, is the real barrier: not his inferiority to Tristan or Iseut's disinterest, but a matter of personal integrity on his part. The text allows us to imagine the virtually unthinkable possibility that Iseut might in fact fall in love with a Muslim – might even give herself to him as she has done with Tristan – while assuring us that this will never happen, because it is Tristan that she loves, and Mark that she is married to.

The adulterous love of Tristan and Iseut is placed in an interesting perspective by its juxtaposition with Palamedes's desperate love. Tristan, in fact, is the perfect partner for Iseut, so much so that her father would have been happy for him to marry her. In response to Tristan's request of Iseut's hand on behalf of King Mark, the Irish king replies:

> Bien avez Yselt deservie, et achetee chierement; et por ce la vos otroi je mout debonerement a ce que vos la preignoiz a moillier, se il vos plest, et se vos ce ne poez faire, que vos soiez si tenuz au roi Marc que vos li doiez livrer, li mariaiges m'en plest mout.
> (Curtis, 1, 216)

> (You certainly deserve Iseut, and have paid dearly for her, and so I gladly agree that you should take her as your wife, if you want to; and if you can't do that, because you're pledged to King Mark to give her to him, that marriage pleases me greatly.)

Their relationship is also accepted and nurtured in Arthur's kingdom, where they live for a time after Tristan succeeds in wresting Iseut away from Mark. Though transgressive in a legalistic sense, their love is noble in and of itself. A love affair with an unconverted Saracen, however, is not simply transgressive; it redefines the very parameters of acceptable relationships, of the boundaries that can be crossed in the name of love. And in a sense, it is from precisely this dangerous, uncharted love that Tristan saves Iseut by interposing himself between her and Palamedes right from the start. Interestingly, the other great thirteenth-century prose romance, *Lancelot*, also features an alternative to the adulterous love that is the hero's abiding passion. Galehaut's love for Lancelot – ultimately as hopeless as that of Palamedes for Iseut – similarly redefines the parameters of love by presenting a version that is not only homoerotic, but also involves a union, or desired union, between a human and a half-breed giant. And it is Galehaut who is responsible for the beginning of Lancelot's adulterous relationship with Guenevere, just as Palamedes is responsible, albeit not of his own volition, for Tristan's relationship with Iseut. In both texts, the transgressive love of adultery is juxtaposed not only with marriage, but also with a queer love that, however noble and heartfelt, can never quite come to fruition, and whose very presence in the text casts a normalizing shadow onto the adulterous couple at its centre.

Eventually Palamedes does accept Christianity. This happens only after Iseut and Tristan are dead, however, as if completely to foreclose any possibility that, as a Christian, he might finally have won her love. Palamedes differs from Galehaut in that he does not die for love; but, like Galehaut, his alterity is of a kind that can be overcome only through an act of submission. Galehaut, who has never done homage to any man and who conquers all in his path, surrenders to Arthur and becomes a companion of the Round Table; Palamedes, the staunch Muslim, submits to Arthur's wishes and adopts Christian law. As knights, both men are unimpeachable; and it is knighthood, rather than love, that offers both men the greatest chance at assimilation. Yet in the end, even membership of the Round Table does not ensure the complete integration of these slightly mysterious figures into the Arthurian world. Galehaut dies alone in his castle, yearning for Lancelot. The death of Palamedes, equally tragic, reflects the extent to which this Saracen knight both is and is not accepted by Arthur's knights, and deserves closer examination.

Even when he is no longer 'passing' as a Christian, Palamedes is admired by the chivalric world, which stands ready to receive him if only he will accept Christianity. Arthur, for example, tells Palamedes that he admires him 'sour tous les cevaliers qui en Dieu ne croient' (Ménard *et al.*, IX, 100: 'above all the knights who don't believe in God') and urges him – unsuccessfully at first – to make his conversion. Only the austere Galehaut refuses Palamedes's company, loftily telling him, 'Vous n'estes mie de nostre compaingnie, puis que vous n'estes crestiens!' (Ménard *et al.*, IX, 93: 'You're not of our company, since you're not a Christian'). In the end, the power of peer pressure from 'li rois et la roïne et tout li baron de la court' (Ménard *et al.*, IX, 248) induces Palamedes to accept baptism. As a Christian he can at last join the Round Table and, consequently, the Grail Quest. Presumably, his outsider days are over. But unfortunately, word travels slowly in the kingdom of Logres, and many of Arthur's knights are unaware of Palamedes's new status. Thus it is that Lancelot, coming upon Palamedes in the forest, decides to test the prowess of the famous Saracen and challenges him to a sword fight. Eventually Palamedes realizes that his combatant is a knight of the Round Table and ends their combat, since both are sworn not to take up arms against their fellows; by then, he has been severely wounded. So serious is the offence that Palamedes cannot resist chastizing his erstwhile adversary:

> Mais toutes voies di je bien que vous vous estes mesfais de ceste bataille durement, car je sui compains de la Table Reonde, pour coi vous ne deüssiés a moi combatre en nule maniere du monde ... Si nel di mie, sire, fait il, pour vantance, mais pour vostre mesqueance et pour ce que vous vous gardés autre fois de cevalier estrange asaillir que vous ne connissiés. (Ménard *et al.*, IX, 263)

> (But anyway, I'm telling you that you transgressed badly in this battle, because I'm a companion of the Round Table, so you shouldn't fight me in any way. I don't say this, sir, as a boast, but to let you know your misdeed, and that you should be careful another time about attacking a strange knight that you don't know.)

Already this event has reminded the reader of the vulnerability of the foreign or unknown knight, who can find himself in a fight to the death for no other reason than to satisfy the curiosity of a local knight. But the real tragedy ensues when the wounded Palamedes, unable to defend himself, is attacked yet again, this time by Gauvain and Agravain. Ignoring Palamedes's pleas – he is a Companion of the Round Table, he is too badly wounded to defend himself, and he should not be attacked by two knights at the same time – Gauvain runs Palamedes through with his sword and leaves him to die. Palamedes is not, of course, the only knight of the Round Table to be attacked or killed by the implacable sons of King Lot. Nonetheless, his death has a special poignancy, coming as it does so quickly in the wake of his admission to the Arthurian fellowship. Admired by all, yet denied the love of the woman he has adored throughout his chivalric career; admitted to the Round Table only to be killed through the whims of one of his fellow knights and the vindictive wrath of another: Palamedes occupies a liminal position that even his baptism cannot overcome. Though he dies a good Christian death and we can assume that his soul enters the company of the blessed, in his life on earth he never quite escapes that aura of alterity, that sense of being not quite 'one of us'.

Throughout medieval French literature, we find a range of exotic beings and the problems surrounding their relations with the dominant court society. Some are resolutely other, to the extent that it is impossible to maintain a relationship with them while also retaining allegiance to the court. Others make a significant contribution to their host society, but true integration is extremely difficult. Whether difference is expressed through religious belief, bodily gigantism or shape-shifting, or outright magical powers, the divide between 'us' and 'them' proves difficult to overcome. Those marked by these differences of culture, ethnicity, or magic are often tremendously attractive and desirable, but rarely can they lose their aura of exoticism and danger.

Thus we find these texts pervaded by conflicting impulses of attraction and repulsion, admiration and fear. In *Melusine* the giant's death, like that of the sinister son Oruble, is a vital step in the elimination of civilization's enemies. The marriages of Melusine's other sons, the possibility of extracting benefits from Melior while remaining unseduced by her beauty, and the eventual liberation of Palestine, in contrast, mark the domestication and absorption of those forces. Similarly, the death of the Golden-Haired Giant is a victory for the march of civilization, as is the marriage and courtly education of his daughter. The political context is all the more evident when more familiar ethnic differences are at stake, as in the fascination exerted by the heroic Saracen. Moving between extermination on the one hand, colonization, exploitation and assimilation on the other, medieval authors endlessly consider and reconsider both the permeability and the intractability of those boundaries that separate 'us' from 'them'.

## Notes

1. *An Anonymous Old French Translation of the Pseudo-Turpin Chronicle*, ed. R. N. Walpole (Cambridge, MA, The Mediaeval Academy of America, 1979), pp. 60–5.
2. See S. Kinoshita, *Medieval Boundaries: Rethinking Difference in Old French Literature* (Philadelphia, University of Pennsylvania Press, 2006), pp. 105–38; R. H. Bloch, *The Anonymous Marie de France* (Chicago University Press, 2003).
3. *Medieval Boundaries*, p. 106.
4. Jean d'Arras's *Melusine* is cited from Vincensini's edition. On this text see D. Maddox and S. Sturm-Maddox, *Melusine of Lusignan: Founding Fiction in Late Medieval France* (Athens, GA, University of Georgia Press, 1996).
5. *Perceforest: Deuxième partie*, ed. G. Roussineau, I. See my *Postcolonial Fictions in the Roman de Perceforest: Cultural Identities and Hybridities* (Cambridge, D. S. Brewer, 2007).
6. Kinoshita, *Medieval Boundaries*, pp. 46–73.
7. I cite the following volumes of the prose *Tristan*: Curtis, I and Ménard *et al.*, IX (this volume ed. L. Harf-Lancner, 1997).

# APPENDIX: REFERENCE WORKS FOR
# OLD AND MIDDLE FRENCH

This Appendix seeks to give a brief critical guide to reference works and pedagogical tools for the Old and Middle French language. The editorial standards of websites may be less rigorous than those of the published sources cited, and the sites themselves may not be permanent.

## A. Dictionaries

### (a) Research dictionaries

The best dictionary for the early Old French period (i.e. to c.1300) is the multivolume *Altfranzösiches Wörterbuch* (often referred to as Tobler/Lommatzsch or TL).[1] TL glosses words in German, offering extensive examples and cross-referencing to other dictionaries, particularly Godefroy and *FEW* (see below). The older multivolume dictionary by Godefroy is useful for both the Old and Middle French period:[2] it glosses in French and has two alphabetical sequences, the second, which extends and supplements the first, beginning in volume 8. Though more specialized in some respects, the *Anglo-Norman Dictionary* (*AND*),[3] which glosses in English, is frequently invaluable, though it is in the course of major revision.

For fourteenth- and fifteenth-century French usage, the only complete published research dictionary remains Godefroy. Unfortunately it only includes words or glosses that differ from Modern French. The multivolume dictionary of the sixteenth century by Huguet (glosses in French) can be a useful supplement,[4] though it likewise only glosses words or acceptances not found in Modern French. A new online dictionary of Middle French is available at www.atilf.fr.blmf; for additional lexographical resources, see www.lexilogos.com/francais_dictionnaire_ancien.htm.

### (b) Pocket dictionaries

A number are available: Greimas's *Dictionnaire de l'ancien français* and Godefroy's *Lexique de l'ancien français* are the two most readily available

French-language dictionaries; Brian Levy *et al.*'s *Old French–English Dictionary* is in English.[5] The disadvantage of pocket dictionaries is that they are little more than word lists, so the glossaries to critical editions are often more useful.

### (c) Etymological dictionaries

The best dictionaries of Modern French provide etymological information (particularly the *Robert* and the *Littré*). The real etymologist's etymological dictionary is the *Französisches etymologisches Wörterbuch* (*FEW*),[6] but it takes some getting used to as it is organized by etymon, with separate sequences for Latin, Germanic, Oriental, etc. etymons. In other words, you need to know the etymon of the word you want to look up to find the relevant entry. Fortunately, all but the first few volumes have useful indices to help non-initiates. *FEW* is gradually being replaced by the as yet very incomplete *Dictionnaire étymologique de l'ancien français* (for further details see www.deaf-page.de).

## B. Histories of the language

One of the best short overall histories of the language in English is Price's *The French Language*, unfortunately now out of print.[7] In French, Picoche and Marchello-Nizia's *Histoire de la langue française* is generally regarded as the gold standard.[8] For Old French, Raynaud de Lage's short *Introduction à l'ancien français* is readily available and has the merit of including helpful examples from Old French literary texts.[9] For Middle French, the best overall account is Marchello-Nizia's *La Langue française aux XIVe et XVe siècles*.[10] It too contains lots of examples. A useful supplement to these more formal histories is Ayres-Bennett's *History*,[11] which guides students through the history of the language through sustained commentaries on longer extracts.

## C. Phonetics and phonology

Most traditional histories of the language are primarily devoted to phonology, so this is the most widely covered area of the history of the language. The specialist work remains Fouché's *Phonétique historique*,[12] but a user-friendly introduction to Old French pronunciation may be found at www.geocities.com/Athens/Acropolis/8716/course.html.

## D. Dialects

Linguists swear by Dees's *Atlas*,[13] an analysis of the usage of documents from different areas of France. However, Pope's monumental *From Latin to*

*Old French* – strictly for initiates – has useful appendices on dialect with especially good coverage of Anglo-Norman, while for Picard, Gossen's *Grammaire de l'ancien picard* may be consulted.[14]

## E. Syntax

Ménard's *Syntaxe de l'ancien français* is a thorough traditional syntax and preferable to Foulet's *Petite Syntaxe*, which is based exclusively on thirteenth-century romances.[15] For Middle French, see Martin and Wilmet's *Syntaxe du moyen français*, and for a more historical perspective, see Harris's *The Evolution of French Syntax*.[16]

## G. Discourse

Cerquiglini's *La Parole médiévale* has become a classic in this area.[17] See also Fleischman's influential work, particularly chapter 4 of *Tense and Narrativity*.[18] For envisaging medieval French works in performance, visit the thought-provoking website euterpe.bobst.nyu.edu/mednar/index.php.

## H. Lexis

Hollyman's, *Développement du vocabulaire féodal* is an historical study of the evolution of a few key terms, while Matoré's *Vocabulaire de la société médiévale* is a more theoretical study of broader semantic fields, and Andrieux-Reix's *Fiches de vocabulaire* is designed specifically for the French post-graduate curriculum.[19]

## I. Websites and searchable databases of interest

The database *Frantexte* contains a searchable corpus of Middle French texts on atilf.atilf.fr/dmf.htm. Some medieval texts are also available on line at gallica.bnf.fr/.

## Notes

1. A. Tobler and E. Lommatzsch, *Altfranzösisches Wörterbuch*, 11 vols., Berlin and Stuttgart, Weidmannsche and F. Steiner Verlag, 1925–2002, now also available on CD and DVD ROM, for more information, see www.uni-stuttgart.de/lingrom/stein/tl/.
2. F. Godefroy, *Dictionnaire de l'ancienne langue française et de tous ses dialectes du IXe au XVe siècle*, 10 vols. (Paris, F. Vieweg, 1880–1902).

3. L. W. Stone and W. Rothwell, *Anglo-Norman dictionary*, 7 fascicules (London, MHRA, 1977–92); in the course of major revision and also available online at www.anglo-norman.net. The online edition is a hybrid work (consisting of unrevised and revised material), but covering the whole alphabet.

4. E. Huguet, *Dictionnaire de la langue française du seizième siècle*, 7 vols. (Paris, Champion, 1925–67).

5. A. Greimas, *Dictionnaire de l'ancien français jusqu'au milieu du quatorzième siècle* (Paris, Larousse, 1968); F. Godefroy (with J. Bonnard and A. Salmon), *Lexique de l'ancien français* (Paris, Champion reprint, 1982); B. Levy, A. Hindley, and F. W. Langley, *Old French–English Dictionary* (Cambridge University Press, 2000).

6. W. von Wartburg *et al.*, *Französisches etymologisches Wörterbuch*, 25 vols. to date (Bonn, Schröder, 1922–).

7. G. Price, *The French Language: Present and Past* (London, Edward Arnold, 1971).

8. J. Picoche and C. Marchello-Nizia, *Histoire de la langue française* (Paris, Nathan, 1989).

9. G. Raynaud de Lage, *Introduction à l'ancien français*, 9th edn (Paris, SEDES/CDU, 1975).

10. C. Marchello-Nizia, *La Langue française aux XIVe et XVe siècles* (Paris, Nathan, 1997).

11. W. Ayres-Bennett, *A History of the French Language through Texts* (London, Routledge, 1996).

12. P. Fouché, *Phonétique historique du franccais*, 2nd edn, 3 vols. (Paris, Klincksieck, 1956 and 1969).

13. A. Dees (with M. Dekker, O. Huber and K. van Reenen-Stein), *Atlas des formes linguistiques des textes littéraires de l'ancien français* (Tübingen, Niemeyer, 1987).

14. M. K. Pope, *From Latin to Modern French with Especial Consideration of Anglo-Norman: Phonology and Morphology*, 2nd edn (Manchester University Press, 1952); C. T. Gossen, *Grammaire de l'ancien picard*, 2nd edn (Paris, Klincksieck, 1970).

15. P. Ménard, *Syntaxe de l'ancien français*, 4th edn (Bordeaux, Bière, 1994); L Foulet, *Petite Syntaxe de l'ancien français*, 3rd edn, CFMA (Paris, Champion, 1965).

16. R. Martin and M. Wilmet, *Syntaxe du moyen français* (Bordeaux, Sobodi, 1980); M. Harris, *The Evolution of French Syntax: a Comparative Approach* (London, Longman, 1978).

17. B. Cerquiglini, *La Parole médiévale: discours, syntaxe, texte* (Paris, Minuit, 1981).

18. S. Fleischman, *Tense and Narrativity: from Medieval Performance to Modern Fiction* (London, Routledge, 1990).

19. J. Hollyman, *Le Développement du vocabulaire féodal en France pendant le haut Moyen Age: étude sémantique* (Geneva, Droz, 1957); G. Matoré, *Le Vocabulaire de la société médiévale* (Paris, PUF, 1985); N. Andrieux-Reix, *Ancien français: fiches de vocabulaire* (Paris, PUF, 1989).

# BIBLIOGRAPHY OF MEDIEVAL FRENCH TEXTS

This bibliography contains full references to the editions of all the medieval French texts that are substantively discussed in this *Companion*. Some additional references to works we think important are also included.

CCMA = Champion Classiques: Moyen Age
CFMA = Classiques français du moyen âge
SATF = Société des anciens textes français
TLF = Textes littéraires français

Adam de la Halle, *Le Jeu de la feuillée* and *Le Jeu de Robin et Marion*, in *Œuvres complètes*, ed. P.-Y. Badel, Lettres gothiques, Paris, Livre de poche, 1995.
Alexandre de Paris, *Le Roman d'Alexandre*, ed. E. C. Armstrong *et al.*, trans. L. Harf-Lancner, Lettres gothiques, Paris, Livre de poche, 1994.
*Ami et Amile*, ed. P. F. Dembowski, CFMA, Paris, Champion, 1969.
*Aucassin et Nicolette*, in *Nouvelles courtoises occitanes et françaises*, ed. S. Méjean-Thiolier and M.-F. Notz-Grob, Lettres gothiques, Paris, Livre de poche, 1997, pp. 632–701.
Benoît de Sainte-Maure, *Le Roman de Troie*, ed. L. Constans, 6 vols., SATF, Paris, Firmin-Didot, 1904–12.
Bodel, Jean, *La Chanson des Saisnes*, ed. A. Brasseur, 2 vols., TLF, Geneva, Droz, 1989.
*Le Jeu de Saint Nicolas*, ed. A. Henry, TLF, Geneva, Droz, 1981.
*Cent Nouvelles nouvelles*, ed. F. P. Sweetser, 2nd edn, TLF, Geneva, Droz, 1996.
*Chanson de Guillaume*, ed. P. E. Bennett, London, Grant and Cutler, 2000.
*Chanson de Roland*, ed. I. Short, Lettres gothiques, Paris, Livre de poche, 1990.
*Chanson de Roland, The Song of Roland: the French Corpus*, ed. J. J. Duggan *et al.*, 3 vols., Turnhout, Brepols, 2005.
Charles d'Orléans, *Ballades et rondeaux*, ed. J.-Cl. Mühlethaler, Lettres gothiques, Paris, Livre de poche, 1992.
*Poésies*, ed. P. Champion, 2 vols., CFMA, Paris, Champion, 1923–7.
*Charroi de Nîmes*, ed. D. McMillan, 2nd edn, Paris, Klincksieck, 1978.
Chartier, Alain, *The Poetical Works of Alain Chartier*, ed. J. C. Laidlaw, London, 1974.
*Le Cycle de la belle dame sans mercy*, ed. D. F. Hult and J. E. McRae, CCMA, Paris, Champion, 2003.

Châtelain de Couci, *Les Chansons attribuées au Chastelain de Coucy*, ed. A. Lerond, Paris, PUF, 1964.

*Châtelaine de Vergy*, in *Nouvelles courtoises occitanes et françaises*, ed. S. Méjean-Thiolier and M.-F. Notz-Grob, Lettres gothiques, Paris, Livre de poche, 1997, pp. 450–503.

Chrétien de Troyes, *Le Chevalier au lion*, ed. D. F. Hult, Lettres gothiques, Paris, Livre de poche, 1994.

*Le Chevalier de la charrette*, ed. C. Méla, Lettres gothiques, Paris, Livre de poche, 1992.

*Cligès*, ed. C. Méla and O. Collet, Lettres gothiques, Paris, Livre de poche, 1994.

*Le Conte du graal*, ed. C. Méla, Lettres gothiques, Paris, Livre de poche, 1990.

*Erec et Enide*, ed. J.-M. Fritz, Lettres gothiques, Paris, Livre de poche, 1992.

Christine de Pizan, *Cent Ballades d'amant et de dame*, ed. J. Cerquiglini-Toulet, Paris, 10–18, 1982.

*Ditié de Jehanne d'Arc*, ed. A. J. Kennedy and K. Varty, Medium Aevum monographs 9, Oxford, Society for the Study of Medieval Languages and Literature, 1977.

*Epistre au dieu d'amours*, in T. S. Fenster and M. C. Erler (eds.), *Poems of Cupid, God of Love*, Leiden, Brill, 1990.

*Epistre de la prison de vie humaine*, in *The Epistle of the Prison of Human Life with An Epistle to the Queen of France and Lament on the Evils of the Civil War*, ed. and trans. J. A. Wisman, New York, Garland, 1984.

*Epistre Othea. Edition critique*, ed. G. Parussa, TLF, Geneva, Droz, 1999.

*Le Livre de l'advision Cristine*, ed. C. Reno and L. Dulac, Paris, Champion, 2001.

*Le Livre de la cité des dames, La città delle donne*, ed. E. J. Richards, trans. P. Caraffi, Milan, Luni, 1997.

*Le Livre de la mutacion de Fortune*, ed. S. Solente, 4 vols., SATF, Paris, A. & J. Picard, 1959–66.

*Le Livre des fais d'armes et de chevalerie: The Book of Fayttes of Armes and of Chyvalrye. Translated and printed by William Caxton*, ed. A. T. P. Byles, Early English Text Society, Oxford University Press, 1932.

*Le Livre des trois vertus*, ed. E. Hicks and C. C. Willard, Paris, Champion, 1989.

*Le Livre du chemin de longue étude*, ed. A. Tarnowksi, Lettres gothiques, Paris, Livre de poche, 1998.

*Le Livre du corps de policie*, ed. A. Kennedy, Paris, Champion, 1998.

*Le Livre du duc des vrais amants*, ed. T. S. Fenster, Medieval and Renaissance Texts and Studies, Binghampton, NY, Center for Medieval and Renaissance Studies, 1995.

*Œuvres poétiques de Christine de Pisan*, ed. M. Roy, 3 vols., SATF, Paris, Firmin-Didot, 1886.

Clemence of Barking, *The Life of St Catherine*, ed. W. Macbain, Oxford, Anglo-Norman Text Society / Blackwell, 1964.

Conon de Béthune, *Les Chansons de Conon de Béthune*, ed. A. Wallensköld, CFMA Paris, Champion, 1921.

*Continuations of the Old French Perceval of Chrétien de Troyes*, ed. W. Roach, 5 vols., Philadelphia, University of Pennsylvania Press, 1949–83.

Coudrette, *Le Roman de Mélusine*, ed. L. Harf-Lancner, Paris, Flammarion, 1993.

*Couronnement de Louis: les rédactions en vers du couronnement de Louis*, ed. Y. G. Lepage, TLF, Geneva, Droz, 1978.

*Débat sur le Roman de la Rose*, ed. E. Hicks, Paris, Champion, 1977.

Deschamps, Eustache, *Art de dictier*, ed. D. Sinnreich-Levi, East Lansing, Colleagues Press, 1994.

*Œuvres poétiques*, ed. le marquis de Queux de Saint Hilaire and G. Raynaud, 11 vols., SATF, Paris, Firmin-Didot, 1878–1903.

Etienne de Fougères, *Le Livre des manières*, ed. R. A. Lodge, TLF, Geneva, Droz, 1979.

*Fabliaux érotiques*, ed. L. Rossi and R. Straub, Lettres gothiques, Paris, Livre de poche, 1992.

*Floire et Blancheflor, Le conte de Floire et Blancheflor*, ed. J.-L. Leclanche, CFMA, Paris, Champion, 1980.

Froissart, Jean, *Ballades et rondeaux*, ed. R. S. Baudouin, TLF, Geneva, Droz, 1978.

*Chroniques*, ed. Kervyn de Lettenhove, 28 vols., Brussels, Heussner, 1867–77.

*La Prison amoureuse*, ed. A. Fourrier, Paris, Klincksieck, 1974.

*L'Espinette amoureuse*, ed. A. Fourrier, Paris, Klincksieck, 1963.

*Le Joli Buisson de Jonece*, ed. A. Fourrier, TLF, Geneva, Droz, 1975.

*Meliador*, ed. A. Longnon, 3 vols., SATF, Paris, Firmin-Didot, 1895–9.

*Le Voyage en Béarn*, ed. A. Diverres, Manchester University Press, 1953.

Gace Brulé, *The Lyrics and Melodies of Gace Brulé*, ed. S. N. Rosenberg and S. Danon, music ed. H. van der Werf, New York, Garland, 1985.

Gautier d'Arras, *Eracle*, ed. G. Raynaud de Lage, CFMA, Paris, Champion, 1976.

*Ille et Galeron*, ed. Y. Lefèvre, CFMA, Paris, Champion, 1988.

Gerson, Jean, *Œuvres complètes*, ed. P. Glorieux, 10 vols., Paris, Desclée & Cie, 1968.

Greban, Arnoul, *Le Mystère de la passion*, ed. O. Jodogne, 2 vols., Brussels, Académie royale de Belgique, 1965–83.

Guillaume de Lorris and Jean de Meun, *Le Roman de la rose*, ed. F. Lecoy, 3 vols., CFMA, Paris, Champion, 1968–70.

*Le Roman de la rose*, ed. A. Strubel, Lettres gothiques, Paris, Livre de poche, 1992.

Heldris de Cornualle, *Le Roman de Silence*, ed. S. Roche-Mahdi, East Lansing, MI, Colleagues Press, 1992.

*Huon de Bordeaux*, ed. P. Ruelle, Brussels, Presses Universitaires de Bruxelles, 1960.

Jakemes, *Le Roman du Castelain de Couci et de la Dame de Fayel par Jakemes*, ed. J. E. Matzke and M. Delbouille, SATF, Paris, Firmin-Didot, 1936.

Jean d'Arras, *Mélusine, ou la noble histoire de Lusignan*, ed. J.-J. Vincensini, Lettres gothiques, Paris, Livre de poche, 2003.

Jean Renart, *L'Escoufle*, ed. F. Sweetser, TLF, Geneva, Droz, 1974.

*Le Lai de l'ombre*, in *Nouvelles courtoises occitanes et françaises*, ed. S. Méjean-Thiolier and M. -F. Notz-Grob, Lettres gothiques, Paris, Livre de poche, 1997, pp. 578–31.

*Le Roman de la rose ou de Guillaume de Dole*, ed. F. Lecoy, CFMA Paris, Champion, 1969.

*Jeu d'Adam, Ordo representacionis Ade*, ed. W. Noomen, CFMA, Paris, Champion, 1971.

*Lancelot do Lac, the Non-Cyclic Old French Prose Romance*, ed. E. Kennedy, 2 vols., Oxford University Press, 1980.

*Lancelot, roman en prose du XIIIe siècle*, ed. A. Micha, 9 vols., TLF, Geneva, Droz, 1978–83.

la Sale, Antoine de, *Jehan de Saintré*, ed. J. Blanchard, trans. M. Quereuil, Lettres gothiques, Paris, Livre de poche, 1995.

Le Franc, Martin, *Le Champion des Dames*, ed. R. Deschaux, CFMA, 5 vols., Paris, Champion, 1999.

*Livre du graal*, ed. D. Poirion with P. Walter *et al.*, 2 vols. to date, Bibliothèque de la Pléiade, Paris, Gallimard, 2001–3.

Machaut, Guillaume de, *Le Livre de la Fontaine amoureuse*, ed. J. Cerquiglini-Toulet, Paris, Stock, 1993.

   *Le Livre du Voir dit*, ed. P. Imbs with J. Cerquiglini-Toulet and N. Musso, Lettres gothiques, Paris, Livre de poche, 1999.

   *La Louange des dames*, ed. N. E. Wilkins, Edinburgh, Scottish Academic Press and London, Chatto & Windus, 1972.

   *Œuvres complètes*, ed. E. Hopepffner, 3 vols., SATF, Paris, Firmin-Didot, 1908.

Manessier, *La Troisième Continuation du Conte du graal*, ed. W. Roach, ed. and trans. M.-N. Toury, CCMA, Paris, Champion, 2004.

Marie de France, *Lais*, ed. A. Micha, Paris, Garnier-Flammarion, 1998.

Michel, Jean, *Le Mystère de la passion (Angers 1486)*, ed. O. Jodogne, Gembloux, Duculot, 1959.

*Miracles de Nostre Dame par personnages*, ed. G. Paris and U. Robert, 8 vols., SATF, Paris, Firmin-Didot, 1867–83.

Molinet, Jean, *Les Faictz et dictz de Jean Molinet*, ed. N. Dupire, 3 vols., SATF, Paris, Firmin-Didot, 1936–9.

*Mort le roi Artu, roman du XIIIe siècle*, ed. J. Frappier, 3rd edn, TLF, Geneva, Droz, 1964.

*Narcisse, Lai de*, in *Pyrame et Thisbé, Narcisse, Philomena. Trois contes du XIIe siècle français imités d'Ovide*, ed. E. Baumgartner, Paris, Gallimard, 2000.

*Nouveau Recueil complet des fabliaux*, ed. W. Noomen and N. van de Boogaard, 10 vols., Assen, Van Gorcum, 1983–98.

*Ovide moralisé. Poème du commencement du quatorzième siècle*, ed. C. de Boer, *Verhandelingen der Koninklijke Akademie van Wetenschapen te Amsterdam. Afdeeling Letterkunde*, vol. 1, books I–III, n.s. XV, 1915; vol. 2, books IV–VI, n.s. XXI, 1920; vol. 3, books VII–IX, ed. C. de Boer, M. G. de Boer, and J. Th. M. van't Sant, n.s., XXX, 1931; vol. 4, books X–XIII, ed. C. de Boer, M. G de Boer, and J. Th. M. van't Sant, n.s. XXXVII, 1936; vol. 5, books XIV and XV with two appendices, ed. C. de Boer, n.s. XLIII, 1938.

*Pathelin, Maistre Pierre Pathelin, farce du XVe siècle*, ed. R. T. Holbrook, CFMA, Paris, Champion, 1986.

*Perceforest, Roman de*, ed. J. H. M. Taylor, TLF, Geneva, Droz, 1979; subsequent vols. (7 to date) ed. G. Roussineau, TLF, Geneva, Droz, 1987–

*Philomena*, in *Pyrame et Thisbé, Narcisse, Philomena. Trois contes du XIIe siècle français imités d'Ovide*, ed. E. Baumgartner, Paris, Gallimard, 2000.

*Première Continuation de Perceval*, ed. W. Roach, trans. C. A. Coolput-Storms, Lettres gothiques, Paris, Livre de poche, 1993.

*Prise d'Orange*, ed. C. Régnier, 7th edn, Paris, Klincksieck, 1986.

*Pseudo-Turpin: an Anonymous Old French Translation of the Pseudo-Turpin Chronicle*, ed. R. N. Walpole, Cambridge, MA, The Mediaeval Academy of America, 1979.

*Pyrame et Thisbé, Narcisse, Philomena. Trois contes du XIIe siècle français imités d'Ovide*, ed. E. Baumgartner, Paris, Gallimard, 2000.

*Queste del Saint Graal*, ed. A. Pauphilet, CFMA, Paris, Champion, 1923.

*Quinze Joies de mariage*, ed. J. Rychner, TLF, Geneva, Droz, 1963.

*Raoul de Cambrai*, ed. S. Kay, trans. W. Kibler, Lettres gothiques, Paris, Livre de poche, 1996.

René d'Anjou, *Le Livre du Cœur d'amour épris*, ed. and trans. F. Bouchet, Lettres gothiques, Paris, Livre de poche, 2003.

*Renaut de Montauban: édition critique du manuscrit Douce*, ed. J. Thomas, TLF, Geneva, Droz, 1989.

*Roman d'Eneas*, ed. A. Petit, Lettres gothiques, Paris, Livre de poche, 1997.

*Roman de Renart*, ed. J. Dufournet, 2 vols., Paris, Flammarion, 1985.

*Rutebeuf, œuvres complètes*, ed. M. Zink, Lettres gothiques, Paris, Livre de poche, 2001.

Thomas de Kent, *Le Roman d'Alexandre ou le Roman de toute chevalerie*, ed. B. Foster and I. Short, trans. C. Gaullier-Bougassas and L. Harf-Lancner, CCMA, Paris, Champion, 2003.

*Tristan et Iseult, les poèmes français, la saga norroise*, ed. D. Lacroix and P. Walter, Lettres gothiques, Paris, Livre de poche, 1989.

*Tristan en prose*, ed. R. L. Curtis, 3 vols., vol. I, Munich, Max Hueber, 1963; vols. II and III, Cambridge, D. S. Brewer, 1985.

*Tristan en prose*, ed. P. Ménard *et al.*, 9 vols., TLF, Geneva, Droz, 1987–97.

*Vie de Sainte Paule*, ed. K. Grass, Halle, Niemeyer, 1908.

*Vie de Saint Alexis*, ed. C. Storey, Oxford, Basil Blackwell, 1946.

*The Vie de Saint Alexis in the Twelfth and Thirteenth Centuries*, ed. and commentary by A. G. Elliott, North Carolina Studies in the Romance Languages and Literatures, Chapel Hill, University of North Carolina Press, 1983.

Villehardouin, Geoffrey de, *La Conquete de Constantinople*, ed. E. Faral, 2nd edn, 2 vols., Classiques de l'histoire de France au moyen âge, Paris, Les Belles Lettres, 1938–9.

Villon, François, *Poésies complètes*, ed. C. Thiry, Lettres gothiques, Paris, Livre de poche, 1991.

*Le Testament Villon*, ed. J. Rychner and A. Henry, 2 vols., TLF, Geneva, Droz, 1974.

*Voyage de Charlemagne à Jerusalem et à Constantinople*, ed. P. Aebischer, TLF, Geneva, Droz, 1965.

Wace, *Le Roman de Brut de Wace*, ed. I. Arnold, 2 vols., SATF, Paris, Firmin-Didot, 1938–40.

*Le Roman de Rou de Wace*, ed. A. J. Holden, 3 vols., SATF Paris, Picard, 1970–3.

*La Vie de Sainte Marguerite*, ed. E. J. Francis, CFMA Paris, Champion, 1932.

# SUGGESTED FURTHER READING

Where the same work is suggested for more than one chapter, full references are provided at the first mention and subsequent mentions indicate with respect to which chapter that mention occurred. These suggestions for further reading relate to the general topic covered by each chapter, not just to their specific content.

### Introduction (Broad-ranging studies of medieval French literature)

Bloch, R. H., *Medieval French Literature and Law*, Berkeley, California University Press, 1977.
   *Etymologies and Genealogies: a Literary Anthropology of the French Middle Ages*, Chicago University Press, 1983.
Burgwinkle, W. E., *Sodomy, Masculinity, and Law in Medieval Literature*, Cambridge University Press, 2004.
Burns, E. J., *Bodytalk: When Women Speak in Old French Literature*, Philadelphia, University of Pennsylvania Press, 1993.
Busby, K., *Codex and Context: Reading Old French Verse Narrative in Manuscripts*, 2 vols., Amsterdam, Rodopi, 2002.
Cerquiglini, B., *L'Eloge de la variante: histoire critique de la philologie*, Paris, Seuil, 1989.
Fleischman, S., *Tense and Narrativity: from Medieval Performance to Modern Fiction*, London, Routledge, 1990.
Gaunt, S., *Retelling the Tale: an Introduction to Medieval French Literature*, London, Duckworth, 2001.
   *Gender and Genre in Medieval French Literature*, Cambridge University Press, 1995.
   *Love and Death in Medieval French and Occitan Courtly Literature: Martyrs to Love*, Oxford University Press, 2006.
Gravdal, K., *Ravishing Maidens: Writing Rape in Medieval French Literature and Law*, Philadelphia, University of Pennsylvania Press, 1991.
Huchet, J.-Ch., *Littérature médiévale et psychanalyse: pour une clinique littéraire*, Paris, PUF, 1990.
Huot, S., *From Song to Book: the Poetics of Writing in Old French Lyric and Lyrical Narrative Poetry*, Ithaca and London, Cornell University Press, 1987.
   *Madness in Medieval French Literature: Identities Found and Lost*, Oxford University Press, 2003.
Kay, S., *The Chansons de geste in the Age of Romance: Political Fictions*, Oxford University Press, 1995.

*Courtly Contradictions: the Emergence of the Literary Object in the Twelfth Century*, Stanford University Press, 2001.

Kay, S., Cave, T. C., and Bowie, M., *A Short History of French Literature*, Oxford University Press, 2003.

Kinoshita, S., *Medieval Boundaries: Rethinking Difference in Old French Literature*, Philadelphia, University of Pennsylvania Press, 2006.

Köhler, E., *L'Aventure chevaleresque: idéal et réalité dans le roman courtois*, trans. Eliane Kaufholz, Paris, Gallimard, 1974.

Krueger, R. L., *Women Readers and the Ideology of Gender in Old French Verse Romance*, Cambridge University Press, 1993.

Marnette, S., *Narrateur et points de vue dans la littérature française médiévale*, Bern, Peter Lang, 1998.

McCracken, P., *The Romance of Adultery: Queenship and Sexual Transgression in Old French Literature*, Philadelphia, University of Pennsylvania Press, 1998.

Solterer, H., *The Master and Minerva: Disputing Women in Medieval French Culture*, Berkeley, California University Press, 1995.

Spiegel, G. M., *Romancing the Past: the Rise of Prose Historiography in Thirteenth-Century France*, Berkeley, California University Press, 1993.

Vance, E., *Mervelous Signals: Poetics and Sign Theory in the Middle Ages*, Lincoln and London, University of Nebraska Press, 1986.

*From Topic to Tale: Logic and Narrativity in the Middle Ages*, Minneapolis, Minnesota University Press, 1987.

Zumthor, P., *Essai de poétique médiévale*, Paris, Seuil, 1972.

### Chapter 1 (*The* Chanson de Roland*)*

Boutet, D., *La Chanson de geste: forme et signification d'une écriture épique au Moyen Age*, Paris, PUF, 1993.

Daniel, N., *Heroes and Saracens: an Interpretation of the Chansons de geste*, Edinburgh University Press, 1984.

Duggan, J. J., *La Chanson de Roland: Formulaic Style and Poetic Craft*, Berkeley, California University Press, 1973.

Gaunt, S. *Gender and Genre*. [See Introduction]

Haidu, P., *The Subject of Violence: the Song of Roland and the Birth of the State*, Bloomington, Indiana University Press, 1993.

Kay, S., *The Chansons de geste in the Age of Romance*. [See Introduction]

Kinoshita, S., *Medieval Boundaries*. [See Introduction]

Nichols, S. G., *Romanesque Signs: Early Medieval Narrative and Iconography*, New Haven and London, Yale University Press, 1983.

Rychner, J., *La Chanson de geste: essai sur l'art épique des jongleurs*, Geneva, Droz, 1955.

Suard, F., *La Chanson de geste*, new edn, Paris, Que sais-je?, 2003.

Vance, E., *Reading the Song of Roland*, Englewood Cliffs, NJ, Prentice-Hall, 1970.

### Chapter 2 (*The Old French Vulgate cycle*)

Bogdanow, F., *The Romance of the Grail*, Manchester University Press, 1966.

Bloch, R. H., *Etymologies and Genealogies*. [See Introduction]

Burns, E. J., *Arthurian Fictions: Reading the Vulgate Cycle*, Columbus, Ohio State University Press, 1985.

Dover, C. (ed.), *A Companion to the 'Lancelot-Grail' Cycle*, Cambridge, D. S. Brewer, 2003.

Griffin, M., *The Object and the Cause in the Vulgate Cycle*, Oxford, Legenda, 2005.

Kennedy, E., *Lancelot and the Grail*, Oxford University Press, 1986.

Kibler, W. (ed.), *The Lancelot-Grail Cycle: Text and Transformations*, Austin, University of Texas Press, 1994.

Lacy, N. (gen. ed.), *Lancelot-Grail: the Old French Arthurian Vulgate and Post-Vulgate in Translation*, 5 vols., New York and London, Garland, 1995.

Leupin, A., *Le Graal et la littérature*, Geneva, L'Age d'Homme, 1982.

McCracken, P., *The Romance of Adultery*. [See Introduction]

## Chapter 3 *(The* Roman de la rose*)*

Brownlee, K. and Huot, S. (eds.), *Rethinking the 'Romance of the Rose': Text, Image, Reception*, Philadelphia, University of Pennsylvania Press, 1992.

Fleming, J. V., *Reason and the Lover*, Princeton University Press, 1984.

Guynn, N., *Allegory and Sexual Ethics in the High Middle Ages*, New York, Palgrave Macmillan, 2007.

Heller-Roazen, D., *Fortune's Faces: the 'Roman de la rose' and the Poetics of Contingency*, Baltimore, Johns Hopkins University Press, 2003.

Hult, D. F., *Self-fulfilling Prophecies: Readership and Authority in the First 'Roman de la rose'*, Cambridge University Press, 1986.

Huot, S., *The 'Romance of the Rose' and its Medieval Readers: Interpretation, Reception, Manuscript Transmission*, Cambridge University Press, 1993.

Kay, S., *The Romance of the Rose*, London, Grant and Cutler, 1995.

Kelly, D., *Internal Difference and Meanings in the 'Roman de la rose'*, Madison, University of Wisconsin Press, 1995.

Poirion, D., *Le Roman de la rose*, Paris, Hatier, 1973.

Regalado, N. F., '"Des contraires choses": la fonction poétique de la citation et des *exempla* dans le *Roman de la rose*', *Littérature*, 41 (1981), 62–81.

## Chapter 4 *(François Villon)*

Demarolle, P., *L'Esprit de Villon: Etude de style*, 2nd edn, Paris, Nizet, 1992.

*Villon: un testament ambigu*, Paris, Larousse, 1973.

Dérens, J., Dufournet, J., and Freeman, M. (eds.), *Villon hier et aujourd'hui: Actes du colloque pour le cinq-centième anniversaire de l'impression du 'Testament' de Villon, Bibliothèque historique de la Ville de Paris, 15–17. décembre 1989*, Paris, Bibliothèque historique de la Ville de Paris, 1993.

Dufournet, J., *Nouvelles Recherches sur Villon*, Paris, Champion, 1980.

*Villon: ambiguïté et carnaval*, Paris, Slatkine, 1992.

Freeman, M., *François Villon in his Works: the Villain's Tale*, Amsterdam, Rodopi, 2000.

Hunt, T., *Villon's Last Will: Language and Authority in the 'Testament'*, Oxford University Press, 1996.

Regalado, N. F., '*Effet de réel, Effet du réel*: Representation and Reference in Villon's *Testament*', *Yale French Studies*, 70 (1986), 63–77.

'Gathering the Works: the Œuvres de Villon and the Intergeneric Passage of the Medieval French Lyric into Single-Author Collections', L'Esprit Créateur, 33 (1993), 87–100.

Taylor, J. H. M., The Poetry of François Villon: Text and Context, Cambridge University Press, 2001.

Vitz, E. B., The Crossroad of Intentions: a Study of Symbolic Expression in the Poetry of François Villon, The Hague, Mouton, 1974.

## Chapter 5 (Chrétien de Troyes)

Haidu, P., Aesthetic Distance in Chrétien de Troyes: Irony and Comedy in 'Cligès' and 'Perceval', Geneva, Droz, 1968.

Kelly, D. (ed.), The Romances of Chrétien de Troyes: a Symposium, Lexington, KY, French Forum Monographs, 1985.

Köhler, E., L'Aventure chevaleresque. [See Introduction]

Krueger, R. L., Women Readers and the Ideology of Gender. [See Introduction]

Lacy, N. J. and Grimbert, J. T. (eds.), A Companion to Chrétien de Troyes, Cambridge, D. S. Brewer, 2005.

Lacy, N., Kelly, D., and Busby, K. (eds.), The Legacy of Chrétien de Troyes, 2 vols., Amsterdam, Rodopi, 1987–8.

Maddox, D., The Arthurian Romances of Chrétien de Troyes: Once and Future Fictions, Cambridge University Press, 1991.

Pickens, R. (ed.), The Sower and the Seed: Essays on Chrétien de Troyes, Lexington, KY, French Forum Monographs, 1983.

## Chapter 6 (The Châtelain de Couci and trouvère lyric)

Butterfield, A., Poetry and Music in Medieval France: from Jean Renart to Guillaume de Machaut, Cambridge University Press, 2002.

Dragonetti, R., La Technique poétique des trouvères dans la chanson courtoise, Bruges, Tempel, 1960.

Guiette, R., D'une Poésie formelle en France au moyen âge, new edn, Paris, Nizet, 1972.

Huot, S., From Song to Book. [See Introduction]

Rosenberg, S, Switten, S. and Le Vot, G. (eds.), Songs of the Troubadours and Trouvères: an Anthology of Poems and Melodies, New York and London, Garland, 1998.

Switten, M. L., Music and Poetry in the Middle Ages: a Guide to Research on French and Occitan Song, 1100–1400, New York and London, Garland, 1995.

Vance, E., Mervelous Signals. [See Introduction]

Zaganelli, G., Aimer, sofrir, joïr: i paradigmi della soggettività nella lirica francesa dei secoli XII e XIII, Florence, La Nuova Italia, 1982.

Zumthor, P., Essai de poétique médiévale. [See Introduction]

## Chapter 7 (Guillaume de Machaut)

Brownlee, K., Poetic Identity in Guillaume de Machaut, Madison, WI, University of Wisconsin Press, 1984.

Calin, W., A Poet at the Fountain: Essays on the Narrative Verse of Guillaume de Machaut, Lexington, University Press of Kentucky, 1974.

Cerquiglini-Toulet, J., 'Un engin si soutil': Guillaume de Machaut et l'écriture au XIVe siècle, Paris, Champion, 1985.

Earp, L., Guillaume de Machaut: a Guide to Research, New York and London, Garland, 1995

Huë, D. (ed.), préface de J. Cerquiglini-Toulet, 'Comme mon cœur désire'. Guillaume de Machaut, 'Le Livre du Voir dit', Orléans, Paradigme, 2001.

Huot, S., From Song to Book. [See Introduction]

Guillaume de Machaut: Poète et compositeur. Actes et colloques. Reims (19–22 avril 1978), Paris, Editions Klincksieck, 1982.

McGrady, D., Controlling Readers: Guillaume de Machaut and his Late Medieval Audience, Toronto University Press, 2006.

Williams, S. J., 'An Author's Role in Fourteenth-Century Book Production: Guillaume de Machaut's "livre où je met toutes mes choses"', Romania, 90 (1969), 433–54.

## Chapter 8 (Christine de Pizan)

Altmann, B. K., and McGrady, D. L. (eds.), Christine de Pizan: a Casebook, New York and London, Routledge, 2003.

Brown-Grant, R., Christine de Pizan and the Moral Defence of Women: Reading beyond Gender, Cambridge University Press, 1999.

Desmond, M. (ed)., Christine de Pizan and the Categories of Difference, Minneapolis, University of Minnesota Press, 1998.

Desmond, M. and Sheingorn, P., Myth, Montage and Visuality in Late Medieval Manuscript Culture: Christine de Pizan's Othea, Ann Arbor, University of Michigan Press, 2003.

Hicks, E. (ed.), Le Débat sur le Roman de la rose, Paris, Champion, 1977.

Laidlaw, J., 'Christine de Pizan – an Author's Progress', Modern Language Review, 78 (1983), 532–50.

'Christine de Pizan – a Publisher's Progress', Modern Language Review, 82 (1987), 35–75.

Solterer, H., The Master and Minerva. [See Introduction]

Willard, C. C., Christine de Pizan: her Life and Works, New York, Persea, 1984.

## Chapter 9 (Narrative genres)

Baader, Horst, Die Lais. Zur Geschichte einer Gattung der altfranzösischen Kurzerzählungen, Frankfurt am Main, Klostermann, 1966.

Busby, K., Codex and Context. [See Introduction]

Gnädinger, Louise. Studien zur altfranzösischen Heiligenvita des 12. und 13. Jahrhunderts, Tübingen, Niemeyer, 1972.

Jauss, H. R., Toward an Aesthetic of Reception, trans. T. Bahti, Minneapolis, Minnesota University Press, 1982.

Jodogne, O., Le Fabliau, Turnhout, Brepols, 1975.

Kay, S., The Chansons de geste in the Age of Romance. [See Introduction]

Kelly, D., The Art of Medieval French Romance, Madison, University of Wisconsin Press, 1992.

*Medieval French Romance*, New York, Twayne, 1993.

Mölk, U. (ed.), *Französische Literarästhetik des 12. und 13. Jahrhunderts*, Tübingen, Niemeyer, 1969.

Payen, J.-C., *Le Lai narratif*, Turnout, Brepols, 1985. [Supplement to Jodogne]

Schmolke-Hasselmann, B., *The Evolution of Arthurian Romance: the Verse Tradition from Chrétien to Froissart*, trans. M. and R. Middleton, Cambridge University Press, 1998.

Suard, F., *La Chanson de geste*. [See Chapter 1]

Zumthor, P., *Essai de poétique médiévale*. [See Introduction]

## Chapter 10 *(Late medieval lyric poetry)*

Armstrong, A., *Technique and Technology: Script, Print and Poetics in France, 1470–1550*, Oxford University Press, 2000.

Boulton, M., *The Song in the Story: Lyric Insertions in French Narrative Fiction, 1200–1400*, Philadelphia, University of Pennsylvania Press, 1993.

Butterfield, A., *Poetry and Music in Medieval France*. [See Chapter 6]

Cerquiglini-Toulet, J., *La Couleur de la mélancolie: la fréquentation des livres au XIVe siècle, 1300–1415*, Paris, Hatier, 1993.

Johnson, L. W., *Poets as Players: Theme and Variation in Late Medieval French Poetry*, Stanford University Press, 1990.

Kelly, D., *Medieval Imagination: Rhetoric and the Poetry of Courtly Love*, Madison, WI, University of Wisconsin Press, 1978.

Poirion, D., *Le Poète et le prince: l'évolution du lyrisme courtois de Guillaume de Machaut à Charles d'Orléans*, Paris, PUF, 1965.

Taylor, J. H. M., 'Research on the French Medieval Lyric: an *Etat présent*', *French Studies*, 61 (2006), 69–83.

*The Making of Poetry: Poetic Anthologies in Late-Medieval France*, Turnhout, Brepols, 2007.

Wimsatt, J. I., *Chaucer and his French Contemporaries: Natural Music in the Fourteenth Century*, University of Toronto Press, 1991.

Zumthor, P., *Le Masque et la lumière: la poétique des Grands Rhétoriqueurs*, Paris, Seuil, 1978.

## Chapter 11 *(The short comic tale)*

Bloch, R. H., *The Scandal of the Fabliaux*, Chicago University Press, 1986.

Brownlee, K., 'Discourse as Proueces in *Aucassin et Nicolette*', *Yale French Studies*, 70 (1986), 167–82.

Cobby, A. E., *Ambivalent Conventions: Formula and Parody in Old French*, Amsterdam, Rodopi, 1995.

Dubuis, R., *Les Cent Nouvelles nouvelles et la tradition de la nouvelle en France au Moyen Age*, Presses Universitaires de Grenoble, 1973.

Fein, D. A., *Displacements of Power: Readings of the Cent nouvelles nouvelles*, Lanham, MD, University Press of America, 2003.

Martin, J. H., *Love's Fools: Aucassin, Troilus, Calisto, and the Parody of the Courtly Lover*, London, Tamesis, 1972.

Nykrog, P., *Les Fabliaux. Etude d'histoire littéraire et de stylistique médiévale*, Copenhagen, Munksgaard, 1957.

Vance, E., *Mervelous Signals*. [See Chapter 6]

## Chapter 12 (Theatre)

Bordier, J.-P., *Le Jeu de la passion: le message chrétien et le théâtre français du XIII–XVIe siècles*, Paris, Champion, 1998.

Bouhaïk-Gironès, M., *Les Clercs de la Basoche et le théâtre comique (Paris 1420–1550)*, Paris, Champion, forthcoming.

Dominguez, V. *La scène et la croix: le jeu de l'acteur dans les Passions dramatiques françaises (XIVe–XVIe siècles)*, Turnhout, Brepols, 2007.

Enders, J., *The Medieval Theater of Cruelty*, Ithaca and London, Cornell University Press, 1999.

*Death by Drama and Other Medieval Legends*, Chicago University Press, 2002.

*Rhetoric and the Origins of Medieval Drama*, Ithaca and London, Cornell University Press, 1992.

Hindley, A. (ed.), *Drama and Community: People and Plays in Medieval Europe*, Turnhout, Brepols, 1999.

Hüe, D., and Smith, D. (eds.), *'Maistre Pierre Pathelin': lectures et contextes*, Presses Universitaires de Rennes, 2000.

Knight, E. A., *The Stage as Mirror: Civic Theatre in Late Medieval Europe*, Woodbridge, D. S. Brewer, 1997.

Koopmans, J., *Le Théâtre des exclus au moyen âge*, Paris, Imago, 1997.

Rousse, M., *La Scène et les tréteaux: le théâtre de la farce au moyen âge*, Orléans, Paradigme, 2004.

Runnalls, G., *Etudes sur les mystères*, Paris, Champion, 1998.

Solterer, H., *Medieval Roles for Modern Times: Theater and the Battle for the Third French Republic*, forthcoming.

Symes, C., 'Appearance of Early Vernacular Plays: Forms, Functions and the Future of Medieval Theater', *Speculum*, 77 (2002), 778–831.

*A Common Stage: Theater and Public Life in Medieval Arras*, New York, Cornell University Press, 2007.

Tydeman, W. (ed.), *Theater in Europe: a Documentary History, the Medieval European Stage, 500–1550*, Cambridge University Press, 2001.

## Chapter 13 (Feudalism and kingship)

Bradbury, J., *Philip Augustus: King of France, 1180–1223*, London, Longman, 1998.

Duby, G., *Guerriers et paysans: VIIe-XIIe siècle: premier essor de l'économie européenne*, Paris, Gallimard, 1973.

*Les Trois Ordres ou l'imaginaire du féodalisme*, Paris, Gallimard, 1978.

Dunbabin, J., *France in the Making 843–1180*, Oxford University Press, 1985.

Ganshof, F. L., *Feudalism*, new edn, London, Longman, 1979.

Jordan, W. C., *The Penguin History of Europe: Europe in the High Middle Ages*, London, Penguin, 2002.

Reynolds, S., *Fiefs and Vassals: the Medieval Evidence Reinterpreted*, Oxford University Press, 1994.

Smith, J. M. H., *Europe After Rome: a New Cultural History 500–1000*, Oxford University Press, 2005.

Spiegel, G. M., *Romancing the Past*. [See Introduction]

Kantorowicz, E. H., *The King's Two Bodies: a Study in Medieval Political Theology*, Princeton University Press, 1957.

S. Kay, *The Chansons de geste in the Age of Romance*. [See Introduction]

J. R. Simpson, *Fantasy, Identity and Misrecognition in Medieval French Narrative*, Bern, Peter Lang, 2000.

## Chapter 14 (Clerks and laity)

Bullington, R., *The Alexis in the St Albans Psalter: a Look into the Heart of the Matter*, New York and London, Garland, 1991.

Cazelles, B., *The Lady as Saint: a Collection of French Hagiographic Romances of the Thirteenth Century*, Philadelphia, University of Pennsylvania Press, 1991.

Corbellari, A., *La Voix des clercs: littérature et savoir universitaire autour des dits du XIIIe siècle*, Geneva, Droz, 2005.

Dembowski, P. F., 'Literary Problems of Hagiography in Old French', *Medievalia et Humanistica*, n.s. 7 (1976), 117–30.

Duby, G., *Le Chevalier, la femme et le prêtre: le Mariage dans la France féodale*, Paris, Hachette, 1981.

Fanous, S. and Leyser, H. (eds.), *Christina of Markyate: a Twelfth-Century Holy Woman*, New York and London, Routledge, 2005.

Johnson, P. and Cazelles, B., *'Le Vain Siècle guerpir': a Literary Approach to Sainthood through Old French Hagiography of the Twelfth Century*, Chapel Hill, University of North Carolina Press, 1979.

Kay, S., 'Courts, Clerks, and Courtly Love', in R. L. Krueger (ed.), *The Cambridge Companion to Medieval Romance*, Cambridge University Press, 2000, pp. 81–96.

Laurent, F., *Plaire et édifier: les récits hagiographiques composés en Angleterre aux XIIe et XIIIe siècles*, Paris, Champion, 1998.

Wogan-Browne, J., *Saints' Lives and Women's Literary Culture c.1150 – 1300: Virginity and its Authorizations*, Oxford University Press, 2001.

## Chapter 15 (Marriage and sexuality)

Baldwin, J., *The Language of Sex: Five Voices from Northern France around 1200*, Chicago University Press, 1994.

Boswell, J., *Same-Sex Unions in Premodern Europe*, New York, Vintage, 1994.

Brundage, J. A., *Law, Sex, and Christian Society in Medieval Europe*. Chicago University Press, 1987.

Burgwinkle, W. E., *Sodomy, Masculinity, and Law*. [See Introduction]

Freccero, C., and Fradenburg, L. (eds.), *Premodern Sexualities*, New York and London, Routledge, 1996.

Karras, R. M., *Sexuality in Medieval Europe: Doing unto Others*, New York and London, Routledge, 2005.

McCarthy, C. (ed.), *Love, Sex and Marriage in the Middle Ages: a Sourcebook*, London and New York, Routledge, 2004.

Murray, J. and Eisenbichler, K. (eds.), *Desire and Discipline: Sex and Sexuality in the Premodern West*, Toronto University Press, 1996.

### Chapter 16 (Others and alterity)

Cohen, J. J., *Of Giants: Sex, Monsters, and the Middle Ages*, Minneapolis, University of Minnesota Press, 1999.

Friedman, J. B., *The Monstrous Races in Medieval Art and Thought*, Cambridge, MA, Harvard University Press, 1981.

Hahn, T., 'The Difference the Middle Ages Makes: Color and Race before the Modern World', *Journal of Medieval and Early Modern Studies*, 31 (2001), 1–38.

Huot, S., 'Love, Race, and Gender in Medieval Romance: Lancelot and the Son of the Giantess', *Journal of Medieval and Early Modern Studies*, 37 (2007), 373–91.

   *Postcolonial Fictions in the Roman de Perceforest: Cultural Identities and Hybridities*, Cambridge, D. S. Brewer, 2007.

Kabir, A. J., and Williams, D. (eds.), *Postcolonial Approaches to the European Middle Ages: Translating Cultures*, Cambridge University Press, 2005.

Kinoshita, S., *Medieval Boundaries*. [See Introduction]

Maddox, D., and Sturm-Maddox, S., *Melusine of Lusignan: Founding Fiction in Late Medieval France*, Athens, GA, University of Georgia Press, 1996.

Sinclair, F., 'Conquering Constantinople: Text, Territory and Desire', in M. Topping (ed.), *Eastern Voyages, Western Visions: French Writing and Painting of the Orient*, Bern, Peter Lang, 2004, pp. 47–68.

# INDEX

# Cambridge Companions to ...

## AUTHORS

## TOPICS